Colección Támesis

SERIE A: MONOGRAFÍAS, 236

A COMPANION TO FEDERICO GARCÍA LORCA

A Companion to Federico García Lorca provides a clear, critical appraisal of the issues and debates surrounding the work of Spain's most celebrated poet and dramatist. It considers past and current approaches to the study of Lorca, and also suggests new directions for further investigation. An introduction on the often contentious subject of Lorca's biography is followed by five chapters – poetry, theatre, music, drawing and cinema – which together acknowledge the polymath in Lorca. A further three chapters – religion, gender and sexuality, and politics – complete the volume by covering important thematic concerns across a number of texts, concerns which must be considered in the context of the iconic status that Lorca has acquired and against the background of the cultural shifts affecting his readership. The *Companion* is a testament to Lorca's enduring appeal and, through its explication of texts and investigation of the man, demonstrates just why he continues, and should continue, to attract scholarly interest.

FEDERICO BONADDIO lectures in Modern Spanish Studies at King's College London.

A COMPANION TO
FEDERICO GARCÍA LORCA

Edited by

Federico Bonaddio

TAMESIS

First published 2007
by Tamesis, Woodbridge
Reprinted in paperback 2010

Transferred to digital printing

ISBN 978-1-85566-141-7 hardback
ISBN 978-1-85566-212-4 paperback

Tamesis is an imprint of Boydell & Brewer Ltd
PO Box 9, Woodbridge, Suffolk IP12 3DF, UK
and of Boydell & Brewer Inc.
668 Mt Hope Avenue, Rochester, NY 14620, USA
website: www.boydellandbrewer.com

A CiP catalogue record for this book is available
from the British Library

This publication is printed on acid-free paper

CONTENTS

List of illustrations   vi

List of contributors   ix

Acknowledgements   xi

Introduction: Biography and Interpretation   1
   FEDERICO BONADDIO

1   Poetry   16
   CHRISTOPHER MAURER

2   Theatre   39
   SARAH WRIGHT

3   Music   63
   D. GARETH WALTERS

4   Drawing   84
   JACQUELINE COCKBURN and FEDERICO BONADDIO

5   Cinema   101
   XON DE ROS, ANTONIO MONEGAL and ALBERTO MIRA

6   Religion   129
   ERIC SOUTHWORTH

7   Gender and Sexuality   149
   CHRIS PERRIAM

8   Politics   170
   NIGEL DENNIS

Suggested Further Reading   190

Bibliography   195

Index   209

ILLUSTRATIONS

between pages 84 and 85

The drawings below are reproduced by kind permission of the Fundación García Lorca, Madrid.

Teorema de la Copa y la Mandolina (1927)
Retrato de Salvador Dalí (1927)
Amor Intelectualis (1927)
San Sebastián (1927)

LIST OF CONTRIBUTORS

Federico Bonaddio is Lecturer in Modern Spanish Studies at King's College London. He has published articles on Lorca's poetry, including 'Lorca's "Romance sonámbulo": the Desirability of Non-Disclosure', and on Spanish theatre and popular cinema. He is co-editor of *Crossing Fields in Modern Spanish Literature*.

Jacqueline Cockburn is Head of History of Art at Westminster School and an Associate Lecturer at Birkbeck College, University of London. She has published essays on Lorca's drawing ('Learning from the Master: Lorca's homage to Picasso' and 'Gifts from the poet to the art critic') as well as *The Spanish Song Companion* (with Richard Stokes). She is currently lecturing on Spanish art and researching Catalan artists.

Nigel Dennis is Professor of Spanish at the University of St Andrews. Although primarily interested in the prose writers of the pre-Civil War period, he has also written extensively on poets, especially Rafael Alberti and Lorca. He is the author of *Vida y milagros de un manuscrito de Lorca: en pos de 'Poeta en Nueva York'* and contributed one of the introductory essays to *Federico García Lorca (1898–1936)*, the catalogue of the exhibition held at the Museo Nacional de Arte Reina Sofía in 1998 to mark the centenary of the writer's birth. Other recent work on Lorca includes: '*Viaje a la luna*, de Federico García Lorca, y el problema de la expresión' and 'Lorca en el espejo: estrategias de (auto)-percepción'. With Andrew Anderson he has published the only extant autograph version of 'Tu infancia en Menton' from *Poeta en Nueva York*: 'The Manuscript of Lorca's "Tu infancia en Menton" '.

Christopher Maurer is Professor of Spanish at Boston University. His works include editions of Lorca's *Collected Poems* and *Selected Poems, Poet in New York, Conferencias* (2 vols) and (with Andrew A. Anderson) the *Epistolario completo*. He is also the author of two books on southern art, *Fortune's Favorite Child: The Uneasy Life of Walter Anderson* and *Dreaming in Clay on the Coast of Mississippi: Love and Art at Shearwater*, and the translator of Baltasar Gracián's *The Art of Worldly Wisdom*.

Alberto Mira is Reader in Film Studies at Oxford Brookes University, where he teaches film narrative, issues of gender and film and Spanish culture and society. He has published on film and homosexuality, as well as on Spanish theatre and theory of translation. His monograph *De Sodoma a Chueca*, published in 2004, is a cultural history of homosexuality in Spain. He is the editor of *24 Frames: The Cinema of Spain and Portugal*. He is now working on a monograph on Catalan writer Terenci Moix. His first novel appeared in 2005.

Antonio Monegal teaches literary theory, comparative literature and film at the Universitat Pompeu Fabra in Barcelona. Among other publications, he is the author of *Luis Buñuel de la literatura al cine* and *En los límites de la diferencia: Poesía e imagen en las vanguardias hispánicas*. He has edited the anthology *Literatura y pintura*, and García Lorca's *El público* and *Viaje a la luna*, and was a member of the national advisory board for the García Lorca centenary celebration. His current research is on the representation of wars in literature and the visual arts. In 2004 he co-curated an exhibition entitled 'At War' at the Centre de Cultura Contemporània de Barcelona.

Chris Perriam is Professor of Hispanic Studies at the University of Manchester. His research interests are: poetry in Spanish, queer writing in Spain, and contemporary Spanish cinema. His publications include *A New History of Spanish Writing from 1939 to the 1990s* (ed. and co-author) and *From Banderas to Bardem: Stars and Masculinities in Recent Spanish Cinema*.

Xon de Ros is University Lecturer and Fellow of Lady Margaret Hall, Oxford. She has published articles on Lorca in collective volumes and journals ('Science and Myth in Lorca's "Llanto"', 'Ignacio Sánchez Mejías Blues'), as well as more generally on Spanish film. Her book, *Primitivismo y Modernismo: Maria Blanchard y los escritores de 1927*, will be published in 2007 by Peter Lang AG.

Eric Southworth is University Lecturer in Spanish, and Fellow of St Peter's College, Oxford. He has written on his long-standing interests Galdós, Machado, Valle-Inclán and Lorca; on the latter, he has published 'Lorca's "San Rafael (Córdoba)" and Some Other Texts' in the *Modern Language Review*.

D. Gareth Walters is Professor of Hispanic Studies at the University of Exeter. Among numerous articles are studies of Manuel de Falla and Lorca, while his more recent books include *'Canciones' and the Early Poetry of Lorca: A Study in Critical Methodology and Poetic Maturity* (2002) and *The Cambridge Introduction to Spanish Poetry* (2002). A book on the Catalan poet Salvador Espriu is in press.

Sarah Wright is Senior Lecturer in Hispanic Studies at Royal Holloway, University of London. She is author of *The Trickster-Function in the Theatre of García Lorca* and has research interests in Spanish culture, theatre and film. She is currently working on an interdisciplinary approach to the legendary Spanish seducer, Don Juan.

ACKNOWLEDGEMENTS

The editor wishes to extend his thanks to Manuel Fernández-Montesinos García and the *Herederos de Federico García Lorca* for permission to reproduce Lorca's texts and to William Peter Kosmas for his help and advice in this matter. He also gratefully acknowledges the authors of translations that have been cited in this book: Catherine Brown, Ian Gibson, Will Kirkland, John London, Christopher Maurer, Greg Simon and Stephen F. White. The editor would also like to thank Stephen Hart of Tamesis and Elspeth Ferguson and the editorial team at Boydell & Brewer, and is grateful to the Department of Spanish and Spanish American Studies, King's College London, for its assistance with the costs of publication.

Introduction

Biography and Interpretation

FEDERICO BONADDIO

Personality

Lorca's personality – the distinguishing characteristics of the man as they relate to his life story – weighs heavily, it seems, on the criticism of his work. 'García Lorca', writes Paul Julian Smith, 'is perhaps the most extreme case of proprietorial authorship in Spanish literature: it seems impossible to approach his texts without acknowledging his person, and it is almost an article of faith amongst critics that in Lorca literature and life are one.'[1] For Smith, writing in the late 1980s, the problem with Lorca criticism is that it has sought in his work characteristics of homogeneity and uniformity by which to link it to the person himself. This has given rise, according to Smith, to a number of shared critical preconceptions: that, for instance, Lorca is 'at once universal and particular' (p. 107), or that he, like all authors, 'must be equipped with an *oeuvre* whose value is consistent, whose conceptual field is coherent, whose style is unified' (p. 108). Smith reminds us also that critical judgements of Lorca are historically specific: the fact, for example, that 'the anti-fascism and homosexuality repressed or condemned by early critics are proclaimed and celebrated by later ones' (p. 107) demonstrates just how treacherous the path connecting authors with their texts can be. Smith's Foucauldian approach to Lorca is one that considers the author to be 'not a person but a function' (Smith, p. 106) and that deems it necessary for the author to 'be deprived of his role as originator' (p. 107), thus undermining traditional criticism's maintenance of the direct relation between the personality of the author and the ideas of the text. The implications of this approach are that questions like 'Who really spoke? Is it really he and not someone else? With what authenticity or originality? And what part of his deepest self did he express in his discourse?' give way to other questions such as 'What are the modes of existence of this discourse? Where has it been used, how can it circulate, and who can appropriate it for himself? What are the places in it

---

[1] Paul Julian Smith, *The Body Hispanic: Gender and Sexuality in Spanish and Spanish American Literature* (Oxford: Oxford University Press, 1989), ch. 4 ('Lorca and Foucault'), 105–37 (p. 107).

where there is room for possible subjects? Who can assume these various subject-functions?'[2]

Whether or not we are persuaded by the Foucauldian approach, Smith's analysis is important in that it encourages us, at the very least, to enquire into the relationship between an author's life and his work and the extent to which our own approach to Lorca's texts should be governed, and in which ways, by an understanding of the personality to whom those texts have been ascribed. There have always been, and there still are, critics who attempt to look at Lorca's work with little or no regard for personal or biographical context, even though their approaches may not necessarily meet the anti-humanist criteria advocated by Smith. Among them we can find histories of Lorca's aesthetic development, formal and linguistic analyses, and symbological studies.[3] Recently, reader-oriented theories, discourse studies and performance studies have played their part in shifting emphasis away from origins and on to questions of reception and delivery.[4] And, of course, there is the ever-increasing interest in translating Lorca.[5]

It is always significant when critics make a special point of distancing their work from the suggestion of allusions to the 'real-life' circumstances of the author, being – as it seems they are – ever aware of that 'personality' (with all its dangers, with all it implies) looming just overhead. For example, Carlos Ramos-Gil (p. 12) presents his study as 'an analysis from within, leaving outside

---

[2] Michel Foucault, 'What is an author?', in David Lodge (ed.), *Modern Criticism and Theory. A Reader* (London and New York: Longman, 1988), 196–210.

[3] See, for example, Marie Laffranque's seminal *Les idées esthétiques de Federico García Lorca* (París: Centre de Recherches Hispaniques, 1967); David William Foster, 'Reiterative Formulas in García Lorca's Poetry', *Language and Style*, 9, 3 (Summer 1976), 171–91, or Salvador López Quero, 'Formas de atribución en la poesía de Federico García Lorca', *Alfinge*, 13 (2001), 143–7; Rupert C. Allen's *The Symbolic World of Federico García Lorca* (Albuquerque: University of New Mexico Press, 1972) and his *Psyche and Symbol in the Theatre of Federico García Lorca. Perlimpín. Yerma. Blood Wedding* (Austin and London: University of Texas Press, 1974), or Carlos Ramos-Gil, *Claves líricas de García Lorca. Ensayos sobre la expresión y los climas poéticos lorquianos* (Madrid: Aguilar, 1967).

[4] See, for example, Luis Beltrán Fernández de los Ríos, *La arquitectura del humo: una reconstrucción del 'Romancero gitano' de Federico García Lorca* (London: Tamesis, 1986), Dennis Perri, 'Lorca's Suite "Palimpsestos": Keeping the Reader at Bay', *Romance Quarterly*, 38, 2 (May 1991), 197–211, or D. Gareth Walter's recourse to Stanley Fish, in *'Canciones' and the Early Poetry of Lorca: A Study in Critical Methodology and Poetic Maturity* (Cardiff: University of Wales Press, 2002), 33–4, 38 and 39; Robin Warner's *Powers of Utterance: A Discourse Approach to Works of Lorca, Machado and Valle-Inclán* (Bristol: Hiplam, 2003); and María Delgado's 'Lluis Pasqual's unknown Lorcas', in Sebastian Doggart and Michael Thompson (eds), *Fire, Blood and the Alphabet: One Hundred Years of Lorca* (Durham: University of Durham, 1999), 81–106, or her *Other Spanish Theatres: Erasure and Inscription on the Spanish Stage* (Manchester: Manchester University Press, 2003).

[5] See, for example, Merryn Williams, 'Translating Lorca', *Vida Hispánica*, 18 (September 1998), 25–8; Eric Keenaghan, 'Jack Spicer's Pricks and Cocksuckers: Translating Homosexuality into Visibility', *Translator*, 4, 2 (November 1998), 273–94; or the section 'Translating Lorca' in Doggart and Thompson, 225–82.

– unless indispensable – curiosities, source-hunting, forced comparisons and secondary detail'. For its aim is 'to strike up a dialogue with those readers [. . .] for whom human interest, the world of pure creation and poetic vision count for more than mere anecdote, private goings-on, picturesqueness and the glamour of García Lorca's poetry' (Bonaddio's translation). Luis Beltrán Fernández de los Ríos (p. 256), commenting on the frequency with which 'pechos o senos' [breasts] appear in *Romancero gitano* [*Gypsy Ballads*], explains that his intention is not 'in any way to identify García Lorca's possible sexual inclinations, but to take note of the existence of yet another component that tends to confirm the logic of [his] reconstruction [of the text]' (Bonaddio's translation). And Rupert C. Allen, in order to clarify his recourse to psychoanalysis in his exploration of symbol in the theatre, explains that his intention is not 'to treat [Lorca's] work as biographical material contributing toward a psychoanalytic understanding of Lorca the man' (Allen 1974, p. 32). What he is interested in, rather, is the dramatic potential Lorca saw in Freudian theory. Allen also sees his own work on the poetry as being not 'about a foreign poet so much as [. . .] about the world of symbols which all of us inhabit and the transformation of that world into poetry' (Allen 1972, p. viii). Moreover, for Allen, 'What is essential to Lorca transcends the limits of nationality'; what Allen is concerned with is the 'understanding of the symbol as the *substance* of poetry – with Lorca as [. . .] principal exhibit' (p. viii). 'The dreams that you and I had last night', writes Allen, 'are the same that Lorca had and wrote about in his day' (Allen 1972, p. ix).

Different critics, then, have had their own reasons for excluding the man's life from their evaluation of his work. Others, by contrast, have decided that there are indeed legitimate reasons to delve into this domain.[6] In this respect, it is worth noting Stanley Fish's reaffirmation of the inescapability of biography in his essay 'Biography and Intention'. Fish argues that 'if [in modern literary theory] the self has been dissolved', it does not follow that 'the notion of an intentional agent with a history and biography must dissolve too'.[7] For (and here

---

6 Daniel Devoto claims in his article '¿Tesis, o prótesis?', *Bulletin Hispanique*, 89, 1–4 (1987), 331–58 (p. 343), that 'all artistic creation is autobiographical, and doubly so: by virtue of belonging, as an event, to its author's biography, and because it feeds on that biography' (trans. Bonaddio). David Johnston, in his *Federico García Lorca* (Bath: Absolute Press, 1998), writes: 'The present book contains discussions of most of [Lorca's] plays and poetry, on the basis that one cannot separate Lorca's life from his work' (p. 8). 'This is not to say', adds Johnston, 'that [. . .] everything Lorca wrote is autobiographical, or can be explained only by reference to his personal circumstances. There is no simple relationship between biography and creativity.' Compare these with the view expressed by John Butt in his review article of Leslie Stainton's biography, *Lorca: A Dream of Life*, entitled 'I'm not a happy poet', *London Review of Books*, 1 April 1999, pp. 27–8: 'The obliqueness and obscurity of [Lorca's] texts means that biographies are of no use when it comes to understanding his poems and plays' (p. 28).

7 Stanley Fish, 'Biography and Intention', in William H. Epstein (ed.), *Contesting the subject: essays in the postmodern theory and practice of biography and biographical criticism* (West Lafayette, IN: Purdue University Press, 1991), 9–16.

he cites Foucault's 'What is an Author?') 'we have "merely transposed the empirical characteristics of an author to a transcendental anonymity" ' (Fish, p. 13). He continues:

> That is, if the originating author is dissolved into a series of functions [. . .], then we have not done away with intention and biography but merely relocated them. In principle it does not matter whether the originating agent is a discrete human consciousness or the spirit of an age or a literary tradition or a culture or a language itself; to read something as the product of any one of these 'transcendental anonymities' is to endow that anonymity with an intention and a biography. The choice [. . .] is not between reading biographically and reading in some other way (there is no other way) but rather between different biographical readings that have their source in different specifications of the sources of agency. The only way to read unbiographically would be to refrain from construing meaning – to refrain, that is, from regarding the marks before you as manifestations of intentional behaviour; but that would be not to read at all. (Fish, pp. 13–14)

Fish explains that to say that meaning and biography are inextricable 'does not direct us to prefer one mode of interpretation to another'. Nor does pointing to the inescapability of biography remove any of the 'traditional questions [. . .] about what constitutes a biography, about what is and is not biographical evidence, about what kind of entities can have biographies, and so on'. Yet 'we will always be reading [an author's] words as the intentional product of the person or nonperson we now understand him to be' (Fish, p. 15).

Returning to Lorca, it is clear that the idea of the man and artist that has emerged from biographical investigation is by no means a uniform one; nor indeed is the significance that has been attributed to his 'intentional product', the impact of biography on his texts having led to a number of problematic or contradictory readings. To begin with, Lorca's death at the hands of the Nationalists at the outbreak of the Civil War and the status of martyr consequently conferred upon him have prompted some critics to look for evidence in his texts of political engagement in order to make sense of his brutal murder, while others continue to doubt Lorca's political credentials, seeing him above all as a man devoted to the arts. The abrupt end to his life has also meant that references in his work to death have been interpreted, retrospectively, as presaging his tragic fate (as Smith, p. 110, notes), even though we might presume that if human beings can be sure of anything, it is surely that they will one day have to die. Then there is the matter of Lorca's sexuality, which, some would say, has given rise to a number of generalizations or misconceptions. For example, that his homosexuality was a source of anguish that inevitably permeates his entire work; that his work cannot be understood without taking account of his homosexuality (although some argue that it can and should);[8] or that he had a kind of

---

[8] Johnston (p. 22), making clear that the suggestion is not 'that Lorca's work is intelligible only in terms of a homosexual reading', argues nonetheless 'that Lorca's sexuality, and

insider's understanding of the sensibilities of women and the predicaments that they faced (see Smith again, p. 110). There is also the question of the level of erudition of this versatile talent, some critics finding in the details of Lorca's personal library evidence to support their view that he was well-read, others perhaps confusing the complexity of their own theoretical approach with complexities in the texts that can only be the product of an erudite thinker, and others still, finding it difficult to reconcile their idea of an academic low-achiever, yet undoubted instinctual talent, with notions of intellectual prowess or polymathy.[9] And then there is the way in which, from a foreign perspective primarily, Lorca has come to embody the clichés associated with Spain and particularly Andalusia, whether it be in terms of his ' "Latin" temperament' (Smith, p. 135) or the perceived folkloricism of some of his texts. There is always the danger that what some find so attractive about the man and his work may in fact obscure from them subtleties both in the personality of that man and in the texts themselves.

Biographies

It is, of course, in biographies of Lorca that critics have tended to seek the information by which to support their respective theses, although it is also true that the idea that some have of the man has arisen from their very reading of his texts – an approach, however, which raises certain epistemological concerns. Luis Fernández-Cifuentes alerts us to these concerns when he chides the biographer Ian Gibson for claiming that Lorca's early poetry is mainly autobiographical,[10] Gibson taking his cue, it seems, from Lorca's preface to his *Libro de*

---

above all the crisis of being homosexual in a society that gifted the word *macho* to the world, is a key to the very distinctive sense of life that informs his work'. Walters, on the other hand, in his *'Canciones' and the Early Poetry of Lorca*, emphasizes the alternative reading: 'In the mass of writing about Lorca's supposed tragic situation as a homosexual and the frustrations he would thereby have experienced both as a man and a writer it is easy to forget that his poetry contains a variety of perspectives on love [. . .]. We must, even then, be wary not to fall into the trap [. . .] which results from reading all of Lorca's utterances on amatory subjects as homosexually oriented, in defiance of the evidence' (p. 191).

9 See, for example, Butt's reference, in respect of Stainton's biography, to the 'suspicion [. . .] that Lorca was shallow as an artist and as a person', or that he was 'a man who enjoyed a relatively easy emotional life and had few, and rather conventional, intellectual preoccupations' (p. 27). Butt concludes his review article by affirming his belief that Lorca was 'not an idiot savant with an adventitious gift for unexpected metaphors, but an adult writer who reflected intensely if not very systematically about Modernism in the arts, and moved in sophisticated avant-garde circles without ever losing a child's capacity for wonder' (p. 28). Stainton herself notes that Lorca 'once claimed to have read only two books in the world', although he also once 'bragged of having gone through periods when he read two books a day "as an intellectual exercise" ', adding that 'Martínez Nadal eventually concluded that Lorca read far more than anyone suspected', but that 'he was no pedant', taking 'from books, and from conversations about books, only what he needed for his writing'. In Leslie Stainton, *Lorca: A Dream of Life* (London: Bloomsbury, 1998), 124.

10 See Luis Fernández-Cifuentes, 'Ian Gibson, *Federico García Lorca 1: De Fuente*

poemas [*Book of Poems*], in which the poet declares that the book is 'la imagen exacta de mis días de adolescencia y juventud' [the exact image of the days of my adolescence and youth] and 'el reflejo fiel de mi corazón y de mi espíritu' [the faithful reflection of my heart and soul].[11] Fernández asks how it is possible to make such a claim for poetry, since 'it contradicts all notions of polysemy established by contemporary literary theory' (Bonaddio's translation). Yet, without wishing to detract from the validity of Fernández's point, it must be said that it is extremely tempting to see autobiography in a body of work that is, in part, highly lyrical, at times very self-conscious (we might note here the obvious example of the title *Poeta en Nueva York* [*Poet in New York*]), and in which critics have pointed to identity and selfhood as being major preoccupations. Indeed, in *Poeta en Nueva York*, the constant use of the first person, the inclusion of the figure of the poet, the references to the inhabitants of New York, to places and to landmarks, all seem to favour the possibility of an autobiographical reading of the poems whose content, regardless of the epistemological problems, has often been treated by critics as evidence of Lorca's social and political concerns.

In any case, when critics take the opposite route, when they 'use the life to interpret the work', rather than 'the work to interpret the life',[12] they should bear in mind, nonetheless, that the work of the biographer cannot be equated automatically with the truth. In his book, *The Nature of Biography*, John A. Garraty affirms that the biographer's domain is reality, yet he also makes clear the necessarily interpretative aspect of biographical work: 'Instead of steering clear of interpretations, instead of stifling his imagination, instead of attempting the impossible task of refusing to select the important from the trivial in the interest of an unattainable objectivity, the biographer must interpret, imagine, and select constantly if he is to approach the reality he seeks.'[13] A 'record of a life' (Garraty, p. 3) biography may be, but ultimately the biographer's aim is to portray a personality; a portrayal whose technical difficulties are essentially artistic (see Garraty, p. 9) and whose success is no guarantee of accuracy. For given the complexities of the human personality, the biographer's interpretation of character can at best only be convincing, but it can never be given with absolute certainty (see Garraty, p. 11).

There are numerous biographical works on the subject of Lorca, some combining his life-story with interpretations of the texts, a few focusing on the important relationship between Lorca and Dalí (and Buñuel), and others taking

Vaqueros a Nueva York, 1898–1929 (review article)', *Nueva Revista de Filología Hispánica*, 34 (1985–6), 224–32 (p. 231).

11 Federico García Lorca, *Obras completas*, I, ed. Arturo del Hoyo, 3 vols, 22nd edn (Madrid: Aguilar, 1986), 5.

12 The citations are from Susan Sontag's introduction to Walter Benjamin's *'One-Way Street' and Other Writings*, trans. Edmund Jephcott and Kingsley Shorter (London: Verso, 1985), 7–28 (p. 9).

13 John A. Garraty, *The Nature of Biography* (New York: Alfred A. Knopf, 1957), 19.

the form of memoirs which, like autobiography for Garraty, '[result] from remembrance', unlike biography, which is the product of 'reconstruction' (Garraty, p. 26).[14] It is perhaps because of the perceived partiality or subjectiveness of memoir that literary critics have most often had recourse to biography proper, although their choice is arguably founded upon a miscalculation of the degree to which biographies represent objective accounts. In English, the best-known and most widely used biographies are Ian Gibson's *Federico García Lorca: A Life* (1989), first published in Spanish in two volumes (1985 and 1987 respectively)[15] and Leslie Stainton's *Lorca: A Dream of Life* (1998).

In terms of the amount of factual information it contains, Gibson's biography is currently unparalleled, which is why, no doubt, it has become a standard reference for scholars requiring precise dates, details of place, records of conversations and events, lists of acquaintances, and so forth. It has arguably also played its role, along with Gibson's later work, *Lorca–Dalí: El amor que no pudo ser* [*Lorca–Dalí: The Love That Could Never Be*], in helping to dismantle what Johnston (p. 13) calls 'the wall of silence which has been constructed around Lorca's homosexuality, the result of either explicit denial or the dismissive view which holds that his sexuality is just another streak of colour in the boldly painted flamenco legend'.[16] Yet so packed is Gibson's biography with contextual information that Lorca himself seems, at times, to disappear amidst it all, the book falling into that category described by Garraty (p. 24) as being 'closer akin to history than biography'. This is one of the points made by Fernández-Cifuentes in his review article of the book, which is overall highly critical of Gibson's approach to biography. '[Gibson's] historical characters', writes Fernández (p. 226), 'are often figures drowned by that very passion for documentation which seeks to recuperate them' (Bonaddio's translation). It is in, among other things, this passion for documentation that we sense, according to

---

14 On Lorca and Dalí, see Agustín Sánchez Vidal, *Buñuel, Lorca, Dalí: el enigma sin fin*, 2nd edn (Barcelona: Planeta, 1996) or Ian Gibson, *Lorca–Dalí: El amor que no pudo ser* (Barcelona: Plaza & Janés, 1999). For memoirs, see Carlos Morla Lynch, *En España con Federico García Lorca: páginas de un diario íntimo (1928–1936)* (Madrid: Aguilar, 1957); José Mora Guarnido, *Federico García Lorca y su mundo: Testimonio para una biografía* (Buenos Aires: Losada, 1958); Jorge Guillén, *Federico en persona. Semblanza y epistolario* (Buenos Aires: Emecé Editores, 1959); Francisco García Lorca, *Federico y su mundo*, ed. Mario Hernández, 2nd / revised edition (Madrid: Alianza, 1981); and Isabel García Lorca, *Recuerdos míos* (Barcelona: Tusquets, 2002). See also Marcelle Auclair's biography, *Enfances et mort de García Lorca* (Paris: Seuil, 1968).

15 See Ian Gibson, *Federico García Lorca, 1. De Fuente Vaqueros a Nueva York, 1898–1929* (Barcelona: Grijalbo, 1985); *Federico García Lorca, 2. De Nueva York a Fuente Grande, 1929–1936* (Barcelona: Grijalbo, 1987) and *Federico García Lorca: A Life* (New York: Pantheon / London: Faber & Faber, 1989).

16 See Johnston's introduction (Johnston, pp. 11–22) for his account of the silences and absences in Lorcan scholarship, the opposing positions taken up during the 1998 centenary celebrations, and the gaps in the centenary exhibition held at Madrid's Reina Sofía Museum, in whose catalogue Gibson 'raises one of the few dissident voices among the rather more neutral scholars assembled there' (p. 19).

Fernández, the personality of the biographer bearing down upon the text at the expense, regrettably, of the personality of his subject. In the quest for truth, understood here as material fact, what is missing perhaps is the imaginative detail required to bring the subject to life (see Fernández-Cifuentes, pp. 227–8).

Stainton's biography, on the other hand, is less inundated by the particulars of context and is able thus to give prominence to Lorca's engagement with the arts, his artistic development, and the friendships and acquaintances that helped him in his career, although like Gibson, perhaps, she arguably misses the opportunity to delve deeply into Lorca's relationship with his close family. In his appraisal of Gibson's book, Fernández (pp. 229–30) refers to the way that biography, since Freud, has tended to make a priority of familial relationships, and how Gibson, at most, only alludes to the importance that Lorca's relationship with his father may have had in the writer's development. Stainton herself only goes so far as to remind us periodically of Lorca's almost constant financial dependence on his father as well as Don Federico's anxieties and doubts about his son's career prospects. John Butt, in a review of the book, states that Stainton's biography 'sticks close to the ascertainable facts of Lorca's life and [. . .] is as strong on detail as it is reluctant to speculate' (Butt, p. 28). Yet we can sense in the selection of detail (like the references to Lorca's constant requests for money to his father) certain reservations on the part of the biographer in respect of her subject, even though her portrayal of Lorca is ultimately not unkind. The cumulative effect of this selection is summarized thus by Butt:

> It may seem odd to ask whether a poet whose mind was an inexhaustible source of sparkling metaphors had a rich inner life, but Stainton evidently has her misgivings about Lorca's natural frivolity. She takes more note than Gibson of his disastrous academic record, of his 'petulance and immaturity, his incessant and puerile need for adulation', of his mendaciousness, of his hysterical streak, of the absence of books in his rooms and his habitual preference for partying over reading, and of his dislike for intellectual discussions, during which he tended to slope off to the piano. (Butt, p. 27)

Whether we agree with him or not, what is interesting about Butt's observations (other than the fact that they point once again to the impact of the biographer's own personality on the text) is the way that they allude to a perceived contradiction between, on the one hand, Lorca's undoubted creative ability – a sign of 'a rich inner life' – and, on the other, aspects of his behaviour that signal some sort of deficiency or lack. For it is quite possible that, far from undermining Lorca – the man and artist – in any way, this contradiction is, instead, the very key to unlocking the secrets of his personality that biographers have tended to overlook, and one that deserves further investigation, either in terms of a psychoanalytical reading or some other theoretical approach.

One of the obstacles for biographers in search of that 'inner life' has been, no doubt, the fact that Lorca seems not to have kept a personal diary. The absence of intimate detail that a diary might have afforded means that biographers have had to look primarily to Lorca's correspondence for the reconstruction of their subject, as well as to the testimonies of those who met or knew the man.[17] Of course, neither of these sources can necessarily be taken at face value. Take, for example, the letters that Lorca wrote to his family from New York in which there is little sense of the anguish that permeates the poetry that he produced in the metropolis. We might ask ourselves in which of these sets of texts resides the truth about Lorca's New York experience, but it can never be as straightforward as this. What is clear is that, in approaching either, we should be aware of the strategies and context of textual practice.[18] The letters cannot be read, for example, without taking into account the identity of the recipients or without speculating on the aims of the sender. Bound as they are to contextual considerations, they must be subjected to an interpretative process that takes these considerations into account, just as other individual testimonies should be, given that a whole series of conditions (personal tastes, mutual interests, political beliefs, and so forth) are relevant to our assessment of other people's representations of the biographical subject.

Interpretation

Thus we find ourselves, it seems, on a slippery slope – sliding from the uncertainties surrounding critical practice, to the limitations of biography and the doubts that are raised by biographical sources. In each case we are left to contend with the nature of textuality, which means that in our reconstruction of either the work or the man we can never totally escape the speculative character of our task. And nor, perhaps, should we try to. For, if anything, the limitation of some biography is marked by its very tendency to focus on the facts rather than on the relation between them; a relation that opens up a space for the biographer, just as the relation between texts, or between authors, their texts and the world, opens up a space for the critic, to enter and not simply describe, but also interpret.

Interpretation is not to be taken here in the sense that Susan Sontag deplores in her seminal essay 'Against Interpretation', as that which places the stress on content, as an exercise of translation (as Sontag puts it), uncovering meaning 'in

---

[17] As Christopher Maurer remarks in his prologue to the collected letters, *Epistolario completo*, ed. Andrew A. Anderson and Christopher Maurer (Madrid: Cátedra, 1997), 7–17 (pp. 16–17), despite the efforts of scholars, the body of correspondence available is still incomplete, a fact which he attributes to a life brutally cut short and the scant attention that Lorca paid to collecting and ordering his paperwork. Johnston also laments the 'frustrating litany of unpublished correspondence and withheld private papers', although his suggestion is that it is the very nature of the content of these intimate items, as in the case of 'a huge portion of the potentially explosive correspondence with Salvador Dalí', that has prevented our access to the them (Johnston, pp. 19–20).

[18] See, for example, Federico Bonaddio, 'Lorca's *Poeta en Nueva York*: Creativity and the City', in 'The Image of the City', *Romance Studies*, 22 (Autumn 1993), 41–51, for an interpretation of the poetry in the context of personal and creative preoccupations.

order to set up a shadow world of "meanings" '.[19] Nor is it to be understood 'in the broadest sense, the sense in which Nietzsche (rightly) says, "There are no facts, only interpretations" ' (Sontag 1967, p. 5). To interpret, here, is to evaluate the implications of relations that are not confined to content.[20] In biography these may take the form of relations between facts, between testimony and the context of its delivery, whether its context be personal or more broadly cultural. In literature, the relations may be intertextual, the context might be a literary genre or mode, or even social.[21] And where these relations are between the text and the circumstances of its production, biographical information is an important element in the interpretative process.

What, in effect, Gibson and Stainton describe in their works – the former with his detailed references to the members of the circles in which Lorca moved, the latter with her emphasis on Lorca's dependence on friendships and acquaintances – is the circumstances of Modernist production.[22] The first decades of the twentieth century saw a proliferation of groups, journals and manifestos, along with the collaboration that such enterprises entailed. Writers and artists knew of each other's work, sought alliances and recognition, and interaction was an integral part of the literary and artistic scene. With this in mind, we can look, for

[19] Susan Sontag, 'Against Interpretation', in Susan Sontag, *Against Interpretation and other essays* (London: Eyre & Spottiswoode, 1967), 3–14 (pp. 5 and 7).

[20] That there is no single view among critics of where the limits of interpretation lie is clearly illustrated by Devoto's concerns about the extent to which some criticism – here the guilty parties in his mind are Eutimio Martín's *Federico García Lorca, heterodoxo y mártir* and Michèle Ramond's *Psychotextes. La question de L'Autre dans Federico García Lorca* – can lose sight of interpretation and use the text instead as a springboard for critical invention: 'Their critical interpretation of Lorcan texts jubilantly transcends interpretation and criticism, and rises without pausing to the heights of the highest and purest invention. Judged in terms of the humble task of the critic, they might recall that there is no more incorrigible philologist than he who has no wish to see the text he has before him' (Devoto, p. 358; trans. Bonaddio).

[21] See, for example, Sandra Cary Robertson's evaluation of Lorca's work in relation to the poetry of Spain's oral tradition, in her *Lorca, Alberti, and the Theatre of Popular Poetry* (New York: Peter Lang, 1991); or Xon de Ros's readings of *Llanto por Ignacio Sánchez Mejías [Lament for the Death of Ignacio Sánchez Mejías]* in relation to the poetic elegy and jazz blues, in 'Ignacio Sánchez Mejías Blues', in *Crossing Fields in Modern Spanish Culture*, ed. Federico Bonaddio and Xon de Ros (Oxford: Legenda [European Humanities Research Centre], 2003), 81–91, and in the context of the social and political circumstances of the Second Republic, in 'Science and Myth in Lorca's "Llanto"', *Modern Language Review*, 95, 1 (2000), 114–26.

[22] It should be noted that critics often make a distinction between Modernism, to which we are referring above, namely the, among other things, highly self-conscious literary production of groups and individuals writing in the West in the first twenty to thirty years of the twentieth century, and *modernismo*, a term used to define the work specifically of Latin American and Spanish poets influenced by trends of the nineteenth-century French *fin-de-siècle* (parnassian, decadent, symbolist) and founded by the Nicaraguan poet, Rubén Darío, in the early 1890s. For a general survey of Modernism, see Malcolm Bradbury and James McFarlane (eds), *Modernism* (Harmondsworth: Penguin, 1976). For a discussion that sets *modernismo* in the broader context of Modernism, see Matei Calinescu, *Five Faces of Modernity* (Durham, NC: Duke University Press, 1987), 68–85.

example, to the theorist Pierre Bourdieu for a possible model for the analysis and interpretation of creativity in such circumstances.[23]

For Bourdieu, who has affinities with Foucault,[24] context and relational factors are paramount. Speaking in terms of the 'field of cultural production', Bourdieu stresses the importance of defining the field and 'of understanding works of art as a *manifestation* of the field as a whole, in which all the powers of the field, and all the determinisms inherent in its structure and functioning, are concentrated' (Bourdieu, p. 37). A whole number of relational factors now come into play, such as the personal disposition of the artist (for example, class, wealth or temperament), the dominant definitions of art (for example, as anti-bourgeois), the specific knowledge or mastery that access to the field presupposes, or the position of art in the market economy. Bourdieu thus provides a theoretical framework in which we can reinterpret not only Lorca's associations with other artists and influential members of the contemporary artistic scene, but also the shifts in his artistic development, which can now be understood as something other than the mere product of artistic influence at any given moment: namely the manifestation of positions taken up by Lorca within the field of art with a view to gaining recognition therein.[25] This position-taking is synonymous with both the dynamics of association – the adoption of the principles that hold sway – and differentiation, by which the artist stakes his claim to the established and indispensable virtues of originality. All this is not to detract in any way from the value of Lorca's work in itself or to suggest that none of his associations took place in the context of what we might call friendship and all that this commonly implies. Instead it is to accept that artistic production is not exempt from social processes and, moreover, that it itself has a role in shaping and ordering society by virtue, for example, of the way it reinforces, or undermines, definitions of art (as in the case, for instance, of art-for-art's sake) that limit access to the field. It is to see the self (the author) in terms of the 'variety

23 See Pierre Bourdieu, *The Field of Cultural Production. Essays on Art and Literature*, ed. and introd. Randal Johnson (Cambridge: Polity Press, 1993), in particular the essays 'The Field of Cultural Production, or: The Economic World Reversed' (pp. 29–73), 'Field of Power, Literary Field and Habitus' (pp. 161–75) and 'The Historical Genesis of a Pure Aesthetic' (pp. 254–66).

24 In his introduction, Randal Johnson notes that 'Like Foucault, Bourdieu sees power as diffuse and often concealed in broadly accepted, and often unquestioned, ways of seeing and describing the world; but unlike Foucault, in Bourdieu's formulation this diffuse or symbolic power is closely entwined with – but not reducible to – economic and political power' (Bourdieu, p. 2). Moreover, Bourdieu himself explains how Foucault 'refuses to relate works in any way to their social conditions of production', arguing on the contrary that 'it is not possible [. . .] to make the cultural order [. . .] a sort of autonomous, transcendent sphere, capable of developing in accordance with its own laws' (Bourdieu, p. 33).

25 Although she makes no reference to Bourdieu, Jacqueline Cockburn, in her article 'Gifts from the Poet to the Art Critic', in Federico Bonaddio and Xon de Ros (eds), *Crossing Fields in Modern Spanish Literature* (Oxford: Legenda [European Humanities Research Centre], 2003), 67–80, argues that Lorca's drawings provided him with a means to enter into debates on art by adopting, in effect, the same currency.

of interpersonal systems that operate through it'.[26] And it is also to establish the relevance to artistic production of much biographical information that otherwise risks falling into the irrelevance of what Ramos-Gil called 'mere anecdote, private goings-on, picturesqueness'.

If we take Stainton's biography, for example, there are innumerable pronouncements by the poet and remarks attributed to him that can be interpreted as signs of Lorca's position-taking and of the knowledge of the field that it presupposes. Thus we come face to face with a poet who appropriates for himself the myth of the natural and indispensable character of poetic ability: ' "I was born a poet and an artist, just as others are born lame, blind, or handsome" ' (Stainton, p. 73); ' "I want to be a Poet through and through, living and dying by poetry" ' (p. 144). A poet who defines himself as innovative and anti-bourgeois: ' "The fight I must wage is enormous, for on the one hand I have before me the old school, and on the other I have the new school. And here I am, from the newest school, chopping and changing old rhythms and hackneyed ideas" ' (Stainton, p. 78); 'Spurred by his deepening zeal for the avant-garde, he sat in cafés with friends in Granada and mocked the vulgar tastes of the local bourgeoisie' (p. 116). A poet who affirms the peculiarity of the work by marking out the limits of its accessibility: ' "I have to defend these poems against incomprehension, dilettantism, and benevolent smiles" ' (p. 263). A poet who is aware and takes advantage of the hierarchies structuring his field: 'Lorca relished his sudden status as an international celebrity. To a young man from rural Cuba who introduced himself as a "poet," Lorca smiled indulgently and said, "Local, I take it?" ' (p. 253); ' "As you can see," Lorca informed his parents, "I've become a fashionable little boy after my useful and advantageous trip to America" ' (p. 268). And, finally, a poet who is able to change position according to aesthetic shifts, here from art-for-art's sake to social art: ' "I know very well how to do semi-intellectual theatre, but that's not what counts. In our day, the poet must open his veins for the people. That's why [. . .] I've devoted myself to the theatre, because it permits a more direct contact with the masses" ' (pp. 403–4).

Yet another model for our interpretation of Lorca's artistic production within its context is to be found in Edward Said's *The World, the Text, and the Critic* – a model that is, we might argue, potentially more affective than Bourdieu's. Here Said develops the notions of filiation and affiliation in his discussion of critical consciousness, the former corresponding to the ties connecting members of the same natal culture or same family, the latter to the construction of a new order of relationships: 'What I am describing', writes Said, 'is the transition from a failed idea or possibility of filiation to a kind of compensatory order that, whether it is a party, an institution, a culture, a set of beliefs, or even a world-vision, provides men and women with a new form of relationship, which I have

---

[26] Jonathan Culler, *Structuralist Poetics: Structuralism, Linguistics, and the Study of Literature* (Ithaca, NY: Cornell University Press, 1975), 28; cited by Fish, p. 13.

been calling affiliation but which is also a new system.'[27] Said explains that in the new affiliative mode of relationship 'we will find the deliberately explicit goal of using that new order to reinstate vestiges of the kind of authority associated in the past with filiative order' (Said, p. 19). He continues:

> Thus if a filial relationship was held together by natural bonds and natural forms of authority – involving obedience, fear, love, respect, and instinctual conflict – the new affiliative relationship changes these bonds into what seems to be transpersonal forms – such as guild consciousness, consensus, collegiality, professional respect, class, and the hegemony of a dominant culture. The filiative scheme belongs to the realms of nature and of 'life,' whereas affiliation belongs exclusively to culture and society. (Said, p. 20)

It is not difficult to see how this model, which Said applies to his investigation of the bonds forged by critics, may be applied equally to a discussion of the groups and associations that sprang up in the Modernist period. The implication for our study of Lorca would be that he, as a result of the failed possibility of filiation, sought via his artistic production to enter into a community of an affiliative order. We could conceive of this failed possibility of filiation in terms of, for example, Lorca's sense of estrangement from the ideals of the bourgeois society into which he was born, which might equally explain both his attraction to the avant-garde and the allure of popular forms of expression, such as the *cante jondo* [flamenco deep song].[28] However, we might also conceive of filiation in regenerative terms. Said notes how 'Childless couples, orphaned children, aborted childbirths, and unregenerately celibate men and women populate the world of high modernism with remarkable insistence, all of them suggesting the difficulties of filiation' and he suggests (though arguably overstating his case) that consequent upon this pattern is 'the pressure to produce new and different ways of conceiving human relationships' (Said, p. 17).

Of course, we should be careful not to jump to conclusions about the relation between Lorca's homosexuality and his creative impulse, between childlessness and the need to forge alternative relationships. For it is one thing to see filiative limitation in terms of lack, that is, from the perspective of a value system that considers childlessness in wholly negative terms, and another to appreciate, as Said clearly does, the social character of human beings for whom relationships and belonging are vitally important.[29] Yet it is perhaps worth noting that

---

27 Edward W. Said, *The World, the Text, and the Critic* (Cambridge, MA: Harvard University, 1983), 19.

28 Stainton (p. 313) remarks that 'Despite the fact that he and his family belonged to it, Lorca despised Spain's middle class.'

29 In this context, see the poem from the New York series entitled 'Pequeño poema infinito' [Little Infinite Poem] (*Obras completas*, I, 547–8), where we find the line 'Equivocar el camino / es llegar a la mujer' [To take the wrong road / is to arrive at woman]. Translation from Federico García Lorca, *Collected Poems*, revised bilingual edition, ed. Christopher Maurer (New York: Farrar, Straus and Giroux, 2002), 763.

Stainton, echoing Gibson (see Gibson 1989, pp. 317 and 356), perceives child-lessness in her biography as both a source of inspiration and anguish for Lorca. She notes that he often 'summons the motif of the unborn child' in his works (Stainton, p. 288), that 'his own inability to engender a child [. . .] was both a poetic conceit and a private preoccupation' (p. 332), that 'while his own child-less condition freed him to live and work impulsively [. . .], it also removed him from the most basic of human cycles, and this was a fact to which he never entirely reconciled himself' (p. 333), and that 'as the oldest son of a wealthy Andalusian landowner' he knew that 'he was expected to engender offspring to perpetuate his family's name' (p. 397). She also cites the remark made by Lorca's close friend, the dancer and singer Encarnación López Júlvez ('La Argentinita'), at the opening of his play Yerma [Yerma], which focuses on the childless condition of its central character, a woman whose name provides the play's title: ' "The work is Federico's own tragedy. What he'd like most in the world is to get pregnant and give birth [. . .] Yerma is Federico, the tragedy of Federico" ' (p. 397).

Whatever we make of the suggestion that Lorca was frustrated (and inspired) by his childlessness, it is not, as we have implied, this element of biographical speculation that most concerns us in pointing to the possible application to his circumstances of the notions of filiation and affiliation. Rather it is the possi-bility that, as an alternative to Bourdieu's model, Lorca's associations at a pro-fessional level may be understood as representing a means for him to enter into a community where he is not so much seeking recognition in terms of status as instead looking for acceptance that can translate itself into a sense of belonging. The implications for our interpretation of, for example, the aesthetic shifts in his texts are that these be taken as signs of a desire for proximity, while the perceived originality of any of his works can be read as fulfilling a criterion of that affiliative order, that new cultural system, to which the artist wishes to belong. If the sense of belonging is indeed of primary importance here, then it is perhaps not at all surprising that so many of Lorca's artistic associates were also, as a glance at any of the biographies will tell us, some of his closest and most intimate friends. In any event, biography is once more, as Fish (p. 15) puts it, 'the winner', insofar as biographical evidence, in the broadest sense, provides the context for the interpretation of the motivations behind the author's work and insofar as that work remains connected to the very personality of the author. The only debate is, as ever, about how to define that personality. What is clear is that, in the context of Bourdieu or Said, our assessment of personality must never lose sight of either interpersonal or transpersonal systems.

Conclusion

Whatever our approach to his work, whether or not we feel that the details of his life are essential to our reading, the fact remains that it is difficult to come to his work in total ignorance of his biography, such has been our exposure, partic-ularly over the last twenty years or so, to the personality we call Lorca. If we decide to put our knowledge of what has been said about the man to use, then it is advisable, at the very least, to attempt to scrutinize the myths and the clichés that surround him. It is advisable also to question the very nature of biography, to identify its limitations, as well as find new theoretical frameworks in which to apply biographical fact. Ultimately, we are faced, at every level – biography, criticism and, indeed, the author's own texts – with the uncertainties of textual practice and interpretation. What is almost certain, however, is that whatever we uncover through our study of the man and his work is bound to add yet another Lorca to the many Lorcas who already exist.

1

Poetry

CHRISTOPHER MAURER

In an essay on one of his brother's plays, Francisco García Lorca points out that, although a 'process of maturation is visible in the work of all artists', there is no 'clear line of evolution' in Federico's work. 'As a poet and as a playwright, what Federico undergoes is a continuous metamorphosis,' rather than a clear evolution in any one direction. What he does is to 'adapt technical procedures to artistic intentions that vary with every work'.[1] Luis Fernández Cifuentes adds a further warning about sweeping generalizations: that Lorca's critics seem to be on a continual, reductive search for totality, continuity and unity in his work.[2]

Despite these caveats, one does discover in Lorca's poetry – both lyrical and dramatic – certain constant thematic and stylistic elements. He is, to begin with, an elegiac poet who looks beyond presence into absence, often evoking not what *is*, but what *is not*, what *was*, or what *might have been*. Lorca is a poet of desire, rather than love; of longing, rather than fulfilment. As the American poet Robert Bly once wrote, García Lorca is always saying 'what he wants, what he desires, what barren women desire, what water desires, what gypsies desire, what a bull desires just before he dies, what brothers and sisters desire'.[3] Although one of his biographers, Ian Gibson, has written insistently of Lorca's poetry and theatre as an expression of 'erotic frustration' by a gay artist surrounded by intolerance and unable to express his desire openly, such an approach, which has found wide popular acceptance, restricts desire – erroneously, perhaps – to homoerotic desire, when it is really, in Lorca, a much more general phenomenon. If Lorca's characters had 'followed the call of instinct' rather than 'yielding to socio-economic pressures', Gibson writes, '[their tragedies] would not have occurred'.[4] On the contrary, the desire that is found everywhere in Lorca's

---

[1] Francisco García Lorca, *In the Green Morning* (London: Peter Owen, 1989), 232.

[2] Luis Fernández-Cifuentes, 'Qué es aquello que relumbra? (Una última cuestión): Examen de agotamientos', in Andrés Soria Olmedo, María José Sánchez Montes and Juan Varo Zafra (eds and introd.), *Federico García Lorca, clásico moderno (1898–1998)* (Granada: Diputación de Granada, 2000), 223–5.

[3] Robert Bly (ed. and trans.), *Lorca and Jiménez. Selected Poems* (Boston: Beacon Press, 1997), 101.

[4] Ian Gibson, *Federico García Lorca: A Life* (New York: Pantheon, 1997), 341. Carlos

poetry and drama cannot be 'frustrated' for it has no identifiable object. To put it as broadly as possible: Lorca's poetic characters – both in his theatre and in his narrative poetry – cannot identify what it is that they want, and the poet often suggests that, even if they could, and could achieve those desires, they would be no 'happier': new desires would take their place. In one of his earliest prose pieces, Lorca writes:

> The tragic, sinister thing about the human heart, and the terrifying, incomprehensible thing about the desires of men is that if they achieve the dreams they were longing for, they do not find [happiness]. They nourish an illusion that is their constant torment, and if, after long suffering, they find it, its possession leads to a devastating ennui.[5]

An epitome of this unspecified desire – which is, in fact, sometimes symbolized by homoerotic longing – would be that of the rose in Lorca's 'Casida de la rosa' [Casida of the Rose] in *Diván del Tamarit* [*Diwan of the Tamarit*]:

> La rosa
> no buscaba la aurora:
> casi eterna en su ramo,
> buscaba otra cosa.
>
> La rosa
> no buscaba ni ciencia ni sombra;
> confín de carne y sueño,
> buscaba otra cosa.
>
> La rosa
> no buscaba la rosa:
> inmóvil por el cielo,
> buscaba otra cosa.
>
> [The rose
> was not seeking the dawn
> almost eternal on its branch
> it was seeking something else.

Jerez-Farrán, a more subtle and thorough reader, shares a similar point of view, regarding Lorca's entire *oeuvre* as a code: 'Lorca's work is a work written in code, full of impossible loves, of illicit sexual relations, of sexual frustration and of frustrated paternity, like his personal life' (review of Robin Warner, *Powers of Utterance; A Discourse Approach to Works of Lorca, Machado and Valle-Inclán*, in *Bulletin of Spanish Studies*, 81 (2004), 392; Maurer's translation. For Jerez-Farrán in many cases the 'code' – Lorca's 'corpus literario' – has 'the purpose of recreating mentally and in writing personal realities difficult to articulate in the Spain of his time' ('Mundo étnico y circunstancia personal en el *Romancero gitano* de García Lorca', *Cuadernos Americanos*, 109 (2005), 103–31 (p. 103); Maurer's translation.
  5 Federico García Lorca, *Prosa inédita de juventud*, ed. Christopher Maurer (Madrid: Cátedra, 1994), 37. All translations are Maurer's, unless specified.

The rose
was seeking neither science nor shade
juncture of flesh and dream,
it was seeking something else.

The rose
was not seeking the rose
immobile in the sky
it was seeking something else.][6]

In Lorca's view, poetry points toward that 'otra cosa', that 'something else,' that *wanting* (in both senses of the word) that is an ineluctable part of all life.

Another constant in Lorca's work is his elegiac evocation – more pronounced, perhaps, than in other poets – of absent styles. As in his dramatic poetry, García Lorca often writes his lyrical and dramatic poetry '*à la manière de . . .*', evoking another art form, an earlier artistic style or a specific artist. The celebratory wedding scene of *Bodas de sangre* [*Blood Wedding*] is meant to suggest a cantata of Bach; *La casa de Bernarda Alba* [*The House of Bernarda Alba*] evokes a black and white 'photographic documentary'; *Doña Rosita la Soltera o El lenguaje de las flores* [*Doña Rosita the Spinster or the Language of Flowers*] and *Mariana Pineda* [*Mariana Pineda*] draw inspiration from the aesthetics of engraving. The play *El amor de don Perlimplín con Belisa en su jardín* [*The Love of Don Perlimplín for Belisa in Their Garden*] alludes to the eighteenth-century world of Scarlatti but is also meant to suggest the perspective of early-Renaissance Italian painting. The poetry is no less 'stylized' – no less allusive to previous styles – than the theatre. Certain rather melodramatic poems of *Poema del cante jondo* [*Poem of the Deep Song*] – for example, 'Sorpresa' [Surprise] – aim to capture the luridness of a nineteenth-century steel engraving, and the rest of the book, the lyrics of *cante jondo* [deep song]. Two 'waltzes' in *Poeta en Nueva York* [*Poet in New York*] evoke Vienna, and *Diván del Tamarit*, the great classical collections of Arabic verse forms like the casida and the ghazal. Two of Lorca's books – *Poema del cante jondo* and *Romancero gitano* [*Gypsy Ballads*] – are described by the poet as *retablos*, meaning a reredos or carved altarpiece.

Foremost among the elements of style in Lorca's poetry are the genres and forms of traditional verse, including the traditional ballad, the lullaby and popular songs of the sort he sings and comments on in the 1933 recital-lecture 'Cómo canta una ciudad de noviembre a noviembre' [How a City Sings From November to November].[7] Among the qualities he associated with traditional verse, and which made it a sort of touchstone for his own poetry, were its brevity and thematic concentration; its fragmentary nature and habit of beginning *in*

---

[6] Federico García Lorca, *Collected Poems*, revised bilingual edition, ed. Christopher Maurer (New York: Farrar, Straus and Giroux, 2002), 794–5.

[7] Federico García Lorca, *How a City Sings from November to November*, ed. and trans. Christopher Maurer (San Francisco: Cadmus Editions, 1984).

medias res (which helped turn the lyrics into a mysterious story only half told); its circular structure, use of the refrain and of assonant rhyme (rhyming of vowels but not consonants); its sparing use of metaphor; and its vividness and ability to visually 'enact' rather than narrate.

The closeness of words and music in traditional song is another enduring characteristic of Lorca's own work, and it is no coincidence that he composed tunes for some of his own ballads and, later in life, his own arrangements of folk tunes, which he played and recorded with the singer and dancer Encarnación López Júlvez, *La Argentinita*. Throughout his poetry, from his juvenilia (circa 1916) until the end of his life, one finds a conscious effort to bring together literature and music, a characteristic that is not surprising, given his earliest artistic training as a classical pianist and his early attempts at musical composition for the piano. At first the effort consists in a belief – inspired perhaps by the nineteenth-century poet Gustavo Adolfo Bécquer – in the inadequacy of language; the constant use of musical metaphors (as when the landscape gives off 'modulaciones' [modulations] or 'acordes' [chords]; and an ingenuous faith in the evocative power of musical titles.[8] In his first book, *Libro de poemas* [*Book of Poems*] (1921), there are compositions with titles like 'Canción otoñal' [Autumn song], 'Canción menor' [Minor Song], 'Balada triste' [Sad Ballade] and 'Madrigal de verano' [Summer Madrigal] or 'Aire de nocturno' [Nocturne Breeze]. Before that, in his early poetry and prose, his titles, and sometimes the structure of his pieces, attempt to find literary equivalences for popular airs, circus music, nocturnes, scherzos, symphonies, duos, romanzas, psalms and sonatas.

Other enduring characteristics of Lorca's work are his habit of seeing 'reality', particularly the natural world, through the lens of myth; the cultivation of 'mystery' and narrative uncertainty as an essential quality of all enduring poetry ('Only mystery makes us live,' he wrote beneath one of his drawings. 'Only mystery.')[9]; the ability to combine the forms and themes of traditional art with avant-garde elements prevalent in the 1920s and 1930s; and a deep faith in the oral dimension of poetry and the power of live performance.

Lorca's existence as a poet begins in 1916, in Granada, when the death of his piano teacher, Antonio Segura Mesa (an admirer of Verdi and the author of a number of operas never performed), leads him to put aside any thought of a musical career. In an early essay, 'Las reglas en la música' [The Rules in Music], García Lorca describes music as the most perfect of the arts, for it transports the listener to a 'realm of ideas' and emotion to which the poet has only partial

---

[8] See Christopher Maurer, 'Lorca y las formas de la música', in Andrés Soria Olmedo (ed.), *Lecciones sobre Federico García Lorca* (Granada: Edición del Cincuentenario, 1986), 237–50.

[9] Mario Hernández, *Libro de los dibujos de Federico García Lorca* (Madrid: Tabapress / Fundación Federico García Lorca, 1990), 113, no. 290.6.

access.[10] Lorca's earliest work reflects admiration for the verbal music of Rubén Darío, the early Juan Ramón Jiménez and minor Andalusian poets like Salvador Rueda or Francisco Villaespesa. It was not until around 1920, until after he had moved from Granada to the more cosmopolitan Residencia de Estudiantes, Madrid, and his aesthetic tastes had widened beyond Spanish Romantic and *modernista* poetry, that García Lorca began to consider publishing his verse. He did so with much editorial help from a friend – the painter and printer Gabriel García Maroto – and from his brother Francisco (the habit of relying on others to help him ready his works for publication was to endure). *Libro de poemas* begins with a few 'Words of Justification' in which he apologizes for his 'youthful ardor, torment, and unbounded ambition', but claims to offer an 'exact image of the days of my adolescence and boyhood', a 'passionate childhood, as I ran through the meadows of the Vega against the backdrop of the Sierra [Nevada]' (*Collected Poems*, p. 890). In *Libro de poemas* one detects many of the thematic concerns of later books: a boundless love of the natural beauty and folk culture of the river plain – the Vega – where the poet had spent his childhood and earliest youth; a search for spirituality in the midst of a materialistic world; regret for the loss of childhood innocence; and an elegy for all manner of lost possibilities, particularly those of unrequited love (for example, 'Elegía a doña Juana la Loca' [Elegy to doña Juana la Loca])[11]; as well as the celebration of nature and the yearning of the poet to draw as close to it as possible ('Cigarra' [Locust]). In a series of ode-like poems dominated by epithet, metaphor and the use of 14-syllable Alexandrines, the poet celebrates natural phenomena like water and poplars, laurel and honey. A second distinct group of poems, written somewhat later, shows the combination of metaphor and whimsical humour that Lorca would have admired in the writing of Ramón Gómez de la Serna, whom he had met – and whose *greguerías*, or humorous metaphorical aphorisms, he would have read – during his first years in Madrid.

By the time he published *Book of Poems* Lorca was already at work on a book based on structural principles he considered radically new in Spanish poetry: *Suites*. Revised throughout his life and published posthumously (1983), *Suites* was conceived as an open-ended collection of sequences of short poems, distantly analogous in structure to the musical suites of Debussy or to the theme and variations of classical composers; an alternative title was *Diferencias* [*Differences*], which evokes sixteenth-century Renaissance Spanish composers like Luis Milán or Antonio de Cabezón. It was around 1921[12] that Lorca, along with other Spanish and Latin American poets, became aware of haiku and of the

---

[10] Federico García Lorca, *Obras completas*, IV, ed. Miguel García-Posada (Barcelona: Galaxia Gutenberg / Círculo de Autores, 1997), 42.

[11] On Lorca's poetic treatment of the spinster, see D. Gareth Walters, 'The Queen of Castile and the Andalusian Spinster: Lorca's Elegies for Two Women', in Robert Harvard (ed.), *Lorca: Poet and Playwright* (Cardiff: University of Wales Press, 1992), 9–30.

[12] *Epistolario Completo*, ed. Christopher Maurer and Andrew A. Anderson (Madrid: Cátedra, 1997), 107.

four- or five-line lyrics of *cante jondo*, and, through them, of the expressive possibilities of the short poem. Lorca's Bergsonian intuition, perhaps, was that a natural phenomenon – the sea, the nocturnal sky, the world of the snail or palm tree – could be rendered better in a series of discrete 'moments', snapshots or discontinuous partial views than it could by means of a longer, more unified and discursive poem. A page from his early poetic manuscripts – the revisions made to a poem about the bat ('Murciélago') – reveals his discovery of the short poem, and a new desire for simplicity and brevity:

Early version:

> El murciélago
> (elixir de la sombra)
> se disuelve en el aire.
>
> Sin murciélagos
> no habría noche.
> Ellos dan el color
> al silencio
> y lo hacen
> invisible.
>
> Muerden el talón
> del día
> y despiertan al perro
> y a la rana
>
> . . . y son los verdaderos
> amantes de la estrella.

> [The bat
> (elixir of shadow)
> dissolves in the air.
>
> Without bats
> there would be no night.
> They give color
> to silence
> and make it
> invisible.
>
> They nip at the heel
> of day
> and awaken the dog
> and the frog
>
> . . . and are the true
> lovers of the star.]

Revised version:

> El murciélago,
> elixir de la sombra,
> verdadero amante de la estrella,
> muerde el talón del día.

> [The bat,
> elixir of shadow,
> true lover of the star,
> nips at the heel of day.]   (*Collected Poems*, pp. xxxiii–xxxiv)

One of the earliest suites, written in 1921, was inspired by the world of *cante jondo*, the Andalusian musical genre of flamenco, and grew into a unified book of its own. It was the brief lyrics of *cante jondo* that had taught Lorca and other poets, he said, how best to go about 'pruning and caring for the overluxuriant lyric tree left to us by the Romantics and post-Romantics'.[13] The previous summer, 1920, a year before publishing *Libro de poemas*, the poet had been exposed for the first time to the study of Spanish 'traditional' art, accompanying the great Spanish philologist Ramón Menéndez Pidal as he transcribed oral folk ballads in a Gypsy neighbourhood of Granada. It was about the same time, in daily conversation with the composer Manuel de Falla and other friends from Granada (for example, the painter Manuel Ángeles Ortiz, the journalist José Mora Guarnido and the future literary critic José Fernández-Montesinos), that Lorca had become deeply interested in *cante jondo*, or flamenco – another form of traditional poetry and music. Results of that interest were a fervent lecture in defence of *cante jondo* (a genre disdained as vulgar by the Spanish bourgeoisie) (for the text, see *Deep Song*, pp. 23–41) and the book of poems *Poema del cante jondo*, published in 1931. Both texts were written in connection with an amateur *cante jondo* competition organized by Falla in Granada on the Feast of Corpus Christi, June, 1922 – an event that Falla and Lorca hoped would dignify *cante jondo* as an art form, elevate it to the status of a 'high art'[14] and save it from the supposed commercial adulteration of flamenco cafés and 'flamenco opera' (the massive flamenco concerts held in bullrings).

An ebullient letter from Lorca to his friend the music critic Adolfo Salazar, contains the first news of *Poema del cante jondo*:

> I have gone back over the *Suites* for the last time and am now putting the golden roof tiles on *Poem of the Deep Song*, which I am going to publish to coincide with the [*cante jondo*] festival. It is something different from the *Suites* and filled with suggestions of Andalusia. The rhythm is popular in a stylized way, and I bring out all of the old *cantaores* [singers of *cante jondo*],

---

[13] Federico García Lorca, *Deep Song and Other Prose*, ed. and trans. Christopher Maurer (London: Marion Boyars, 1980), 30.
[14] Timothy Mitchell, *Flamenco Deep Song* (New Haven: Yale University Press, 1994).

all the fantastic flora and fauna that fill these sublime songs. Silverio, Juan Breva, Loco Mateo, La Parrala, el Fillo . . . and Death! It's a great carved altarpiece . . . it's . . . a jigsaw puzzle, if you know what I mean. The poem begins with a motionless sunset, and then the *siguiriya*, the *soleá*, the *saeta*, and the *petenera* come filing across it. The poem is full of gypsies, tapers, forges, and it even contains allusions to Zoroaster. It's the first thing I've done with a *completely different orientation*, and I still don't know what I can say about it . . . but it *does* have novelty. The only person who knows it is Falla [. . .]. Spanish poets have never even *touched* this theme, and I deserve a smile, at least, for my daring. (*Collected Poems*, pp. 893–4)

The last sentence is significant. 'Spanish poets', including some whose works Lorca knew quite well – Rueda, Manuel Machado – had, in fact, written abundantly on *cante jondo*, but, in contrast to Lorca, they had attempted to compose their own versions of the four- and five-line lyrics of flamenco forms like the *siguiriya*, the *saeta*, or the *soleá*. Influenced by Falla's peculiar aesthetic of imitation – one of allusion and gentle suggestion rather than of direct imitation or quotation of folk documents – Lorca's homage to *cante jondo* was strikingly different from that of other poets. Rejecting the direct imitation of traditional *cante jondo* lyrics that had prevailed until then and fleeing from pastiche, he chooses instead to evoke, in a series of sequences or 'suites', not only the most famous of the *cantaores* but also the thematic world of *cante jondo* (love and death), along with its rural setting and its most characteristic objects: the guitar, castanets, olive groves, oil lamp, knife, etc. His guiding idea, in some of these groupings, was to allow his own poetic sequences to mimic the slow progression of, say, a *siguiriya*. Thus, for example, '*Poema de la siguiriya gitana*' [Poem of the Gypsy Siguiriya] begins with an evocation of the Andalusian setting ('*Paisaje*' [Landscape]), and continues with the initial thrumming of the guitar ('*Guitarra*' [Guitar]), the melismatic 'Ay!' of the *cantaor* ('El grito' [The Cry]), the resonating silence that follows the 'cry' ('El silencio' [The Silence]), the hypnotic aftermath of the song ('Después' [Afterwards]) and the song's effect on the spiritual and physical landscape ('Y después' [And After That]).

The book was indeed shared first with the Spanish composer Manuel de Falla, a close friend to whom, years later, Lorca would devote an unorthodox 'Ode to the Most Holy Sacrament'. Falla's influence on Lorca's aesthetics was profound.[15] He provided the young poet with the moral example of an artist selflessly devoted to his craft; introduced him to the music of composers like Stravinsky, Debussy and Ravel, and Spaniards like Ernesto Halffter and Oscar Esplá; and, above all, taught him how he might best incorporate traditional art into his poems and plays. Falla's teaching may be felt vividly in Lorca's 1922 lecture on deep song, a text that sheds much light on *Poema del cante jondo*. Not

---

15 See also D. Gareth Walters, 'Parallel Trajectories in the Careers of Falla and Lorca', in Federico Bonaddio and Xon de Ros (eds), *Crossing Fields in Modern Spanish Culture* (Oxford: Legenda [European Humanities Research Centre], 2003), 92–102.

only does Lorca rely on the composer for historical information, one also feels Falla's influence on Lorca's perception of deep song as an anonymous, traditional music created by the Andalusian people (primarily, gypsies), rather than music created by individual *cantaores*. One also 'hears' Falla in Lorca's comments on pastiche. The difference between a *cante jondo* lyric invented by a modern poet such as Manuel Machado or Salvador Rueda or Ventura Ruiz Aguilera and the traditional lyric that 'the people created themselves' is, Lorca says, 'the difference between a paper rose and a natural one!'

> The poets who compose 'popular' songs cloud the clear lymph of the true heart. How one notices, in their poems, the confident ugly rhythm of the man who knows grammar. Nothing but the quintessence and this or that trill for its coloristic effect ought to be drawn straight from the people. We should never want to copy their ineffable modulations: we can do nothing but blur them. Simply because of education. (*Deep Song*, p. 33)

Those words are in consonance with Falla's treatment of traditional song in his own works. The following words, written by Falla's disciple and Lorca's close friend Adolfo Salazar, who was then writing for the Madrid daily *El Sol*, apply not only to works like Falla's *Retablo de Maese Pedro* [*Master Peter's Puppet Show*], which Falla was working on around the time of the Festival, but also to Lorca's poetry:

> Evocation is, today, an element of beauty, a source of emotion; it doesn't try to reconstruct or bring anything back to life. It constructs and lives things anew, for their own sake, and the reference to things from the past is merely a password, a countersign. The 'traditional' theme dissolves into pure fantasy.[16]

Contrasting Falla to earlier composers like Isaac Albéniz, Salazar writes of Falla's *La vida breve* [Short Life] in words that aptly describe the aesthetic of Lorca:

> The localist, Spanish cliché disappears, yielding to a suggestiveness produced by extremely simplified elements. The indigenous element is reduced to its vital nucleus. . . The composer places himself on a poetic plane that is far from direct impression . . . He acquires a greater capacity for evocation . . . He proceeds not by 'presentation' but by 'reflection'. (Maurer 2000, p. 33)

An article by the literary critic Enrique Diez-Canedo identifies the same characteristics in Lorca's own *Poema del cante jondo*:

> The fact that we run into the name of Falla at the very beginning of Lorca's apprenticeship, tells us much about the character of Lorca's poetry, where the popular motif, taken directly from the people, turns into free artistic creation,

---

[16] Christopher Maurer, *Federico García Lorca y su 'Arquitectura del cante jondo'* (Granada: Comares, 2000), 33.

merely alluding to the original theme. Pressing this comparison, and supporting it with another one [. . .] we could find a similar relation between Lorca and Manuel Machado, on the one hand, and Falla and Isaac Albéniz, on the other. (Maurer 2000, p. 33)

Although Lorca would eventually reject Falla's Romantic vision of *cante jondo* as 'traditional', non-commercial, rural art and come to see it as the creation or recreation of sophisticated urban *cantaores* like Manuel Torres or Pastora Pavón rather than the anonymous product of the people, Falla's aesthetics of imitation would also influence much of his later production including *Canciones* [*Songs*], *Suites* and *Romancero gitano*. Besides Falla's insistence on 'the truth without the authenticity' (a phrase he applied to the 'Andalusian' music of Debussy), Lorca also learned from him – and from the example of some of the productions of the Ballets Russes – that local folklore – stories, ballads, song and other music – can, if treated with intelligence, sensitivity and a touch of irony, have a broad international appeal. The lesson of *cante jondo* for Lorca was that rather than fleeing from the local and the provincial, the artist can turn it into something universal, and that, rather than rebelling against foreign notions of the 'typically Spanish', one can treat them affectionately or ironically (while others railed against the false vision of Andalusia that had been propagated by Romantic travellers like Gautier, Lorca and his circle of friends commemorated the French writer's visit with a ceramic plaque). When they defend *cante jondo* not as a symbol – or deformation – of the Andalusian character but as the ancient source of a 'supranational' music, as old as 'the first sob and the first kiss' (*Deep Song*, p. 30), and when they plan for a theater troupe (never realized) called 'Los títeres de Cachiporra de Granada' [The Billy Club Puppets of Granada] to perform traditional Andalusian puppet plays in London and other European capitals (*Epistolario*, p. 138), both Lorca and Falla have in mind the international successes of the Ballets Russes.

On completing *Poema del cante jondo*, Lorca returned to the composition of *Suites*, on which he worked actively over the next two years, through the summer of 1923, ranging enjoyably over a variety of themes: whimsical visions of animals (cuckoo, parrot, turtles, snails) and of nature (palm tree, sky, sea, river); 'musical' compositions divided into 'moments' ('*Seis canciones de anochecer*' [Six Songs at Nightfall]); celebration of the beauty of Andalusia ('*Surtidores*' [Water Jets]) and of its popular culture ('*Ferias*' [Fairs]); playful parodies of the clichés of Romanticism ('*Album blanco*' [White Album]) and philosophical meditations on identity ('Suite de los espejos' [Mirror Suite]) or ontological reflections on lost possibilities ('En el jardín de las toronjas de luna' [In the Garden of the Lunar Grapefruits], a long, ambitious sequence in which Lorca explores, in his own words, 'the garden of possibilities, the garden of what is not, but could [and at times should] have been, the garden of theories that passed invisibly by and children who have not been born').[17] On the whole, *Suites*, like

---

[17] On the textual history of *Suites*, see the edition of Melissa Dinverno (Madrid: Cátedra,

some of the *cante jondo* poems, reflects a rejection of the post-Romantic solemnity and earnestness of his earliest poetry, and an ambitious lyrical experiment tinged with irony, humour, and light-hearted parody.

While composing and revising his *Suites*, Lorca was also at work on other poems – short lyrical poems, sonnets, ballads – which were *not* conceived as sequences, and in 1926/7, five years after the publication of his first book, amid growing concern among his friends about his slowness in publishing, Lorca entered on a period of intense revision and ordering of all that he had written since 1921. From his papers emerged several distinct groups of poems: *Poema del cante jondo*, *Suites*, *Canciones* (short lyrical poems, some of which had belonged originally to the sequences of *Suites*), and an incipient book of ballads on Andalusian themes.

In ordering his *Canciones,* Lorca divided them, like *Suites*, into lyrical 'chapters'. Published in 1927 by his friends the poets Emilio Prados and Manuel Altolaguirre at their tiny print shop (*Sur*) in Málaga, the book was meant to have, as Lorca told his friend Jorge Guillén, 'the high air of the sierra'; it was, he declared, a 'sharp, serene lyrical effort' (*Collected Poems*, p. 913). While an introductory section called 'Teorías' [Theories] playfully questions the structure of human knowledge – why, for example, does the rainbow have only *seven* colours? 'Why weren't there nine? / Why weren't there twenty?' (*Collected Poems*, p. 443) – later groups delve into the poetic universe of children; the landscapes of Andalusia, seen, at times, through the stylizing lens of Romanticism ('*Granada 1850*' or '*Canción de jinete (1860)* [Rider's Song (1860)]; personal identity ('De otro modo' [In Another Manner]); unfulfilled love and erotic frustration (the section entitled '*Eros con bastón*' [Eros With a Cane]); the celebration of the seasons ('Agosto' [August]); and the mysteries of poetic expression and of artistic creation (for example, the 'portraits' of Juan Ramón Jiménez, Debussy and Verlaine). Throughout, *Canciones* incorporates many of the thematic and formal features of traditional verse (most notably, parallelism, the refrain and circular structure).

The series of ballads, written between 1921 and 1926 and published in 1928 by the prestigious *Revista de Occidente* (directed by the philosopher José Ortega y Gasset) as *Primer romancero gitano, 1924–1927* (commonly referred to as *Romancero gitano* and translated as *Gypsy Ballads*, but more accurately, *First Gypsy Ballad Book*), reflect, on the one hand, Lorca's abiding interest in the traditional ballad – over the years he had continued to collect ballads and write his own, some of which he used in his theatre – but also a fascination with the life of the Spanish gypsies; a life-long interest in mythology; passion for the mythopoetic power of verse; and his growing admiration for the poetics of the seventeenth-century master poet Luis de Góngora, the 300th anniversary of whose death was being celebrated in 1927 (Lorca's poetic group – the Genera-

---

in press), which, unlike the first edition by André Belamich, carefully reconstructs successive textual versions of the book.

tion of 1927[18] – would draw its name from this important event, which had wide repercussions throughout the Spanish and Latin American literary world).

Lorca's interest in the gypsies, and in their contribution to Andalusian culture, dates as far back as the *cante jondo* festival of 1922, and was strengthened by his travels throughout Andalusia (see, for example, the letter to his brother written from Lanjarón in 1926 [*Epistolario*, pp. 329–31]). Lorca's primitivistic image of the gypsies, a group harshly marginalized by Spanish society, feeds on the conviction that they live in greater harmony with nature than others and enjoy greater imaginative freedom from societal constraints; see for example, the 'Romance de la Guardia Civil española' [Ballad of the Spanish Civil Guard] or the 'Escena del teniente coronel de la Guardia Civil' [Scene of the Lieutenant Colonel of the Civil Guard], a dialogue appended to *Poema del cante jondo*. 'Although [my book] is called Gypsy, the book as a whole is the poem of Andalusia,' Lorca wrote years later, 'and I called it Gypsy because the Gypsy is the loftiest, most profound and aristocratic element of my country, the most deeply representative of its mode, the very keeper of the glowing embers, blood, and alphabet of Andalusian and universal truth' (*Deep Song*, p. 105).

Of all the traditional poetic forms admired by Lorca, the ballad was the one that left the deepest mark on his poetry and theatre. The traditional ballad is a narrative poem, with lines of eight syllables and feminine rhyme, accompanied by music and transmitted orally by a mostly illiterate folk community. Lorca's title alludes to the existence of a subgroup of these traditional ballads transmitted by the Gypsies from one generation to another: poems he had first heard of, years earlier, in 1920, on his ballad-hunting excursion with Menéndez Pidal. Among the qualities Lorca associated with the ballad and with traditional verse – qualities that made it a sort of touchstone for his own poetry – were its brevity and concentration; its fragmentary nature; use of the refrain and other sorts of parallelism; and its thematic range, from Spanish history and the lives of saints and heroes (a section of the book is called 'Three Historical Ballads') to the lyrical expression of tragic love and loneliness.[19] Years later, Lorca would speak of his effort to blend lyricism with narration:

> From my very first steps in poetry, in 1919 [sic], I devoted much thought to the ballad form, because I realized it was the vessel best shaped to my sensibility. The ballad had gone nowhere from the last exquisite ballads of Góngora until the Duque de Rivas made it sweet, fluent and domestic and Zorrilla filled it with water lilies, shades, and sunken bells.
>
> The typical ballad had always been a narration, and it was the narrative

---

[18] For a detailed history of the term, and these poets' self-awareness as a group, see Andrew A. Anderson, *El veintisiete en tela de juicio: Examen de la historiografía generacional y replanteamiento de la vanguardia histórica española* (Madrid: Gredos, 2005).

[19] For a good introduction to the traditional ballads, see C. Colin Smith, *Spanish Ballads*, 2nd edn (Bristol: Classical Press, 1996) and Roger Wright, *Spanish Ballads* (Warminster: Aris & Phillips, 1987).

element that made its physiognomy so charming, for when it grew lyrical without an echo of anecdote it would turn into a song. I wanted to fuse the narrative ballad with the lyrical without changing the quality of either.

(*Deep Song*, p. 105)

The traditional ballad makes little use of metaphor, but Lorca's ballads do, revealing the poet's love of Góngora, and his habit – well established by then – of recreating traditional forms rather than imitating them strictly. Like that of the short poem, the importance of metaphor in Spanish poetry had been growing steadily since the early 1920s, when the writer Gómez de la Serna and the literary movement called *Ultra* (a derivative of Italian Futurism) made it the central element in poetry. At a time when Spanish and Latin American poets like Guillermo de Torre, Gerardo Diego, or the early Jorge Luis Borges, reacting against the *modernismo* of Rubén Darío and others, spoke dogmatically of purging poetry of sentimentality and 'personality' and engaging, through metaphor, with the 'modern world' (the crescent moon could be a telephone receiver rather than a trite Romantic symbol), the work of poets such as Góngora, dominated by the Baroque conceit, was eagerly received, even when imperfectly understood. A 1926 essay by Lorca, 'La imagen poética de don Luis de Góngora' [The Poetic Image of Don Luis de Góngora], explains what attracted him to the 'aristocratic solitude' of the Cordovan poet: his lexical wealth ('an inborn necessity for fresh beauty made him cast language in a new way'); his capacity, 'unprecedented in Spanish, for hunting and molding metaphors'; his unsentimental, unrelenting love of 'objective beauty – pure, useless beauty, devoid of communicable anxieties'; his powers of synaesthesia ('A poet', Lorca wrote, 'must be a professor of the five bodily senses'); his deep knowledge of classical mythology and his power to turn everything he touches into myth (*Deep Song*, pp. 62–6). There was also a psychological dimension to Góngora: what Lorca admires, perhaps above all, is Góngora's apparent restraint as a creator, his prodigious ability not to yield to sudden inspiration, to 'the jewels that genius happens to place in our hands':

> Because Góngora [ties] up his imagination, he can detain it at will, and does not allow himself to be dragged about by the dark natural forces of the law of inertia, nor by the fleeting mirages where careless poets die like moths in a lamp. [. . .] Neither pale nor coloured images nor overly brilliant ones can frighten him in his mental landscape. He hunts the image that no one else sees (so unrelated does it seem to anything else), the white straggling image that livens his startling poetical moments. His fantasy counts on his five bodily senses and they obey him blindly, like five colorless slaves, and do not cheat him as they do other mortals. (*Deep Song*, pp. 67, 73)

There are moments, in *Romancero gitano*, of direct homage to Góngora, as when a boy bathes in a stream (*buey de agua*; literally 'water-ox') at night, wading in the reflection of the crescent moon:

Los densos bueyes del agua
embisten a los muchachos
que se bañan en las lunas
de sus cuernos ondulados

[Dense oxen of water
charge at the boys
bathing in the moons
of their rippling horns]   (*Collected Poems*, pp. 588–9)

The same shimmering moonlight appears in the most famous of the ballads, 'Romance sonámbulo' [Sleepwalking Ballad], where a body floats in a cistern:

Un carambano de luna
la sostiene sobre el agua.

[An icicle of the moon
holds her over the water.]   (*Collected Poems*, p. 559)

At such times one feels in *Romancero gitano* a proud display of metaphorical power. But there is also, in tension with that metaphorical virtuosity, the fragmented sense of narrative mystery that Lorca and other major poets of the time (Antonio Machado, Juan Ramón Jiménez) admired in traditional art. A poem like 'Romance sonámbulo', where the outlines of the story (a *contrabandista* [smuggler], fleeing from the Guardia Civil, takes refuge in the house of his beloved, who has 'long awaited' him), are artistically blurred. 'It seems to have a story, but it doesn't,' Lorca's friend the painter Salvador Dalí remarked.[20] A third element – that of myth – derives only in part from Góngora. It is not that Lorca reworks classical mythology in the *Romancero;* what happens is that his vision of phenomenological reality is itself imbued with mythical and religious elements.[21] In 'Preciosa y el aire' [Preciosa and the Wind], for example, where a gypsy girl is pursued by the 'sword' and 'tongues' of a sexually charged wind, Lorca draws not only, as Góngora would have done, on the Ovidian myth of Boreas, ravisher of Oreithyia, but also on the personification of the wind in the lyrics of *cante jondo* and on traditional lyrics where the wind acts like a lover or an erotic threat. Lorca is not imitating Góngora directly but claiming, for his own verse, a quality he admired in the Baroque poet – the ability to invent myths of his own: 'This way of animating and vivifying Nature is characteristic of Góngora. He needs the elements to be conscious. He hates what is deaf, he hates dark forces that have no limits. [. . .] the poet transforms all that he touches. His

20 See Jorge Guillén's introduction to the Aguilar edition of Lorca's complete works, *Obras completas*, ed. Arturo del Hoyo, 17th edn (Madrid: Aguilar, 1972), xlvii.
21 Two classic discussions are Ángel Álvarez de Miranda's anthropologically oriented *La metáfora y el mito* (Madrid: Taurus, 1963) and the Lacanian treatment of the tragedies by Carlos Feal Deibe, *Lorca: tragedia y mito* (Ottawa: Dovehouse Editions, Ottawa Hispanic Series 4, 1989).

sublime theogonic feeling gives personality to the forces of nature' (*Deep Song*, p. 80).

A third major influence on Lorca's art in the 1920s – beside the composer Manuel de Falla and the Baroque poet Góngora – was that of the painter Salvador Dalí. The two of them met in early 1923, in the Residencia de Estudiantes, Madrid, when Lorca was 24 and Dalí was a timid 18-year-old enrolled at the Special School of Drawing at the Academy of San Fernando.[22] Their daily camaraderie at the 'Resi' – and in Toledo with Luis Buñuel, Pepín Bello and others – came to a halt when Dalí was expelled from the Academy, but the friendship survived thanks to visits, letters and other writings – documents that provide invaluable insight into the art of both. During Easter Week 1925 Lorca visited Dalí on the Costa Brava (his first trip ever to Catalonia), and in 1926, inspired, perhaps, by Cocteau's 'Ode to Picasso', he published in the *Revista de Occidente* a long poem celebrating the aesthetics of Dalí's painting of the previous few years and immortalizing their friendship as one of 'love, friendship' and intellectual 'fencing'. In Barcelona, in the summer of 1927, Dalí designed the stage settings for one of Lorca's plays, *Mariana Pineda*, and arranged for an exhibition of the poet's drawings at the prestigious Dalmau gallery. By the time of their estrangement in 1928, after Dalí wrote Lorca a long letter attacking *Romancero gitano* as bound, 'hands and feet, to the old poetry' (*Sebastian's Arrows*, p. 101), the world of each had been deeply altered. It is clear, for example, that the friendship with Lorca gave Dalí new faith in his writing, and helped the poet regard his own drawings as an integral part of his poetic world (see, in particular, Lorca's letters to the Catalan critic Sebastià Gasch).

If Manuel de Falla drew Lorca in the direction of 'tradition', it was Salvador Dalí who tried to draw him, more forcefully than anyone else toward what the painter called the 'eurhythmia' of contemporary civilization: photography and the cinema, dance, sport, the perspectives of contemporary science. The 'tradition' Dalí invoked, when he invoked it at all, was the drawing of Raphael or Ingres or the careful brushwork of Vermeer. For Dalí, tradition was the product of intelligence and patient technique, not of a rustic 'popular' muse like the one to whom Lorca had attributed popular ballads and *cante jondo*, and it led to 'clarity', not to the 'mystery' Lorca held out as a necessary condition of art. '¡No hay claridad!' – 'There is no clarity!' – the poet often heard Dalí say. In Dalí's thought of the mid-1920s, as expounded in the prose poem 'Saint Sebastian' and other writings, emotion and pathos led straight to the trite, vulgar sentimentality he called 'putrefaction' (he begged Lorca, in vain, to supply an introduction to a satirical book of sketches, *Los putrefactos* [*The Putrefact*], some of which were published posthumously by the Catalan critic Rafael Santos

---

[22] For their collected correspondence, with a brief history of their friendship, see *Federico García Lorca, Salvador Dalí, Sebastian's Arrows: Letters and Mementos*, ed. Christopher Maurer (Chicago: Swan Isle Press, 2004). See also the books by Ian Gibson, Rafael Santos Torroella, Antonina Rodrigo and Agustín Sánchez Vidal, cited in the Bibliography.

Torroella). What mattered to Dalí in his pursuit of modernity was the epidermis of things: the surface was *all there was*: there were no 'inner depths'. 'Fleeing the dark thicket of incredible forms, / Your fantasy reaches as far as your hands,' Lorca wrote in his 'Ode to Salvador Dalí' and Dalí, who was opposed to any sort of 'mystery', surely took it as a compliment (*Sebastian's Arrows*, pp. 8–9). '[For me] the inside of things is still a superficial reality,' he wrote to a friend in 1927. 'What is deep is still an epidermis . . . Things *have no other meaning besides their strict objectivity*; and to me this accounts for their miraculous poetry [. . .]. I don't see any question to answer in the world which *surrounds* us; I only see objectivities to register.'[23] *Santa Objetividad* – Blessed Objectivity – was a saint he often invoked.

Lorca contrasts his own aesthetics with those of Dalí in two texts from around 1927, an unfinished dialogue titled 'Corazón bleu y Coeur azul' (respectively the Spanish and French for 'blue heart') and a narrative entitled *'Santa Lucía y San Lázaro'* [Saint Lucy and St Lazarus], where the two aesthetics are brought sharply into contrast by means of imagery rather than analysis.[24] On the one hand, Dalí / St Lucy: 'the exterior of things, the clean airy beauty of the skin, the charm of slender surfaces', 'contours, transparency and surface'. On the other, Lorca / St Lazarus: 'dark physiologies of the body, the central fire, and the funnels of night', the 'spurt of blood' versus 'the tranquillity of agates and the shadowless nudity of the jellyfish'.[25]

While the early Dalí – 1923 to 1926 – had represented an aggressive push toward objectivity, contemporaneity and his own peculiar style of representational realism (the portraits of his sister and father; 'Basket of Bread', etc.), at a slightly later but distinct moment in his development – 1927 to 1929 – he seemed to open to García Lorca the possibilities of what Max Ernst called the 'aesthetics of collage' and to diminish the attractions of the traditional metaphor. Dalí's pursuit of 'objectivity' had transcended the celebration of the visual world (a trait he shared with Góngora) and the rejection of sentimentality and symbolism to an epistemological questioning of whole objects of any sort and the effort to reduce the object – any object – to its individual parts. It was this idea of systematic disorganization that he set forth in a letter and subsequent essay ('Realismo y surrealismo' [Realism and Surrealism]) directed to Lorca, against the *Romancero gitano*:

---

23 Antonio Monegal, 'Las palabras y las cosas, según Salvador Dalí', *El aeroplano y la estrella: El movimiento de vanguardia en los Paises Catalanes (1904–1936)*, ed. Joan Ramon Resina (Amsterdam / Atlanta: Rodopi, 1997), 151–76 (p. 152). See also, for a helpful discussion of Dalí's early aesthetic of objectivity in literature and painting, Monegal's *En el límite de la diferencia: Poesía e imagen en las vanguardias hispánicas* (Madrid: Editorial Tecnos, 1998).

24 Federico García Lorca, *Poemas en prosa*, ed. Andrew A. Anderson (Granada: Comares / La Veleta, 2000), 91–2 and 57–66 respectively.

25 For an excellent discussion, see Terence McMullan, 'Federico García Lorca's *Santa Lucía y San Lázaro* and the Aesthetics of Transition', *Bulletin of Hispanic Studies*, 67 (1990), 1–20.

The minute-hands of a clock (never mind my examples, I'm not exactly looking for poetic ones) begin to have real value at the moment they stop pointing out the hours and, losing their *circular* rhythm and the arbitrary role our intelligence has subjected them to (pointing out the hours), they *evade* the clock entirely and occupy the place that would correspond to the sex organs of little bread crumbs.

You move within accepted, anti-poetic notions – you talk about a rider, and you suppose that he's riding a horse, and that the horse is galloping, *and this is already too much*, for in reality it would be better for you to ask whether it is really the rider who is on the horse; if the reins aren't really an organic extension of his very hands; if, in reality, the little hairs on the rider's balls aren't much faster than the horse; and if the horse isn't something immobile, fastened to the earth by vigorous roots. Etc. etc. [. . .] We must leave things *free of* the conventional ideas to which intelligence has subjugated them. At that moment those handsome little things will begin to act in accordance with their real, *consubstantial* manner of being. Let the things themselves decide where their shadows fall! (*Sebastian's Arrow*, pp. 102–3)[26]

It was a programme of voluntary aphasia, the refusal to recognize the objects of everyday life in their normal context, and each of those phenomena – the liberated hands of a clock, the sex organs of little bread crumbs, the reins as an extension of the hands – would be described by Dalí, who borrowed the phrase from Le Corbusier (Finkelstein, p. 57) as an 'hecho poético', a 'poetic act' or 'poetic fact' or 'poetic event' (the word *hecho* implies all three), and it was the 'poetic fact' that Lorca would celebrate (adapting Dalí's and Le Corbusier's concept of the *fait poétique*) in his own writing and poetry over the next few years, first in a serious of narrations commonly also known as 'prose poems' and later in his *Poeta en Nueva York* and related works. The revised version of Lorca's lecture on Góngora[27] and a new lecture on poetry, 'Imaginación, inspiración, evasión' [Imagination, Inspiration, Evasion] (both given in 1930), give evidence of the waning attraction, for him, of the metaphor based, like Góngora's, on logical analogy and of Lorca's desire to grant a larger role to the subconscious and to the irrational during the process of composition, without, however, resorting to the automatic writing of the Surrealists, of which he had been aware since 1926.[28] That aesthetic would be evident in his next major collection of poems, *Poeta en Nueva York*.

---

[26] For the text of the essay, Haim Finkelstein (ed.), *The Collected Writings of Salvador Dalí* (Cambridge: Cambridge University Press, 1998), 94–8.

[27] Federico García Lorca, *Conferencias*, I, ed. Christopher Maurer, 2 vols (Madrid: Alianza Editorial, 1984), 91–125.

[28] 'Surrealism uses the dream, the intensely real world of dreams and there one finds truly authentic poetic norms, but this evasion by means of dream or the subconscious is, although very pure, not very clear! // We Spaniards want profiles and visible mystery. Form and sensuality. In the north Surrealism can take hold – for example, modern German art – but Spain defends us from the strong liquor of dream' (*Sebastian's Arrows*, pp. 160–1). See also his comments to Sebastià Gasch regarding his drawings: 'You're right in all you tell me. But

Written during a life-changing visit to New York, Vermont and Cuba (June 1929–April 1930), *Poeta en Nueva York* departs in several important ways from earlier works: its mostly urban setting and the absence of the form and themes of traditional Spain; the more pronounced and deliberate presence of social criticism (for example, the 'Oda a Roma' [Ode to Rome] and the section 'Los negros' [The Blacks]); the explicit treatment of homosexuality ('Oda a Walt Whitman' [Ode to Walt Whitman]).[29] There are structural differences as well: the predominance of free verse and the reduced presence of metaphor; the use of a narrative structure – that of a journey – to bring unity to the book (chapter headings trace the poet's progress to New York, to Vermont, back to the city, and his escape from there to Havana, Cuba); the intended combination of written expression with the use of drawings, postcards and photographs (only the drawings were included in the posthumous first edition). In *Poet in New York*, North America and the metropolis are attacked as a symbol of racial injustice, materialism, spiritual cowardice, cruelty and the crowd's indifference to nature and to tiny, helpless things – from 'abandoned children' to the 'butterfly drowned in the inkwell'. For these the poet serves as redeemer and spokesman.[30] A ubiquitous theme is that of the search for identity that has been lost in the depersonalizing crowds of the metropolis. The poet's injunction to the blacks to reconnect with their African roots and to Americans to re-embrace the democratic agrarian ethos of Walt Whitman, is analogous to his own search for a time in his childhood, 'when all the roses spilled from my tongue' (*Collected Poems*, p. 685): presumably, when poetic wonder was intact, and its expression less clouded by rhetoric. Fractured by his sojourn in the New World, the subject of the poems feels pulled between the 'crystal-seeking forms' of (perhaps) science and technology and the 'curves' of poetry, nature, and the imagination ('Vuelta de paseo' [Back from a Walk]). Many readers – most recently and lucidly, Nandorfy – have detected in *Poeta en Nueva York* the influence of the biblical book of Revelation, and some of the poems ('Oda al rey de Harlem' [Ode to the King of Harlem]) sound an apocalyptic note, predicting a vague, vengeful rebellion by blacks against the white power structure. Although such documents should not be allowed to overdetermine the meaning of the poems, *Poeta en Nueva York*

---

my state is not one of *perpetual dream*. I expressed myself badly. I have *skirted* dream sometimes, but without falling fully into it, and always preserving a lifeline of laughter and a sturdy wooden scaffolding. I never venture into terrains which do not belong to man, for I turn around immediately and almost always *rip up* the product of my journey. [. . .] I loathe the art of dream' (*Epistolario*, pp. 518–19).

29 Lorca's treatment of both blacks and gays reveals, as Paul Julian Smith and others have pointed out, a deeply ambivalent attitude. See 'New York, New York: Lorca's Double Vision', *Journal of Iberian and Latin American Studies*, 6, 2 (2000), 171.

30 On *Poet in New York*, see Richard L. Predmore, *Lorca's New York poetry: Social Injustice, Dark Love, Lost Faith* (Durham, NC: Duke University Press, 1980); Derek Harris, *Federico García Lorca: Poeta en Nueva York*, Critical Guides 24 (London: Grant & Cutler, 1978); and Martha Nandorfy, *The Poetics of Apocalypse: García Lorca's 'Poet in New York'* (Lewisburg, PA: Bucknell University Press / London: Associated University Presses, 2003).

may be read in the context of a series of other documents: the letters Lorca
wrote to his parents from New York – charming humorous observations on the
US and on his surroundings at Columbia University and elsewhere; the 1932
lecture-recital entitled 'Un poeta en Nueva York' [A Poet in New York], where
the poet emphasizes the social criticism of his collection; a film script called
Viaje a la luna [*Trip* (or *Journey*) *to the Moon*] that was to have been realized by
the Mexican photographer Emilio Amero; and the play *El público* [*The Public*
or, perhaps more precisely, *The Audience*], which was begun in Havana in
1930.[31] Together, with poems not collected in the book (for example, 'Infancia
y muerte' [Childhood and Death]), these texts form a cycle of writing that marks
a new point of departure for the poet. The fact that *Poeta en Nueva York* was not
published during Lorca's lifetime – he delivered a rough version of the manuscript to his friend José Bergamín for publication in Madrid but it was not
published until 1940 when Bergamín was in exile in Mexico – created textual
problems affecting both the composition of the book and the meaning of individual verses and poems. Bergamín's edition appeared almost simultaneously
with a bilingual edition published by the poet and translator Rolfe Humphries in
New York. The reappearance of the manuscript Lorca had given to Bergamín
(sold at auction in London in 2003 and acquired by the Fundación Federico
García Lorca) helps to solve many of those problems, though, as with the *Suites*
and with other Lorca works, no edition will ever be considered final and definitive.[32]

Lorca's return to Spain and the advent of the Second Republic in 1931
brought new involvement with its cultural programmes (for example, the travelling theatre group La Barraca, dedicated to giving rural Spain access to the classical theatre of Lope de Vega, Cervantes, Tirso de Molina and others), and a will
to address social problems through the theatre, which Lorca conceived both as a
form of poetry – 'the poetry which rises from the book and becomes human'
(*Obras completas*, III, p. 630) and as a forum for social justice, 'a school of
laughter and lamentation, an open tribunal where the people can introduce old
and mistaken mores as evidence, and can use living examples to explain eternal
norms of the human heart' (*Deep Song*, p. 124). His ideas on poetry and the
theatre are found in the 1935 talk 'Charla sobre el teatro' [A Talk about Theatre]
(*Deep Song*, pp. 123–6) and in the numerous interviews he gave during the last
five years of his life. Although some of Lorca's earliest dramatic works were
written during his life at the Residencia de Estudiantes, Madrid, those for which
he is best known – *Bodas de sangre*, *Yerma*, *La casa de Bernarda Alba*, *Doña*

---

[31] All of these documents, except for *El público*, are collected in Christopher Maurer
(ed.), Greg Simon and Steven F. White (trans.), *Poet in New York* (New York: Noonday Press,
1998). For *El público*, see the edition and introduction of Antonio Monegal in Federico García
Lorca, *Viaje a la luna [Guión cinematográfico]* (Valencia: Editorial Pre-Textos, 1994).

[32] For the most recent account of the textual history and rediscovery of the manuscript,
see Nigel Dennis, *Vida y milagros de un manuscrito de Lorca: En Pos de 'Poeta en Nueva
York'* (Santander: Sociedad Menéndez Pelayo, 2000).

Rosita la soltera, etc. – were mostly written during the first half of the 1930s. In each of them, poetry (understood not primarily as verse for the stage but as vivid, rhythmic, memorable, often metaphorical speech, often accompanied by music) is an essential ingredient. During the same period, particularly during a trip to Buenos Aires in 1933/4 during which he directed hugely successful productions of *Bodas de sangre* and other plays, Lorca was also active as a lecturer, presenting new versions of several lectures and his last prolonged statement on the process of poetic composition and poetic inspiration. In 'Juego y teoría del duende' [Play and Theory of the Duende], which supersedes the earlier essay entitled 'Imaginación, inspiración, evasión', poetic inspiration is attributed to any of three transcendent forces: the angel, the muse, or the *duende* (the first two much less clearly differentiated than the *duende*). In Lorca's view, the *duende* – a popular Spanish expression for an impish household spirit and for a mesmerizing, inexplicable sort of charm – is a mysterious chthonic force responsible not only for inspired creation but also for the successful transmission and comprehension of works of art. Found most frequently among bullfighters, dancers and flamenco artists, the *duende* thrives on live performance, preferring spontaneity and instinct to calculated 'style' and 'form' and leaping sometimes from an inspired audience to a dull performer, rather than the other way round. Elements of the *duende*'s *je ne sais quois* are, in Lorca's view, its irrational, diabolic nature, its deep connection with the earth and an intense awareness of death on the part of creator and audience.[33]

The poems written during Lorca's last five years of life (studied most carefully by Andrew A. Anderson) are far less numerous than those written in the five years preceding the trip to New York, but no less intense. The posthumously published book *Diván del Tamarit* is a grave meditation on love and death in imagery meant to suggest the 'divans' (collections), composed of ghazals and casidas, of Arab-Andalusian poets in whom Lorca had been interested since the early 1920s (the 'Tamarit' was a country estate owned by an uncle). Offering an alternative to the colourful Orientalist visions of earlier poets like Zorrilla (whose imitators had been hilariously parodied by Lorca and his circle of friends in Granada),[34] the *Diván del Tamarit* was published with a prologue by Emilio García Gómez, one of Spain's most renowned scholars on Andalusian literature in Arabic. In these poems a relentlessly grave poetic voice, the martyr of unrequited love, declares from his own garden of Gethsemane (using Granada and the Vega as poetic backdrop), the universal presence of death. Lorca's poetic discourse is more spare, intense and difficult here than in previous works. The poetic 'addressee' of the poems can be deduced to be a male, and another aspect

---

[33] For an English translation of the lecture, see Federico García Lorca, *In Search of Duende*, ed. and trans. by Christopher Maurer (New York: New Directions, 1998), 48–62. See also Edward Hirsch, *The Demon and the Angel. Searching for the Source of Artistic Inspiration* (New York: Harvest Books, 2003).

[34] On Andalusian themes in Lorca, see C. Brian Morris, *Son of Andalusia. The Lyrical Landscapes of Federico García Lorca* (Nashville: Vanderbilt University Press, 1997).

of the book's 'Arab-Andalusian' character arises, as Alberto Mira suggests, from the fact that the association of Arab culture and southern Spain had been 'tinged' with homoerotic elements after the publication of García Gómez's 1931 anthology, *Poemas arábigoandaluces* [*Poems of Al-Andalus*].[35]

Written slightly later, *Seis poemas galegos* [*Six Galician Poems*] is a homage to the language and poetry of Galicia, particularly to the melancholy poetry of Rosalía de Castro and to the spiritual unity of Galicia in Spain and among the emigrants of the New World. The book reflects Lorca's contact not only with the hilly rural country of northwest Spain and its capital Santiago de Compostela, which he had first visited as a student, but also his contact, in 1933/4, with the Galician community of Buenos Aires. Anderson has pointed out that these poems, written in 1932–4 and published by a small press in Santiago in 1935, were

> composed originally, in written or oral form, in Castilian or defective Galician. Thereafter, they were translated or copied out, certainly with linguistic and probably also aesthetic corrections by [Lorca's close friend] Ernesto da Cal and possibly another. Finally they were transcribed again, with further ortho-graphic, linguistic, and aesthetic revisions by [the noted Galician author] Eduardo Blanco Amor. The received text is the result of an accretion of several redactions and versions, and certainly not all of these were supervised, corrected, or directly checked and approved by Lorca himself.[36]

Lorca's *Llanto por Ignacio Sánchez Mejías* [*Lament for the Death of Ignacio Sánchez Mejías*], published in 1935, is his last major book, an elegy to the death of his close friend, the Sevillian bullfighter gored to death in the bullring in the summer of 1934 at the age of 43, after an unexpected return from retirement. In one of his finest critical essays, Lorca's brother Francisco has drawn attention to the *Llanto*'s musical structure: in each of the poem's four sections, there are marked changes in tone, theme and rhythm, analogous to the movements of a symphony. In the *Llanto*, a narrator, who officiates at a rite of his own invention, gives lyrical voice to four distinct stages of shock and grief: (1) the narrative enumeration of details of the 'Goring and Death' in part I, where events imag-ined to happen 'at exactly five in the afternoon' crowd simultaneously into the poet's consciousness; (2) psychological denial in the imaginary wake entitled 'Cuerpo Presente' [The laid-out body]; (3) a philosophical meditation in which the indifference and inert permanence of stone (mountains, the mortuary slab)

---

[35] Alberto Mira, 'Modernistas, dandis y pederastas: articulaciones de la homosexualidad en "la edad de plata"', *Journal of Iberian & Latin American Studies*, 7, 1 (2001), 27–35 (p. 72). For a discussion of Lorca's influence in modern Arabic-language poetry, see Yair Huri, 'In Your Name this Death is Holy: Federico García Lorca in the Works of Modern Arab Poets', in *Ciberletras*, 13 (2004), at http://www.lehman.cuny.edu/ciberletras/v13/huri.htm

[36] Andrew A. Anderson, 'Who Wrote *Seis poemas gallegos* and in What Language?', in C. Brian Morris (ed.), *'Cuando yo me muera . . .' Essays in Memory of Federico García Lorca* (Lanham, MD: University Press of America, 1988), 139.

are contrasted with the fragility and fleetingness of human life ('Cuerpo ausente' [Absent Body]); and (4) a final commemoration of Ignacio's excellence ('Alma ausente'; 'Absent Soul'), inspired by the fifteenth-century elegy 'Coplas por la muerte de su padre' [Verses for the Death of His Father] by Jorge Manrique. Throughout the poem, Ignacio is imagined as a martyred Christ figure, except that, in Lorca's vision, his death has little, if any, redemptive value: the protagonist is imagined, brutally, as destined for a 'heap of snuffed-out dogs', and only the poet's loyalty and the poem itself will keep his memory alive. Xon de Ros views the poem as an articulation of 'the tensions of a nation torn between faith and reason, tradition and modernity'.[37] In his essay, Francisco García Lorca notes the poet's ability – evident in all his works – to move from specific detail to abstraction, setting up a contrast between tangible objects and their occult and universally valid meaning.[38]

In the months before he was murdered by Francoist troops during the early days of the Spanish Civil War, Lorca was working on a collection of sonnets, *Jardín de los sonetos* [*Garden of Sonnets*], which would have brought together some of the many he had written over the course of his lifetime – a sign of a trend in Spanish poetry thatt Lorca described as a return to 'traditional forms after a wide-ranging and sunny stroll through the freedom of metre and rhyme' (*Obras completas*, III, p. 633). The most important sequence in that book was to have been the *Sonetos del amor oscuro* [*Sonnets of Dark Love*], a collection of eleven homoerotic love sonnets written in 1935 and inspired by Rafael Rodríguez Rapún, the young engineering student who had worked as Lorca's assistant in La Barraca. Some of these sonnets are more heavily revised and polished than others, although all of them were eagerly and indiscriminately incorporated into the canon of the work after the posthumous publication of the sequence in a pirated edition in 1983 and the official first publication in the Madrid newspaper *A.B.C.* The final version – if ever Lorca prepared a draft that he considered final – has been lost. It is saddening that the two Lorca works that deal most boldly and directly with homoeroticism exist, today, only in 'unfinished' versions, and that some of Lorca's closest friends chose not to publish complete versions of the letters he wrote to them.[39]

From the advent of the Franco regime, in 1939, until the Generalísimo

---

[37] Xon de Ros, 'Science and Myth in Lorca's "Llanto" ', *Modern Language Review*, 95, 1 (2000), 118.

[38] Francisco García Lorca, *Federico y su mundo*, ed. Mario Hernández, 2nd edn (Madrid: Alianza Editorial, 1980), 232.

[39] See, for example, the truncated letter in Rafael Martínez Nadal, *Federico García Lorca. Mi penúltimo libro sobre el hombre y el poeta* (Madrid: Editorial Casariego, 1992), 298; and the fragments of a letter to Jorge Zalamea in *Epistolario completo*, 576–8. Lorca's letters to Dalí have been stolen or lost (see Ian Gibson, *The Shameful Life of Salvador Dalí* [New York: W.W. Norton, 1998], 651). On the suppression or mutilation of Lorca's works, see Daniel Eisenberg, 'Lorca and Censorship: The Gay Artist Made Heterosexual', *Angélica* (Lucena, Spain), 2 (1991), 121–45. updated version posted at http://users.ipfw.edu/jehle/deisenbe/

himself authorized the first edition of his *Obras completas* [Complete Works], edited in a censored version by the indefatigable Arturo del Hoyo in 1953, Lorca's poetry, plays, drawings, music, lectures and letters were published much less frequently in Spain than abroad. Over the past several decades, particularly since the advent of a democratic regime in 1975, Lorca has become a protean and highly contested cultural and political icon, moving between the worlds of popular kitsch and high culture and frequently invoked in discussions of social, linguistic and sexual politics.[40] He is probably Europe's best-known twentieth-century poet, and his poetry – both lyrical and dramatic – as well as his poetic of the 'duende' have profoundly influenced the course of European and – through the early translations of Robert Bly, Ben Belitt, Roy Campbell, Rolfe Humphries and others – American poetry.[41]

[40] For a recent discussion, see the essays and discussions in Sebastian Doggart and Michael Thompson (eds), *Fire, Blood and the Alphabet: One Hundred Years of Lorca* (Durham: University of Durham, 1999).

[41] On Lorca in American poetry, see Robert Bly, *American Poetry: Wildness and Domesticity* (New York: Harper & Row, 1990).

2

Theatre

SARAH WRIGHT

In close-shot, a bloodied bullet is submerged in a glass of water. The anguished strains of *cante jondo* [deep song] erupt into the surround sound. This sequence forms the opening titles of Marcos Zurinaga's 1996 film *Muerte en Granada* [Death in Granada], released in the US as *The Disappearance of García Lorca*. Hollywood actor Andy García steps into the role of the poet and playwright to recreate the circumstances surrounding Lorca's murder. The film is a noirish thriller. It features a journalist-cum-literary critic turned detective, who becomes embroiled in a plot involving the same suspects responsible for Lorca's death years earlier. In this opening scene, a series of dissolves cross-cuts footage from the Spanish Civil War with shots of García, playing Lorca, dressed in a striking white suit in a cell awaiting execution. He is reciting Lorca's famous poem *Llanto por Ignacio Sánchez Mejías* [*Lament for the Death of Ignacio Sánchez Mejías*]: its chorus line 'a las cinco de la tarde' [at five in the afternoon] tolls above the orchestral crescendo. '[Lorca's] murder was one of the enigmas of the war,' the credits inform us. The film acknowledges a debt to Ian Gibson's *The Assassination of García Lorca* and his *Lorca: A Life*, which underscores the importance of Gibson's biographical work in the 1970s. Knowing it would be seized on internationally, the Franco regime suppressed information about Lorca's death. Gibson not only revealed details about the murder, but also shed light on Lorca's homosexuality (an aspect that is omitted from Zurinaga's thriller).

Zurinaga's film illustrates well the 'seductiveness'[1] of Lorca as icon: the patchy trail of homosexual liaisons, partially glimpsed or wholly suppressed, and the enigma of his murder, create the desire to turn detective and find out more. But the opening sequence of the film also illustrates the way that the circumstances of Lorca's death have come to influence interpretations of his work: the poem 'Llanto por Ignacio Sánchez Mejías' deals with the death of a

---

[1] Paul Julian Smith, *The Theatre of García Lorca: Text, Performance, Psychoanalysis* (Cambridge: Cambridge University Press, 1998), draws on Luis Fernández-Cifuentes, *García Lorca en el teatro: la norma y la diferencia* (Zaragoza: Prensas Universitarias de Zaragoza, 1986), to write persuasively of Lorca's capacity for seduction.

matador in the bullring. But in the Zurinaga film it signifies Lorca's status as
martyr at the hands of Fascism, in a neat elision of *oeuvre* and biography, of
work and life.

Paul Julian Smith has alerted us to the 'extreme case of proprietorial authorship' represented by the work of García Lorca. 'It seems impossible', he writes,
'to approach his texts without acknowledging his person, and it is almost an
article of faith that in Lorca literature and life are one.'[2] To read Lorca's life (or,
more specifically, his death) into his work is to seek and find confirmation of a
series of preconceived assumptions: namely that Lorca's work can be seen to
articulate metaphors that in different ways express the struggle between freedom
and repressed desires; that the backdrop of a Spain threatened by Fascism can be
seen as the *mise-en-scène* (in varying degrees of disguise) for his plays. Such an
approach can prove fruitful in approaching some of Lorca's theatrical output.
Lorca's *La casa de Bernarda Alba* [*The House of Bernarda Alba*], for example,
with its damning indictment of the silent menace of repressive regimes, can be
productively read against tensions in the opening stages of the Spanish Civil
War and the growing threat of Fascism internationally in the 1930s. If we were
to try to imagine what the 'standard adjective in English derived from [García
Lorca's] name, equivalent to the familiar "Brechtian"' (Smith 1998, p. 140)
might connote, it would surely be a theatrical experience that allows the spectator to engage with a search for passionate bursts of life amidst encroaching,
stultifying repression. Simultaneously, if the name 'Lorca' has come to signify
'martyr', this in itself is an important and always timely reminder of the cruel
effects of certain repressive regimes (Lorca's name has recently taken on fresh
resonance in Spain as an agent of cultural memory, in the struggle against the
so-called 'pact of silence', as a debate continues about whether to exhume his
grave).[3] If Lorca's seductiveness derives in part from the enigma of his murder,
his continuing appeal may partly have to do with our desire to engage and come
to terms with a violent moment in history. Most English-language productions
are accompanied by the outline of events of the Spanish Civil War, information
about Lorca's death and glossy reproductions of early photographs of a young,
glamorous Lorca gazing soulfully at the camera. Perhaps we might say that part
of the attraction of attending a production of one of Lorca's plays springs from a
desire on the part of the audience and director to revisit the trauma of his
untimely death in a process of collective mourning.

---

[2] Paul Julian Smith, 'Lorca and Foucault', in *The Body Hispanic: Gender and Sexuality
in Spanish and Spanish American Literature* (Oxford: Oxford University Press, 1989),
105–37 (p. 107).

[3] Commentators of Spanish history have alluded to the 'Pact of Silence', a tacit agree-
ment among the Left after the death of Francisco Franco not to enter into criticisms of Spain's
past for the sake of a peaceful transition to democracy. Weekend exhumations of bodies
dumped into mass graves (much like the one Lorca was buried in) are seen as part of attempts
to re-engage with a painful aspect of the Spanish past. See Elizabeth Kolbert, 'Looking for
Lorca: A Poet's Grave and a War's Buried Secrets', *The New Yorker*, 22 and 29 December
2003, pp. 64–78.

But to approach Lorca's theatre armed with a checklist of 'Lorca issues' distilled from our knowledge of the way he died is inevitably to overlook other important aspects of his dramaturgy. Lorca was a playwright of extraordinary versatility and virtuosity. He is most famous as the creator of the so-called 'rural trilogy', comprising *Bodas de sangre* [*Blood Wedding*], *Yerma* [*Yerma*] and *La casa de Bernarda Alba*. These large-impact tragedies are seen to be rooted in the Spanish earth and have generally been regarded as the most accomplished of Lorca's works for the theatre. But Lorca also made great inroads into the theatre of the avant-garde, culminating in his strikingly modernist works, *Así que pasen cinco años* [*Once Five Years Pass*] and the theatrical *tour de force*, *El público* [*The Public*, or *The Audience*]. Lorca experimented with the bio-drama of an historical figure (*Mariana Pineda*), and the private drama of a Spanish old maid (*Doña Rosita la Soltera o El lenguage de las flores* [*Doña Rosita the Spinster or the Language of Flowers*]. He wrote tragi-comic farces (*Amor de Don Perlimplín con Belisa en su jardín* [*The Love of Don Perlimplín for Belisa in Their Garden*] and *La zapatera prodigiosa* [*The Shoemaker's Prodigious Wife*]) and a series of puppet-plays (*La tragicomedia de don Cristóbal y la Señá Rosita* [*Tragi-comedy of Don Cristobal and Mam'selle Rosita*], *Retablillo de Don Cristóbal* [*Don Cristobal's Puppet Play*] and *El maleficio de la mariposa* [*The Butterfly's Evil Spell*]. Short, experimental pieces included *Quimera* [*Chimera*], *El paseo de Buster Keaton* [*Buster Keaton's Outing*] and *La doncella, el marinero y el estudiante* [The Maiden, the Sailor and the Student]. A series of unfinished works provides tantalizing clues as to projects to be taken up later or discarded for good; some are no more than a list of dramatis personae, others are semi-complete: *Los sueños de mi prima Aurelia* [*Dreams of my Cousin Aurelia*], *La bola negra* [*Black Ball*], *La destrucción de Sodoma* [*The Destruction of Sodom*], *Lola la comedianta* [*Lola the Actress*], *Dragón* [*Dragon*] and *Comedia sin título* [*Play Without a Title*].[4]

The relatively recent publication of early drafts and unfinished theatrical projects has given rise to new ways of addressing Lorca's theatrical output. Lorca's juvenilia, which includes the playlet *Cristo. Tragedia religosa* [*Christ. Religious Tragedy*], *Jehová* [*Jehovah*], *Místicas* [*Mystics*], *Sombras* [*Shadows*] and *La viudita que se quería casar* [*The Little Widow Who Wanted to Wed*] appeared in 1994 and certainly warrants more critical attention than has been afforded it to date.[5] It reveals a Lorca who is at once playful, experimental and intellectual, as well as directing attention to the important role of religious imagery in Lorca's work: the remaking of Biblical legends; the reworking of the sacrificial imagery of the Christ-figure. Alongside Lorca's interest in the Gypsy

---

[4] See Marie Laffranque, *Federico García Lorca: Teatro inconcluso. Fragmentos y proyectos inacabados* (Granada: Universidad de Granada, 1987).

[5] Federico García Lorca, *Teatro inédito de juventud*, ed. Andrés Soria Olmedo, Letras Hispánicas 385 (Madrid: Cátedra, 1994). For a study of early juvenilia, see Eutimio Martín, *Federico García Lorca, heterodoxo y mártir. Análisis y proyección de la obra juvenil inédita* (Madrid: Siglo XXI, 1986).

roots of his Spanish motherland, we now have the urban dreamscape of *Así que pasen cinco años* and the arena of classical antiquity of *El público*. Against a fascination with strong female characters we have love (and sex) between men. Primitive passions are to the fore in many of Lorca's plays, but behind others we find a thinker and intellectual who used theatre to work out moral, ethical and philosophical issues. Lorca the Andalusian competes with Lorca the surrealist and the American Lorca. Lorca studies proliferate in new, and often contradictory, directions, from the historical and textual, the folkloric and the biographical, the psychoanalytic and the performance-based; we also have feminist studies, gay readings and cultural studies. Paul Julian Smith has explored what he terms the 'cult' of García Lorca and the way that his name has been pressed into service for a variety of causes and personal investments. Describing Lorca as a 'site of struggle', Smith writes that Lorca 'refuses to be confined to any one side of the paradigm – tradition and modernity, centre and periphery, gay and straight' (Smith 1998, pp. 139, 143).

One aspect of consensus among critics appears to be the notion that Lorca was a committed theatre practitioner: he strove to see his work produced on stage. His project with La Barraca (a troupe of itinerant players who would set up a space for theatre in town squares to bring the classics to the locals) bears witness to his belief in the importance of theatre as live act as well as his need to engage with an audience. To factor Lorca's commitment to performance into the way we view his theatrical output has meant new ways of classifying the development of his theatre. For some years, critics tended to view Lorca's theatre as a journey towards the 'rural trilogy'.[6] According to this reading, certain works are seen as minor experiments *en route* to the major tragedies. But recently, critics have begun to question these schemata. Some of Lorca's works simply were not palatable for the time in which he lived, forcing him to shelve them in favour of other projects. In fact, in statements uttered in the 1930s, Lorca consistently names *El público, Así que pasen cinco años* and *El sueño de la vida* [*The Dream of Life*] as '*mi* obra' [*my* plays]. In 1933 Pablo Suero wrote, 'Si le habláis de *Bodas de sangre* habla con entusiasmo de dos obras que no ha podido representar y que son, según él, el teatro que quiere hacer. Estas obras se titulan *Así que pasen cinco años* y *El público*' [If you mention *Blood Wedding* he talks with enthusiasm of two plays that he hasn't been able to put on stage, and that are, according to him, the theatre that he wants to do. These plays are called *Once Five Years Pass* and *The Audience*].[7] Fernández Cifuentes has shown how

---

[6] Andrew Anderson notes that while Lorca spoke of a trilogy (the first two plays of which were *Bodas de sangre* and *Yerma*), he intended the third to be a Biblical work entitled either *El drama de las hijas de Loth* [*Drama of Loth's Daughters*] or *Destrucción del Sodoma*, which existed 'at least in rudimentary form, for during the summer of 1935, Lorca gave a reading of it to two friends [. . .] Rodríguez Rapún and Sáenz de la Calzada, and the latter has in fact given a two-page resumé of the plot'. See Anderson, 'The Strategy of Federico García Lorca's Dramatic Composition, 1930–36', *Romance Quarterly*, 33 (1986), 211–29.

[7] Pablo Suero, 'Crónica de un día de barco con Federico García Lorca', in Federico

Lorca was badly affected by the hostile reception afforded his early lyrical transposition of the world of beetles and butterflies to the stage, *El maleficio de la mariposa*, which closed after four performances (Fernández-Cifuentes 1986, pp. 29–44).[8] At the same time, Lorca was to find enormous critical and commercial success with some of the stage-actresses of his time. María Delgado, studying Lorca's collaborative projects with Margarita Xirgu, has suggested that the influence on Lorca's writing of the success he achieved with the major actresses of his time may have been underestimated: 'the plethora of roles written by García Lorca for women may remain as the most permanent attestation for even the most entrenched literary critic that the theatrical climate in which the dramatist worked, dominated by companies run by actresses, shaped his dramatic climate'.[9] Christopher Soufas makes the distinction between commercial theatre (appropriate for the times) and the experimental, 'impossible', theatre that Lorca really wanted to stage; he views Lorca's work as an ongoing dialogue with his historical audience, a conservative milieu that had dictated the theatre agenda of the Madrid theatre scene during the 1920s.[10] A tactician, rather than a strategist, Lorca responded reactively to the contemporary theatre climate. *El público*, at once theatrically daring, and 'de tema francamente homosexual' [frankly homosexual in theme],[11] was perceived by Lorca to be 'muy difícil, y por el momento irrepresentable. Pero dentro de diez años será un exitazo, ya lo verás' [very difficult, and for the moment, unperformable. But in ten years' time it will be a huge success, you'll see].[12] In fact Lorca's *El público* had to wait until 1986 to be performed for the first time, not ten but fifty years later.

Now that we have access to Lorca's *oeuvre* almost in its entirety, and now that critics are working to contextualise Lorca's writing for the theatre within the time in which it was conceived or performed, we can begin to have a more complete vision of Lorca's theatrical output. To view Lorca's theatre now is to have the benefit of access to the range of Lorca's works, and at times to have the possibility of seeing some works in production. By juxtaposing the lyrical with the surrealist, the experimental with the classical, we can start to spawn fresh connections, drawing new, exciting conclusions about Lorca's theatre. Theatre,

García Lorca, *Obras completas*, III, ed. Arturo del Hoyo, 3 vols, 22nd edn (Madrid: Aguilar, 1986), 539–53 (pp. 544–5).

8 See also María Francisca Vilches de Frutos and Dru Dougherty, *Los estrenos teatrales de Federico García Lorca (1920–45)* (Madrid: Tabapress / Grupo Tabacalera / Fundación FGL, 1992), 23–32.

9 María Delgado, *Other Spanish Theatres: Erasure and Inscription on the Spanish Stage* (Manchester: Manchester University Press, 2003), 52.

10 C. Christopher Soufas, *Audience and Authority in the Modernist Theater of Federico García Lorca* (Tuscaloosa and London: University of Alabama Press, 1996).

11 Federico García Lorca, *Espitolario completo*, ed. Andrew A. Anderson and Christopher Maurer (Madrid: Cátedra, 1997), 690.

12 Rafael Martínez Nadal, *El público: amor y muerte en la obra de Federico García Lorca* (Madrid: Ediciones Hiperión, 1970), 17.

after all, ought to be less about confirming our expectations than challenging them. Lorca studies today provides fertile ground for finding new ways of approaching Lorca's exciting imagery and exhilarating vision for the theatre.

Vexed Eros: unstageable love in *Amor de Don Perlimplín con Belisa en su jardín*, *El público* and *Bodas de sangre*

Amor de Don Perlimplín con Belisa en su jardín (1926) is a brief work that for many years was regarded as a minor piece unworthy of extensive attention.[13] While the play has been turned into operetta, and is often staged with puppets, full theatrical performances are rare.[14] Tellingly, a lavish production of 1990 (whose sumptuous set-design was described as 'demasiado para tan poca cosa' [too much for such a small thing])[15] at the Teatro Bellas Artes in Madrid, directed by José Luis Gómez, sold the production of this little-known work on the basis of its two 'heavyweight' stage and screen actors, Héctor Alterio and Sonsoles Benedicto, as much as on Lorca's name,[16] and twinned the play with another brief piece, *Quimera*, conceived as a bad dream of Perlimplín.

Amor de Don Perlimplín con Belisa en su jardín tells the tale of Don Perlimplín, a fifty-year-old virginal male and confirmed bachelor, who is persuaded to marry Belisa, a beautiful and sensual young woman. They seem to be the 'perfect' match: he has a lot of lands; she possesses youth and beauty. On their wedding night, two *duendes* (sprites) draw a veil over the marriage chamber and insinuate that Belisa will commit adultery. Out of revenge for the dishonour brought upon him by his wife's infidelity, Perlimplín invents a fantasy Young Man in the Red Cape (Perlimplín in disguise) who writes letters to Belisa. When Perlimplín kills himself at the end of the play, he leaves Belisa searching endlessly for the mysterious lover.

In the second tableau, two tricksterish sprites emerge out of the twilight to comment on proceedings. These figures may remind us of Lorca's early play, *Sombras*, where shadowy spirits emerge out of the mist into a garden to offer a mocking commentary on faith (Soria Olmedo, pp. 45–50). The characters in

---

[13] Fernández-Cifuentes, *García Lorca en el teatro*, Pamela Bacarisse, 'Perlimplín's Tragedy', in Robert Havard (ed.), *Lorca: Poet and Playwright* (Cardiff: University of Wales Press, 1992), 71–92, and Margarita Ucelay (ed.), *Amor de Don Perlimplín con Belisa en su jardín*, Letras Hispánicas 313 (Madrid: Cátedra, 1992) argue that the play should not be regarded as minor.

[14] For example, Heymann Micro-Teatro, who staged a puppet-version at the Centro Cultural de la Villa, Madrid in 1998; A Tarumba, who have toured internationally with their puppet-play; Poul Rovsing Olsen's one-act opera, *Belisa*; Miguel Ángel Coria's opera *Belisa* and Conrad Susa's opera version, which received its première in 1984 at the San Francisco Opera Center.

[15] Eduardo Haro Tecglen, 'Estampa pequeña', *El país*, 17 October 1990, n.p.

[16] Héctor Alterio had by then starred in *La historia oficial* [*The Official Story*] by Luis Puenzo and *Yo, la peor de todas* [*I, the Worst of All*] by Luisa Bemberg; Sonsoles Benedicto had had a role in *Un hombre llamado flor de otoño* [*A Man Named Flower of Autumn*) by Pedro Olea among others.

Sombras appear to have been drawn from Plato's *The Symposium*, which presents a dialogue on differing forms of love.[17] Interestingly, most critics of *Amor de Don Perlimplín* concur that it is an exposition on the nature of love, with spiritual love thrown into relief by carnal desire.[18] The play can also be read as a complex twinning of the theme of love with that of the search for 'truth' amidst the deceptiveness of appearances.[19]

Plato's *The Symposium* consists of a series of encomia to different forms of love (*erôs*) between men. Distinctions are drawn between Heavenly love and Common love: the latter is purely physical, the former is also ethical and virtuous. Emerging from the dialogues is a model relationship first introduced by Pausianus: that of an older male lover who takes sexual gratification from a younger male and in exchange educates him in the meaning of virtue. Diotima (a wise woman) expands on this 'asymmetrical' coupling to suggest that a modified (non-sexual, philosophical) form of this relationship should be the ideal form of love. Paradigmatic of this relationship is the one expressed between Socrates and Alcibiades. We can see clear echoes of this model in the union of Perlimplín and Belisa. Perlimplín is a 'monigote sin fuerza' [lifeless rag doll] (*Obras completas*, II, p. 495), the grotesque side of the pairing of 'lo lírico y lo grotesco' [the lyrical and the grotesque],[20] but he has a noble spirit: in similar fashion, Socrates is snub-nosed with bulging eyes like Silenius, the satyr, but is possessed of inner beauty.[21] Perlimplín is happiest when immersed in his books, much as Socrates is representative of contemplative, philosophical life. Belisa is represented by her body ('pues si la viera por dentro, ¡como de azúcar!' [you should see her on the

---

[17] Earlier titles for the work were 'Diálogos de Sombras' [*Dialogues of Shadows*] and 'Banquete final' [*Final Banquet*] – Plato's *The Symposium* is also known as *The Banquet*. The *Sombra de Sócrates* [*Socrates' Shadow*] is a character in Lorca's play, while Socrates also appears as a character in Plato's work (see Soria Olmedo, p. 45). Plato's *The Symposium* was present in Lorca's personal library: *El banquete o El amor*, with a critical study by Ralph W. Emerson; and a 'Discurso sobre las pasiones del amor/de Blas Pascal'; translation, prologue and notes by Rafael Urbino (Madrid: Francisco Beltrán, 1923). See Manuel Fernández-Montesinos, *Descripción de la biblioteca de Federico García Lorca (Catálogo y estudio). Tesina para la licienciatura presentada en la Universidad Complutense de Madrid*, 13 September 1985, p. 211. For access to this text, the author is grateful to Rosa María Illán of the Fundación Federico García Lorca.

[18] See for example, A. Lewis, *The Contemporary Theater* (New York: Crown Publishers, 1971), who writes that '[Perlimplín's] love for Belisa is so selfless that he has created the image by which she can discover love [. . .]. He gives his life that she will learn the meaning of love' (p. 248).

[19] See Sarah Wright, 'Perlimplín's Seduction: Masquerade and the *trompe l'oeil*', in Sarah Wright, *The Trickster-Function in the Theatre of García Lorca*, Colección Támesis 185 (Woodbridge: Tamesis, 2000), 39–61.

[20] 'Lo que me ha interesado en Don Perlimplín,' stated Lorca, 'es subrayar el contraste entre lo lírico y lo grotesco y aun mezclarlos en todo momento' [My interest in Don Perlimplín has been to underline the contrast between the lyrical and the grotesque and even to mix the two at any moment] (*Obras completas*, III, p. 521).

[21] Plato, *The Symposium*, 215b, trans. and intro. Christopher Gill (London: Penguin, 1999), p. 54.

inside, like sugar!], her mother brazenly asserts) (*Obras completas*, II, p. 465),[22] while Alcibiades too, is marked out by his physical beauty. Lorca's tale, like *The Symposium*, is by turns comic and tragic; both present shifting forms of love from the sacrificial to the sexual, the platonic and fatherly to the educative.

In *The Symposium*, a model relationship is characterized in terms of stages in an ascent towards 'the good', when Diotima (a wise woman) claims that the goal of love is to attain 'immortality along with the good' through reproduction and 'birth in beauty' (Plato 206e, p. 44). Reproduction can take place through men (here she contrasts physical and mental ways of immortalizing oneself, seen as a form of reproduction) for 'the ethical improvement of the boyfriend is [. . .] the means by which the lover can immortalize himself' (she compares this to 'immortal fame', which motivates people to die for others) and 'everything that grows old and goes away leaves behind another new thing of the same type' (Plato 208b, p. 45). In the relationship between Socrates and Alcibiades, the ethical education of the latter occurs when he realises that Socrates does not want him sexually: this impresses Alcibiades so much that it produces a mixture of humiliation, bafflement, anger and admiration and he becomes 'more completely enslaved to [Socrates] than anyone ever has been to anyone' (Plato 219e, p. 59). Diotima's model is thus played out: Alcibiades learns about love and truth, while Socrates gains a form of immortality by possessing Alcibiades mentally '*forever*'. Like the liaison between Socrates and Alcibiades ('when I got up next morning I had no more *slept with* Socrates than if I'd been sleeping with my father or elder brother [Plato, 219d, p. 59]), Perlimplín's relationship with Belisa remains unconsummated (Perlimplín wakes up instead with enormous horns on his head, symbolizing her adultery). Perlimplín invents the Young Man in the Red Cape (we could say he gives birth to the young, beautiful lover) and sacrifices himself,[23] in order to educate Belisa in the ways of love. While the Young Man in the Red Cape speaks to Belisa of her body, Perlimplín is withheld from her sexually (in fact there are suggestions that he is unable to perform sexually). At the end of the play, Belisa also has a revelation of sorts: '¡Nunca creí que fuese tan complicado!' [I never realized he was so complicated!], she cries, left endlessly trying to solve the enigma (who was the Young Man in the Red Cape?), which recalls the bafflement, anger and admiration expressed by Alcibiades. Through his masquerade, Perlimplín has managed to possess Belisa forever (achieving immortality – he dies for her love, and will remain forever in Belisa's imagination).

[22] The Mother's description of Belisa chimes with Alcibiades' description of Socrates' discussions: they may seem ridiculous at first, but 'if you can open them up and see inside, you'll find they're the only ones that make any sense' (Plato, 222a, p. 61). In both Lorca's play and the Platonic text, a dialectic between inner and outer is established. In both, the question of the deceptiveness of appearances is mooted as theme.

[23] The play also has strong religious overtones. See Patricia McDermott's excellent study, 'Subversions of the Sacred: The Sign of the Fish', in Derek Harris (ed.), *The Spanish Avant-garde* (Manchester: Manchester University Press, 1995), 204–17.

Socrates uses the dialogic method to 'reduce people to confusion and [make them] realise that they need to reconsider what they think they understand'.[24] In *Amor de Don Perplimplín*, the *duendes* warn the audience not to trust too much to appearances (making them realize they cannot trust what they understand): the play turns into a search for knowledge (the truth), but one that can never reach a conclusion. This is also true of *The Symposium*, where the Socratic method presents philosophy as a 'continuing search for objective truth', but simultaneously emphasizes 'the difficulty or incompleteness of this search'.[25] Significantly, this search, in both works, has erotic power, drawing the lover constantly towards an ever-receding goal.

Given the similarities of the Platonic text with the tale of Perlimplín and Belisa, it is intriguing to see that Lorca's play can be considered to be a veiled exploration of an ideal form of love between men. Behind Belisa, who appears to be the archetypal sensual young woman, we find a beautiful young man. Is this a further twist on the theme of the deceptiveness of appearances, the audience observing love between men recast for the times in a disguise? Reading back into Lorca's theatrical trajectory from (the unstaged) *El público*, conceived as the type of theatre Lorca was committed to, but which was ideologically as well as theatrically too daring for 1920s and 1930s Spain, it is tempting to see Lorca's theatre as a series of veiled attempts to stage variations on love between men. As it was, *Amor de Don Perlimplín* was subject to censorship: although it finally received its première as part of a 'gala function' two-parter with *La zapatera prodigiosa* at the Teatro Español in Madrid in 1933, the first attempt to stage the play in 1929 with the group El Caracol under the direction of Cipriano Rivas Cherif at the Sala Rex, Madrid, was thwarted. Already sensitive to the activities of El Caracol, whose previous production, *El sueño de la razón* [*The Dream of Reason*] had lesbianism as its theme,[26] the *guardia civil* confiscated the text of *Amor de Don Perlimplín* (placing it in the 'departamento de pornografía' [pornography department]) and closed the performances.

We must be wary, however, of readings that do not fully explore the richness of Lorca's complex achievement for the theatre. Don Perlimplín and Belisa are stock figures of farce taken from a kind of vignette known as the *aleluya*. As Margarita Ucelay has shown, in her companion piece to the play, early drafts show experimentation with the *grand guignol* of the *aleluyas* while a brief, early fragment, named *Teatro de aleluyas*, shows that one of Lorca's projects for the theatre was to create emotional distance from the spectators (Ucelay, pp. 36–7).

---

24 See Christopher Gill's 'Introduction' to Plato's *The Symposium* (London: Penguin, 1999), xxxviii.

25 In Plato's *The Symposium*, daimôns or spirits (in this case *erôs*) hold the truth (God communicates with humans, whether awake or asleep, through the medium of spirits).

26 The subtitle for the play was *Un engendro de lesbos* [*a procreation of Lesbos*]. It presented two women, Livia and Blanca, who perpetuate their love with a child conceived with the aid of a young prince who had fallen on hard times. The play is published in Juan Aguilera Sastre and Manuel Aznar Soler (eds), 'Cipriano de Rivas Cherif: Retrato de una utopía', *Cuadernos el Público*, 42 (Madrid, December 1989), 61–100.

Here, reference is made to 'Historia [story] de Don Perlimplín y Belisa en su jardín'. The important theme of love is added to title and theme in later drafts. The tale of the old man and the young girl is as 'old as the hills', and recasting a Platonic version of love between men as a tale of mismatched heterosexuality permits Lorca to harness a range of intertextual metanarratives for this couple, from the Beauty and the Beast, to Edmond Rostand's *Cyrano de Bergerac* (1897) and Fernand Crommelynck's *Le cocu magnifique* [*The Magnificent Cuckold*] (1921). A relationship often viewed as the 'perfect match' is made grotesque, revealing the sinister power play at work in this battle for sexual dominance through suggestion and fantasy. The play draws on a tradition that sees the search of knowledge as a journey towards truth veiled in feminine form (yet how intriguing to imagine, in a further twist, the deceptiveness of the visual now aligned with masculinity) (Wright, pp. 39–61). At every turn, the play betrays its philosophical origins, presenting an intricate and multi-layered meditation on the seductiveness of appearances, on the thwarted search for truth, and on shifting variations of the nature of love.

It is a fascinating coda to this alternative reading of *Amor de Don Perplimplín* to observe that the staging of a play that features a young man disguised as a young woman, in a love story with an older man, against intolerant times, is the theme dramatically played out in Lorca's 1930 play, *El público*. The action revolves around the storm that has erupted surrounding the Director's attempts to stage a scandalous production of Shakespeare's *Romeo and Juliet* in which 'Romeo era un hombre de treinta años y Julieta un muchacho de quince. La denuncia del público fue eficaz' [Romeo was a man of thirty and Juliet a boy of fifteen. The public's denouncement was effective] (*Obras completas*, II, p. 657). The reference is to the Elizabethan era, when young boys often played the roles of female characters: 'El Director de escena evitó de manera genial que la masa de los espectadores se enterase de esto' [The Theatre Director skilfully managed to prevent the mass of spectators from finding this out] (*Obras completas*, II, p. 658), in the traditional suspension of disbelief, which fails to see a boy in drag in the role of Juliet. This is the 'teatro del aire libre' [theatre of the open air] where artifice and inauthenticity reigns, presided over by its master of illusion the *Prestidigitador* [Magician]. If the love story between men had been couched in contextual alibi (a temporary madness, perhaps, such as that which causes a woman to fall in love with an ass in *A Midsummer's Night's Dream*), that would have been acceptable to the audience. But, the Director's story of love between men was simply too apparent, too easily seen-through and now the audience is baying for the Director's blood. Outside the walls of the theatre, the crowd advances like an angry lynch mob: 'piden la muerte del Director de escena' [they are demanding the death of the Theatre Director] (*Obras completas*, II, p. 647). Inside the theatre, the audience has set upon and killed the actors. The First Man would like the Director to direct theatre that is 'beneath the sand' (which tells the truth of tombs) rather than of the 'open air' (which dwells in illusion), but the Director expresses his fears: '¿Qué hago con el público si quito las barandas al puente? Vendría la máscara a devorarme. Yo vi una vez a un hombre devorado por la máscara [. . .]. Los jóvenes más fuertes de la ciudad, con picas ensangrentadas, le hundían por el trasero grandes bolas de periódicos abandonados' [What do I do with the audience if I take away the handrails? The mask would come to devour me. I once saw a man devoured by the mask (. . .). The strongest youths in the city, with bloody pick-axes, stuffed great balls of old newspapers into his back-side] (*Obras completas*, II, p. 604). This is an audience that is homophobic, intolerant, fearful of alterity.

In some senses, *El público* can be seen as part of an ongoing dialogue between Lorca and his audience that can be found throughout much of Lorca's writing for the theatre. A number of Lorca's plays feature the figure of the Author/Director or Poet who appears as an *agent provocateur* in a prologue to the play and addresses the audience. In *El público* we see the opening up of the prologue as a discrete section into a theatrical space that offers an extended provocation to the audience. In *El público* the fourth wall is broken down, the audience is metaphorically trapped within the theatrical space, assaulted by a theatrical experience that by turns moves and offends. This exhilarating experimental theatre, at once moving and provocative, would have been anathema to the conservative theatre-going audiences of the 1930s.

The 'teatro bajo la arena' [theatre beneath the sand] emerges from the sepulchre scene of *Romeo and Juliet* (itself a meditation on the dangers of artifice – Juliet's sleep is mistaken for death). Romeo and Juliet are caught within a tape-loop, repeating, night after night, their love story with a fatal end. This is at once a statement about the staleness of theatrical productions, doomed endlessly to repeat the same old themes, but also expresses the anxiety of the *theatrum mundi*, the idea that all the world might be a stage. In the play, the Director is now encouraged to inaugurate a new theatrical space. The Prestidigitador accuses him of recycling old drama, but the Director is adamant that in his theatre the characters do not pretend to die, but 'queman la cortina y mueren de verdad en presencia de los espectadores' [they burn the curtain and die for real in the presence of the audience] (*Obras completas*, II, p. 666). This new theatre is like the non-theological stage of Artaud's theatre of cruelty, which, as Derrida writes, 'is not a *representation*. It is life itself, in the extent to which life is non-representable.'[27] In order to inaugurate this new type of theatre, the First Man is crucified (the transposition to a hospital bed makes his wounds seem more immediate, life-like and visceral). Lorca attempts to get close to original representation, the closest we can ever get to the limit of representation, at once a philosophical statement, and an invigoration of the theatre of his time.

As with *Amor de Don Perlimplín*, *El público* appears to offer a debate on

---

[27] Jacques Derrida, 'The Theater of Cruelty and the Closure of Representation', in A. Bass (trans.), *Writing and Difference* (London: Routledge, 1990), 232–50 (p. 234). Xon de Ros also compares this play to the work of Artaud. See her 'Lorca's *El público*: An Invitation to the Carnival of Film', in Derek Harris (ed.), *Changing Times in Hispanic Culture* (Aberdeen: University of Aberdeen Press, 1996), 110–20.

shifting variations of love. Like Plato's *The Symposium*, it takes place in a male arena, filled with classical marble statues and flute-players of antiquity. For Carlos Jerez Farrán, the play offers an ambivalent critique of an almost encyclopaedic set of variations on homosexual masculinity, while privileging the First Man, at once self-sacrificing and celibate (we are reminded here of Diotima's model for male love in *The Symposium*),[28] based on Adam, who, as Patricia McDermott reminds us, is the 'original androgyne before the separation and limitation of gender'.[29] But the revelation of the First Man as paragon is as double-edged as the crucifixion scene/hospital bed that offers the hope of transcendence while rooting the First Man firmly in his body. It is a short-lived 'flash of insight', for in this play 'there can be no escape into freedom' (Smith 1989, p. 134). As Smith has pointed out, in his Foucaldian reading of the play, the theatre of authentic experience is also a 'theatre of death and confinement'. For Smith, the shifting scenarios of desire and love, revealing of private struggles for dominance in the sexual sphere, are accompanied by a painful awareness of the impossibility of the transcendence of the structures of power and pleasure (Smith 1989, pp. 134–5). The play ends, as it begins, with the audience being shown into the theatre. But this time the performance begins in another time and space (off-stage), ushering the audience into a new type of theatre that is at once collective, fleetingly revelatory and painfully aware of the limitations of humanity.

At once an example of, and a manifesto for, the 'theatre beneath the sand', *El público* lived up to its label of 'unstageable' theatre until it finally received its première in 1986 at the Teatro Piccolo Studio in Milan. Lluís Pasqual's dazzling production set the action on 'an expansive, almost circular playing area of sparkling blue sand' (Delgado, p. 209), which evoked a circus-ring, gladiatorial arena and oneiric beach. The Horses were memorably rendered as bare-chested, jodhpur-wearing cenotaurs, with white mohicans to suggest reins. The performance stressed its theatricality; costumes evoked the carnivalesque with its attendant suggestion of the performative of gender, while the register was polyphonic, as characters vied for dominance in language that was by turns poetic and provocative. As María Delgado has noted, revelation was the key theme of this production: 'the relevation of García Lorca's "unknown" play never previously produced in Spain, the revelation of an "unknown" García Lorca which refuses to re-confirm the populist associations of his best known works' (Delgado, p. 212). Arguably the most significant of Lorca productions in recent times, Pasqual's version brought male love and 'unstageable' theatre together for a live public for the first time.

[28] Carlos Jerez-Farrán, *Un Lorca desconocido: Análisis de un teatro 'irrepresentable'* (Madrid: Biblioteca Nueva, 2004). Jerez-Farrán draws out the full range of homosexual symbolism, and bases his studies on medical accounts of the 1930s and a reading of classical imagery.

[29] P. McDermott, 'Lorca's Trip Back to a Future Surrealist Theatre and Cinema', in Robert Havard (ed.), *A Companion to Spanish Surrealism* (Woodbridge: Tamesis, 2004), 183–203.

Bodas de sangre, which received its première in Madrid in 1933 (Vilches de Frutos and Dougherty, pp. 73–8) presents interpretative challenges for those who wish to bring it to the stage.[30] It is often seen to be rooted in the Andalusian earth (in fact it was based on a story that Lorca read in a newspaper of a feud between rival gangs in Níjar, Andalusia) and begins with an easy naturalism in the first act. But by Act Three the tone is overtly lyrical, and populated by strange, anti-naturalistic characters such as the Moon and the Woodcutter/ Death, sinister portents of what is to come. A recent production of the play at the Almeida Theatre, London in May 2005, in English translation (by Tanya Ronder) sought to liberate the work from its 'ubicación, contexto, cante jondo, guitarra, castañuelas' [setting, context, deep song, guitar, castanets], to quote its star Mexican actor Gael García Bernal.[31] It achieved this in part through the exhilarating dialogic clash of accents from the international cast, and the mélange of incidental music drawn from the global stage. This move confounded a British press intent on seeing the play as 'obstinately rooted in an Andalusian world of honour or pride', which, predictably, seemed to be a cover for seeking an 'authentically latin',[32] hot-blooded García Bernal, 'guaranteed to turn up the heat' and aiming, apparently, through Lorca, to make 'English audiences thaw, to become aware of emotions we have mislaid, passions we will now be able to name'.[33] Less predictably, the cacophonous blend of backgrounds and sounds served to blur rather than offer a coherent critique of the themes of heredity, blood-line and caste that run through the play.

Interestingly, the production begins with the sinister figure of Death (Daniel Cequeira) walking backwards centre-stage in a suit on back to front and with a wig that initially shrouded his face (with resonances of Magritte's paintings) before being slowly twisted round to reveal his features. This provided a bridge between the naturalistic and surreal elements in Lorca's play, serving to divorce the play from its naturalistic setting, and propel it into a world of visual lyricism and symbolism.

Arguably, it is the Moon, rather than Death, who carries the responsibility for this bridging between poetic worlds in the play. The Moon appears in Act Three,

[30] For a discussion of an important 1935 production in New York in a translation by José Weissberger, see Smith 1998, 44–70.

[31] Lourdes Gómez, 'He logrado desmitificar el teatro inglés', *El País*, 23 May 2005, p. 48.

[32] Michael Billington, 'Blood Wedding', *The Guardian*, 13 May 2005: http://arts/ reviews/story/0,,1483199,0.html (accessed 15 May 2005).

[33] Kate Kellaway, 'The Language of Love', *The Observer*, 1 May 2005: http://arts/ reviews/story/0,,1473999,0.html (accessed 15 May 2005). Bernal in fact refuted the attribution of remarks about passion: 'me atribuyeron palabras que yo no dije en entrevistas previas al estreno. Me preguntaban si *Bodas de sangre* iba a traer una pasión que ellos desconocen. Respondí que no, que todos tenemos y compartimos estas pasiones' [I have been attributed remarks that I never made in interviews prior to the opening night. I was asked if *Blood Wedding* would bring with it a passion unknown to them. I said no, we all have and share these passions] (Lourdes Gómez, p. 48).

in the forest where the lovers, Leonardo and the Bride, have taken flight. In the Almeida production, Assly Zandry, playing the Moon, was repeatedly winched up through a trap door on a trapeze to address the audience, spotlights dancing on her naked skin. But in Lorca's play the Moon is a 'leñador joven, con la cara blanca' [young woodcutter with a white face], (*Obras completas*, II, p. 776) while referring to him/herself in the feminine 'vengo helada' [I am frozen] and speaking of 'los montes de mi pecho' [the mounds of my breasts] (*Obras completas*, II, p. 776). Plato's *The Symposium* describes the moon as 'a combination of sun and earth' that represents the third gender (androgyny). In Aristophanes' speech, he explains how Zeus created genders: in the beginning there were three genders, one male, one female and one androgynous. To lessen their power, he cleft these in two (Plato, 189d–191a, pp. 23–4). Freud picked up on the story of the cleaving of the third gender to account for the sexual drive (two halves looking for each other), which he also related to the death drive.[34] In *Bodas de sangre*, the Moon prefigures the coming together in death of the two lovers: Leonardo and the Bride. Leonardo and the Bride are caught up in a passion that is stronger than both of them: they seem irrevocably to be swept along in sexual desire. This is the *Liebestod* fantasy – the perfect union of male and female counterparts in death, a variation on countless versions that have come before. Yet this official, seemingly prefigured, end is belied by the workings of the plot. For it is not Leonardo and the Bride who die together in love, but rather Leonardo and the Bridegroom: 'en un día señalado, entre las dos y las tres, / se mataron los dos hombres del amor. / Con un cuchillo, con un cuchillito / que apenas cabe en la mano, pero que penetra fino / por las carnes asombradas' [on the specified day, between two and three o'clock, two men died for love, with a knife, a little knife, which scarcely fits in the hand, but which finely penetrates the astonished flesh] (*Obras completas*, II, p. 798). As Ángel Valente has written, it is the two men, 'que se acoplan [. . .] en una lucha a muerte, que es la única expresión real del eros en *Bodas de sangre*. Un eros que se consuma en la muerte, bajo la luna "neutra luna de piedra sin semilla", la luna del Adán oscuro' [who come together in a fight to the death, which is the only real expression of eros in *Blood Wedding*. An eros that is consumed in death, beneath the moon, 'neutral moon of stone without seed', the moon of dark Adam].[35] In the 2005 Almeida production, the Bride (Thekla Reuten) appears to the Mother (Rosaleen Linehan) on-stage, her wedding dress drenched with the mix of blood of her lover, Leonardo (Gael García Bernal), and the Groom (Björn Hlynur Haraldsson). Off-stage, mutely, the passionate love between two men has been played out. On-stage, in the Almeida production, the two men are strapped

---

[34] Sigmund Freud, *Beyond the Pleasure Principle* (1920), in *The Standard Edition of the Complete Psychological Works of Sigmund Freud*, VIII, trans. and ed. J. Strachey, 23 vols (London: The Hogarth Press, 1974), 1–64.

[35] Ángel Valente, 'Pez luna', *Trece de nieve: homenaje a Federico García Lorca*, 1–2 (Madrid, 1976), 191–201 (p. 200).

together, bare-chested before being carried away. A link can be drawn between the eroticism of male desire, and a theatre that takes place off-stage, but is present in Lorca's drama: 'if the desirable male body is the lost object of *Bodas de sangre*, exiled off stage, so García Lorca's "unrepresentable" or "unplayable" plays are the absent centre of his dramatic career' (Smith 1998, p. 70). Once again, unplayable theatre and male love come together in an unrepresentable space, somewhere off-stage.

Postponing desire: *Así que pasen cinco años* and *Doña Rosita la Soltera o El lenguaje de las flores*

Así que pasen cinco años (1931) was never performed in Lorca's lifetime. Margarita Xirgu was uncomfortable with it (declaring it 'unstageable') when Lorca approached her in 1930, preferring *La zapatera prodigiosa*, although later she expressed a desire to see its surrealist atmosphere created with designs by Salvador Dalí (Delgado, pp. 45, 50).[36] It belongs to the exciting period Lorca spent in the Americas (1929–30). It is populated by characters drawn from the tangled urban sprawl, such as the shop window Mannequin, the Typist and the American-football player. In the play, the Young Man is engaged to marry his Fiancée upon her return from a journey of five years' duration. When she returns, however, she rejects him in favour of the American-football player. On the rebound, the Young Man seeks solace in the arms of his Typist, whose advances he had previously rejected. She agrees that they should consummate their love only once five years have passed. Two friends and an Old Man offer him advice on his thwarted journey to find love. A Dead Cat, a Dead Child, a Mask, a Mannequin, a Girl, a Harlequin and a Clown also interrupt the action. The Young Man participates in a game of cards at home and dies when the ace of hearts is played.

Most critics concur that the play should be read as a journey into the mind of the Young Man. This is a retreat into the inner world of the psyche, signified by the blue light that fills the stage. The play has been seen as influenced by aesthetic movements such as Expressionism (whether German, French or Russian) or by Lorca's awareness of Freud's theories of psychoanalysis.[37] The play is an exploration into different accounts of masculinity, presented to the Young Man as alternatives to follow.[38] The American-football player is like the

---

[36] For a discussion of the première in Paris in 1958, see Smith 1998, 71–104.

[37] See Robin Warner, *Powers of Utterance: A Discourse Approach to Works of Lorca, Machado and Valle-Inclán* (Bristol: Hiplam, 2003); Andrew Anderson, '*El público, Así que pasen cinco años y El sueño de la vida*: tres dramas expresionistas de García Lorca', in Dru Dougherty and María Francisca Vilches de Frutos (eds), *El teatro en España: entre la tradición y la vanguardia, 1918–39* (Madrid: CSIC / Fundación FGL / Tabacalera, 1992), 215–26; and Julio Huélamo Kosma, 'La influencia de Freud en Federico García Lorca', *Boletín de la Fundación Federico García Lorca*, 6 (1989), 59–83.

[38] See Sarah Wright, '*Así que pasen cinco años. Leyenda del tiempo*: Masochism and the Limits of Masculinity', in Wright 2000, 62–86.

matinee idols of the silent screen. His shoulder-pads suggest enhanced masculinity, while the fact that he never speaks gives the impression that he is no more
than a figment of the Fiancée's imagination, tailor-made to her desires, and a
foil to the limp Young Man. The two friends, meanwhile, offer more masculine
alternatives, from the Don Juanesque First Friend, who keeps photographs of all
the women with whom he sleeps (like notches on the bed-post) and never has
enough time to keep all of his dates, to the wistful Second Friend, who dreams
of keeping his perfect woman suspended within a raindrop. None of these characters offers the model of a close relationship with a woman; each trades in
different ways in distance and fantasy. The Old Man, meanwhile, stands as a
warning to the Young Man not to waste his life dreaming of a love that will
never come; the Dead Child represents a boy whose life has been cut off before
manhood. The Old Man lives on his memories of the past; the Dead Child
dreams of his impossible future. These characters exist in a kind of virtual
reality, unable to engage fully with life, caught in a limbo between tenses. Smith
contends that these characters should not all be presented as fragments of a split
psyche. Drawing on Gide's *Corydon* and Freud's *Dora*, he suggests that we pay
closer attention to the homoeroticism between the Young Man and the First
Friend (Smith 1998, pp. 91–8). Given the constant 'staggering of heterosexual
desire that remains resolutely nonreciprocal' (Smith 1998, p. 92), perhaps this
character (the First Friend) holds the key to the meaning of the piece, evidence
of homosexual desire. But there is something strange and yet disconcertingly
familiar in this tale of deferred love.[39] This is a play whose formal aspects are
stunning. The circularity of the play's structure, formalised by the broken
engagements, brakes the action (like a Shklovskian retardation) of this peculiar
love story, with expressive force, mimicking melodrama's delaying of the
denouement and mocking the spectators' desire for narrative resolution. For do
not most tales of romantic love contain similar scenarios of deferred consummation? Is not most love a tricky negotiation of interruptions before the final,
blissful union? *Así que pasen cinco años* is, like Breton's *l'amour fou*, an *ars
poetica* on the vicissitudes of love. The fact that the Young Man's waiting-game
may be entirely self-imposed merely adds ambiguity to this multi-layered variation on the classical love-story. Lorca, like Breton, wanted to 'remake the world
through the emotions', to refashion the relationship between interior and exterior worlds to 'reveal more about both than the rational mind could possibly
detect': 'I have wanted to show what precautions and what ruses desire takes',
wrote André Breton in 1937, 'in search of its object and evading it.'[40] Lorca's
play *Así que pasen cinco años*, like Buñuel and Dalí's *L'Âge d'Or* [*The Golden*

---

[39] Fernández-Cifuentes makes the case for Lorca's plays to be read as 'cartografías de
desasosiego' [disconcerting cartographies], a term he defines with recourse to Freud's
'unheimlich'. See Luis Fernández-Cifuentes, *Cartografías de desasosiego: el teatro de
García Lorca* (Madrid: Ediciones del Orto / University of Minnesota, 2003).

[40] André Breton, *Mad Love*, trans. Mary Ann Caw (Lincoln and London: University of
Nebraska Press, 1987), xiii.

Age], articulates beautifully a love of the irrational and the irrational nature of love.

In *Doña Rosita la Soltera o El lenguaje de las flores* (1936), Rosita, identified with the rose, described in the *ballad of the rosa mutabilis* at the centre of the drama, is engaged to her cousin. Lorca declared that 'la rosa mudable, encerrada en la melancolía del *carmen*' [the *rosa mutabilis*, enclosed in the melancholy of the *carmen*] was the setting for the play within a house in Granada at the turn of the century.[41] Rosita's cousin announces in the first act that he must go to Tucumán, in Argentina, to manage the family estates. In the following two acts, she will wait in vain for her lover to return, while being visited by a variety of characters – some of them suitors – and agreeing to a marriage by proxy with her cousin – a marriage that never materialises. During the course of the play her costume will change from a scarlet dress to one of the palest pink, to mimic the petals of the rose that lasts for just a single day. The three acts encompass the whole of Rosita's life, from youth to old age. Characters enter, flitting briefly through, to remind Rosita of the passing of time outside the walls of the house.

Doña Rosita la Soltera was staged for the first time in Barcelona in 1935, with Lorca's favourite actress Margarita Xirgu in the title role. It was regarded as a 'gran éxito' [great success] (Dougherty and Vilches de Frutos, p. 107). As the curtain went up at the Principal Palace Theatre at the opening of this play on 12 December 1935, Lorca was heard to exclaim, '¡Qué mal gusto tan magnífico!' [What marvellous bad taste!].[42] In 1935 he wrote of this play, 'recojo toda la tragedia de la cursilería española y provinciana, que es algo que hará reír a nuestras jóvenes generaciones, pero que es de un hondo dramatismo social, porque refleja lo que era la clase media' [I gather together all the tragedy of Spanish and provincial tweeness, which is something that will make the younger generations laugh, but which constitutes a deep social drama, because it reflects what the middle class once was] (*Obras completas*, III, p. 619). *Cursilería* (defined as being applied to a 'persona que presume de fina y elegante sin serlo' [person who tries to be fine and elegant without being so] and to anything that appears elegant but is in fact 'ridículo y de mal gusto' [ridiculous and in bad taste])[43] runs throughout this play, which seems to delight in bad

---

41 The word *carmen* derives from the Arabic for 'vineyard' and used to describe villas in the Albaicín in Granada, which have indoor gardens replete with fountains, splashes of colour from the geraniums and roses, and fragrances from the aromatic herbs. The Arabs thought of the *carmen* as the earthly incarnation of Paradise. The *carmen* is peculiarly Arabic, and may be associated in Lorca's mind with the 'city of sighs', which was what Granada became to the Moors after their expulsion. The expression 'Ojalá' [If only] conveys well the constellation of imagery surrounding longing in Lorca's conception of Moorish Spain and fully present throughout this play.

42 Joan Alavedra, 'La mort de la rosa', *Última hora*, 13 May 1935; cited in Antonina Rodrigo, *García Lorca en Cataluña* (Barcelona: Planeta, 1975), 383.

43 Definition of 'cursilería' in *Diccionario de la Lengua Española*, Real Academia Española, 21st edn, 2 vols (Madrid: Espasa-Calpe 1992), vol. I, p. 629.

taste and old-fashioned variations on *kitsch*. The gifts that are presented to Rosita throughout the play, for example, include a barometer, in the shape of a girl dressed in pink and whose skirts open or close according to the humidity. Then there is the pendant in the form of a mother-of-pearl Eiffel Tower over two doves bearing in their beaks the wheels of industry, and the mention of the silver cannon through whose barrel can be glimpsed the Virgin of Lourdes. As Noel Valis has written in her thorough study of 'cursilería' in the work,

> the play brims with small, dated objects used as stage props and verbal arti-facts: Rosita's parasol, the housekeeper's Louis the Fifteenth Thermometer case decorated with a fountain, rose arbour and nightingale, a saint's day card [. . .], and, above all, the names of things – muslin and Marseilles laces, poplinette blouses and buckles with serpents and dragonflies, and the flowers of the subtitle, fuchsia, heliotrope, Louis Passy violet, damask and jasmine.[44]

Valis shows how sentimentalized nostalgia comes to stand for ambivalent modernity, the backwardness of provincial Granada (the figuring of 'home as feminised, dated space') (Valis, p. 245) as well as the sad plight of a Spanish spinster (the Solteronas [Old Maids] with their outmoded language of flowers[45] prefigure Rosita's elegiac end). The play is often viewed as a comment on the limited options available to women in early twentieth-century Spain. Undoubt-edly it expresses this well. But is there not also something irrational about Rosita's endless waiting for love? As in *Así que pasen cinco años*, in *Doña Rosita*, too, there is a sense of a life unlived, a trading on dreams, a willingness to remain in this state. Tragic stasis or immobility against the passing of time, trading on unfulfilled desires: these are elements common to both. But, as Valis notes, what is noteworthy about the later play is that while it is about sentimen-talism, tackiness, shallowness and nostalgia, the play is 'not a *cursi* text, that is, artistically or otherwise lacking the fullness of aesthetic and affective experi-ence' (Valis, p. 245). It is precisely because of the prescribed and clichéd nature of Rosita's situation (the self-awareness of her lurch towards ridiculed spinster-hood and death) that Lorca manages to highlight the full pathos of her condition. *Así que pasen cinco años* highlighted the formal structures of the melodramatic text, in a distancing effect; in *Doña Rosita* Lorca steers a careful course through the pitfalls of formulaic over-sentimentalism to lead the audience to the play's emotional core.

---

[44] Noel Maureen Valis, 'The Culture of Nostalgia, or the Language of Flowers', in Noel Maureen Valis, *The Culture of Cursilería: Bad Taste, Kitsch, and Class in Modern Spain* (Durham, NC and London: Duke University Press, 2002), 244–76 (p. 249).

[45] See Federico García Lorca, *Doña Rosita la Soltera o El lenguaje de las flores*, ed. Mario Hernández (Madrid: Alianza, 1998), 47.

All About Mothers: *Bodas de sangre, Yerma, La casa de Bernarda Alba*

Lluís Pasqual's devised tribute to 'el Lorca más esencial' [the essence of Lorca],[46] *Haciendo Lorca* [*Doing Lorca*] of 1996, featured an extended homage from Nuria Espert to maternal love. On a stage bare except for cranes and winches, and kneading dough under the light of the moon, Espert delivered a soliloquy that was a collage synthesis of fragments of Lorca's plays, but predominantly a reworking of excerpts from *Bodas de sangre*, which expresses the grief of a mother when confronted with the death of her child. There are many mothers in Lorca's plays, from the mother of the Dead Child in *Así que pasen cinco años* who weeps for her little boy who will never reach manhood, to the mad old grandmother in *La casa de Bernarda Alba* who is locked up inside the house. For Pasqual – famous as the director who had shown through his production of the 'unstageable' works that 'no existe el "teatro imposible" de Lorca, sino más bien los directores imposibles de nuestro panorama teatral, miopes o incapaces de ver más allá del costumbrismo o del regionalismo' [Lorca's 'impossible theatre' doesn't exist, just the impossible directors of our theatrical panorama, myopic or incapable of seeing beyond folklorism and regionalism][47] – this is the synthesis of Lorca: a mother's grief. While some reports of the production saw it as cold and sombre,[48] others commented on how the production had affected some women in the audience, who were moved to tears.[49] In the final scenes of Pedro Almodóvar's 1999 film *Todo sobre mi madre*, Marisa Paredes, playing Huma Rojo, is on-stage in a production of *Haciendo Lorca* and pronounces the words included in both Lorca's *Bodas de sangre* and repeated in Pasqual: 'Se tarda mucho. Por eso es tan terrible ver la sangre de una derramada por el suelo . . . Una fuente que corre un minuto y a nosotros nos ha costado años' [It takes time (to grow a child). Which is why it is so terrible to see one's blood spilled on the ground . . . A fountain that runs for a moment that has taken us years to cultivate] (*Obras completas*, II, pp. 756–7). For Almodóvar, and for Pasqual (in *Haciendo Lorca* at least), the quintessence of Lorca is the raw emotion of the grief of a mother for her dead child.

Yerma (1934) focuses on a woman's desperate search to satisfy her desire to have a child. Yerma (whose name means 'barren woman') lives in a rural Spanish village that resembles an archaic landscape of pagan ritual and super-

46 Gonzalo Pérez de Olaguer, 'Pasqual ofrece un frío montaje de Lorca', *El Periódico*, 20 April 1996, n.p. The author is grateful to Berta Muñoz of the Centro Dramático Teatral for press materials.

47 Enrique Centeno, 'Lorca, la magia y la fantasía', *Diario 16*, 28 April 1996, n.p.

48 Pérez de Olaguer, 'Pascual ofrece un frío montaje de Lorca', *El Periódico*, 20 April 1996, n.p.

49 Eduardo Haro Tecglen, 'Palabras en el espacio: Haciendo Lorca', *El País*, 30 April 1996, n.p.

stition. Obsessed with the notion that she must satisfy her maternal desires, Yerma sees fecundity all around her and perceives herself as lacking. At the end of the play, driven to distraction, and seeing no way out of her situation, she will strangle her husband, crying 'He matado a mi hijo' [I have killed my child]. As Fernández Cifuentes has shown, in his reading of the performativity of language in the play, words can be read as performing an act.[50] In Yerma's final pronouncement then, she is creating a role for herself: the mother grieving for her dead child (much like the mother in *Bodas de sangre*), which she deems preferable to her barren state. But the final words of the play (the sisters-in-laws' cries of 'Yerma') can be seen as the 'culminación de la palabra como acto de esterilidad' [culmination of the word as an act of sterility] (Fernández-Cifuentes 1984, p. 298). For how can Yerma escape the pathologizing condition which her name proscribes, which she has internalized, and which has dogged the play since its première in 1934? (see Fernández-Cifuentes 1984, p. 288).

A flamenco-dance version of *Yerma* was staged at the Teatro Español in June 2004. Flamenco diva Cristina Hoyos, dressed in shades of rich brown to evoke the Spanish earth, danced a solo performance as the Pagan Woman. The production's finale, in stylistic balletic violence, played out a scene that unmistakably suggested that Yerma's strangling of her husband was motivated by self-defence after repeated maltreatment from her husband. Domestic violence was the hot topic of that summer in Spain, as the Spanish government's plans for a change in the law (the so-called *ley integral contra la violencia de género* [comprehensive law against domestic violence]) found their way into various forms of popular culture.[51] Such abuse makes Yerma's final action explicable and understandable. When faced with a life of domestic violence, her actions seem like a strike for feminism. But there is no such suggestion in Lorca's play whose ending is troubling and disquieting. Juan, Yerma's husband, is cold and rather reserved, happy to continue with their childless life together, but there is no hint of physical violence of the kind that Yerma metes out to him. Rather than a victim of a violent husband, Yerma can be seen as a victim of patriarchy. *Yerma* can equally be seen as a product of pro-natalist, eugenicist discourses of Spain of the 1930s (Smith 1998, pp. 16–43). She yearns to fulfil her role as mother of an as yet unborn child. Yerma's active, vocal sexual desires are sublimated and disguised as a love for her unborn child: what she wants, needs and

---

[50] Luis Fernández-Cifuentes, 'Anatomía de una transgresión', *MLN*, 99, 2 (March 1984), 288–307.

[51] The *ley integral contra la violencia de género* was passed in October 2004, 'un poderoso instrumento para derrotar al machismo criminal' [a powerful instrument to destroy criminal machismo], according to Spanish premier, José Luis Zapatero. See Charo Nogueira, 'El Congreso aprueba por unanimidad la ley integral contra la violencia de género', *El País*, 8 October 2004, p. 1. The *anteproyecto de ley* [draft bill] was being put forward in June 2004 and controversially included a clause giving the right to positive discrimination in favour of the woman.

is obsessed with is the need for procreation. Yerma equates sexual desire with fecundity; her pleasure in love-making arises only in direct proportion to the possibility for conception. It is Yerma's troubled relationship to her own rebellious body that points up her disquieting condition. Lorca shows how femininity is rewritten as maternity on the female body. The nub of the question for contemporary audiences and scholars (as for those of the play's inception) seems to be just how far Yerma and her condition belong to the past, and how far she inhabits the present. Many studies of the play focus on its world-view of archaic superstitions and primitive passions, thereby locating it either in 1930s Spain, or in a much more distant past. Yet others seek to present the play's timeless quality (the play has been examined for its Biblical imagery and its debt to Greek tragedy) and the ongoing issues it raises for feminism (questions of agency and control) and bio-ethics.[52] Andrew Anderson points out that social and scientific changes ('fertility drug treatments, artificial insemination, in vitro fertilization, surrogate motherhood and experiments with cloning') mean that we must be careful to 'recognise, contextualise and historicise the gulf that separates us from Yerma's world and its *mores* and values'. And, he asks, 'why does she fix, so obsessively, her hopes and desires on this one event, why does she not conceive, and why does she not explore any of the other avenues open to her?'[53] For Silvia Tubert, who sees *Yerma* as a product of pathologizing discourses on femininity, the play demonstrates how 'where maternity is normality, infertility becomes transgression'.[54] Yerma's violent act at the end of the play becomes more comprehensible if we can see Yerma as always already defined as trangressive (Fernández-Cifuentes 1984, p. 288). Although on the face of it, *Yerma* seems less perplexing than Lorca's avant-garde works, nevertheless it offers interpretative challenges to contemporary audiences and scholars alike.

On the face of it, *La casa de Bernarda Alba* (1936) presents the actions of a mother who, after the death of her husband and protector, sentences her daughters to eight years of mourning out of a misguided desire to protect them from the malicious gossips in town.[55] But through a distorting lens, Bernarda

---

[52] Anna Fuse's multimedia performance work 'Yerma's Eggs', at the Riverside Studies, London, May 2003, explored the theme of assisted reproduction technologies and bio-ethics.

[53] Andrew Anderson, *García Lorca: Yerma*, Critical Guides 69 (London: Grant & Cutler, 2003), 76.

[54] Silvia Tubert, 'The Deconstruction and Construction of Maternal Desire: *Yerma* and *Die Frau ohne Schatten*', *Mosaic*, 26, 3 (1993), 69–87.

[55] Such was the interpretation suggested by a recent production of *The House of Bernarda Alba* in a translation by David Hare at the National Theatre in April 2005. The play received its première in 1945 in Buenos Aires with Margarita Xirgu in the title role (Vilches de Frutos and Dougherty, p. 113). Variations of the play include La Chiusa and Nelson's musical *The House of Bernarda Alba* staged at the Lincoln Center, New York, in 2006. Reinaldo Arenas's *Halley's Comet* presents a magical-realist sequel where Adela comes back

becomes a power-crazed individual who, once freed from the shackles of her husband, enjoys flexing her power and inflicts hardship, without reason, on her daughters. Overwhelmingly, however, Lorca's play has been interpreted as an indictment of the effects of repressive regimes. This is a play not so much concerned with motherly love, or the lack of it, as with structures of power.

Smith has drawn attention to the politics of surveillance in the house of the play's title, to illustrate how each of the women in the house keeps control over the other through surveillance, while 'there can be no escape except into ever increasing visibility' (Smith 1984, p. 122). Photographs suggest the notion of the frame, where each perspective includes certain elements within the frame at the expense of others. As an audience we are presented with a theatre set that frames the action, like a static close-up, within the house. This focus reflects the lives of the women of the house, who are confined to a life within its walls. But at the same time we are constantly made aware of events that take place outside the house, and hence beyond our frame of vision. The women protago-nists, and we, hear what is happening outside the walls of the house (either reported by Poncia, or glimpsed by the women themselves). Thus, the harvesters who arrive in town and sing lusty songs are heard but never seen by us; we hear the screams of the unfortunate woman who is pursued by the villagers for attempting to cover up an unwanted pregnancy; we hear the tale of Paca la Roseta who is taken off to the olive grove by the Gypsies. The truth about Adela and Pepe el Romano is learned when one of the sisters hears the hooves of his horse galloping away from Adela's window. As an audience, we never put a face to the stories we hear about Pepe el Romano: for us, as for the women within the house, he becomes a fantasy image, one that threatens to become so large as to absorb all meaning within the house. María Josefa, the mad old grandmother, speaks of him as 'un gigante' [a giant] (*Obras completas*, II, p. 1058). Although never seen by us, we are aware that he is the most impor-tant character in the play. With such an emphasis on what takes place within the house, we get a sense that the smallest of events is blown out of all proportion. Thus when Martirio steals the portrait of Pepe el Romano it assumes supreme importance. We might draw an analogy with the close-up, in which every move-ment becomes distorted out of recognition. At the same time, rather than being 'realistic', the characters threaten almost to become caricatures: María Josefa, for example, is larger-than-life; dressed in a nightdress that doubles as her wedding dress, she dreams of a life living beside the sea with a handsome man and as mother to the little lamb she carries in her arms. Bernarda, meanwhile, is the arch manifestation of repression carried to extremes. Where else is there for Adela to go, but be driven into extremes of rebellion against an unfair power system? Lorca described *La casa de Bernarda Alba* as a 'documental foto-gráfico' [photographic document] (*Obras completas*, II, p. 973). Yet rather than

---

to life and travels with her sisters to Cuba to open a brothel. See Reinaldo Arenas, *Halley's Comet*, trans. Dolores M. Koch, *Hopscotch: A Cultural Review*, 2, 1 (2000), 74–82.

mimesis, *La casa de Bernarda Alba* is like the theatrical rendering of a photographic close-up, absorbing, claustrophobic, suffocating and blown-up into distorting patterns that have their own internal logic. Engulfed by this distortion, we threaten to lose all perspective, dragged along by events until they reach their tragic denouement. Yet the close-up, caricature-like quality of events and characters simultaneously has a distancing effect, allowing us to reflect on the consequences of the discharge of power.

Doing Lorca

The title of Lluis Pasqual's production *Haciendo Lorca* contains the implicit suggestion that all approaches to Lorca's theatre, be they scholarly or performance-based, are necessarily interpretations of the legacy left to us of Lorca's words in print; or of what we understand to be the significance of different aspects of his work and of his life within the context in which he lived. There are countless Lorcas, from the playwright who struggled with his desires to bring homosexual love to the stage, to the writer who was fascinated with the themes of maternal love, the function of longing and repressed desires, and with the discharges of passion and repression. Lorca's theatre maps the urban dreamscape as well as the rural landscape; explores the comic alongside the tragic; is intellectual as well as instinctual and sensual. Scholarly interpretations of Lorca's writing for the theatre have included the historical, the contextual and the psychoanalytic; the folkloric, the performative and the political. Performative versions for the stage constantly rework Lorca's words on the page in myriad different interpretations. It is fascinating to note that Lorca's plays are often staged as canonical classics in full production at major international theatres; at other times they present experimental reinterpretations of those classics, bringing a time and place alive for a contemporary audience, or introducing new scenic perspectives on familiar works. Lorca's avant-garde works are staged less frequently: the best of these stagings work to shake us out of our complacency, revealing new sides to Lorca's writing. Student performances flourish alongside the major international theatre productions. Lorca's work is also often performed in translation, although translations into English are notoriously difficult.[56] Translations often work to transport the audience into a Spanish context, at other times they work to bring the writer home (Spain is converted into, for example, an Irish, South American or Indian context)[57] or operate within a non-specific geographical locale in an attempt to stress at once Lorca's strangeness and the universality of his themes.

---

56 Sebastian Doggart and Michael Thompson (eds), *Fire, Blood and the Alphabet: One Hundred Years of Lorca* (Durham: University of Durham, 1999) contains an excellent section on the difficulties of 'Translating Lorca', pp. 225–82.

57 See Lawrence Venuti, 'Translation as Cultural Politics: Regimes of Domestication in English', *Textual Practice*, 7, 2 (1993), 208–23, who contrasts what he terms the 'domesticating' and 'foreignizing' methods in translation.

In the preceding sections, we have drawn out the ways in which Lorca's theatre can be seen as a love of the irrational (in particular, his explorations into experimental theatre) and also as a presentation of the irrational nature of love (love can be seen to drive all Lorquian characters, to varying degrees, with the exception of Bernarda, whose lack of motherly love stands as a metaphor for the cruel discharges of power). But of course there are myriad alternative interpretations. Lorca has enduring appeal: his plays are performed, attended, read and studied internationally. To 'do Lorca' (whether on the stage or the page) means to engage in an interpretation that contests or complements others that have gone before, in a process of fertile and endless renewal.

3

Music

D. GARETH WALTERS

'La actividad más importante en la vida de Federico García Lorca, fuera de la literatura, fue la música' [Apart from literature, the most important activity in the life of Federico García Lorca was music].[1] If we think of Lorca before the age of eighteen, however, then we could with justice invert the priorities in Federico de Onís's statement. In the years leading up to 1916 the future writer proved himself an immensely talented, if not precocious, musician. Several ancestors on his father's side had been similarly accomplished: his great-grandfather, Antonio García Vargas, was a singer and guitarist and one of his brothers a violinist. One of the great-grandfather's four children, Federico, played the bandurria, a lute-type instrument, in the Café de Chinitas in Malaga, a location that figures as the title of one of the folksongs that Lorca arranged for voice and piano, while another, Baldomero, according to Lorca's mother, had the voice of a seraph. She also claimed that her son learnt to hum before he could speak, although he did not receive any formal musical training for sure until the family moved to Granada in 1909.[2] Indeed, Lorca was not singled out for special training as a musician: his sister Concha and brother Francisco also received piano lessons from Eduardo Orense, the cathedral organist. It was with his next teacher, Antonio Segura Mesa, however, that Lorca was to display his musical gifts. Segura, a timid man of nearly seventy years of age when he took Lorca under his wing, was a follower of Verdi and an unsuccessful composer: his opera *The Daughters of Jepthah* had been a flop. Nonetheless, he was a successful teacher and ensured that Lorca acquired an excellent piano technique and an adequate knowledge of theory and harmony. Apart from the technical aspects of performance, however, the young Lorca responded to the music he played with the same fervour and enthusiasm he was to display in later life when reciting his own poetry or delivering a lecture. According to his brother, Fran-

[1] Cited in Francisco García Lorca, *Federico y su mundo*, 2nd edn (Madrid: Alianza, 1981), 430. On Lorca and music, see the very complete bibliography of Roger D. Tinnell, *Federico García Lorca y la música*, 2nd edn (Madrid: Fundación March, 1998).

[2] It is possible that Lorca had started to study music in the short period (1908–9) spent as a boarder at Almería where he attended the College of Jesus for his first year of secondary education. See Ian Gibson, *Federico García Lorca: A Life* (London: Faber & Faber, 1989), 41.

cisco, the earliest pieces he studied with Segura were arrangements of items from Italian opera (Francisco García Lorca, p. 424). He played the standard classical and romantic repertoire, with a preference for the music of Beethoven. For his *Appassionata Sonata* Lorca had a particular affection, observing that nobody could have reproduced in words such an experience of shattering passion.[3] It was while he was playing a Beethoven sonata in the Granada Arts Club, probably in 1915, that Lorca attracted the attention of Fernando de los Ríos Urruti, Professor of Political and Comparative Law at Granada University, who was to be Lorca's mentor and friend as well as an important political figure in the years of the Second Republic.

That Lorca, the prime poet of Andalusia, should have taken to the piano rather than the guitar is not surprising. The reasons are not entirely social. The piano may have been in Spain, as in other countries, the instrument beloved of the middle classes, but the period when it constituted the prime focus of Lorca's artistic ambition could justifiably be termed the golden age of Spanish piano music. In a space of less than a decade there appeared three of the masterworks of the Spanish piano repertoire: Isaac Albéniz's *Iberia* (1906–9), Manuel de Falla's *Four Spanish Pieces* (1907) and Enrique Granados's *Goyescas* (1912–14). *Iberia* and *Goyescas* are regarded as among the most daunting works written for the piano, on a par with other late Romantic pieces of the same era such as Rachmaninoff's *Third Piano Concerto* and *Second Sonata*. That Andalusia was a favoured region for Spanish music of the period is also evident from the works of Falla and Albéniz. The last of Falla's *Four Spanish Pieces*, a brilliant piece entitled 'Andaluza' [Andalusian], is marked to be played 'avec un sentiment sauvage'; according to Gilbert Chase, it has a 'harsh, almost metallic clang'.[4] The most popular of Granados's twelve *Spanish Dances* is the fifth, entitled *Andaluza*, while even in the *Goyescas*, redolent of the Madrid of the days of Goya, there is an intoxicating piece in the form of an Andalusian dance, *El fandango del candil* [*The Fandango of the Lamp*]. The Andalusian spirit is, however, most evident in the series of pieces by Albéniz, like Granados, a Catalan by birth. Indeed the three pieces that make up the last of the four books into which the work is divided are all of Andalusian inspiration: the rhythms of the *malagueña*, the *zambra* and the *sevillanas* are evident in *Málaga*, *Jerez* and *Eritaña* respectively.

The piano was a constant source of delight for Lorca throughout his life, and not merely as a private pursuit or for entertaining friends, as he did especially when at the Residencia de Estudiantes in Madrid. In 1916 he took part in a study visit for students of the University of Granada organized by the Professor of the Theory of Literature and the Arts, Martín Domínguez Berrueta. This was to be the first of four such events, two of which involved travel beyond Andalusia.

---

[3] 'Las reglas en la música', cited in Leslie Stainton, *Lorca: A Dream of Life* (London: Bloomsbury, 1998), 24.

[4] Gilbert Chase, *The Music of Spain*, 2nd revised edn (New York: Dover Publications, 1959), 186.

The more local visits took place in the town of Baeza where, in 1916, Lorca met Antonio Machado, a friend of Berrueta, for the first time. Machado was in his forties and regarded as one of the leading poets of his day, having published his best-known collection, *Campos de Castilla*, in 1912. He read some of his poems to the group, after which, Lorca gave a short piano recital. In 1933 Lorca collaborated with Rafael Alberti and the singer and dancer Encarnación López, *La Argentinita*, in an event held at the Teatro Español in Madrid celebrating Andalusian song and dance. Everyone who heard him play commented on the inspirational nature of his performances: his impromptu recitals at the Residencia de Estudiantes provoked astonishment, and Andrés Segovia, who heard him play in New York, was no less struck by his ability, declaring that it was 'phenomenal' and that he 'electrified people' (Stainton, pp. 63, 238). There are several photographs of him at the piano; one from 1935, the year before his death, taken at the family home of Huerta de San Vicente in Granada depicts him in a relaxed, almost rapt, state, with hands lightly touching the keys.

Having achieved mastery as a pianist, Lorca then started to compose. Some of his work has unfortunately been lost, while much of what remains is either incomplete or sketchy. He had a talent for improvisation and it is quite likely that he did not feel it necessary to write out his compositions in full in order to be able to perform them. Such a trait would have been consistent with the diffidence he displayed a little later in his life when it came to publishing his poetry; he exasperated friends and editors alike in his cavalier and neglectful attitude to proof-reading and producing finished versions.[5] His musical compositions date from around 1916 when he was eighteen years of age. The first works derived their inspiration from his home town, one composition being entitled *Serenade on the Alhambra*, subsequently shortened to *Granada* (Stainton, p. 25). The title of another piece contains the name of Edward Greig, a favourite composer in middle-class salons of the period, juxtaposed with that of Andalusia. The designation of pieces by names of towns or regions was not unusual for the period: it was a hallmark of Albéniz's music, as in his *Recuerdos de viaje* [*Recollections of Travelling*], *Cantos de España* [*Songs of Spain*] and *Suite española* [*Spanish Suite*], one of the pieces in the last-named of these bearing the title *Granada (Serenata)* [Granada (Serenade)].

On the evidence of what has survived it cannot be asserted that Lorca would have been as genial a composer as he was a poet and dramatist, although his earliest literary productions did not offer much evidence of his greatness as a writer either.[6] The autograph score of his *Lieder heroico* [sic] of 1916–17

---

[5] The most notorious instance of Lorca's uncooperative attitude was in his dealings with Prados concerning the publication of three books of poems in 1926–7. See Christopher Maurer, 'Perspectivas críticas: horizontes infinitos. Two Critical Editions of Lorca's Early Poetry (A Review Article)', *Anales de Literatura Española Contemporánea*, 14 (1989), 223–37.

[6] See D. Gareth Walters, *'Canciones' and the Early Poetry of Lorca: A Study in Critical Methodology and Poetic Maturity* (Cardiff: University of Wales Press, 2002), 43–61.

reveals his shortcomings.[7] The deficiency in notation is explicable given Lorca's inexperience as a composer, but the character of the music is unimaginative and uninspired. It would be unfair to expect a Spanish composer writing in the shadow of Albéniz and Granados to be daring or innovative in respect of tonality or harmony and to betray the influences of such pioneers as Schoenberg or Stravinsky even though Lorca was acquainted with the younger generation of Spanish composers, among them Federic Mompou and Roberto Gerhard. Yet the piece possesses neither the heady lushness of the major Spanish composers of the period nor the impressionistic delicacy of Debussy, a composer whom Lorca especially admired.[8] It is unambiguously tonal – D major – and is undistinguished melodically. The style of writing is unpianistic or, at least, devoid of effects designed to exploit the resources of the instrument and the skill of the performer. In a way, though, it is the equivalence in music to what Lorca would shortly be turning out as his earliest literary productions. There is an analogy between the declamatory and four-square nature of the opening passage of the *Lieder heroico* and the poetry that he produced in vast quantities in 1917–18 – what is now classified as his juvenilia. There is the same monotonous register, the same rhythmic inflexibility, much as we find in lines from his earliest unpublished poem, 'Canción: ensueño y confusión' [Song: Fantasy and Confusion]:

> Toda la locura de los días dulces
> Se llora en las noches del estío feroz.
> Se llora por ansias de amor que no llega.
> Se sufre por carne vista a lo Berlioz.
>
> Y llega la noche negruzca y callada,
> Y llega la carne con fe y esplendor,
> Y llega el placer con el dulce extravío,
> Mas ¡ay! que la muerte llegó y el dolor.[9]
>
> [All the madness of the sweet days
> is lamented in the nights of the fierce summer.
> There is weeping for the pangs of love that does not arrive.
> There is suffering for flesh that is seen like the music of Berlioz.

---

[7] See *Diccionario de la música española e hispanoamericana*, vol. 5, ed. and coord. Emilio Casares Rodicio, 10 vols (Madrid: Sociedad General de Autores y Editores, 1999), 463.

[8] He referred to Debussy as 'ese argonauta lírico, descubridor del nuevo mundo musical' [that lyrical Argonaut, discoverer of the musical new world]. In Federico García Lorca, *Conferencias*, I, ed. Christopher Maurer, 2 vols (Madrid: Alianza, 1984), 42. He also used the composer's name for the title of one of the poems from the 'Tres retratos' [Three Portraits] section in *Canciones* [Songs]. In Federico García Lorca, *Canciones y primeras canciones*, ed. Piero Menarini (Madrid: Espasa-Calpe, 1986), 134.

[9] Federico García Lorca, *Poesía inédita de juventud*, ed. Christian de Paepe (Madrid: Cátedra, 1994), 25.

And there arrives the dark-hued and hushed night,
the flesh decked in faith and splendour,
and pleasure with its whimsical distraction,
but, alas, death arrived and, with it, sorrow.]

Lorca himself drew attention to the relationship between his music and his poetry in an autobiographical note written during his period in New York in 1929–30. He relates his decision to become a poet to thwarted musical ambitions: 'Como sus padres no permitieron que se trasladase a París para continuar con sus estudios iniciales, y su maestro de música murió, García Lorca dirigió (dramático) patético afán creativo a la poesía' [As his parents did not allow him to go to Paris to continue with his initial studies and as his music teacher died, García Lorca turned his (dramatic) pathetic creative urges towards poetry].[10] Yet this statement, like others by the writer, needs qualification. Several commentators have observed that the sentence is in the third person, but not that it was only at this point in the autobiographical jotting that the more usual first-person presentation is abandoned. Perhaps this change of perspective indicates a conscious effort on Lorca's part to supply an interpretation of his musical aspirations in terms of composition – hence the 'pathetic creative urges' – but neither the death of Antonio Segura, his music teacher, nor the inability to study in Paris would obviously have stifled his ambition in this area. More likely they would have been detrimental to his prospects of a career as a performer, as a concert pianist. Lorca had in fact already started to write before the death of Segura, and it may well be that he would have soon realized, if he had not already, that his creative energies were destined to be channelled into a literary rather than musical field.

Yet he did not abandon music by any means, and in the years to come it was to play an important and varied role in his artistic development and his poetical and dramatic works. His most successful compositional undertaking was perhaps his setting of Spanish folksongs, nine of which were recorded in 1931.[11] The singer was *La Argentinita*, accompanied by Lorca himself at the piano. Characteristically, he had not written these down, but the pieces were subsequently transcribed anonymously and published by the Hispanic Institute in New York. As Francisco García Lorca has pointed out (p. 423), the earliest musical experiences of his brother comprised the children's songs and sung ballads that he would have picked up from family servants and wetnurses. In his lecture on lullabies Lorca described the role played by these in the diffusion of traditional music and poetry among the children of well-off families:

Son las pobres mujeres las que dan a los hijos este pan melancólico y son

---

[10] Federico García Lorca, *Obras completas*, 13th edn (Madrid: Aguilar, 1967), 1698.
[11] According to Ronald Crichton, in addition to being a good musician and competent pianist, Lorca was 'a better arranger of folk songs than many of Falla's epigones'. See *Falla*, BBC Music Guides (London: British Broadcasting Corporation, 1982), 49.

ellas las que lo llevan a las casas ricas. El niño rico tiene la nana de la mujer pobre, que le da al mismo tiempo, en su cándida leche silvestre, la médula del país.

Estas nodrizas, juntamente con las criadas y otras sirvientas más humildes, están realizando hace mucho tiempo la importantísima labor de llevar el romance, la canción y el cuento a las casas de los aristócratas y los burgueses. (*Obras completas*, p. 95)

[It is the women who are poor who give their children this melancholy bread and it is they who bring it into the houses of the well-off. The rich child receives the lullaby from the poor woman, who gives him at the same time, with her wild, simple milk, the very marrow of the country.

For a long time these wet-nurses together with maids and other lowly domestic servants have been undertaking that most important task of taking ballads, songs and stories into the homes of aristocrats and the middle classes.]

Lorca's indebtedness to such unlikely mentors cannot be overstated as the songs and folklore he imbibed in his infancy were to leave a mark on the majority of his works, from the poetry of *Libro de poemas* [*Book of Poems*] to plays such as *Bodas de sangre* [*Blood Wedding*] and *Yerma* [*Yerma*]. Yet his knowledge of folksong also involved a more active, even scholarly, interest. He owned ballad books and was familiar with the most significant collections of folksongs, among them the *Cancionero musical popular español* [Book of Spanish Folk Songs] published in four volumes between 1918 and 1922. When Ramón Menéndez Pidal visited Granada in 1920 as part of his project for collecting and transcribing the words of popular ballads surviving in the oral tradition it was Lorca who accompanied him in his visits to the gypsies of the Albaicín and Sacromonte. Pidal was impressed by Lorca's commitment to the subject and, as Ian Gibson has suggested (1989, p. 106), it is likely that the eminent scholar's visit to Granada reinforced Lorca's interest in folk music and in the songs of the local gypsies.

Lorca's folksong arrangements are on the whole beautifully realized: he combines a lightness of touch with imagination and piquancy. The second song in the set, 'Los cuatro muleros' [The Four Muleteers], is a case in point (Example 1).[12] The dissonance of a diminished ninth in the first bar of the song proper dominates the whole piece, imposing itself upon the four-bar *basso ostinato* that provides a rather gruff accompaniment to the cheery song. It evokes very well the ungainly haste of the muleteers as they ride to the river. A dissonant effect is also present in the first song of the group, 'Anda jaleo' [Let's have a good time] (Example 2). Here it is of an almost jazz-like nature: the clash of major and minor third in the second bar of the song proper is enhanced by the syncopations, accentuated in Lorca's arrangement, in the fourth and eighth bars.

---

[12] The music of these songs is reproduced in *Obras completas* (1967), pp. 1865–94.

Example 1

Example 2

In the sixth song, 'Sevillanas' (a characteristic Sevillian dance), the repeated *accaciature* reinforce the tremendous sense of beat in the piano accompaniment in what is a truly exciting arrangement (Example 3). Notably different in mood is the gentle 'Nana de Sevilla' [Lullaby from Seville], the eighth of the set. The augmented fourths, the hint of the Phrygian mode and the semiquaver triplets redolent of *cante jondo* all lend the song an Arabic tinge (Example 4). Lullabies held a special fascination for Lorca. They figure at key points in his late plays: in *Bodas de sangre* when the song Leonardo's wife sings to her baby is replete with symbols that foreshadow the tragic events to come, and at the very opening of *Yerma* when a snatch of a lullaby is heard off-stage.

Lorca's folksong arrangements – and the 'Nana de Sevilla' in particular –

Example 3

bear comparison with Falla's earlier *Siete canciones populares españolas* [*Seven Spanish Popular Songs*]. These were composed in response to a request from a Spanish opera singer making her debut in Paris, where Falla was living at that time. He used traditional tunes and words but with some retouching. For example, the sixth song, entitled 'Canción' [Song] has the same melody as the song that Lorca arranged as the ninth of his own set 'Los Pelegrinitos' [Little Pilgrims] but with a slight variation in the opening phrase of the tune. Falla's piano arrangements are more sophisticated than Lorca's and require more virtuosity from the pianist. Yet, as Ann Livermore has pointed out, these accompaniments are not entirely his own but taken from collections of the ninetheen century: the jaunty opening of 'El paño moruno' [The Moorish Cloth] comes directly from *Flores de España* [*Flowers of Spain*] by Hernández and the long introduction to the last, the impetuous 'Polo', a song of Andalusian origin, is

Example 4

Es — te ga — la — pa — qui — to no — tie — ne ma — re —
Lo pa — rió u — na gi — ta — na lo e — chó a la ca — lle —

no tie — ne ma — re sí no tie — ne ma —
Lo e — chó a la ca — lle lo e — chó a la ca —

taken from an authentically mid-nineteenth-century setting by Ocón.[13] The song settings themselves vary between close adherence to the original song and considerable retouching. One of the songs treated most freely is the fifth, the 'Nana', a lullaby that bears close comparison with Lorca's setting of the 'Nana de Sevilla'. Ronald Crichton's summary of the character of the Falla setting suggests its affinity with Lorca's: 'A lullaby of the oriental, Andalusian type. Descending figures in the piano part: a tonic pedal (the key is E-major-minor, much inflected) sounded every time on the off-beat' (Crichton, p. 30).

Lorca first met Falla when the musician paid a visit to Granada in 1919. Two years later it was to become his home, so entranced was he by its beauty and in particular by the views of the Alhambra.[14] A native of Cadiz, Falla, who was born in 1876, was more than twenty years older than Lorca, and he was already a composer of international renown when he decided to settle in the town. He was a shy, even timid, man, possessed of what Stravinsky described as 'the most unpityingly religious nature I have ever known'.[15] Neat and fastidious in his dress and habits and with an almost monastic devotion to his art, he was temperamentally the opposite of Lorca. Yet this was no obstacle to an immediate friendship and eventual collaboration, although Lorca, out of deference to the age and unassuming dignity of the composer, invariably adressed him as 'Don Manuel'.

In the years preceding his move to Granada, Falla's music betrayed a marked Andalusian inspiration. The first and third movements of his *Noches en los jardines de España* [*Nights in the Gardens of Spain*] (1911–15), entitled 'En el Generalife' [In the Generalife], referring to the Moorish gardens of the Alhambra, and 'En los jardines de la Sierra de Córdoba' [In the gardens of the Sierra of Cordoba] represent what could be termed the Romantic view of the region, with their melancholy Orientalism and lush sounds. In his ballet *El amor brujo* [*Love the Magician*] (1914–15) the music is more astringent, betraying the most obvious traits of *cante jondo*. Falla had assimilated this ancient art so well that he did not need to use a single folksong to convey the spirit and the swagger of gypsy music. The last major work of Andalusian pedigree was the *Fantasía baetica* [Andalusian Fantasy], a piano piece commissioned by Artur Rubinstein, who gave the first performance in 1920, the year after its completion. It is strikingly different from the earliest of these works of Andalusian origin. Within the form of a classical sonata movement (with a slow intermezzo replacing the development section) Falla unleashes some of his harshest and most dissonant effects. He does this especially in the part that corresponds to the second subject

13 Ann Livermore, *A Short History of Spanish Music* (London: Duckworth, 1972), 191.

14 For a first-hand account of Falla's plans for living in Granada, see José Mora Guarnido, *Federico García Lorca y su mundo: Testimonio para una biografía* (Buenos Aires: Losada, 1958), 155.

15 Quoted in Burnett James, *Manuel de Falla and the Spanish Musical Renaissance* (London: Victor Gollancz, 1979), 69.

of the sonata-form design. It occurs with the repetition of a dramatic *cante jondo* recitative. In its first version it could have strayed out of a composition by Albéniz, but when it appears a second time it has the discordant intervals of the seventh and the ninth rather than the kind of octave doubling we get in a piece like Albéniz's *Sevillanas*.

A similar process of engagement with 'lo andaluz' occurs in Lorca, albeit a little later: the full-blown late Romantic hue of evocations of the region and its culture in the poetic juvenilia yields to the sparser, more elemental, manner of the *Poema del cante jondo* [*Poem of the Deep Song*] and to the sharp-edged images and visions of the *Romancero gitano* [*Gypsy Ballads*].[16] Such a rapprochement in aesthetic outlook is not surprising given the close artistic relationship that developed between the older composer and the aspiring writer in the early 1920s. There is, however, rather less evidence of mutual influence at a textual level than one might have supposed. A possible instance might be in a scene towards the end of Act I of Lorca's *La zapatera prodigiosa* [*The Shoemaker's Prodigious Wife*] where the Neighbours crowd the stage in a dance-like fashion when they come in to gloat over the misfortune of the shoemaker's young wife. The scene recalls the 'Neighbours' Dance' in Falla's *El sombrero de tres picos* [*The Three-Cornered Hat*], the plot of which, based on a short novel by Pedro de Alarcón, has affinities with Lorca's play. As an instance of influence in the other direction, it is possible that Falla's puppet-opera *El retablo de Maese Pedro* [*Master Peter's Puppet Show*], based on an episode from *Don Quixote*, emerged from the composer's interest in the puppet theatre, a genre that fascinated Lorca at the same time.

In 1921 Lorca started work on a puppet-play of his own, and soon after planned a joint undertaking with the music critic and composer, Adolfo Salazar, which involved nothing less than the re-establishment of the near-defunct Andalusian guignol. This ambitious project would involve a musical input from Falla and, at one point, Salazar even contemplated the possibility of interesting Diaghilev (Gibson 1989, p. 107). Like a number of other of Lorca's plans, however, it came to nothing, although, in his defence, it coincided with involvement in the preparations for the *Cante Jondo* festival. Equally inconclusive was the attempt by Lorca and Falla to compose a comic opera, entitled *Lola la comedianta* [*Lola, the Actress*]. Neither man, however, had enough enthusiasm to complete the project. In the case of Lorca it can probably be attributed once again to his volatility as a creative artist and to what even his friends started to define as a lack of discipline (Stainton, p. 114). Indiscipline would be the most unlikely of deficiencies to afflict Falla, but, according to Gibson (1989, p. 125) it may have been that the pious composer had misgivings about the morality of

---

[16] For a more detailed account of the evolution of 'lo andaluz' in these artists see D. Gareth Walters, 'Parallel Trajectories in the Careers of Falla and Lorca', in *Crossing Fields in Modern Spanish Culture*, ed. Federico Bonaddio and Xon de Ros (Oxford: Legenda [European Humanities Research Centre], 2003), 92–102.

the work and the depiction of the wiles of the scheming heroine.[17] More successful was the *ad hoc* event that took place in the Lorca home on 6 January 1923 to mark the feast of the Epiphany. This was a sophisticated puppet show, involving a mixture of short items: a thirteenth-century mystery play, an interlude attributed to Cervantes, and a script produced by Lorca himself for the occasion, 'La niña que riega la albahaca y el príncipe preguntón' [The Girl who Waters the Basil Plant and the Inquisitive Prince]. The most striking feature of the entertainment, however, was the eclectic blend of music that Falla had arranged as accompaniment: traditional songs, Latin plainchant, and arrangements of composers such as Debussy, Ravel and Stravinsky. The intimate setting was no impediment to its being reviewed three times, twice by Lorca's friend José Mora Guarnido (Stainton, p. 108).

The event that ensured that the names of Lorca and Falla would be forever connected was the *Cante Jondo* festival or more correctly 'concurso' [competition], held in Granada in 1922. Although these two represented the driving force in an organization that would eventually involve dozens of people it seems likely that the idea came from Miguel Cerón Rubio, a local businessman (Gibson 1989, p. 92). The rationale for the festival, however, was rooted in the belief shared by Falla and Lorca that primitive Andalusian song, or *cante jondo*, was in decline as a result of its commercialization in café entertainment. The festival was conceived as a corrective measure: to restore purity and dignity to the art by reviving it in an uncontaminated form. In a lecture on the subject given to the Arts Club in Granada a few months before the event, Lorca was characteristically exuberant on this issue: 'Es una obra patriótica y digna la que se pretende realizar; es una obra de salvamento, una obra de cordialidad y amor' [What we seek to achieve is a patriotic and worthy enterprise; it is a task that involves recuperation, enthusiasm and love].[18] Yet as Stainton (p. 92) points out, this ideal was flawed: 'neither man was correct to think there was any distinction between "ancient" deep song and "modern" flamenco; the two were intertwined'. The festival itself was to take the form of a competition, and it fell to Lorca, sometimes accompanied by Falla, although more often by his childhood friend Manolo Ángeles Ortiz, to undertake excursions to various parts of Andalusia in search of potential performers.[19] Stainton (p. 94) describes what the process might involve:

> Arriving in a village where singers were said to reside, the two friends would first wander the streets, then sit in a public square in the fading afternoon light

[17] For the text and analysis of the opera, see Federico García Lorca, *Lola la comedianta*, ed. Piero Menarini (Madrid: Alianza, 1981).

[18] Federico García Lorca, *Conferencias*, I, ed. Christopher Maurer, 2 vols (Madrid: Alianza, 1984), 50.

[19] The arrangements for the competition and the rules for entrants, including admission tests and preliminary rounds, are reproduced in Manuel de Falla, *On Music and Musicians*, with an introduction and notes by Federico Sopeña (London: Marion Boyars, 1979), 112–17.

and wait. As Lorca later described it, two elderly men might be seated on a bench across from them, talking, when suddenly one or both would start to sing, Lorca could recognize what he called the 'bloodcurdling' sound of pure *cante jondo* instantly.

The event itself took place on 13 and 14 June 1922. It was preceded by a concert that contained a number of musical items, including Segovia, whose repertoire invariably comprised music written or arranged for classical guitar, unusually playing flamenco. It was Lorca who stole the show, however, according to the reviews in the following day's papers (Gibson 1989, p. 115). During the two days of the competition there were some notable performances, both by old singers, like Diego Bermúdez Cañete who, it was believed, had walked 80 miles to take part, and by newcomers like Manuel Ortega, an eleven-year-old who was to become one of the best-known of flamenco singers (Gibson 1989, p. 115). For Mora Guarnido, a journalist and friend of Lorca, the event was 'acaso la fiesta de mayor trascendencia artística que se haya realizado en España en los últimos tiempos' [perhaps the most momentous artistic festival to have taken place in Spain in recent times].[20] This is not a view that was universally shared. There were those in Granada who disapproved of the event both because of the financial commitments required of the city council and because they held Gypsy and Andalusian folk culture in low esteem. Recent commentators have expressed artistic misgivings, and have been highly critical about the impact of the festival and the quality of the singers. Marion Papenbrok is especially blunt. She suggests that the organizers made a serious error in the choice of performers. By believing that flamenco belonged to all the Andalusian people – Lorca's observation about 'el alma música del pueblo' [the musical soul of the people] (*Conferencias*, I, p. 50) is symptomatic of this view – the organizers excluded professional singers over the age of twenty-one, a kind of inverted artistic snobbery that overlooked the fact that there were fine professional performers who were in no way guilty of popularising their art for the sake of financial reward.[21] Another charge that has been levelled against Lorca and, by inference, Falla is that they did not understand the background and history of flamenco. The most reasoned critique is that provided by Félix Grande. He pulls no punches in outlining Lorca's deficiencies:

> En plena juventud [. . .] García Lorca no sabía sobre la historia del flamenco ni lo que sabía Manuel de Falla, ni, como es natural, lo que podían saber y recordar los mejores cantaores y guitarristas de la época. Incluso es posible pensar que un buen aficionado al flamenco, contemporáneo del poeta, tenía sobre la historia y la geneología de los cantes conocimientos más acertados que los de Federico.[22]

---

[20] Mora Guarnido, *Federico García Lorca y su mundo*, 162.

[21] See Marion Papenbrok, 'History of Flamenco', in *Flamenco: Gypsy Dance and Music from Andalusia*, ed. Claus Schreiner (Portland, OR: Amadeus Press, 1990), 35–48 (p. 45).

[22] Félix Grande, *García Lorca y el flamenco* (Madrid: Mondadori, 1992), 12–13.

[In his youth García Lorca did not know what even Manuel de Falla knew about flamenco nor, as might be expected, what the best singers and guitar players of the period knew and remembered. It is even possible to believe that any of the poet's contemporaries who had a fondness for flamenco would have had a more sure knowledge of the history and origins of the songs than did Federico.]

Yet against this has to be set the more availing force of artistic imagination: 'A Federico ni siquiera le estorbaron las ignorancias que llamé veniales para dejarnos algo que está más allá del saber: el conocimiento poético' [Federico wasn't even sufficiently troubled by a lack of knowledge of the kind I termed 'venial' to leave us something that goes beyond knowledge: poetic awareness] (Grande, p. 13).

Lorca's lecture on *cante jondo*, delivered to the Arts Club in Granada, in February 1922, was entitled 'Importancia histórica y artística del primitivo canto andaluz llamado "cante jondo"' [The Historical and Artistic Importance of Primitive Andalusian Song Known as 'Deep Song']. The essay is in two parts: the first deals with the music of *cante jondo*, the second, with the words. The first draws heavily on an essay that Falla had written in preparation for anonymous publication immediately before the start of the festival proper. It is as a consequence far less original than the second part and cites Falla verbatim on several occasions. Lorca is less concerned with musical analysis and description than Falla, however, and tends more to an evocation of the effects of the music, as when he envisages *cante jondo* in terms of 'ondulación' [ondulation] whereas *cante flamenco* involves 'saltos' [leaps] (*Conferencias*, I, p. 53). Although he does not deal with the material in the same order as his friend, Lorca emphasizes the same four issues: definitions, origins, characteristics and impact. A distinction is drawn between what is believed to be the ancient *cante jondo* and the more recent *cante flamenco* that only achieved its definitive form in the eighteenth century (p. 51). The classic form for the older song is the *siguiriya*, from which other songs such as the *polo* and the *soleá* have emerged. Examples of the *cante flamenco* are forms such as the *malagueñas*, *granadinas* and *peteneras*. Following Falla, Lorca draws attention to the Oriental character of *cante jondo*, specifying the elements that have lent it a distinctive hue: the adoption by the Church of Byzantine chant, the Moorish invasion of the Peninsula in 711 and the Gypsy migrations at the start of the fifteenth century.[23] In short we have 'un canto puramente andaluz, que ya existía en germen en esta región antes que los gitanos llegaran a ella' [a purely Andalusian song, the seed of which had been planted in this region before the Gypsies arrived here] (p. 56). Lorca then reproduces Falla's listing of some of the characteristic features of *cante jondo*: the use of enharmonic intervals as a means of modulation, the use of a melodic range that seldom goes beyond a sixth, the repeated and 'obsessive' use of one note,

---

[23] When he delivered a lecture on the same subject in Salamanca, however, Lorca cited other influences, notably Jewish music. See *Conferencias*, I, p. 55n.

frequently accompanied by an upper or a lower appoggiatura (pp. 56–8). He continues by bemoaning the coarsening of the art in the later decades of the nineteenth century (p. 59) and concludes the first part of his lecture, again following Falla, with an examination of the influence of *cante jondo* on Romantic and modern composers (pp. 60–3). If there are errors in other parts of the survey then in the final section there is distortion: the impact of *cante jondo* on Russian composers of the nineteenth century in the wake of Glinka's visit to Spain in 1847 and its effect on the music of Debussy are overstated.

The other part of the lecture – on the distinctive poetic qualities of the words of the *cante jondo* songs – relates to another venture connected with the festival. In the preceding November, Lorca wrote *Poema del Cante Jondo*, though it was not to be published until 1931 with a couple of additional items. His fascination with the concise yet evocative verse of the genre meant that the work was markedly different from the poetry of Andalusian inspiration written in the first two decades of the twentieth century, Manuel Machado's *Cante hondo* (1912) being a case in point (Walters 2002, pp. 120–1). Admittedly, Lorca's collection contains poems inspired by flamenco performers and by the guitar, while the titles of some of the sections of the work relate to various kinds of flamenco music: the *siguiriya*, the *soleá* and the *petenera*. In one respect, more than others, however, Lorca appears to have tried to make his poetry mimic one of the features of the music of the *cante jondo* pinpointed by Falla.

One of the features of flamenco song is voice modulation enhanced by the use of melismas, an apparently decorative treatment of melody. The qualification 'apparently' is worth underlining because in the best singing such techniques are present, in Falla's words, 'only when the emotional power of the words being sung suggests an expansion or sudden burst of feeling. Thus these embellishments are really more like expanded vocal modulations than ornamental passages.'[24] Christof Jung supplies, in the same piece from which this quotation is taken, a melodic read-out of a *siguiriya* by Manuel Torre, as sung by his son, Tomás, to illustrate such a technique, where the *copla* that begins 'Siempre por los rincones / te encuentro llorando' [I always find you weeping in the corners] is rendered as

> Tiri ti ri ti..ay..ay..ay..ay..i..a..a..ay
> Ti..a..ay..i..
> siempre por loo..siempre por loo..
> rin..in..in.coné..o..ay

This may be compared to Lorca's poem that personifies the *soleá*, where the refrain 'vestida con mantos negros' [dressed in black mantles] is presented on its last appearance as

---

24 Christof Jung, 'Cante flamenco', in Schreiner (ed.), *Flamenco*, 57–87 (p. 64).

> *¡Ay yayayayay,*
> *que vestida con mantos negros!*[25]

Other poems also betray this elaboration – effectively a prolongation – of a refrain. In 'Sevilla', from 'Poema de la saeta' [Poem of the Saeta], the single line 'Sevilla (alternating with 'Córdoba') para herir' is extended at the end to '*Sevilla para herir.* / *¡Siempre Sevilla para herir!* [Seville for wounding. Always Seville for wounding!]. In the sinister poem 'Malagueña' from the section entitled 'Tres ciudades' [Three cities], the brief snatch of the opening – 'La muerte / entra y sale / de la taberna' [Death goes in and comes out of the tavern] (*PCJ*, p. 197) – becomes at the poem's end:

> La muerte
> entra y sale,
> y sale y entra
> la muerte
> de la taberna.

The grammatical ellipsis ('entra' lacks an appropriate particle) is exaggerated, with the result that this magnified dislocation is an appropriate rendering of the effect of emotional heightening achieved by the straining of the melodic line in *cante jondo*. Another way in which the melisma appears to be translated into Lorca's text is supplied in the section entitled 'Gráfico de la petenera' [Graphic of the Petenera]. Here the span is longer, as the first of the eight poems, 'Campana' [Bell] (*PCJ*, p. 174), an eleven-line poem, is lightly varied and extended to seventeen lines in the final poem, 'Clamor' [Clamour] (*PCJ*, p. 183). There is not only a change of singular to plural affecting the opening of the poems ('En la torre / amarilla, / dobla una campana' [In the yellow tower a bell tolls]) but the incorporation of an additional stanza in the later poem. The second part of this extra stanza reads like an equivalence in words of the stubborn, jarring melodic configuration of the melisma:

> Canta y canta
> una canción
> en su vihuela blanca,
> y canta y canta y canta. (*PCJ*, p. 183)

> [It sings and sings
> a song
> in its white *vihuela,*
> and sings and sings and sings.]

Perhaps the most beautiful of such effects of melisma is in the poem '¡Ay!' from 'Poema de la soleá' [Poem of the Soleá]:

---

25 Federico García Lorca, *Poema de cante jondo. Romancero gitano*, ed. Allen Josephs and Juan Caballero, 8th edn (Madrid: Cátedra, 1985), 160. Referred to henceforth as *PCJ*.

El grito deja en el viento
una sombra de ciprés.

(Dejadme en este campo
llorando.)

Todo se ha roto en el mundo.
No queda más que el silencio.

(Dejadme en este campo
llorando.)

El horizonte sin luz
está mordido de hogueras.

(Ya os he dicho que me dejéis
en este campo
llorando.) (*PCJ*, p. 158)

[The cry leaves in the wind
a shadow of cypress.

(Leave me in this field
weeping.)

Everything has broken in the world.
Only the silence remains.

(Leave me in this field
weeping.)

The horizon without light
is bitten by fires.

(I have already told you to leave me
in this field
weeping.)]

It conveys that kind of stillness that we might be tempted to label unworldly until we realize that it is the very embodiment of world. It is a stillness where silence resounds and where the shadow is the picture. In this scene of emptiness the plea for release and abandonment (and how apt an understanding of the emotional nuance of *cante jondo* that is!) is formulated in a refrain that, once again, is expanded on its last appearance in a line of almost painful intensity so emphatically and weightily is it spelled out syllable by syllable.

Such a detailed sensitivity to the effects of music was unprecedented not only in poetry inspired by *cante jondo* but also in Lorca's, admittedly short, poetic career. In his unpublished poetry there are numerous musical references, but of a very different kind from the assimilative and evocative manner evident in the *Poema del cante jondo*. In the vast quantity of verse produced in 1917–18, there is an over-reliance upon musical analogies, as though the musician in Lorca was only letting go with reluctance. He utilizes composers' names as shorthand or code for a desired emotion, such as we saw with the reference to Berlioz in the earliest of these poems. On occasion this practice is embarrassingly trite, as in the line 'Prostituta de ritmo chopinesco' [Prostitute of Chopinesque rhythm] (*Poesía inédita*, p. 94). He also introduces, mainly into the titles or subtitles of poems, technicalities of musical composition, such as tempo markings, key signatures and symphonic or sonata movement names for longer pieces. There is a precedent for such usage in the works of the *modernista* poets. Rubén Darío, a poet who had a considerable influence on the young Lorca, employs titles such as *Sonatina* and *Sinfonía en gris mayor* [Symphony in Grey Major], but he never did so to excess. Fortunately, Lorca soon learnt to drop this habit.

In *Libro de poemas* and *Canciones* [*Songs*], the principal musical influence takes the form of quotations from or references to folksongs and children's songs. The subject has been much studied, and insofar as it is concerned with the words of the songs it is a poetic rather than musical matter.[26] Yet at the same time as he was completing *Libro de poemas* and starting to write the poems that would be included in *Canciones* he was preparing another book of verse whose title and structure betrayed an obvious musical stimulus: *Suites*. Because of a difference of opinion with the intended publisher, Emilio Prados, the work did not appear, as it was intended, at the same time as *Poema del cante jondo* and *Canciones*, and it was only in 1983 that a partly reconstructed edition was to come out.[27]

As Belamich indicates (*Suites*, p. 19), Lorca had two musical models in mind when writing these sets of poems. But it has not been fully appreciated how contradictory they are. The title itself suggests a characteristic kind of composition of the eighteenth century, both for solo instrument – normally the harpsichord, as with Handel – and for larger ensembles, as with Bach. The unifying feature in such compositions is, however, flimsy: merely the key centre, albeit with the alternation of major and minor. Moreover, the suite possesses considerable variety of mood as it comprises a whole range of dance-forms, ranging from the stately sarabande to the lively gigue. But Lorca also had in mind, at least for some of his Suites, a different concept, that of the theme and variations, or, to adhere to the Spanish version that he himself employed: 'diferencias'. This was a kind of composition that pre-dated the Suite proper, and was cultivated by major Spanish instrumental composers of the sixteenth century such as Cabezón, Mudarra and Luis Milán. This kind of work, by definition, presupposed a closer relationship between the various parts that made up the whole.[28]

Perhaps the finest instance of the concept of the unified suite is not in the

---

[26] For a consideration of the way in which Lorca exploits and rewrites the borrowed material, see Ian Gibson, 'Lorca's *Balada triste*: Children's Songs and the Theme of Sexual Disharmony in *Libro de poemas*', *Bulletin of Hispanic Studies*, 46 (1969), 21–38; and Walters 2002, pp. 183–90.

[27] Federico García Lorca, *Suites*, ed. André Belamich (Barcelona: Ariel, 1983).

[28] For an account of how the implications of the term 'suite' works on specific sets of poems in the collection, see Walters 2002, pp. 103–5.

collection that was to become *Suites*, however, but in the *Poema del cante jondo*: the 'Poema de la siguiriya gitana' [Poem of the gypsy *siguiriya*]. This 'flamenco suite' achieves coherence by its continuous sense of sequence. The first poem 'Paisaje' [Landscape] provides a setting, while the next, a famous piece, 'La guitarra' [The Guitar] supplies the opening sounds of the performance. This is succeeded by 'El grito' [The Cry], the first vocal articulation, in the form of repetitions of the exclamation '¡ay!', and then by 'El silencio' [The Silence], indicative of the dramatic and, as the poem rightly notes, *audible* silences that punctuate the melodic flow: 'Oye, hijo mío, el silencio' [Hear, my son, the silence] (*PCJ*, p. 149). A similar sense of continuity characterizes the final three poems of the section, which have their basis in the personification of the *siguiriya* in a procession, hence 'El paso de la siguiriya' [The Passing of the Siguiriya] is followed by 'Después de pasar' [After Passing] and, finally, 'Y después' [And After That]. Just as the music yields to a definitive silence, so too does the final poem of the section:

> Los laberintos,
> que crea el tiempo,
> se desvanecen. (*PCJ*, p. 152)

> [The labyrinths,
> created by time,
> vanish.]

Lorca's most famous book of poetry, *Romancero gitano* has neither the overt nor the implicit musical associations of earlier collections. It suggests, rather, the musicality we would associate with a poet who enjoyed reciting his poetry; it is memorable in the strictest sense of the word. Yet the wonderful diversity of its rhythmic effects – nobody ever exploited the Spanish ballad metre with such verve and imagination – is perhaps a testimony to the training and instinct of a musician. The collection is also as rich in acoustic as it is in visual stimuli. The sounds of the anvil being struck or of horses in motion – typical features of the gypsy's life – occur in poem after poem, and provide through their percussive harshness something of the same dissonant effect as Falla's Andalusian masterpiece, *Fantasía baetica* (Walters 2003, pp. 100–1).

In his early plays Lorca was fascinated by the world of puppets and by the associated concepts of movement and mime. In his last works for the stage, however, music fulfils a more profound and subtle function. Allusion has previously been made to the particular importance of the lullaby in the tragedies: it has an ominous significance in *Bodas de sangre* and a symbolic one in *Yerma*. The conception and structure of the first of these plays also offer an instance of how much Lorca may have been influenced by the music of the great composers. It is partly inspired by Bach's *Cantata* 140, a piece that celebrates the spiritual marriage between the daughters of Jerusalem and Christ, albeit a very different kind of marriage from the one that appears in the play. Bach's work also contains images that are prominent in *Bodas de sangre*: the forest, the moon and death. Indeed, as though to reinforce what Lorca himself acknowledged to be the Bachian flavour of his play, at the first performance an extract from one of the *Brandenburg Concertos* was played between the second and third acts. A more explicit homage to Bach is to be found in a letter that Lorca wrote to Jorge Guillén in 1926. This is one of Lorca's longest and most intriguing letters, which begins with observations about his personal life including thoughts about marriage, which he dismisses no sooner than they are broached.[29] The letter also contained the text of two of the poems that were to appear in *Romancero gitano*, but the main purpose of the letter is to congratulate Guillén on the quality of his poetry. From this Lorca is led to meditate on what he considers the essential virtues of poetry and to attempt to envisage the ideal poem: 'Todavía no se ha hecho el poema que atraviese el corazón como una espada. Yo me admiro cuando pienso que la *emoción* de los músicos (Bach) se apoya y está envuelta en una perfecta y complicada matemática' [The poem that pierces the heart like a sword has not yet been composed. I marvel when I think that the *emotion* of musicians (Bach) is supported and absorbed by a perfect and complicated mathematics] (*Epistolario*, p. 371). Such a reflection is a timely reminder, given the more superficial judgements about the nature of Lorca's work and working methods, prompted in part by an over-reliance on such notions as those advanced in his essay on the *duende*, that, for all his personal and public flamboyance, he was a fastidious craftsman, fully in control of his medium.

Lorca loved a wide range of music. He relished the songs and dances of his native region, the composers of the eighteenth and nineteenth centuries, and, especially after his visit to New York, jazz and blues; among his more positive memories of his stay in that city would be his visits to the clubs of Harlem (Gibson 1989, p. 255).[30] Given his eclectic tastes it is entirely appropriate that his own work should have provided material for a wide variety of musicians and composers. There have been innumerable flamenco-style productions based upon his poetry, the most famous of which is the version of *Bodas de sangre* by the dancer Antonio Gades, filmed by Carlos Saura in 1981.[31] The *New Grove Dictionary of Music and Musicians* supplies a long but not comprehensive list of musical works based on Lorca's writings. The circumstances of his death, at the very start of the Spanish Civil War, have also proved a source of inspiration, as with Poulenc's Sonata for violin and clarinet (1942–43) and Luigi Nono's *Epitaffio per Federico García Lorca* (1952–3). The most moving of all tributes to Lorca, however, is perhaps the one that figures in the greatest of all these

---

[29] Federico García Lorca, *Epistolario Completo*, ed. Andrew A. Anderson and Christopher Maurer (Madrid: Cátedra, 1997), 369.

[30] For an interesting account of the impact of the blues on Lorca's poetry, see Xon de Ros, 'Ignacio Sánchez Mejías Blues', in Bonaddio and De Ros (eds), pp. 81–91.

[31] For an analysis of Saura's flamenco films, including *Bodas de Sangre*, as well as the relevance of flamenco to Lorca's work generally, see Rob Stone, *The Flamenco Tradition in the Works of Federico García Lorca and Carlos Saura. The Wounded Throat*, Spanish Studies 26 (Lewiston / Queenston / Lampeter: Edwin Mellen Press, 2004).

works: Shostakovich's Fourteenth Symphony. This is an unusual symphony as it could more properly be regarded a song-cycle: a setting of eleven poems on the subject of death, comprising poems by Lorca, Apollinaire, Küchelbecker and Rilke. The poems that provide the material for the first two songs come from *Poema del cante jondo*: 'De profundis' and 'Malagueña'. The first is a stark realization, an *adagio* where the dynamic level never exceeds *piano*, while the second piece offers a violent contrast: a sinister and grotesque realization of Death's entry into the tavern, complete with castanets.[32] Perhaps Shostakovich himself realized the unique piquancy of his homage: from a composer who had been subjected to frightening intimidation in the Soviet Union during the years of Stalinism to a victim of an opposing ideology, the poet murdered by Franco supporters in August 1936.

---

[32] See Roy Blokker with Robert Dearling, *The Music of Dmitri Shostakovich; The Symphonies* (Cranbury, NJ: Associated University Presses, 1979), 145.

4

Drawing

JACQUELINE COCKBURN and FEDERICO BONADDIO

Encouraged by Salvador Dalí, Lorca exhibited a number of his drawings at the Dalmau Gallery, Barcelona, between 25 June and 2 July 1927. By exhibiting at the Dalmau he was following in the steps of artists such as Gleizes, Gris, Laurencin, Metzinger, Duchamp, Picasso, Miró, Barradas, Picabia and Dalí himself. Twenty-four drawings were shown.[1] Seven of them were clearly attempts to take advantage of the technical conquests of Cubism and form an interesting collection since they are the only Cubist still-lives that Lorca ever produced (see, for example, Figure 1: *Teorema de la Copa y la Mandolina* [Theorem of the Cup and the Mandolin][2]). These works contain echoes of Picasso's work, and like Picasso, they look back to the conventions of earlier still-lives.[3] The exhibition stimulated some response from both the press and Lorca's own circle. The *Revista de Catalunya* referred to the drawings as 'surrealist art' and the *Ciutat* called them a product of 'post-cubism' (Rodrigo, p. 142). Sebastià Gasch, art critic and friend of Lorca, challenged people to come and see them: 'Que los burócratas del arte, que los miedosos, que los sedentarios pasen de lo largo! Que los trascendentes, que los engreneídos, que los responsables pasen de lo largo! Que los temerosos del ridículo, y de las aventuras inéditas, y los grávidos de preocupación pasen de lo largo!' [Let the bureaucrats of art, the fearful and the sedentary stay away. Let transcendentalists, the pretentious and the responsible stay away! Let those who fear ridicule and hitherto unheard-of adventures, and those who are weighed down with worry stay away!] (Rodrigo, p. 142).

In the September issue of *La Nova Revista* of 1927, Dalí produced his own review of the exhibition under the title 'Federico García Lorca. Exposició de dibuixos acolorits' [Exhibition of colour drawings]. The review begins with a

---

[1] See Antonina Rodrigo, *Lorca–Dalí: Una amistad traicionada* (Barcelona: Planeta, 1981), 140.

[2] Exhibit 19, reproduced in Mario Hernández, *Libro de los dibujos de Federico García Lorca* (Madrid: Fundaciòn Federico García Lorca / Tabapress, 1990), 192.

[3] See Jacqueline Cockburn, 'Learning from the Master: Lorca's homage to Picasso', in *Fire, Blood and the Alphabet: One Hundred Years of Lorca*, ed. Sebastian Doggart and Michael Thompson (Durham: University of Durham, 1999), 23–42.

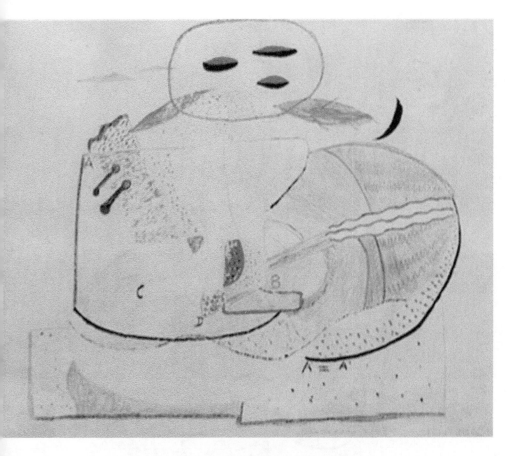

Teorema de la Copa y la Mandolina (1927)

Retrato de Salvador Dalí (1927)

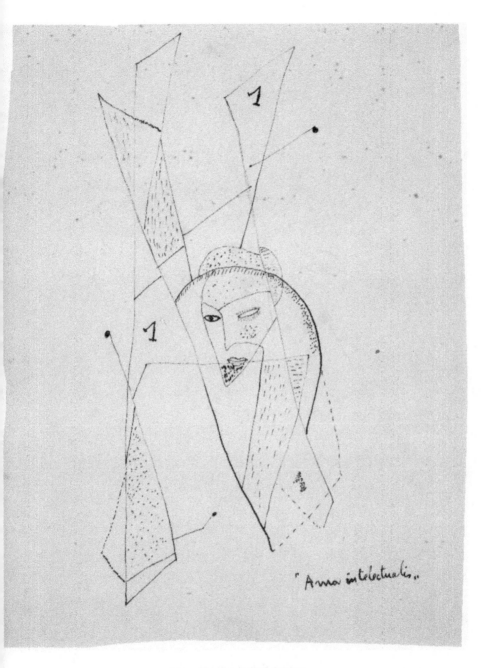

Amor Intelectualis (1927)

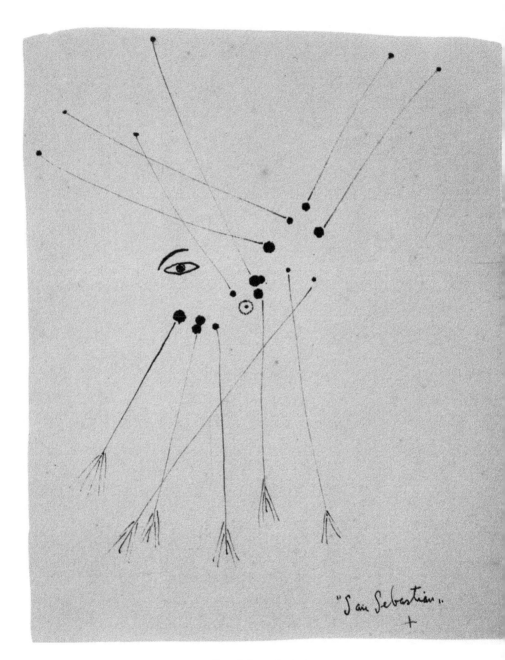

San Sebastián (1927)

discussion of De Chirico and his impact on young artists living in Paris engaged in surrealist activity. Dalí compares these artists with the Cubists whose work he eulogizes. Writing that they are the masters of pure and uncontaminated poetry, he concludes that the Cubists attained a new form of spirituality. Of Lorca's own work, however, he has little to say, and what he does say reveals the reservations he has about his friend's aesthetic engagement: 'El instinto afrodisíaco de Lorca precede siempre a su imaginación. Su espíritu juega en todos los casos un papel secundario. Cuando la imaginación precede a sus dibujos éstos se resienten de ello, quedan limitados a puras ilustraciones, más o menos encantadoras desde el punto de vista popular-infantilista' [Lorca's aphrodisiacal instinct always precedes his imagination. His spirit always plays a secondary role. You can tell when the imagination precedes his drawings because they resent it and end up being restricted to pure illustration, however charming from the popular and child-like perspective].[4] Gasch, on the other hand, continued to champion Lorca's artwork, producing in 1928 an important critical appraisal entitled 'Lorca dibujante' [Lorca the drawer], published in *La Gaceta Literaria*. In it Gasch writes that Lorca,

el poeta, el poeta auténtico, el poeta altísimo, siente a menudo la necesidad, como Jean Cocteau, como Max Jacob, de plasmar sus sueños plásticamente [. . .] y nacen automáticamente sus dibujos [. . .] dibujos presentidos, dibujos adivinados, dibujos vistos en un momento de inspiración, y que pasan directamente de lo más profundo del ser del poeta a su mano [. . .] Pensamos también en los dibujos de Miró, que vive atento a las visiones de su mundo interior, y que las fija rápidamente sobre el papel al presentarse de la misma manera que el poeta anota en su carnet la metáfora que acaba de crear.[5]

[Federico García Lorca, the poet, the authentic poet, the great poet, often needs, like Jean Cocteau, like Max Jacob, to transform his dreams plastically and his drawings are born automatically. Drawings that are premonitions, drawings that are divinatory, drawings seen in a moment of inspiration and that move from the depths of the poet's being to his hand. We are reminded of the drawings of Miró, who lives in awareness of the visions of his inner world, and who submits them quickly to paper in the same way as a poet notes down in his exercise book the metaphor he has just created.]

The fact that Gasch, in writing about Lorca, should have placed him in such illustrious artistic company is evidence of the fact the critic took him seriously as a pictorial artist. Lorca's credentials in the domain of the pictorial arts were further enhanced that year by an important public lecture, 'Sketch de la Nueva Pintura' [Sketch of the New Painting], delivered at the Ateneo [the Athenaeum] in Granada on 26 October. In this lecture it is possible to perceive Lorca's own

4 Salvador Dalí, 'Federico García Lorca. Exposició de dibuixos acolorits', *Nova Revista*, Barcelona, September 1927, pp. 84, 85.
5 Sebastià Gasch, 'Lorca Dibujante', *La Gaceta Literaria*, 30, 15 March 1928, p. 4.

remarkable knowledge of modern art. It begins with criticism of Impressionism and statements very reminiscent of Gasch's article 'Del Cubismo al Super-realismo' [On Cubism and Surrealism], although no mention is made of Gasch himself.[6] Lorca emphasizes the need for form rather than light and attacks the imitation of nature, giving – like Gasch – his full approval to Cubism: 'Con la aparición del primer cuadro cubista se crea ya un abismo entre pintura nueva y pintura vieja' [With the appearance of the first Cubist canvas, an abyss is created between new painting and old].[7] Paying homage to Braque as well as Picasso, Lorca comments on the importance of their work:

> Estaban salvando a la pintura que era un arte de representaciones y la estaban convirtiendo en un arte en sí mismo, en un arte puro, desligado de la realidad. El color y el volumen en la pintura histórica estaban al servicio del retrato, del cuadro religioso; en la pintura moderna color y volumen empiezan, por primera vez en el mundo, a vivir sus propios sentimientos y comunicarse y entrelazarse sobre el lienzo obedeciendo a leyes dictadas por sus esencias. (*Obras completas*, III, pp. 273–4)

> [They were salvaging painting that was an art of representation and were transforming it into an art in itself, pure art, unfettered by reality. Colour and volume in the painting of the past were at the service of portraiture, of religious painting; in modern painting colour and volume begin, for the first time ever, to live their very own sentiments, to communicate with each other and interrelate on the canvas obeying laws dictated by their own nature.]

He pays homage also to Juan Gris (particularly relevant in light of the Cubist images Lorca exhibited at the Dalmau) and provides interesting insights into Italian Futurism and Dadaism. Finally, and dramatically, Lorca asks this question of art: '¿A dónde vamos?' [Where are we heading?] and replies: 'Vamos al instinto, vamos al acaso, a la inspiración pura, a la fragancia de lo directo'. [We're heading towards instinct, towards chance, towards pure inspiration, and the fragrance of the direct]. This is how he introduces Surrealism, which he describes as abandonment to the ultimate heartbeats of the soul. His lecture ended with a number of slides of paintings by Miró, Lorca stating that Miró's paintings are the purest of all images: 'Vienen del sueño, del centro del alma, allí donde el amor está en carne viva y corren brisas increíbles de sonidos lejanos' [They come from dream, from the centre of the soul, there where love is made flesh and incredible breezes of distant sounds blow]. He likens this feeling to the moment a bull is killed in the ring. Lorca's confident conclusion is that 'el

---

[6] See Sebastià Gasch, 'Del Cubismo al Superrealismo', *Gaceta Literaria*, 15 October 1927. In Juan Manuel Rozas, *La Generación de 27 desde dentro: Textos y documentos*, 2nd edn (Madrid: Istmo, 1986), 144–53.

[7] Federico García Lorca, *Obras completas*, III, ed. Arturo del Hoyo, 3 vols, 22nd edn (Madrid: Aguilar, 1986), 273.

arte tiene que avanzar como avanza la ciencia' [Art has to advance just as science does] (*Obras completas*, III, p. 281).

Despite Lorca's evident interest in modern art and the fact that he produced drawings throughout much of his literary career (the first mention of his drawings was made in 1923 by friend, historian and critic Melchor Fernández Almagro [see Hernández, p. 15]), it is perhaps not surprising that his graphic work has been, until relatively recently, largely marginalized, or given only partial treatment by most scholars. For the vast majority of his drawings were never shown publicly and, indeed, were not widely available for viewing until the publication in 1986 of Mario Hernández's momentous catalogue, which is in itself unavoidably incomplete given that some drawings seem to have disappeared. Hernández set about collecting Lorca's graphic work after a posthumous edition of *Poeta en Nueva York*, illustrated with four drawings, came out in 1940. Until the publication of his catalogue, critics had had to work with what drawings were available. Indeed, the very concept of a body of graphic work only unfolded gradually. Hernández points out that 'La primera dificultad se fundaba en su misma dispersión, regalados por el autor a amigos diversos de España y de América a todo lo largo de su corta vida' [The first problem arose from their scattered whereabouts, given as they were by the author as presents to various friends in Spain and America throughout his short life] (Hernández, p. 11). By 1986 Hernández had managed to gather some 381 drawings.

The marginal status of the drawings in Lorcan scholarship is not, however, a question solely of their availability; it is also a question of approach, as a brief survey of the critical attention that the drawings have received will show. For although the last twenty years or so have witnessed an increasing number of critical responses to Lorca's graphic work, some of these have approached the drawings specifically in terms of their relation to images and symbols present in his poetry rather than as objects which may be appreciated and scrutinized in their own right. This is the case of David Loughran's 1978 book, *Federico García Lorca: The Poetry of Limits*, in which one chapter is dedicated to twenty-four drawings, which represented a large proportion of those available at the time; so too Felicia Londré's *Federico García Lorca* and Estelle Irizarry's *Painter-Poets of Contemporary Spain*, both published in 1984.[8] Like Loughran, whose interpretation of the drawings is made in light of his study over several chapters of a pattern of symbolism in the poetry, Londré devotes a whole chapter to the graphic work – she assumes that by then some 150 drawings are known – using it to study the visual imagery in both Lorca's poetry and plays; Irizarry, on her part, analyses in one chapter what she terms the 'iconology' of the drawings and begins to develop the idea that there is a vital relationship between Lorca's poetry and his drawings. Then in 1986, in addition to the publication of

---

8 See David K. Loughran, *Federico García Lorca: The Poetry of Limits* (London: Tamesis Books, 1978); Felicia Londré Hardison, *Federico García Lorca* (New York: Frederick Ungar, 1984); and Estelle Irizarry, *Painter-Poets of Contemporary Spain* (Boston: Twayne, 1984).

Hernández's catalogue, came Helen Oppenheimer's well-known *Lorca, The Drawings: Their relation to his Life and Work*, a volume dedicated entirely to the graphic work. Yet, as the punctuation of the title suggests, this book is primarily about Lorca the man. The drawings seem to fit into a well-documented, meticulously detailed biographical account of the poet's life. Oppenheimer divides them into sections of his life: the naïve early drawings showing Andalusian people locked into their lives; the later drawings depicting struggles of marginalized clowns and sailors; and finally, a later and more experimental period. Yet, despite these divisions, Oppenheimer perceives a unifying thread:

> Lorca's concerns remained the same throughout his artistic career; he was trying to resolve the conflict between the confines and constraints of man's natural condition and his attempts to transcend and improve his lot. The tensions created by this clash recur again and again. Lorca's drawings, so close to the core of his personality, reflect his development as a person and as an artist. They are not political. They are a personal account of his drives and insecurities, a memento of his boundless energy and creativity, as well as a record of the sadness, which lay behind the marvellously sociable entertainer.[9]

In her analysis, Oppenheimer delineates the creative process in such a way as to suggest a fixed way of working with fixed interpretations and symbols. The rationale of such an approach is revealed in the following comments: 'The drawing is useful for understanding verbal images, which might otherwise be difficult. It can stimulate the appropriate visual associations, and prevent the reader from making historical, etymological or other intellectual associations, which would put him on the wrong track' (Oppenheimer, p. 87). Once again the assumption is that Lorca drew primarily for the purpose of extending his poetic repertoire, the drawings thus serving to illuminate the significance of his poems. Importantly, however, Oppenheimer does analyse the relationship between Lorca and Dalí in terms of the act of drawing itself, including the very reasons behind the need to draw. Indeed, it is most significant that Lorca's early forays into drawing should have coincided with his friendship with the Catalan artist.

There are, however, some notable exceptions to the line of criticism outlined above. The first comes from outside the ambit of specifically Lorcan scholarship: Dawn Ades' article 'Morphologies of Desire', in the 1994 catalogue of the exhibition 'Salvador Dalí: The Early Years', held at London's Hayward Gallery. The focus is primarily on Dalí's work, particularly his 'Lorca' period, but it offers some interesting parallels with Lorca's drawings. Ades seeks to identify the vocabulary contained in the work and relate it to the psychoanalytical discourse of the day. The cultural climate, the lectures at the Residencia de Estudiantes and new translations of Freud all have roles to play in an under-

---

[9] Helen Oppenheimer, *Lorca, The Drawings: Their relation to his Life and Work* (London: The Herbert Press, 1986), 125.

standing of influences. Like Ian Gibson, who has produced important biographies of both Lorca and Dalí, she demonstrates how the relationship between the two men is important for an understanding of Dalí's visual images.[10] Moreover, in her exploration of the iconography of a number of Dalí's works, she makes the following important observation:

> Simultaneously with these canvases and with the new manner he adopted to paint them, Dalí published his first text 'Saint Sebastian' dedicated to Lorca. Since 1926 Saint Sebastian had been an emblematic figure for both Dalí and Lorca, part of a shared language which offered a channel for self-dramatisation, though the connotations of the martyr were different for each [. . .] As sado-masochistic object, St Sebastian becomes the sign of *a private language of sexuality*.[11]

This is a crucial point, for in focusing on the vocabulary within visual images, Ades shows how the visual itself can communicate.

Secondly, we have Cecilia Cavanaugh's *Lorca's Drawings and Poems: Forming The Eye of the Reader*, published in 1995.[12] Importantly, Cavanaugh elevates the drawings from their secondary role as illustrations of themes and motifs in the poems and begins to treat them as objects in their own right, thus setting up the possibility of a dialogue between Lorca's visual and verbal texts. This is evident, for example, in her analysis of the drawings' metaphorical dimension, which shifts the emphasis on to messages contained in the graphic work itself. Cavanaugh is aware of possible new approaches to this work and of the challenges awaiting contemporary scholars in the field: 'new discoveries and other correspondences between the drawings and poems remain unexplored. Theatre in Lorca is intrinsically related to the visual and to drawing and painting. Work in this field has only just begun. Different creative approaches to Lorca's visual and verbal texts may yet be applied to their analysis' (Cavanaugh, p. 180).

More recently, Martha Nandorfy's *The Poetics of Apocalypse: Federico García Lorca's 'Poet in New York'*, published in 2003, contains a section entitled 'Sublime Images: Drawing the Unsayable', a section devoted to drawings produced by Lorca in parallel with his New York poetry.[13] What is important about Nandorfy's approach is that it too acknowledges the benefits of the prac-

---

[10] See Ian Gibson's *Federico García Lorca* (London: Faber & Faber, 1989), 143–8, 159–204; and *The Shameful Life of Salvador Dalí* (London: Faber & Faber, 1997), 140–5, 163–8.

[11] Dawn Ades, 'Morphologies of Desire', in catalogue for exhibition *Salvador Dali: The Early Years* (3 March–30 May 1994, London: The Hayward Gallery) pp. 129–59 (p. 140).

[12] Cecilia J. Cavanaugh, *Lorca's Drawings and Poems: Forming The Eye of the Reader* (London: Associated University Presses, 1995).

[13] Martha J. Nandorfy, *The Poetics of Apocalypse: Federico García Lorca's 'Poet in New York'* (Lewisburg, PA: Bucknell University Press / London: Associated University Presses, 2003), 238–64.

tice of drawing beyond the limitations imposed by the category of illustration. She explains that, although he perceived connections between his drawing and writing, Lorca nonetheless made a crucial distinction; namely, 'that drawing is freer from logical constraints and definition than language' (Nandorfy, p. 239). The claim is that 'Lorca attempts to escape from the constraints associated with language in the Western world through drawing, a means of expression that he further privileges by association with the wisdom of childhood consciousness' (Nandorfy, p. 239). Once again, by treating drawing as a means of expression in its own right, Nandorfy makes it possible to read the poetry against the drawings, and vice versa. Thus, for Nandorfy, poetry and drawing in the context of the New York period brings the reader/viewer face to face with 'the *duende*'s double-edged sword: one edge threatens the visionary poet by pushing him to the brink of madness and death, while the other edge concedes him the power of creation to speak and draw the unsayable' (Nandorfy, p. 262).

There are, therefore, ways of approaching the drawings that make it possible for them to be considered as far more than mere adjuncts to Lorca's literary output. It is tempting to see in the relegation of their status to illustrations, or to expansions, of literary concerns a connection with the relatively casual perception and treatment of the gifts that Lorca made of his drawings. In his accompanying essay to his catalogue, entitled 'Líneas de luz y sombra' [Lines of light and shade], Hernández comments on the state of the drawings when he obtained them: 'llama la atención el descuido y desatención con que muchas de estas obras, técnicamente tan delicadas, se han conservado, incluso por familiares muy próximos. El valor afectivo ha superado en muchas ocasiones a la valoración de la obra en sí' [what is striking is the careless lack of attention with which many of these works, technically so delicate, have been conserved, even by close family. Their emotional value in many cases outweighs their value as works of art] (Hernández, p. 19). The drawings were rarely framed or restored, but were kept in the way people keep personal letters or photographs, the implication being that if many of them have been preserved at all it is only because of the sentimental attachment of their owners and not the result of any perceived artistic value of the objects themselves. Moreover, any notion of the inherent value of the drawings is complicated further by the very materials used for their composition: India ink with coloured crayons on paper; pastels on paper; textured drawing paper; India ink and colouring crayons on cardboard; lined exercise paper; pencil and watercolours on watercolour paper; pencil on block of paper; pen on lined diary paper; India ink on drawing paper with a watermark *SAV/écoles*; ink on cloth paper with a school map on the back signed by the boy Paquito Martin; white cardboard cut in an irregular way. Most of the supports appear to be of little monetary value. Indeed, the drawings were often executed on the back of other sketches – one was produced on the inside page of Philip's *Atlas of The World* – or on fragments of letters, photographs, or the inside of books. The paper used is, for the most part, thin, cheap and frequently reflects objects beneath. Indeed, the materials generally smack of supervised classrooms or doodles to while away the boring hours. The drawings are not finished with glazes or surface protection and, as such, it can be assumed that any idea of conservation at the time of production was neither apparent nor relevant.

The value of the drawings, needless to say, does not then reside in the quality of the materials employed, but elsewhere: whether it be in the pure association with the celebrity Lorca has since attained; or as some critics have argued, in what the drawings have to tell us about Lorca's other work and life; or alternatively, in what they have to say independently (to varying degrees) of his *oeuvre* generally. Yet what critics have tended to overlook is that the value of so many of Lorca's drawings is also closely bound up with their function as gifts, the act of gift-giving already implying a degree of worth that may have little, if anything, to do with either monetary or, indeed, artistic value, but resides in the giving itself and the motivation behind this act. Implicit in the following recollection by the artist Gregorio Prieto of his first meeting with Lorca on 7 April 1924 is a sense of the value of the gift conveyed in terms of the spontaneous nature of the act of giving and the concomitant notion of its generosity:

> La primera vez que yo vi un dibujo de Lorca fue el mismo día que lo conocí. Por entonces celebraba yo mi primera exposición en el Museo de Arte Moderno, de Madrid, y se presentó en ella, acompañado de otros estudiantes. Ese mismo día, en su cuarto de la residencia estudiantil vi colgado en la cabecera de su cama el dibujo de la Virgen de los Siete Dolores. Me gustó, se lo dije, y sin decir nada, lo descolgó del muro y me lo ofreció como regalo.[14]

> [The first time I saw a drawing by Lorca was the same day I met him. At that time I was celebrating my first exhibition in the Modern Art Museum in Madrid and he came to it with some other students. That very day in his room in the students' Hall of Residence I saw, hanging above his bed-head the drawing of The Virgin of the Seven Sorrows. I liked it, told him so, and he, without saying a thing, took it off the wall and gave it to me as a present.]

Hernández points to another aspect of the giving of gifts, namely its power of seduction: 'Lorca cultivó muchas veces el dibujo como una forma de amistad. No sólo ilustra libros que dedica y regala, sino que conquista y seduce a quienes aprecia convirtiendo sus cartas en pequeñas y exquisitas obras de arte' [Lorca cultivated his drawings as a token of friendship. He did not merely illustrate books that he dedicated and gave as gifts, but he also conquered and seduced those whom he valued by turning his letters into tiny exquisite works of art] (Hernández, p. 243). Lorca gave more than half of his drawings away as gifts. In light of this, Marcel Mauss's anthropological work on the gift is of great interest.[15] Mauss provides an anthropological analysis of gift-giving as a total social phenomenon involving legal, economic, moral, religious and aesthetic

---

14 In Gregorio Prieto, *Federico García Lorca y la Generación del 27* (Madrid: Editorial Biblioteca Nueva, 1977), 34.
15 Marcel Mauss, *The Gift*, trans. W.D. Halls (London: Routledge, 1990).

dimensions. He stresses that there is no such thing as a free gift. To give is to enhance solidarity. In defining his term for gift as 'potlatch', Mauss affirms that 'each gift is part of a system of reciprocity in which the honour of the giver and recipient are engaged' (Mauss, p. viii).

It is possible, therefore, to understand Lorca's gift-drawings as forming part of an exchange system; a means, if you like, to form bonds and by which to network. In this respect, it is significant that, although he gave many of his draw-ings to close friends and family, many others were sent to important cultural figures of the day, including members of an avant-garde elite, a number of whom would be (or had been) involved in some form of collaboration with him, or else in supporting or promoting his career generally. The list of recipients, then, reads in great part as a who's who of the contemporary literary and artistic scene: the sculptor, Ángel Ferrant; writers such as Rafael Alberti, Dámaso Alonso, José Bergamín, Jorge Luís Borges, José Caballero, Camilo José Cela, J.V. Foix, Jorge Guillén, Gregorio Marañón, Ricardo Molinari, Pablo Neruda, Emilio Prados; artists such as Norah Borges, the painter Benjamín Palencia, or the engraver Hermenegildo Lanz who created the puppet heads for Lorca's puppet shows and theatre (Gibson 1989, p. 120), as well as, of course, the afore-mentioned Gregorio Prieto; the composer, Manuel de Falla, who worked with Lorca on the 1921 *cante jondo* festival and proposed a number of other collabo-rative projects that did not, however, come to fruition; the actress, Margarita Xirgu, who staged a number of Lorca's plays; the editor of *Verso y Prosa*, Juan Guerrero Ruiz; the philologist, Ángel del Río, who proved an invaluable friend during Lorca's first months in New York and who wrote the first full-length study of his work in 1935 (Gibson 1989, p. 248); the French Hispanist, Mathilde Pomès; cultured businessmen such as Miguel Cerón Rubio, a close friend of Falla too, who may have come up with the original idea for the *cante jondo* festival (Gibson 1989, p 109); Hans 'Jean' Gebser, translator of Lorca's literary work into German; and the Chilean diplomat, Carlos Morla Lynch, whose 'home became a refuge for the poet' in 1929 and thereafter.[16] Yet two important figures were to be among the most rewarded by Lorca's gift-giving impulse. These were Dalí and Gasch, two men who, as we have already seen, played an active role in supporting Lorca's drawing habit, and each of whom received in the region of twenty drawings.

In his prologue to *Sebastian's Arrows: Letters and Mementos of Salvador Dalí and Federico García Lorca*, Christopher Maurer, building to an extent on what Gibson has to say about the relationship between Lorca and Dalí, explores the significance of Saint Sebastian in the personal and artistic exchanges between the two men; exchanges that included letters, conversations, poems, but also drawings.[17] As we have mentioned, the importance of these exchanges has

---

[16] Leslie Stainton, *Lorca: A Dream of Life* (London: Bloomsbury, 1998), 213.

[17] See *Federico García Lorca, Salvador Dalí, Sebastian's Arrows: Letters and Mementos of Salvador Dalí and Federico García Lorca*, ed. Christopher Maurer (Chicago: Swan Isle Press, 2004), 3–27. On the relationship between Lorca and Dalí, see also the seminal text by

already been highlighted by Ades; but where she focuses primarily on Dalí's 'Lorca period', Maurer brings into the discussion Lorca's 'Dalí period' too. Maurer notes that both men 'at different moments in their lives turned for aesthetic inspiration to the Catholic liturgy and to the lives of saints and martyrs', and this despite the fact that Dalí declared himself anti-religious and Lorca was unlikely to have described himself as either an orthodox or practising Catholic (*Sebastian's Arrows*, p. 16). Maurer suggests that both men were aware of the homoerotic associations of the saint, who consequently became an emblem of their respective attraction (however reluctant Dalí may have been to accept fully either his or Lorca's desire); but he also points out that each attributed rather differing artistic values to this iconic figure. Dalí, in his written piece, entitled *Saint Sebastian*, alludes to the saint, in line with his own aesthetic of the mid-1920s, 'as protection against the "germs" of emotional "putrefaction," and as a symbol of artistic "asepsia," of irony (solvent of emotion), and objectivity' (*Sebastian's Arrows*, p. 23). Lorca, on the other hand, may have been attracted by the notion of firing arrows itself, a metaphor for the poet's active engagement in the hunt for poetic images, although he would also emphasize the saint's vulnerability, in accordance with the notion of the suffering poet-martyr (see *Sebastian's Arrows*, pp. 19–20).

Through the exchange of items on the theme of Saint Sebastian, both men, therefore, were able to communicate their friendship in a codified form as well as engage in an aesthetic debate. The exchange, however, was not restricted to this saintly motif, but often took the form of portraits of one another, evidence again of their mutual fascination for the personality of the other. Indeed, Dalí's first exhibition at the Dalmau in 1925 contained several works on the theme of Lorca. An example of one of Lorca's gifts to his friend is *Retrato de Salvador Dalí* (Figure 2) (reproduced in Hernández, p. 193), dated around 1927 and one of the works (exhibit 24) that Lorca exhibited at his own show at the Dalmau that same year. The condition in which this drawing was found suggests, intriguingly, that it was once crumpled up and thrown away; salvaged perhaps, but certainly mutilated. Hernández describes it as: 'Roto con posible supresión de título y dedicatoria, en esquinas superior e inferior derecha' [Torn, its title and dedication possibly removed, at the the top and bottom right hand corners] (Hernández, p. 193). In it Lorca depicts Dalí standing in front of a tower behind which we see a crescent moon. Reminiscent of the Cubist practice of displaying surfaces otherwise hidden by naturalist depictions of objects, the moon is not hidden by the tower's 'solid' mass; nor, indeed, is the undulation of hills that intersects the tower's walls. Dalí holds a palette, and on the tips of each of the fingers of his painting hand is a single red fish. Another red fish, though much larger, is situated vertically on Dalí's torso. Dalí wears a helmet embellished by a star. The Catalan painter interpreted this as denoting him as one of the

Rafael Santos Torroella entitled *La miel es más dulce que la sangre: Las épocas lorquiana y freudiana de Salvador Dalí* (Barcelona: Seix Barral, 1984).

Dioscuri.[18] If he was right, then the other is absent and is possibly Lorca himself, leaving us to wonder which of the two mythical half-brothers – Castor or Pollux – is associated with Dalí, and which of the artists is the second brightest star and which the brightest. As for the fish, a clue to their meaning is perhaps provided in the following extract of a letter Lorca sent Gasch on 2 September 1927 on the subject of his own drawings:

> Hay milagros puros como 'Cleopatra', que tuve verdadero escalofrío cuando salió esa armonía de líneas que no había *pensado, ni soñado, ni querido, ni estaba inspirado,* y yo dije '¡Cleopatra ! al verlo, ¡y es verdad ! Luego me lo corrobró mi hermano. Aquellas líneas eran el *retrato exacto, la emoción pura* de la reina de Egipto. Unos dibujos salen así, como las metáforas más bellas, y otros buscándolos en el sitio *donde se sabe de seguro* que están. Es una pesca. Unas veces entra el pez solo en el cestillo y otras se busca la mejor agua y se lanza el mejor anzuelo a propósito para conseguirlo. El anzuelo se llama *realidad.*[19]

> [There are pure miracles like 'Cleopatra'. I felt such a shudder when its linear harmony appeared; a harmony I had not *thought up,* nor *dreamt,* nor *sought, nor had I been inspired,* and I shouted 'Cleopatra!' when I saw it, truly I did! Then my brother confirmed what I had seen. Those lines were the *very likeness, the pure emotion* of the Queen of Egypt. Some drawings just come out like that, like the most beautiful metaphors, and others have to be searched for in places *where we are certain* they will be. It's a fishing trip. Sometimes the fish pops into the net all by itself and other times you have to go looking for the best water and use the best hook in order to catch it. That hook is called *reality.*]

In *Retrato de Dalí*, the multitude of fish denotes, perhaps, Dalí's expert hand. He is the most accomplished of 'fisherman', the large red fish indicating his total devotion to, or embodiment of, the artistic/fishing task, or even the site – the deepest, inner waters – from which inspiration or inspiration's catch may spring. If so, then this portrait of Dalí serves to praise the artist Lorca so admired (this admiration is evident both in his exchanges with Dalí and in a number of letters to Gasch), albeit in codified form, communicating its homage via a visual vocabulary shared between friends and by those privy to the language in which it speaks.

In addition to the question of the content of Lorca's coded graphic messages, there is also the matter of the appropriateness of the graphic medium to which he turned. Pianist turned poet and playwright and now avid drawer, it is perhaps no coincidence that his early graphic output should have coincided, more or less,

[18] Dalí is cited by Robert Descharnes, *The World of Salvador Dalí* (New York: Macmillan, 1962), 21.
[19] In Federico García Lorca, *Epistolario completo*, ed. Andrew A. Anderson and Christopher Maurer (Madrid: Cátedra, 1997), 519.

with his meeting Dalí in 1923; and if he sent drawings to Gasch, it was because he sought the advice and opinion of a man who was already an influential art critic – and, incidentally, a friend of Josep Dalmau – by the time Lorca first met him in the spring of 1927. Indeed, it is possible that if he cultivated his drawing habit at all, it was because actually 'it brought him closer to Gasch and Dalí'.[20] Against the background of artistic manifestos and groups, literary journals and collaborative projects, it was common practice, it seems, to seek associations, although it is interesting to note just how many of his associates Lorca also considered to be his friends. As in the case of his relationship with Dalí, artistic interests and friendship generally went hand in hand, Lorca thus managing to construct a world for himself in which he felt comfortable and which offered him collaborative opportunities, publication outlets or, quite simply, moral support. Drawing offered him another tie to that world; it was yet another of the many languages spoken by members of the creative circles in which Lorca moved. Put another way, Lorca, in respect of both Dalí and Gasch, 'needed to be functioning in the same currency before he could operate on the same level. The "currency" is the primary level of exchange, in that he could seek approval and intellectual nurture more easily' (Cockburn 2003, p. 69). In effect, the drawings sent to Sebastià Gasch – he sent him twenty-two between 1927 and 1928, often with a view to having them exhibited or reproduced in publications – were seductive arrows shot from Lorca's bow into the flesh of his illustrious target: another (appropriately named) Sebastian.

When Lorca entrusted his drawings to Gasch he did so completely. In one letter to him, dated 11 August 1927, and in which he was still using the polite third-person form, he writes: 'Le envío estos dibujos. Si le gustan se los envía a Dalí para que los vea. Si no le parecen dignos de esto, los rompe. Pero son todos de su propiedad y puede hacer de ellos lo que guste' [I'm sending you these drawings. If you like them send them to Dalí to look at. If you don't think they merit this, tear them up. They're all your property and you can do with them what you like'] (*Epistolario*, p. 504). In another, from mid-September 1928, he once more transfers ownership of his artwork: 'Los dos dibujos que publicáis te quedas tú con ellos. Te los regalo. Y te vas haciendo una colleción de pequeñas tonterías' [Keep the two drawings you're going to publish for yourself. They're a gift. That way you can build up a collection of little knick-knacks] (*Epistolario*, p. 589). Lorca seemed to trust Gasch's judgement and often expressed his admiration for him directly in his letters. He also profited from their correspondence by way of the discussions they maintained on art. Gasch advocated the fusion of plasticity and poetry (Cockburn 2003, p. 70), of the technical advances of Cubism and the poetry of Superrealism: 'Esperamos ávidamente la obra genial que aproveche las conquistas técnicas del cubismo, que las enriquezca con la

---

[20] Jacqueline Cockburn, 'Gifts from the Poet to the Art Critic', in Federico Bonaddio and Xon de Ros (eds), *Crossing Fields in Modern Spanish Literature* (Oxford: Legenda [European Humanities Research Centre], 2003), 67–80 (p. 69).

poesía del superrealismo, que fusione, finalmente, la abstracción y la realidad, que una finalmente la inteligencia y la sensibilidad' [Avidly we await that ingenious work which will profit from the technical conquests of Cubism, which will enrich these with the poetry of Superrealism, which will fuse, at last, abstraction and reality, which will at last unite the intelligence and sensibility] (see Rozas, p. 153). As a lyrical poet who had turned his hand to drawing, Lorca, despite his technical limitations (or even because of them, if we consider that the lack of technical accomplishment has contributed to his drawings' apparent naivety and spontaneity, and hence the emotional value associated therewith), was perhaps well placed to produce poetic plasticity. After all, Lorca did himself refer to his graphic art as drawing poetry: 'Ahora empiezo a escribir y a dibujar poesías,' he once wrote Gasch [Now I've begun writing and drawing poems] (*Epistolario*, p. 508). Moreover, in his letter to Gasch dated 2 September 1927 (cited above), he agreed with the critic that the best way forward in art was to 'unir la abstracción a la realidad' [tie abstraction to reality] (*Epistolario*, p. 520). 'Es más,' he adds, 'yo titularía estos dibujos que recibirás [. . .] *Dibujos humanísimos*. Porque casi todos van a dar con su flechita en el corazón' [What's more, I would entitle the drawings you'll be receiving *The Most Human Drawings*. Because nearly all of them will strike their little arrow into the heart]. One of the drawings sent with this letter is *Amor Intelectualis* (1927) (reproduced in Hernández, p. 157, n. 154); another is, rather appropriately in light of Lorca's reference to 'little arrows', *San Sebastián* (1927) (Hernández, p. 102, n. 130).

These two drawings seem to embody the criteria that Gasch, and Lorca, sought for art: poetry and plasticity, reality and abstraction, intelligence and sensibility – the latter duality alluded to in the very title of *Amor Intelectualis* (Figure 3). The very human aspect Lorca refers to in his letter is, at one level, produced by the presence of the human figure in both drawings, albeit metonymically in *San Sebastián* (Figure 4) via the incorporation of the eye. The face in *Amor Intelectualis* appears to be Dalí's; given the reoccurrence of the slender, oval-shaped eye, he may also be the subject in *San Sebastián* – albeit restricted to the now metonymical eye. In *Amor Intelectualis*, the face belongs to the human realm ('*Dibujos humanísimos*'), but is drawn into the domain of abstraction by the lines and shapes emanating from it; lines and shapes that, while remaining geometric, also form the facial features. This fusion of reality and abstraction is evoked also by the eyes: one, open and staring; the other, depicted only as an ellipsis. The open eye is drawn more boldly than the other, as are other figures, lines and shapes (for example, the number 1s, the dots, the curve dissecting the brow). The visual connection this creates sets up in turn a relationship that is possibly conceptual but also emphasizes the geometric character of all these elements. The number 1s (centre left and top right) stand alone but together equal two, reflecting, on the one hand, the integrity of the figure (head joined to lines and shapes) and, on the other, its duality (human form, abstract shapes). In the bottom right-hand corner, a number 1 appears to have been scribbled out: an afterthought perhaps, but nonetheless one that confirms the importance of duality in the drawing by restricting the sum total to 2. Just as the drawing invites us to make this simple addition, so too does it tempt us to decipher its meaning. This is because its combination of geometry and human personality, abstraction and reality, suggests, but never describes, a relation between its elements, thus obliging the viewer to make the connections. If Oscar Wilde's poem of the same name is a significant intertext, then it may point to the nature of the drawing's coded sentiment. The title alone does, in any case, suggest that the drawing may be a metaphorical construction of the notion of intellectual love; a love based on the intelligent evaluation of the mental prowess (denoted by the lines and shapes conjoining the face) of the portrait's human subject. And if the curve dissecting the brow is to be understood as being a halo, then this subject has been canonized, the central, open eye of the total geometrical figure becoming the gaze of the saintly artist – a Saint Sebastian – who, as Lorca saw it, is subjected to and yet can transform (from crude reality to mysterious abstraction) the world that surrounds him.

In the drawing, *San Sebastián*, the saintly associations are clear. Whereas the open eye in *Amor Intelectualis* was central and gazing out amidst abstract shapes, here the single, open eye is off-centre as a number of arrows and lines converge on a central bull's-eye (denoted by a dot contained within a small circle), but fail to hit the mark. The arrows – six in total – are drawn pointing upwards towards and around the bull's-eye; the lines – also six – occupy the top half of the drawing and, like the arrows, seem to approach the central target. The distribution of arrows and lines is only vaguely similar; there is no exact symmetry between the two groupings of objects and forms. Yet in their respective positions in opposite halves of the page, an association – however asymmetrical – is drawn between them given their equal number and the central destination that they have in common: an association, once again, between the abstract (lines) and real (arrows). The eye, as in *Amor Intelectualis*, may be the artist's, once more placed in the service of the creative principle that brings reality and abstraction together. However, in light of the drawing's title and the fact that its recipient was the critic Sebastian, it is tempting to come to a self-referential interpretation of the saintly subject: the eye, in this context, might equally be the critic's, the combination of real and abstract forms having been conceived in accordance with his principles (under his watchful eye) and also with his eventual viewing in mind. In this case, the drawing becomes a self-conscious metaphor for artistic creation in the context of Lorca's exchanges with Gasch; a drawing that offers itself to the critic who must evaluate whether its arrows have, or have not (as the drawing modestly suggests), hit their mark.[21]

Whether or not we all agree on the readings given here, the drawings can clearly be conceived of as metaphors. The product of the fusion of reality and abstraction here – like the fusion of the narrative and lyrical in *Romancero gitano* [Gypsy Ballads] – thus preserves its connection with the experience of the world and also to traditional forms of poetic exegesis. Perhaps too much so

21 For the possibly sexual connotations of this drawing, see Cockburn 2003, p. 77.

for the liking of Dalí whose criticisms of *Romancero gitano* on the basis of its relation to 'the literary commonplace' (see Rodrigo, p. 211) have been well documented and were, rather significantly, referred to by Lorca in one of his letters to Gasch himself (*Epistolario*, p. 585). Dalí's criticisms of Lorca's work, along with his collaboration with Luis Buñuel and Lorca's departure for New York, would produce a schism in the relationship between the two men that not even the gifts that Lorca made of his drawings could avert. As for Lorca's relationship with Gasch, it is perhaps not surprising that there should be no documentation of any correspondence between them during or after Lorca's adventure in New York (1929–30). For on his return, Lorca, although still drawing, immersed himself in the theatre, a domain in which, like drawing, he perceived poetic substance: 'Yo he abrazado el teatro porque siento la necesidad de la expresión en la forma dramática. Pero por eso no abandono el cultivo de la poesía pura, aunque ésta igual puede estar en la pieza teatral que en el mero poema' [I have embraced the theatre because I feel the need to express myself in the dramatic form. But this doesn't mean I'm giving up the cultivation of pure poetry which, in any case, can just as well be found in a theatrical piece as it can in a poem] (*Obras completas*, III, p. 611). In any case, after his exhibition at the Dalmau in 1927, and amidst mixed reviews, Lorca had modestly written to Manuel de Falla to tell him that he had been 'obliged' to show his drawings (*Epistolario*, p. 497); and although Josep Dalmau wrote to him two months after the exhibition to invite him, along with several other artists, to participate in another exhibition in October of that year, Lorca was not to show his drawings again until 1932.

Let us end by returning to the point Nandorfy makes about the childlike aspect of Lorca's drawings; namely the privileging of what she terms 'the wisdom of childhood consciousness'. It is interesting that Prieto and Gasch should also have seen something of the child in Lorca's drawing. Prieto suggests that

> García Lorca componía sus dibujos como un 'entretén', como algo que le divertía y como si estuviera jugando, pero ponía en ellos, al mismo tiempo, esa seriedad que los niños ponen al hacer los suyos, y un interés infantil, como quien desarrolla algo trascendental en su vida (Prieto, p. 34)

> [García Lorca would do his drawings for entertainment, to amuse himself, as if playing, though with that seriousness that children adopt when they do their own, a childlike interest, like someone doing something of the utmost importance in his life]

while Gasch describes Lorca's drawings as

> dibujos vistos en un momento de inspiración, y que pasan directamente de lo más profundo del ser del poeta a su mano. Una mano que se abandona, que no opone resistencia, que no sabe ni quiere saber dónde se la conduce, y que para sin esfuerzo, sin tortura, con optimismo, con alegría, con la misma alegría del

niño que llena de garabatos una pared, esas maravillosas realizaciones que alían la más pura fantasía, el más exacto equilibrio de líneas y colores. (Gasch, p. 4)

[drawings seen in a moment of inspiration, which pass directly from the poet's deepest being to his hand. A hand that lets itself go freely, that offers no resistance, that neither knows nor wants to know where it is being led, and that stops effortlessly, unagonizingly, optimistically, happily, as happily as a child covering a wall with scribble, those most marvellous productions allying the purest fantasy with the most precise balance of line and colour.]

Lorca himself, in his letter to Gasch of 2 September 1927, refers to his drawing and the satisfaction he derived from it in the following terms: 'poesía pura o plástica pura a la vez. Me siento limpio, confortado, alegre, *niño*, cuando los hago. Y me da horror la *palabra* que tengo que usar para llamarlos' [pure poetry or pure plasticity at the same time. I feel clean, comforted, happy, a child, when I do them. And I abhor the word I have to use to name them] (*Epistolario*, p. 519). Whether it be in terms of a child's wisdom, playfulness, lack of self-consciousness or pre-linguistic freedom, what all these observations have in common is that they tap into the myth of childhood innocence untainted by the rational constraints of adult logic and life. The connections with the spirit of Surrealism – though perhaps, in Lorca's case, only the spirit – are clear, as is the connection with the generally anti-discursive modes of the day and the various endeavours to achieve artistic purity. Yet in the context of Lorca's biography, the references to childhood also raise other issues. Lorca was well known – loved even – for his playfulness, his joviality, his desire to entertain, but also his petulance and, much like an egocentric child, his constant need to be the centre of attention. Moreover, biographers have also pointed out Lorca's financial dependence on his parents right into adulthood, as well as Don Federico's anxieties about his son's studies and career, and Lorca's desire to please his father (although they have generally stopped short of any profound analysis of the significance of this parent–child relationship).[22] Together these biographical elements combine to produce the impression of Lorca at once man and child, an impression conveyed equally by the apparent naivety (despite the conceptual sophistication) of many of his drawings – a naivety itself often reinforced by the supports and materials used. Seen in this light, the gifts that Lorca made of his drawings can themselves appear to be childlike gestures; offerings which, with all the naïve and generous simplicity of children's drawings, manage to disarm, charm and seduce their recipients. If we consider Lorca's interest in puppet theatre and lullabies, the playful simplicity of many of his *canciones* [songs] and

[22] This is one of the criticisms that Luis Fernández-Cifuentes makes of Gibson's biography in his review for *Nueva Revista de Filología Hispánica*, 34 (1985–6), 224–32 (p. 230). Lorca's relationship with his parents is a recurring subject in Stainton's biography, although the focus tends to be on Lorca's financial dependence.

suites, or the seemingly unconsidered spontaneity of his drawings, it is not diffi-cult to conclude that Lorca saw the virtue, and indeed made a virtue, of the childlike perspective. Indeed, this was possibly his very own perspective, his temperament. As it turned out, it may also have been his genius.

5

Cinema

XON DE ROS
Cinema in Lorca

ANTONIO MONEGAL
Viaje a la luna [*Journey to the Moon*]

ALBERTO MIRA
Lorca in Cinema

Cinema in Lorca (Xon de Ros)

> It would have been strange if in an epoch when the popular art *par excellence*, the cinema, is a book of pictures, the poets had not tried to compose pictures for meditative and refined minds which are not content with the crude imaginings of the makers of films. [. . .] They want to be the first to provide a totally new lyricism for these new means of expression which are giving impetus to art – the phonograph and the cinema.[1]

Apollinaire's 1917 bugle-call for his fellow poets to work in the cinema heralded an artistic association that would have a lasting impact in the shaping of the European film tradition.

However, among the art forms poetry is arguably the least compatible with cinema, particularly from the current vantage point of a film industry dominated by the action movie. In addition, the narrative drive that the language of film imposes on images puts a limit to their connotative potential. The fact, moreover, that poetry is essentially a linguistic discourse makes it irreducible to the visual image that defines the medium of film. Cinema's emphasis on the visual would have been even more evident during its infancy in the first three decades of the century, before sound became an integral part of the new art. Yet, paradoxically, it was during this period that poetry and film were to be most closely

---

[1] 'The New Spirit and the Poets', *Selected Writings of Guillaume Apollinaire*, trans. with an introduction by Roger Shattuck (London: Harvill, 1950), 227–37 (pp. 228, 237). Apollinaire's speech, delivered at the Théâtre de Vieux-Colombier in 1917, was first published after his death in *Mercure de France*, 491 (December 1918).

associated. Their affinity was promoted within the circles of the French avant-garde, where lyricism became a key laudatory term in film criticism. According to the influential filmmaker Jean Epstein, cinema was 'poetry's most powerful medium', the true incarnation of its verbal artifice.[2] It was a view shared by many critics and cinematographers.

The ascendancy of this movement on their Spanish counterparts may account for the fact that in Spain poetry was to be the literary genre most receptive to the experience of film. Buñuel, who in the mid-1920s had worked as an assistant with Epstein in Paris, was an instrumental figure in this process of artistic fertilization. First contributing film reviews and articles to *La Gaceta Literaria*, where he was in charge of the cinema section, and then from 1928, through his association with the pioneering Cineclub España, Buñuel's preferences and ideas, shaped in Paris, found a fertile ground among the country's literary figures.

Cinema's original status as popular entertainment and the industrial basis of its practice might have alienated the previous two generations of writers who, with a few exceptions such as Valle-Inclán and Blasco Ibáñez, had shown indifference, if not open hostility, towards it. However, Lorca's contemporaries – those born at the same time as the new medium – felt passionately about it. Their enthusiasm contrasted with the paucity of Spanish productions, which suffered from an almost non-existent infrastructure until the 1930s. The widespread appeal and impact of cinema on the cultural history of Spain during the 1920s and 1930s has been well documented by C.B. Morris in his seminal study *This Loving Darkness: Cinema and Spanish Writers, 1920–36*, where he surveys the work of some of the writers who responded creatively to the stimulus of the new medium and its entourage.[3] Morris devotes the central three chapters of his book to discussing the mark left by cinema on the poets of the 1927 group. Among them, Alberti, Cernuda and Lorca are singled out as those whose engagement with cinema shows a greater emotional depth and thematic significance. However, even though Lorca was the only Spanish poet who tried his hand at the new medium by writing a screenplay, in Morris's account he is not given the same prominence as Alberti, who was the most openly partial to cinema both in his poetry and in his declarations. Unlike Alberti, who is granted a chapter to himself, Lorca is given less attention, sharing his chapter with Cernuda. More tellingly, the commentary on Lorca starts by referring to his reticence about reading one of his most cinematic pieces, 'El paseo de Buster Keaton' [Buster Keaton's Outing][4], in the fifth session of the Cineclub español

---

[2] Jean Epstein, 'On certain characteristics of Photogénie' (1924), in Richard Abel (ed. and trans.), *French Film Theory and Criticism: A History/Anthology, 1907–1939*, 2 vols (Princeton: Princeton University Press, 1988), I (1907–29), 314–18 (p. 318).

[3] C. Brian Morris, *This Loving Darkness: Cinema and Spanish Writers, 1920–1936* (Oxford and New York: Oxford University Press, 1980).

[4] All references in the text are to Federico García Lorca, *Obras completas*, ed. Arturo del Hoyo, 3 vols (Madrid: Aguilar, 1991). For the English translation of 'El paseo de Buster

in April 1929. More in line perhaps with the session's title – *Oriente y Occidente* [East and West] – Lorca had chosen to read instead his 'Oda a Salvador Dalí' [Ode to Salvador Dalí] and the romance 'Thamar y Amnón' [Thamar and Amnon]. Morris senses a deep personal conflict expressed in 'El paseo de Buster Keaton', which, in his interpretation, explains Lorca's decision (Morris, pp. 134–9). But the nature of this conflict, which Morris convincingly relates to the problematics of self-perception, and the disparities between public and self-image, can also be understood from the vantage point of Lorca's own ambivalent response to the new medium.

His mixed feelings about cinema should be read in connection with his life-long interest in the theatre. As he stated in an interview in 1936, 'El teatro fue siempre mi vocación' (*Obras completas*, III, p. 673) [Theatre has always been my vocation], and of all the art forms theatre was the closest and therefore the most challenged by the emergence of the so-called seventh art extolled by the likes of Abel Gance, who recommended, above all, that 'it not be theatrical'.[5] In Spain the main and recurrent indictment against indigenous productions was precisely their reliance on theatrical conventions. The antagonism between the two forms had already been articulated in France before the war by the advocates of cinematic specificity, and the debate was reignited with the advent of sound, when the microphone would constrain the mobility of the camera. This constraint would temporarily realign cinema with the theatre and the music hall. By then cinema had become a mass medium, and a more popular form than theatre. That the crisis of the theatre preoccupied Lorca is evident in many of his declarations to the press, and also lies at the heart of his project with La Barraca. His concern was not only with the theatre's loss of agency but also with the dwindling audiences who, even if Lorca never openly acknowledged this fact, were deserting it for the cinema. In 1925 there were almost 1,500 cinemas in Spain. As Buñuel recalls in his memoirs, 'during those years [1917–25] movie theatres were sprouting up all over Madrid and attracting an increasingly faithful public'.[6] It comes as no surprise that among Lorca's plays the one that contains the most explicit references to cinema should be called precisely *El público* [*The Public*, or *The Audience*]. Martínez Nadal reminds us that Lorca often resorted to religious analogies to express his ideas on theatre, comparing it for example to the liturgy of the Mass.[7] Now, however, cinema was appropriating the experience of the numinous. In the words of Buñuel and Giménez Caballero among others, the cinema hall was repeatedly likened to a cathedral.

Keaton', the author has consulted and in some cases adapted John London's translation from his edition *The Unknown Federico García Lorca. Dialogues, Dramatic Projects, Unfinished Plays and a Filmscript* (London: Atlas Press, 1996), 44–8. London points to the fact that there are some discrepancies between the incomplete manuscript held in the Fundación García Lorca and the published version of the text. These discrepancies will only be commented on if they are pertinent to the discussion.

5 Abel Gance, 'A Sixth Art' (1912), in Abel, I, 66–7 (p. 66).

6 Luis Buñuel, *My Last Breath*, trans. by Abigail Israel (London: Fontana, 1985), 75.

7 Rafael Martínez Nadal, *Lorca's The Public* (London: Calder & Boyars, 1974), 221.

'El paseo de Buster Keaton' (*Obras completas*, II, pp. 277–80) was Lorca's first public engagement with the world of film. Written in 1925 and first published in the second and last issue of Lorca's magazine *gallo* in April 1928, it was part of a projected 'book of dialogues' that never came to fruition. The text describes a succession of events without any logical connection around the figure of Buster Keaton, with a caption-length dialogue interspersed with stage directions that often extend into lyrical interludes. The form was probably influenced by a textual format of play in vogue in France after the war consisting of scenarios in which the writers sought to recapture and redeploy through language what they most admired in cinema. As noted by critics, Lorca's piece, framed by the opening image of a cock ('gallo', in Spanish) conjuring up the Pathé newsreel logo, which routinely preceded all film screenings, and a final 'cinematic' kiss, contains a number of cinematographic references. Buster Keaton was one of the favourite heroes of the group of friends attached to the Residencia de Estudiantes in Madrid, and Lorca displays here not only a deep understanding of his character as well as a familiarity with the conventions of comic films in general, but also a knowledge of the current debates on cinema.

Early on, besides the metamorphoses produced by camera tricks, the distinctive features of cinema that were deemed impossible to achieve in the theatre were the actor's performance, which, no longer subordinated to speech, consisted of gestures and movements, and the choice and arrangement of props designed to provide the film with a sense of continuity. While the latter is represented in 'El paseo de Buster Keaton' by the ubiquitous bicycle, the text's cinematic nature is also reinforced by an emphasis on Keaton's movements and facial expressions. These clearly outweigh the character's sparing use of words ('No quiero decir nada ¿qué voy a decir?' [I have nothing to say. What can I say?] [*Obras completas*, II, p. 278]), most pointedly in his whimsical dialogue with the American woman where his gestures totally replace speech. This encounter also introduces the only cinematographic term used in the text ('Buster Keaton sonrie y mira en "gros plan"' [Buster Keaton smiles and stares out in close-up]) (*Obras completas*, II, p. 279). In one article written in 1921 entitled precisely 'Grossissement' [Magnification], Epstein had described the close-up as 'the soul of cinema', its touchstone (Abel, I, p. 236). For him, the close-up and the moving camera shot, which in Lorca's text is recalled in the account of Keaton's bicycle ride, were the main elements of *photogénie*. This concept, which gained currency throughout the silent period, was used to describe cinema's transformative power, linking it to poetry and modern painting. The work of Epstein was known among the Spanish avant-gardists ever since Guillermo de Torre had promoted it from the pages of the *ultraista* magazine *Hélices* (1918–22). That Lorca knew his work was confirmed in 1926 when in his lecture on Góngora he quoted Epstein's definition of metaphor (*Obras completas*, III, p. 230).

Epstein was also one of the first French writers to take notice of Buster Keaton. Like many contemporary comedians, Keaton derived humour from playing out childish misconceptions within an adult framework. His trademark was his dead-pan expression when faced with a range of experiences often associated with the technological age. He would unfailingly rise to such challenges but only to cause a disorder of nightmarish proportions, which he would then confront in an eccentric, matter-of-fact manner. Lorca's treatment of this character gives us the measure of his appreciation of cinema. If at the beginning of the piece Keaton is identified with the sentimental and the slapstick we can also read in his characterization both a rejection of easy trickery ('La bicicleta de Buster Keaton no tiene el sillín de caramelo y los pedales de azúcar' [Buster Keaton's bicycle has neither a caramel saddle nor pedals of sugar], and a lyrical impulse ('Sus ojos, infinitos y tristes [. . .] sueñan lirios, ángeles y cinturones de seda' [His eyes, infinite and sad dream of lilies, angels and silk sashes]) (*Obras completas*, II, p. 278).

At the same time, the underlying sense of nostalgia for a natural, uncomplicated world that suffuses Keaton's films is also present in 'El paseo de Buster Keaton'. The protagonist's resigned attitude towards his own alienation ('Quisiera ser un cisne. Pero no puedo aunque quisiera' [I wish I were a swan. But I can't be, even though I'd like to] [*Obras completas*, II, p. 279]) recalls the inevitability with which the traps of the modern world are met by his filmic counterpart. But in Lorca's invocation of the swan there is also a longing that has to do with poetic symbolism. The urban, manufactured and mechanical world looming in the background of Lorca's text and repeatedly identified with Philadelphia, may be sophisticated but it is blind to poetic nuance:

> *Los habitantes de esta urbe ya saben que el viejo poema de la máquina Singer puede circular entre las grandes rosas de los invernaderos, aunque no podrán comprender nunca qué sutilísima diferencia poética existe entre una taza de té caliente y otra taza de té frío.* (*Obras completas*, II, pp. 278–9)

[The inhabitants of this metropolis already know that the old poem of the Singer sewing machine can circulate among the great greenhouse roses, although they will never understand what an extremely subtle poetic difference exists between a cup of hot tea and another cup of cold tea.]

Eventually, the protagonist's estrangement seems to stem from his inability or unwillingness to conform to a Manichean vision that can be easily identified with a cinematic tradition that represents the world in terms of heroes and villains:

AMERICANA
    ¿Tiene usted una espada adornada con hojas de mirto?
(BUSTER KEATON *se encoge de hombros y levanta el pie derecho.*)
AMERICANA
    ¿Tiene usted un anillo con piedras envenenadas?
(BUSTER KEATON *cierra lentamente los ojos y levanta el pie izquierdo.*)
AMERICANA
    ¿Pues entonces?   (*Obras completas*, II, p. 279)

[AMERICAN WOMAN: Do you have a sword decorated with myrtle leaves?
BUSTER KEATON *smiles and raises his right foot.*
AMERICAN WOMAN: Do you have a ring with poisoned jewels?
BUSTER KEATON *slowly shuts his eyes and raises his left foot.*
AMERICAN WOMAN: Well then?]

The view of nature mediated by mechanical reproduction is reasserted at the end of the piece ('Un gramófono decía en mil espectáculos a la vez: «En América hay ruiseñores»' [A gramophone played simultaneously in a thousand movie-houses: 'In America there are nightingales'] [(*Obras completas*, II, p. 280]).[8] This is followed by one of the silent films' staples, the presence of the police, whose lights flashing on the horizon suggest the restoration of the order that Keaton has disrupted. This conclusion takes us back to the farcical opening scene in which (an out-of-character) Keaton stabs to death his own four children with a wooden knife, a detail that gives the scene a theatrical slant. It is tempting to see in Keaton's four children the four dramatic productions of Lorca to date and in their killing a reference to the radical dissociation between these two art forms promoted by the avant-gardists.[9] The obliteration of anything theatrical had become almost a requisite for a progressive cinema. The cock crowing a second time, symbolic both of betrayal and of a new dawn, suggests the mixed feelings of guilt and trepidation that this phantasmatic incursion into the new language of cinema might have provoked in the poet-playwright.

The protagonist's apparent detachment after the event is accompanied by his distorted perceptions as he takes a ride on his bicycle, ending in a typical comic stunt. At this point, the stage directions draw attention to Keaton's eyes. While the emphasis on them serves to inscribe the figure of the spectator within the narrative, the recurrent motif of eyes – a favoured trope of Surrealism – in the works of Lorca, Buñuel and Dalí has often been associated with the modern transformation of traditional forms of perception, for which the cinema was both expression and effect.[10]

Among the specific changes of perception that cinema brought was a phenomenon related to the acting performance. It concerns the identification between actor and character effected by the screen, particularly prominent in the tradition of the silent comic film that Keaton represents. The ontological confu-

[8] The manuscript differs at this point from the published version. In London's translation: 'In America there are no nightingales' (London, p. 48).
[9] *El maleficio de la mariposa* [*The Butterfly's Evil Spell*] (1920), *Los títeres de la cachiporra* [*The Billy-Club Puppets*] (1922), *La niña que riega la albahaca y el príncipe preguntón* [*The Girl Who Waters the Basil and the Prying Prince*] (1923), *Mariana Pineda* [*Mariana Pineda*] (1925). The undated opera libretto *Lola la comedianta* [*Lola the Actress*] is not included within this list because strictly speaking it falls outside the category of play.
[10] See Antonio Monegal, 'Shall the Circle Be Unbroken? Verbal and Visual Poetry in Lorca, Buñuel, and Dalí', in *Lorca, Buñuel, Dalí: Art and Theory*, ed. Manuel Delgado Morales and A.J. Poust (London and Toronto: Associated University Presses, 2001), 148–58 (p. 156).

sion implicit in Keaton's last words ('Señorita Eleonora, ¡perdóneme que yo no he sido!' [Miss Eleonora, please forgive me! It wasn't me!] [*Obras completas*, II, p. 280]) can be understood as alluding to this collusion between the film actor and his screen persona, which here Keaton tries unsuccessfully to dispel.[11] The point is anticipated shortly before in the character's acknowledgement that he cannot part with the features of his screen image ('¿Dónde dejaría mi sombrero? ¿Dónde mi cuello de pajarita y mi corbata de moaré? ¡Qué desgracia!' [Where would I put my hat? And my wing collar and moiré tie? What a shame!] [*Obras completas*, II, p. 280]).

The conflict between theatre and cinema is again recalled through the name of Eleonora, which, it has been suggested, could be identified with Eleonora Duse, mistress of the Italian poet Gabriele D'Annunzio, and an international stage actress of the stature of Sarah Bernhardt. Duse's death in 1924 while on tour in the United States had been widely publicised in the press.[12] This connection may help explain Eleonora's fainting fit at her encounter with a character whose impassive countenance was in itself a reminder of the way the craft of acting was being undermined by cinema, which in turn was the reason for the difficulties in integrating celebrated stage actors such as Duse to the screen. But if cinema's assault on the acting profession might have caused some discomfort in someone as partial to theatre as Lorca was, there is another, more disturbing phenomenon represented by the presence of the black man eating his straw hat, which Keaton fails to notice. A stock character in silent films and often the target of ridicule, the black man's incongruous presence here is a reminder of the damaging stereotypes that current cinema naturalized.[13] The obliteration of a sense of social awareness in the audience was a corollary of the conflation between the actor's self and role, which, as already stated, was particularly relevant to the star system dominating American cinema in the 1920s. This 'suspension of judgement' effected by the screen is in contrast to the social dimension of the theatre, where the gap between actor and role is preserved.

Therefore, after all these implicit caveats, it is not surprising that the piece's initial exhilaration should eventually change into a more sombre mood as an

---

[11] Román Gubern, in *Proyector de luna: La generación del 27 y el cine* (Barcelona: Anagrama, 1999), 446–7, cites Ian Gibson's account of the collage Dalí sent Lorca in 1925 made up of press cuttings of Buster Keaton's wedding, highlighting the discrepancy between life and fiction, and argues that it might have prompted Lorca's piece. The lack of a precise chronology makes it equally likely that the collage is a response to 'El paseo de Buster Keaton'. The writing that figures at the end of the manuscript suggests that it was a version addressed to Dalí (see London, pp. 118–19).

[12] The connection is made by Rupert C. Allen in 'A commentary on Lorca's *El Paseo de Buster Keaton*', *Hispanófila*, 48 (1973), 23–35. Despite the error in the dating of the text, which leads to an anachronistic interpretation, Allen's article, which considers the tension between film and theatre, contains many valid insights. See also a refutation of Allen's thesis in Robert G. Havard, 'Lorca's Buster Keaton', *Bulletin of Hispanic Studies*, 54 (1977), 13–20.

[13] Morris recalls his presence in Keaton's *The Blacksmith* (1922) and *Seven Chances* (1925), as well as in other films of this period (Morris, 1980, p. 135).

autumnal shade symbolically enters the text ('el Otoño ha invadido el jardín, como el agua al geométrico terrón de azucar' [Autumn has invaded the garden, just as water works its way into a geometrical lump of sugar] [*Obras completas*, II, p. 279]). In his career Lorca's allegiance would remain with the dramatic art. Nevertheless, even if 'El paseo de Buster Keaton' may contain some images whose meaning is difficult to ascertain, what is clear is that Lorca's understanding of the limitations and the possibilities of the new medium was already deep and well-informed. His interest was probably fuelled by his friendship with Buñuel, whose expertise had already been hinted at by Lorca when, in a significant gesture, he had dedicated one of the sections in his poetry collection *Canciones* [*Songs*] (1921–4) to the head of Luis Buñuel 'En grand plain [sic]' (*Obras completas*, I, p. 327).

Notwithstanding his insight into the new art form, the reality is that, apart from his film script *Viaje a la luna* [*Journey to the Moon*], which will be discussed in the next section, the references to cinema in Lorca's work are few and scattered. For instance, the stage directions in the second act of *La zapatera prodigiosa*, where the remark 'Esta es casi una escena de cine' [This is almost a scene from the cinema] (*Obras completas*, II, p. 336) is used to highlight the characters' silent exchange of meaningful glances. In a similar laconic manner *La casa de Bernarda Alba* [*The House of Bernarda Alba*] opens with the poet's statement announcing that the three acts of the play 'tienen la intención de un documental fotográfico' [are intended to be a photographic documentary] (*Obras completas*, II, p. 973). The character don Alhambro from Lorca's presentation of *gallo*, falls asleep 'en el fondo rizado de un interminable *film* de brisa que la ventana proyectaba' [in the curled background of an endless film of breeze projected from the window] (*Obras completas*, III, p. 382). These references, just like his comparison, in an interview for an Italian newspaper, of the eponymous protagonist of *Doña Rosita la soltera o El lenguaje de las flores* [*Doña Rosita the Spinster or the Language of Flowers*] with a well-known Italian film star from the pre-war period, (*Obras completas*, III, p. 640) belong to the imaginary of the time and are only an indication of the penetration of the world of cinema into the realm of everyday life.

It is in his most experimental play, *El público*, where at one point the stage directions indicate that the lights should acquire the silvery hue of a cinema screen (*Obras completas*, II, p. 657), that cinema acquires once more thematic significance. El público explores the crisis in modern theatre through different dramatic discourses. Among them, the language of cinema is evoked through a number of visual strategies that can only be successfully realized in film. For instance, the characters' rapid transformations and the folding screen bring to mind the effects of superimposition or dissolve and fade in/out technique, respectively, which belong to the lexicon of silent cinema. Also, the simultaneity of actions on stage seems to require the device of double or multiple exposure. And in the words of the PRESTIDIGITADOR [Magician, or Conjuror] we could read an allusion to the cinematic technique of the iris: 'Construyan ustedes un arco de alambre, una cortina, y un árbol de frescas hojas, corran y descorran la cortina a tiempo y nadie se extrañará de que el árbol se convierta en un huevo de serpiente' [You could build an arch with wire, a curtain and a tree with green leaves, then draw and undraw the curtain in time and nobody will find it strange that the tree should be transformed into a snake's egg] (*Obras completas*, II, pp. 664–5).

All these techniques figured prominently in his screenplay *Viaje a la luna*, as did the disembodied harlequin that reappears here, and which would be difficult to stage without recourse to film. But it is in the Cuadro Sexto [Sixth Scene] where the allusions to cinema become more explicit, particularly around the character of the PRESTIDIGITADOR, whose insistence on visual tricks brings to mind the figure of George Méliès. Méliès, who had been until 1914 the director of the Theatre Robert-Houdin, the foremost magic theatre in Paris, was a pioneer filmmaker described as having 'appropriate[d] photography and the visual world to the conjuror's sphere'.[14] He represents an approach to cinema that values its expressive function above the representational; famous among his films is *Le Voyage dans la lune* [*Journey into the Moon*], which, in his memoirs, Buñuel recalls seeing as a child. Méliès's fantasy films provoked the later enthusiasm of the Dada-Surrealists. Such a connection seems to be made in *El público* through the huge eye that presides over part of the stage in Cuadro Sexto. This prop, together with the references to a 'mano cortada' [severed hand] and a 'hormiga vivísima' [lively ant] linked to the figure of the PRESTIDIGITADOR, inescapably conjure up the surrealist cinema of Dalí and Buñuel.

Precisely in this equation of cinema and the avant-garde we find an alternative to the type of drama represented by *El público*, which Lorca deemed unperformable because 'los espectadores enseguida se levantarían indignados e impedirían que continuara la representacion' [the members of the audience would immediately stand up infuriated and would prevent the play from continuing] (*Obras completas*, III p. 557). This is in fact what happens in the play within the play. In *El público*, as the title suggests, the protagonist is the audience, whose disciplinarian gaze seems to be the cause of much of the conflict dramatized within it.[15] A contrasting attitude is articulated by Lorca two years later precisely with regard to the films of the French avant-garde:

Si te las explican . . . te quedas aún más en ayunas que antes. Y esto es lo grande que tienen estas producciones. La ninguna responsabilidad que asumen. Pueden ser buenas o malas, bellas u horrendas, lógicas o absurdas

---

[14] Eric Rhode, *A History of the Cinema: from its Origins to 1970* (London: Penguin, 1978), 34.

[15] Lorca's concern with the public reaction of his work, exacerbated with the critical reception given to his 1928 poetry collection *Romancero gitano* [*Gypsy Ballads*] and his play *El amor de don Perlimplín con Belisa en su jardín* [*The Love of Don Perlimplín for Belisa in Their Garden*] by his friends of the Residencia, has been well-documented. This preoccupation resonates for instance in the AUTOR's [Author's] *captatio benevolentia* of the prologue to the contemporary play *La zapatera prodigiosa* [*The Shoemaker's Prodigious Wife*], read by Lorca himself at the opening on Christmas Eve 1930.

..., es igual. El autor se contenta con que las interprete a su antojo cada cual. Peor para quien no las entiende de ninguna manera . . . Allá ellos![16]

[If you have them explained to you . . . you understand even less than before. And that is the great thing about these films. They accept no responsibility for being good or bad, beautiful or horrendous, logical or absurd . . . it makes no difference. The director is quite happy for each of us to interpret them as we will. Hang those who do not understand a thing about them. It's their loss!]

This view could easily be applied to *El público* itself, a play informed by a Carnivalesque spirit in which cinema participates, bringing with it an openness of response and instability of meaning that the play appropriates. At the same time, however, the flippancy and unfeelingness that the character of the PRESTIDIGITADOR displays in his confrontation with the DIRECTOR reveal that the conflict between theatre and the cinema was still unresolved in Lorca's mind.

Lorca, however, was not only a dedicated and accomplished playwright but also, above all, a poet, whose rich visual imagination invites us to make a connection between the poet and the potential filmmaker. Unsurprisingly critics have seen in some of his imagery the imprint of film. Morris suggests correspondances between Lorca's disturbing vision of New York in his collection *Poeta en Nueva York* [*Poet in New York*] and the dystopian world portrayed in Lang's *Metropolis*, and also between the stylized figures that feature in *The Cabinet of Dr Caligari* and the black and white ones that appear in *Así que pasen cinco años* [*Once Five Years Pass*] (Morris, p. 124). On a similar note Román Gubern sees in the scenography of *El amor de Don Perlimplín con Belisa en su jardín* not only the influence of Robert Wiene's aesthetics but also of Soviet cinema, for which in 1935 Lorca declared his interest in one opinion poll carried out by the magazine *Nuestro Cinema* (Gubern, p. 102). More generally, the plasticity of some poetic images can easily be visualized in filmic terms. For instance, his poem 'Reyerta' [The Feud] from *Romancero gitano*, with its impressionistic *mise-en-scène*, can be seen as a dramatic montage sequence. A similar perspective is adopted with regard to 'Romance sonámbulo' [Sleepwalking Ballad] by Derek Harris, who sees it as a film scenario.[17] Whereas these readings are suggestive and intriguing they also raise the issue of the interpenetration of artistic languages, as many of the effects that we now identify as cinematic can be found among the traditional resources of poetry. One of them, quite prevalent in Lorca's poetry, is the sudden change of focal length whose cinematic equivalent is the zoom shot. The close involvement of the audience created by the zoom-in is replicated in the sense of intimacy, often

[16] Carlos Morla Lynch, *En España con Federico García Lorca* (Madrid: Aguilar, 1957), 312. The English translation is from Morris, p. 123.
[17] Federico García Lorca, *Romancero gitano*, ed. by Derek Harris, Grant & Cutler Spanish Texts (London: Grant & Cutler, 1991), 26–31.

erotically charged, of his use of the diminutive. This form of spatial dislocation became more self-conscious around the time of his rediscovery of Góngora's poetry on the three hundredth anniversary of his death. In his lecture 'La imagen poética de don Luis de Góngora' [The Poetic Image of Don Luis de Góngora] Lorca highlights this juxtaposition of perspectives: '[Góngora] une las sensaciones astronómicas con detalles nimios de lo infinitamente pequeño, con una idea de las masas y las materias desconocida en la Poesía hasta que él las compuso' [unites astronomical sensations with tiny details of infinitesimal things, with a sense for the masses and materials that had been unknown to poetry] (*Obras completas*, III, p. 231).[18] Perhaps the analogy with cinema was not far from his mind when in the same lecture he chose to quote from Epstein, the champion of the close-up.

At the same time, Lorca's use of the adjective 'astronomical' inevitably brings to mind the figure of his then close friend Salvador Dalí, who would refer to it as an aesthetic category opposed to the conventional and sentimental, designated as 'putrefacto' [rotten].[19] 'Astronomical' is significantly one of the adjectives chosen by Lorca to describe Charlie Chaplin in a text written in September 1928 with the title 'Meditaciones a la muerte de la madre de Charlot' [Meditations on the death of Charlie Chaplin's mother]: 'Charlot con alas. Charlot de los cisnes. Charlot de los lirios del valle. Charlot del lenguaje de los abanicos y el rubor de novia. Cursi. Bello. Femenino. Astronómico' [Chaplin with wings. Chaplin of the swans. Chaplin of the lilies of the valley. Chaplin of the language of fans and bride's coyness. Mannered. Beautiful. Astronomical].[20] The manuscript has some pages missing and was never published in Lorca's life. The extant text is a mixture of the lyrical and the incongruous ('Que se ha muerto la

---

[18] The English translation is from Christopher Maurer, *Federico Garcia Lorca: Deep Song and Other Prose* (London: Marion Boyars, 1980), 59–85 (p. 66).

[19] In a letter to Pepín Bello in December 1925 Dalí had explained the dichotomy in these terms: 'la putrefacción es el SENTIMIENTO (con mayúsculas). Por lo tanto algo inseparable de la naturaleza humana. Mientras haya atmósfera terrestre hay putrefacción. Lo único fuera de nuestra atmósfera es la "astronomía". Por eso oponemos la astronomía a la putrefacción' [putrefaction is SENTIMENT (with capital letters). Therefore something inseparable from human nature. As long as there is atmosphere there is putrefaction. The only thing outside our atmosphere is astronomy. That's why we place astronomy in opposition to putrefaction]. Quoted by Rafael Santos Torroella in *'los putrefactos' de Dalí y Lorca: Historia y antología de un libro que no pudo ser* (Madrid: Residencia de Estudiantes / CSIC, 1995), 38. See also Lorca on Góngora: 'quiso que la belleza de su obra radicara en la metáfora limpia de realidades que mueren, metáfora construida con espíritu escultórico y situada en un ambiente extraatmosférico' [he wanted the beauty of his work to be rooted in the clean metaphor of realities that die, metaphor constucted with sculptural spirit and situated in an extra-atmospheric environment] (*Obras completas*, III, p. 229).

[20] Federico García Lorca, *Poemas en prosa*, ed. Andrew A. Anderson (Granada: Comares / La Veleta, 2000), 93–100 (p. 96). The English translations are the author's. A published translation of the text by Greg Simon and Steven F. White can be found in Federico García Lorca, *Collected Poems*, ed. Christopher Maurer (New York: Farrar, Straus and Giroux, 1991), 784–86.

madre de Charles Chaplin / muerta la llevan en un calcetín' [Chaplin's mother is dead / they carry her dead inside a sock] [*Poemas en prosa*, p. 94]), and consists of two meditations in prose separated by a section of six rhymed couplets with the title 'Voz del Pueblo' [Vox populi], followed by a number of couplets, with some more on the reverse of two of the pages, one of them bearing the title 'Transverberación de Charlot' [Chaplin's Transverberation]. There is some disagreement among critics about the exact date of the piece, since the date that figures in one of the pages can be read as either 1 or 7 September, and around the question whether or not Lorca had by then read Dalí's harsh letter criticizing his recent collection *Romancero gitano*.[21] Certainly the theme of bereavement could be related to the increasingly deep rift between the two friends, and there are some indications suggesting that the piece may have in fact been written in reaction to Dalí's contempt.[22] Moreover, even if Chaplin was not yet the target of scorn that he would become a year later at the hands of Dalí and Buñuel, the celebration of this quintessential, sentimental antihero may represent a pre-emptive stance on the part of Lorca, whose allegiance to the idea of a dehumanized art was, unlike theirs, less than wholehearted.[23] His identification with the character of Chaplin was first pointed out by Christopher Maurer in his presentation of the piece in 1989.[24] The split between self and appearance that characterizes the comic was part of the experience of the poet who felt himself increasingly alienated from his public persona, particularly after the sensation caused by the publication of his *Romancero gitano* and the subsequent estrangement from his friends. However, the religious undertones of the piece, related to self-sacrifice and the *vía negativa*, also give a redemptive tone to the experience, which would be at odds with a purely biographical interpretation.

At the centre of the text Lorca considers whether Chaplin's unexpected reaction to his mother's death is consistent with the expectations set out by his character on screen, conjured up by a number of allusions to his films. After a brief aside in which the possibility of discourse is entertained and then abandoned, the meditation ends with a playful description of the funeral proceedings through a series of images that combine the humorous ('Como cae la nieve en grandes masas, se teme que Noruega intervenga en el asunto y haya reclamaciones por

[21] See letter xxxvi in 'Salvador Dalí escribe a Federico García Lorca', ed. Rafael Santos Torroella, special double issue of *Poesía*, 27–28 (1987), 88–94.

[22] The piece's insistence on incongruous rhymed couplets might be taken as a protest against Dalí's recommendation to renounce rhyme. This together with the fact that 'San Gabriel' and 'mijitas de pan' [breadcrumbs] – both referred to here by Lorca (*Poemas en prosa*, p. 99) – also appear in Dalí's letter, do seem to suggest that Lorca had read his letter by then.

[23] See Dalí's commentary published in *L'Amic de les Arts*, 31 March 1929: 'Keaton [. . .] es un místico y Charlot un putrefacto' [Keaton is a mystic and Chaplin a putrefact]; also Buñuel's commentary in *La Gaceta Literaria*, 56 (April 1929): '[Chaplin] intenta hacernos llorar con los más vivos lugares comunes del sentimiento' [tries to make us cry with the most acute sentimental clichés]. Quoted by Gubern, pp. 307 and 305 respectively.

[24] Christopher Maurer, 'Millonario de lágrimas', *El País*, 3 December 1989, p. 15.

parte del ministerio de Estado' [As snow is falling in large quantities it is feared that Norway may intervene in the matter and there could be claims made by the Ministry of State] [*Poemas en prosa*, p. 98]) and the surreal ('Don Benito Musolini [sic] ha enviado una [corona] de balas de fusil en cuyo centro se abre una hermosa ópera italiana de plata maciza' [Don Benito Musolini has sent a wreath of rifle bullets with a beautiful Italian opera made of solid silver in the middle] [*Poemas en prosa*, p. 97]), with the downright absurd ('La madre de Charlot fue amortajada por su perro favorito ayudado por una monja que se llama Clara Bontsw' [Chaplin's mother was laid out by her favourite dog helped by a nun called Clara Bontsw] [*Poemas en prosa*, p. 97]).

But 'Meditaciones a la muerte de la madre de Charlot' does not only consist of a series of absurd and disjointed images around Chaplin and his mother. As Andrew Anderson observes, the text also contains an allusion to the 'hecho poético' [poetic event] in Lorca's commentary on Chaplin's *llanto* [lament] (*Poemas en prosa*, p. 51):

En ninguna estética se ha usado el llanto de una manera tan pura. El llanto ha sido siempre una consecuencia. Charlot hace del llanto la causa, fuente aislada sin relaciones con el tema que lo produce. Llanto en redondo. Llanto en sí mismo. (*Poemas en prosa*, p. 95)

[No aesthetics has used lament in such a pure way. The lament has always been a consequence. Chaplin makes of it the cause, an isolated source without any links with the issue that is provoking it. A full stop lament. A lament in itself.]

What Lorca referred to as 'hecho poético' was a key concept in his new poetics that he would expound in his lecture 'Imaginación, inspiración, evasión' in October of the same year. [25] It has been well documented that the year 1928 was a turning point both in Lorca's personal life and his aesthetic orientation.[26] A reassessment of his artistic alignments is manifest in many of his writings of this period. 'Meditaciones a la muerte de la madre de Charlot' shows how cinema might have contributed to the process of shaping and articulating his new poetics. In this context, the death of Chaplin's mother, of whom Lorca says: 'Tu tragedia como actriz ha sido lo más emocionante del teatro moderno' [Your tragedy as an actress has been the most moving one in modern theatre] (*Poemas*

[25] In 'Lorca at the Crossroads: "Imaginación, inspiración, evasión" and the "Novísimas estéticas"', *Anales de Literatura Española Contemporánea*, 16 (1991), 149–73 (p. 152), Andrew A. Anderson defines 'hechos poéticos' as 'free-standing images devoid of any analogical meaning whose creation, internal functionings and interrelations are now determined only by a "lógica poética" [poetic logic].'

[26] Eloquent in this respect is Lorca's letter to Jorge Zalamea of September 1928 (*Obras completas*, III, pp. 978–9); for an overview, see Ian Gibson, *Federico García Lorca, 1. De Fuente Vaqueros a Nueva York, 1898–1929* (Barcelona: Grijalbo, 1985), ch. 21, 530–85.

en prosa, p. 94) takes up the symbolic significance of a break with a filiative system identified with representational art.

Certainly Lorca's creative mindset was about to take a more experimental turn. The amalgamation of bodily senses that he had postulated for the poet in his lecture on Góngora was being translated into an active interest in visual technologies and multimedia practices. In 1931 he recorded a compilation of traditional Spanish songs scored by himself in which he played the piano to *La Argentinita*'s singing. His book *Poeta en Nueva York* was designed to include photographs and drawings. Moreover, there are indications that within this new aesthetic orientation cinema would have played a larger role in his work. Some months after 'Meditaciones a la muerte de la madre de Charlot', in a letter home from New York, Lorca declared that he had become a fervent admirer of the talking pictures and that he wanted to try his hand at them (*Obras completas*, III, pp. 855–6). Shortly afterwards he wrote his script *Viaje a la luna*, and in his last recorded interview he told of his plans to make a film about the world of bullfighting. Lorca might have finally taken up Apollinaire's call quoted above, even if almost twenty years later. While cinematographic modes of thought and expression had long preceded the invention of cinema, never before had the imagination enjoyed such a protean referent. Even if Lorca did not live long enough to fulfil his potential in the new medium, its stimulus and influence have left an indelible trace in his work.

Viaje a la luna [*Journey to the Moon*] (Antonio Monegal)

When, during his travels to New York and Havana between 1929 and 1930, Lorca wrote his one and only film script, *Viaje a la luna*, journeying transcended the category of real-life experience to become a theme in the artist's work. His collection of poems, *Poeta en Nueva York*, is, in some respects, an instance of travel writing too, but it is in *Viaje a la luna* that the journey represents more than either a motive or pretext to become the text's very mode of articulation and prime mover. No journey as such is represented in the script; instead we witness its metaphorization, its use as a vehicle for metaphor, resulting in the most curious of paradoxes: journey is the very vehicle in which we travel. It does not refer us to any concrete experience, yet is still anchored in the experience of the journey that Lorca undertook in 1929.

Lorca's New York journey was, in many senses, responsible for the enigmatic character of the work produced there. It gave rise to a new kind of writing that, although indebted in great part to Lorca's influence by, and previous contact with, the Spanish avant-garde and friends such as Dalí and Buñuel, also owed something to his personal discovery of America. The catalyst and impulse for this writing was his experience of a city steeped in a modernity that Spain could only dream of at the time. Yet Lorca saw the sinister side of such modernity: it was a space and time of alienation, of anguish and anxiety. He struggled with the tension between the familiar and the strange, searching for points of reference and identity that might allow him to bridge the cultural gap and bring other worlds closer to his own. The experience led Lorca to adapt his poetry so that he might respond to the very challenge of speaking the unspeakable.

In the wake of the challenge to the writer have come those facing readers and, in particular, critics who have constantly struggled not only with the difficulty of establishing definitive versions of the texts of Lorca's American cycle – namely *Poeta en Nueva York, El público, Así que pasen cinco años* and, of course, the film script, *Viaje a la luna* – but also with their complexity and opaqueness. If these texts are enigmatic, it is not only because of the experience that they seek to communicate, but also because of the poetics they follow and the strategies they adopt. Despite their generic differences, the texts cited clearly have a common poetic approach. They present us with systems of unlikely associations where there is a complete disregard for logical and semantic continuity, thus producing fractures in the production of meaning that are often irreparable. Lorca had already tested such an approach in his *Poemas en prosa* [*Prose Poems*], in which the traces of his aesthetic dialogue with Dalí are clearly visible. This suggests that Lorca's new artistic phase began in the summer of 1928. However, it was during his time in New York, and subsequently Havana, that this new Lorcan tendency would come into its own.

What is significant about this journey is not the fact of journeying itself but the crisis engendered as the poet comes face to face with the imperatives of modernity and of desire. The avant-garde found in the dynamism of the urban landscape, in the movement of machines and in the accompanying dehumaniza-tion, the very engine of modernity. The city emerges as a signifying machine that devours the old values binding together artistic tradition. Of all the machines participating in the construction of this new world's language, none is so closely linked technologically or symbolically to the aesthetic transformation of urban and industrial society as the cinematographic one. What is new about cinema is not its message but the medium itself. Being the only art form in which movement is an inherent property, cinema was allowed to establish itself as the emblem of the dynamic pace of modernity. In *Viaje a la luna*, Lorca ventures into an art form that both exemplified novelty and was new to him.

The journey into the unknown thus acquires additional connotations. For Lorca, writing this text meant demonstrating his ability to adapt to changing circumstances and to the demands of a different medium and aesthetic. His intention was not merely to write a film script, but rather a script that could be turned into an avant-garde film.

Lorca wrote *Viaje a la luna*, in just a few days, in response to conversations he had in New York with the Mexican filmmaker and painter, Emilio Amero. The kind of films Amero made, as well as the subject of his conversation with Lorca, no doubt had an influence on the script. Amero had just finished shooting an abstract, avant-garde short about calculating machines, entitled *777*, which he showed to Lorca. According to Amero, 'Lorca vio la posibilidad de hacer un guión más o menos como el mío, con el uso directo del movimiento' [Lorca envisaged writing a script more or less like my own, with the direct use of movement].[27] Given that Lorca later gave Amero his manuscript as a gift, telling him that he could do with it as he pleased, that something might just come out of it, it would not be too fanciful to presume that during the writing Lorca had kept in mind the style of the person possibly destined to shoot the film. In fact, Amero did begin shooting the film in Mexico after Lorca's death, in homage to the poet, but never managed to finish it.

We also know from Amero himself that the two men spoke about the première in Paris, in June 1929, of *Un chien andalou* [An Andalusian Dog]. Although it is unlikely that Lorca would have seen Buñuel's and Dalí's film, he must have known enough about it for a number of echoes to emerge in *Viaje a la luna* and, above all, for his script to have been in some respects a riposte to a film in which he apparently perceived a personal attack on himself, believing, as Buñuel tells us, that he was the 'perro andaluz' [Andalusian dog] referred to in the title.[28] Insofar as the increasingly close relationship between Dalí and Buñuel, culminating in this collaboration, coincides with Dalí's criticism of Lorca's aesthetic and the increasing distance between the two artists, it is difficult to draw a line between emotional tensions and artistic controversy.[29] For at least a short period, towards the end of the 1920s, the three artists influenced one another and shared certain characteristics that concurred with the poetic renovation that would determine the direction of the Spanish vanguard. Yet although in this work, as with others of the cycle, we may see converging, even thematically, preoccupations both of a personal and artistic kind, what is important about the contribution of *Viaje a la luna* is that it turns its attention to the cinema.

Since its birth, both as technology and art form, the cinema has meant the consummation of the desire to see, which has traditionally been associated with realistic representation. However, the aesthetic direction with which *Viaje a la luna* engages is not that of the realistic gaze, to which the cinema has most accustomed us, but that of the poetic gaze, corresponding to the author's own

[27] Amero's testimony can be found in Richard Dier's introduction to Federico García Lorca, *Trip to the Moon*, *New Directions*, 18 (1964), 33–5.

[28] Although Lorca passed through Paris in June on his way to New York, there is no evidence that he managed to see his friends' film before speaking to Amero. On the other hand, we know that he felt that the 'perro andaluz' was an allusion to him (see Luis Buñuel, *Mi último suspiro* [Barcelona: Plaza y Janés, 1982], 154, and the interview in *Contracampo*, 16 [1980], 33), although Buñuel himself has denied any connection. A plausible explanation, given by Marie Laffranque ('Equivocar el camino. Regards sur un scénario de Federico García Lorca', in Michèle Ramond (ed.), *Hommage à Federico García Lorca*, Travaux de l'Université de Toulouse-Le Mirail, Série A20 [Toulouse: Université de Toulouse-le-Mirail, 1982], 91, is that Lorca received news about the film via publications relating to its opening, like the review by Eugenio Montes in *La Gaceta Literaria* (15 June 1929). He might also have become acquainted with its script by reading a number of magazines, like, for example, *La Révolution Surréaliste* (15 December 1929).

[29] Agustín Sánchez Vidal provides a thorough study of the relations and exchanges between the three artists in 'El viaje a la luna de un perro andaluz', *Valoración actual de la obra de García Lorca*, eds Alfonso Esteban y Jean-Pierre Étienvre (Madrid: Casa de Velázquez / Univ. Complutense, 1988), 141–61, and in his book *Buñuel, Lorca, Dalí: El enigma sin fin*, 2nd edn (Barcelona: Planeta, 1996).

inclinations, but equally to tendencies within avant-garde cinema at the time. In Lorca's script what we witness is the conjunction of two distinct definitions and orders of image: the visible image that cinema provides and the poetic image that is a construction belonging to the order of discourse.

What Lorca intended to put before our eyes was not the image as an object of desire that stimulates our senses, but the image as poetic figure, the object of our desire to interpret. The enigmatic quality deriving from the poetic construction of these images presents spectators with an invitation and challenge to read with their gaze. This text, exceptional in terms of the trajectory of Lorca's *oeuvre*, is a fascinating illustration of the double nature of the concept of the image, of the difference between visual and poetic images.

The oneiric and poetic universe that is constantly invoked in order to explain the unusual associations populating the works of the New York cycle acquires a different dimension in the context of its treatment by film. The images projected in a film cannot be read in the same way as the written word; when reading the script we have to try to visualize it, implying that any definitive conclusions about it are dependent on our having seen the filmed product.

What we have, then, concentrated in this film, are two distinct manifestations of a desire for the visual: Lorca's desire to realize the film and our desire to be able to see it. *Viaje a la luna* was, until a few years ago, what we might call a virtual film, merely the idea of a film. Lorca embarked on his project wanting to show that he too could do cinema; that he too could put, as his friends had done, his poetic images onto a screen. It has been up to us to imagine the film of the script, to read not as readers but as spectators. Up until the centenary of Lorca's birth the object of our desire was an unmade film. Today, however, we can satisfy our desire by watching an actual film of the script directed by the artist Frederic Amat.

Amat devoted many years to the rigorous reading of *Viaje a la luna*. During these years his interpretation of the text took shape in the form of a storyboard in which he drew each and every shot. This impressive pictorial collection constitutes the first translation into images of *Viaje a la luna*, which, although indebted to Lorca's work, can only be understood from the painter's own viewpoint and in relation to his own work. Amat remained faithful to the script, but without compromising his own artistic vision: a vision as original as it is revitalizing for the text, and one that makes sense of the decision to make the film in the present day. Amat knew how to take on the double role of interpreter and creator. The script does not lend itself to a conventional cinematic treatment. It contains few narrative or dramatic elements as it is constructed as a visual poem consisting of images that have a metaphorical value. For this reason it required the attention of someone who lay at the intersection of artistic systems, who could both read a poem and visualize it, and produce an interpretation of its images.[30] With these images as his starting point, Amat shot a film that is the projection of a dream, the very culmination of a desire.

---

30 In addition to the film itself and the painted storyboard, of which there have been several exhibitions, there is a published record of Amat's work, with images of the story-

We ought to bear in mind that visual images are a primary source of desire, that desire is stirred by the act of looking. The eye is one of our sexual organs. Hence the voyeuristic component associated with the cinematographic phenomenon since its inception. This tendency has been expressed by way of the complicity of the spectator's gaze and the camera. Both vehicle and receptacle for desire, cinema projects our fantasies onto the screen but, what is more, as an image in time, also permits the sequential unfolding of the very process of desire. Lorca exploits this dual dimension of the cinematographic image and, should we need to find a unifying theme for *Viaje a la luna*, this is none other than desire itself. The text presents us with a succession of images of desire, as well as its opposites: fear, aversion and frustration. But it does not do so by presenting us with desirable images in a conventional sense, but instead with metaphors for the act, the very process, of desire.

Lorca turns the desiring subject into a theme via, among other things, the constant references to the eye and visual perception. In section 4, there appears a 'Cabeza asustada que mira fija un punto y se disuelve sobre una cabeza de alambre con un fondo de agua' [Frightened head staring at a point and fades out to a wire head, against a background of water].[31] In 13 we have 'un gran plano de un ojo sobre una doble exposición de peces' [close-up of an eye, double-exposed above fish] (*Viaje*, p. 62 / *Trip*, p. 634). And in 18 'La luna se corta y aparece un dibujo de una cabeza que vomita y abre y cierra los ojos' [The moon is cut open, and a drawing of a head appears, vomiting, blinking] (*Viaje*, p. 63 / *Trip*, p. 634). These strange images are striking and in stark contrast with the kind of cinema to which we are accustomed. The eye-motif, of course, performs an important function, also in association with the moon, in *Un chien andalou*. Buñuel's film presents us with a cloud passing across the moon and the cutting of an eye; in Lorca's script we have fish passing across an eye and a splitting moon. The erotic content of the metaphor constructed by Buñuel has been studied at length, the conjunction of round and long figures generally interpreted as an evocation of sexual penetration.

Before the possibility of watching a film of the script *Viaje a la luna* materialized, our desiring gaze found partial satisfaction in another set of visual manifestations of Lorca's imagination, namely his drawings, to which Amat himself turned in the process of making his film. In these drawings there are numerous instances where Lorca has focused on the motif of the gaze. Licence to substitute or satisfy our desire vicariously by gazing at the drawings instead of the

---

board, the film and the shooting, in an illustrated edition of *Viaje a la luna* (Barcelona: Edicions de l'Eixample-Centre de Cultura Contemporània de Barcelona-Comisión del Centenario de Federico García Lorca-Institut d'Edicions de la Diputació de Barcelona, 1998).

[31] Quotations of the script in Spanish are from Federico García Lorca, *Viaje a la luna*, ed. Antonio Monegal (Valencia: Ed. Pre-Textos, 1994) and translations into English from Federico García Lorca, *Trip to the Moon*, trans. by Greg Simon and Steven F. White, in *Collected Poems*, ed. Christopher Maurer (New York: Farrar, Straus and Giroux, 1991), 631–9. *Viaje*, p. 60 / *Trip*, p. 633.

film has, in a sense, been given by Lorca's inclusion of drawings in his script, as in section 18, cited above, or in 38, 'Doble exposición de barrotes que pasan sobre un dibujo: *Muerte de Santa Rodegunda*' [Double-exposed iron bars that pass over a drawing: The Death of St Radegunda] (*Viaje*, p. 68 / *Trip*, p. 636). The title is that of an actual drawing by Lorca, dated New York 1929 (that is to say, in the period during which the script was written) and now with the Fundación García Lorca. Moreover, this drawing of the martyrdom of a saint matches the description made in section 18 of 'una cabeza que vomita y abre y cierra los ojos' [a head appears, vomiting, blinking].[32]

The drawings, along with the multiple echoes in other works of the New York cycle, serve as an extensive intertextual framework that renders the script neither as strange nor as undecipherable as it seemed at first sight, or at the first reading. What we have is a productive dialogue between the arts, and artists, that must inevitably be considered in any analysis and interpretation. In order to do cinema Lorca has recourse to drawing and, above all, to poetry, and he makes use of images and motifs that he shares with his friends, as well as those that have sprung from his own particular poetic universe.

The poetic and visual images of the script together convey the dynamic of desire and frustration. It is in the representation of this dynamic that we intuit something in the nature of a plot line, however unconventional or elusive it may be. Desire is represented as a journey, but not a journey in space – a movement between two points – rather, a journey in time, that is to say, both across real-life time and filmic time or sequence. It is the choice of shot sequence, often combining seemingly unconnected images, that gives rise to the allusions and associations between images, allowing meaning to be constructed and unfold, yet evade us nonetheless, as if we were pursuing an object (of desire) constantly beyond our reach. At the same time, the film presents a journey through the stages of life: we find reference to childhood, in the child given a beating and the two children who walk along singing with their eyes shut; and to adolescence, with the boy in a bathing suit whose mouth another man covers with a harlequin's costume. These are violent images associated with punishment and the repression of desire. The character grows and splits into a young man in a harlequin's costume and into a nude on whose body the circulatory system is drawn, like on an anatomical doll. These two figures are associated, since the nude initially appears holding the harlequin's costume, and although they both go their separate ways they actually turn out to be the same character. The harlequin's costume may thus be understood to be a disguise by which to mask the truth of the desire, a truth represented by the man whose veins are exposed.

As of section 56 of the script there is a series of shots in which a young woman and the harlequin take part. These offer a degree of continuity:

---

32 The drawing is catalogued at no. 161 in Mario Hernández, *Line of Light and Shadow: The Drawings of Federico García Lorca*, trans. Christopher Maurer (Durham, NC: Duke University Press, 1991); drawing no. 162, untitled, is another possible variation on the same theme.

56.   [. . .]. La muchacha y el arlequín suben en el ascensor.
57.   Suben en el ascensor y se abrazan.
58.   Plano de un beso sensual.
59.   El muchacho muerde a la muchacha en el cuello y tira violentamente de sus cabellos.
60.   Aparece una guitarra. Y una mano rápida corta las cuerdas con unas tijeras.
61.   La muchacha se defiende del muchacho, y éste con gran furia le da otro beso profundo y pone los dedos pulgares sobre los ojos como para hundir los dedos en ellos. (*Viaje*, pp. 73–4)

[56.   The harlequin and the naked girl go up in the elevator.
57.   They go up in the elevator and embrace.
58.   Shot of a sensual kiss.
59.   The boy bites the girl's neck and pulls violently on her hair.
60.   A guitar appears, and a hand quickly cuts the strings with scissors.
61.   The girl defends herself against the boy, and he, furiously, gives her another deep kiss, and covers her eyes with his thumbs, as if to plunge them in.] (*Trip*, p. 638)

The harlequin shows himself to be a violent figure. In the act of blinding we also find an echo from *Un chien andalou* and the association between eroticism and knowledge, between desire and the gaze: the thumbs appear to want to penetrate the eyes, in a metaphorical rape. The play on shape connects the eye and the moon once more, and recalls also a number of Dalí's paintings where fingers have phallic connotations. Once the violent confrontation has been set up along with the barrier posed by his disguise, the male character adopts his other facet:

62.   Grita la muchacha y el muchacho de espaldas se quita la americana y una peluca y aparece el hombre de las venas.
63.   Entonces ella se disuelve en un busto de yeso blanco y el hombre de las venas la besa apasionadamente.
64.   Se ve el busto de yeso con huellas de labios y huellas de manos. (*Viaje*, pp. 74–5)

62.   The girl screams, and the boy, back turned, removes his sport coat and a wig, and the veined man appears.
63.   Then she fades out to a white plaster bust, and the veined man kisses her passionately.
64.   Shot of the plaster bust with lip and hand prints.] (*Trip*, p. 639)

The revelation of hidden passion does not lead to the positive consummation of the relation with the girl, but to her subsequent movement towards a more abstract form. The man with exposed veins does not succeed in gaining access to the woman in flesh and blood, but instead to an idealized representation in the form of the plaster bust. This constitutes, in a sense, a fetishistic displacement that corresponds with the shots in *Un chien andalou* where the male character finally manages to caress the woman's body. Her body turns first into a bust and then into a pair of buttocks; impersonal objects that are suggestive of the ambiguous nature of the man's sexual impulses. In section 66 of *Viaje a la luna*, in face of woman transformed into archetype, there is a violent gush of 'grifos que echan agua de manera violenta' [faucets violently gushing water] (*Viaje*, p. 75 / *Trip*, p. 639), as a metaphor for sexual climax.

In section 67, the consummation of erotic desire is accompanied by the death of the character with exposed veins, 'sobre periódicos abandonados y arenques' [among discarded newspapers and herrings] (*Viaje*, p. 75 / *Trip*, p. 639). In 68, 'aparece una cama y unas manos que cubren un muerto' [A bed appears, and hands that cover a corpse] (*Viaje*, p. 75 / *Trip*, p. 639). The repetition of the image of the bed, with which the script opened, closes the circle and initiates the culmination of the journey. That the sexual climax should lead to death, and that the satisfaction of desire should, therefore, be achieved in death itself, is a theme reiterated in literary tradition and in Lorca's work in particular. In his symbolic system, the moon, among other things (including love and eroticism), signifies death, and it is this significance that, undercover till this point, now surfaces in our reading of *Viaje a la luna*. The final destination of the journey is split between eroticism and death, two aspects of one desire, thus revealing the dark side of the moon.

But *Viaje a la luna* does not conclude with this rather obvious ending. Nor is it here that the script itself ends. What follows is a series of final images that are themselves laden with irony:

69.   Viene un muchacho con una bata blanca y guantes de goma y una muchacha vestida de negro. Pintan un bigote con tinta a una cabeza terrible de muerto. Y se besan con grandes risas.
70.   De ellos surge un cementerio y se les ve besarse sobre una tumba.
71.   Plano de un beso cursi de cine con otros personajes.
72.   Y al final con prisa la luna y árboles con viento. (*Viaje*, p. 76)

[69.   A boy appears in a white coat and rubber gloves comes in, and a girl dressed in black. They paint a mustache with ink on a terrible dead man's head. And they kiss with much laughter.
70.   A cemetery emerges from them, and they are seen kissing over a tomb.
71.   Shot of a vulgar cinematic kiss with other people.
72.   And finally a quick shot of the moon and trees in the wind.] (*Trip*, p. 639)

The superimposition of the kiss and the cemetery emphasizes the final meaning of the journey and sets it in an ironic frame. Parody is brought to the fore by the fact that other characters perform the 'cinematic kiss'. In his film, Amat addresses this detail by incorporating an extract from an old film by Thomas Edison: the very first kiss in cinema history. This shot, like a knowing wink to the spectator, succeeds in bringing the irony home; after all, it is not the characters, but the very text that distances itself from its own tragic message. The insertion of a discourse so contradictory in tone thus opens the way for a new reading of the script as a critique of the conception of sexual relations dominant in contemporary romantic cinema. The journey, far from coming to a close, opens on to other vistas, as many vistas as there are possible interpretations of the meaning of the script.

Lorca in cinema (Alberto Mira)

Human lives rarely have a point or a meaning. And, we need to be reminded, this applies equally to the lives of significant historical figures: events just happen, shaped by chance, just as with everybody else. Later, history, tradition and scholarship slowly attach a meaning to haphazard lifelines. The lives of characters in narrative or in film, however, need to have a point. This distinction is the key to the relationship between historical figures, biographical accounts and fictional treatments, including the biopic. When put into any kind of narrative, certain aspects of the historical individual have to disappear; others will become more prominent. In featuring an actual character, something essentially dramatic in his or her existence has to be identified and structured.

In the case of Federico García Lorca, there are added difficulties in that the historical figure is a writer. What a writer does is not very interesting visually: sports people, dancers, actors, even painters or scientists do things that can be seductive in cinematic terms, from winning a championship to finding a formula that will save lives. Writers, more often than not, face blank pages or hit the keys of their typewriters. The creative process in their case is invisible, pointedly unspectacular. Of course writers do other things: Lorca became the artistic director of a theatre company, travelled, met famous people and, as the films discussed below remind audiences, played the piano. Still, writing remains as the justification of his fame, and somehow needs to be brought into focus when representing the historical figure.

Of course, attempts have been made to make writing resonant in other levels of experience. For instance, Virginia Woolf's overcoming of writer's block in Stephen Daldry's *The Hours* seems to have an impact on the lives of other women decades later. If Lorca sitting at the table while he pens the New York poems lacks interest, his experience of New York can be easily dramatized. Besides a number of clear dramatic through-lines, the cinematic representation of a historical figure needs structure. A narrative arch has to be introduced, sometimes even invented, to make the character work dramatically. Such an arch will end up falsifying the truth (lives do not proceed in terms of neatly organized structures) and oversimplifying it. In the case of García Lorca, such a narrative arch comes naturally from biographical accounts, as his life is riddled with highs and lows, both personal and historical (his upbringing in colourful Granada, encounters in the Residencia de Estudiantes, relationships with such luminaries as Buñuel and Dalí, literary success, his trip to New York and Cuba, the proclamation of the Second Republic, the Civil War and all that piano playing as a background) and ends with a shooting that can easily be taken as a symbol of the political turmoil of the times.

Lastly, and again Lorca is a case in point, countless biographical accounts contain an official truth that must be engaged with in one way or another, whether it be to challenge it or uphold it. It is significant that Lorca's biographer Ian Gibson was involved in two of the three films we will be discussing, partly as a guarantee that it was the 'truth' itself that was being represented. Yet narrative choices (what to include, what not to include) are clearly political, as well as artistic, decisions. Lorca's politics, for example, can be emphasized or not, depending on the audiences to which the text is addressed, as is the case too with Lorca's sexual orientation. The fact that his homosexuality is often a touchy subject with biographers implies that, for some, giving it any prominence at all is tantamount to placing a blemish on the character portrayed (after all, there is a tendency for biopics to become hagiographies – hagiographies, of course, that obey the logic of the authors' own ideals).

The three representations of Lorca on film that we will discuss here serve to illustrate different approaches to the writer, as well as different ways in which a historical figure can be represented in narrative terms. The first is an extended biopic: the TV mini-series *Lorca: Muerte de un poeta* [*Lorca: Death of a Poet*] (1987) – the only film that focuses strictly on the life of the poet himself. The other two instances, *The Disappearance of García Lorca* (1997) and *A un dios desconocido* [*To an Unknown God*] (1977), present Lorca as a secondary figure, albeit one who is central to the films' meaning.

Lorca as biopic – *Lorca: Muerte de un poeta*

As a film genre, the biopic can be regarded as a balancing act between two sets of conventions: the biography and classical film narrative. Both seem to pull the text in different directions. On the one hand, the serious biographical work calls for truth and thoroughness. Biographical narratives are often fragmentary, full of gaps, discontinuities and unresolved issues. Events do not always make sense, they are seldom wholly justified; hypotheses are put forward, but not necessarily confirmed. All of which goes clearly against the main impulse behind classical Hollywood discourse, which aims for consistency, linearity, a clear, strong narrative arch, a single central action. Following the needs of classical narrative, the protagonist has to be presented as a man or a woman with a wish or something to be achieved in the course of the narrative; the narrative itself deals with a single action as far as possible: truth and accuracy are easily betrayed in favour of narrative impact. Of course, around such single action, one can place diversions and episodes that 'really happened': whereas the classic George Arliss biopics made for Warners in the 1930s emphasize the dramatic and show little respect for actual events, modern biopics such as Scorsese's *The Aviator* are more careful about the truth and variety of the subject's life. Still, the convention demanding a secure narrative arch – the fact that the narrative 'must know where it is going' – is strong.

Although *Lorca: Muerte de un poeta* was conceived as a six-hour TV miniseries, rather than a feature film (a two-hour film was subsequently released commercially, focusing on the poet's last days), it nonetheless reveals some of the issues attending to the representation of the writer in biopics. The series was conceived of as a prestigious enterprise, and is part of a number of government-funded quality mini-series for Spanish Television. Many of these dealt with long, substantial literary works by the likes of Blasco Ibáñez, Pérez Galdós, Clarín or Torrente Ballester, although other series at the time included ones on the scientist Ramón y Cajal, the painter Francisco de Goya and Saint Teresa. *Muerte de un poeta* was directed by highly regarded anti-Franco director Juan Antonio Bardem and boasted a number of cameos from famous performers (like Nuria Espert, Lola Gaos, Margarita Lozano or José Maria Pou). Biographer Ian Gibson is listed as writer together with Bardem and filmmaker Mario Camus.

The challenge was to turn Lorca's story into a consistent arch. To this end, it would have been necessary to establish just what lay at the centre of the principal character and what should be developed as his main motivation. It is telling, therefore, that the biographer should be listed as scriptwriter, thus blurring the limits between biography and biopic. For the writer of biopics needs to be flexible with the truth and favour the dramatic needs of the story. In enlisting the help of Gibson, the team responsible for the series suggests an emphasis on truth that can only work against this. In fact, the writers cannot quite make up their minds as to what the central motivation of the character is: consequently, Lorca, played by the British actor Nickolas Grace (dubbed into Spanish), remains as the passive centre of events; he moves from one famous location to another and things just happen to him. In spite of some brief childhood memories presenting him in communion with nature at the beginning, it is hard to know what moves the poet. This is not surprising: biographical accounts of Lorca's life tend to be based on testimonies of people surrounding him, and the differences between all of these testimonies render the character a cipher for which the final meaning is provided by the biographer himself. Classical film narration requires character consistency, otherwise narration moves into the experimental domain (as in *Citizen Kane*) and consciously goes for an ambiguity that was not in the writer's agenda.

The script may, nonetheless, be summarized in terms of three classical Hollywood narrative 'acts' of almost equal length: act 1 (episodes one and two in the series) includes the poet's upbringing and education up until the success of his *Romancero gitano*; act 2 (episodes three and four) covers his successful years as a writer, his trip to the United States and the proclamation of the Spanish Republic; finally, act 3 (comprising the last two episodes, five and six) focuses on the writer's last days, narrated in some detail and moving away from the protagonist himself in order to present the set of political circumstances that framed his death. The death of the poet is shown at the start of each episode – a reminder of the narrative thrust. In this way, the event becomes the teleological centre of the narrative, the suggestion being that everything in Lorca's life led eventually to his death. Yet it is an odd suggestion and one that is not borne out by the narrative events represented. What is more, even if we take account of the difficulties of incorporating writing activities effectively into cinematic narratives, in *Muerte de un poeta* Lorca's creative influences and the sources of his inspiration are conspicuously absent. Highly reductive in this respective is, for example, the representation of Lorca's New York trip: images of a series of postcards of the city filling in as background for the poet in different poses.

The narrative strategy in *Muerte de un poeta* is clear: to select a number of episodes that are representative of Lorca's life. The format allows for any number of such episodes. However, the problem is that, in attending firstly to the needs of biography (attempting as they do to pack a great deal of biographical information into each scene), the creators consistently ignore the needs of dramatization. Consequently, the narrative is barely more than a series of juxtaposed vignettes: in some of them there is violence, in others Lorca does a variety of things (including, of course, the opportunity to hit those piano keys several times).

One key example of what is wrong with the portrayal of Lorca here is its treatment of the poet's 'confession' to Cipriano Rivas Cherif about his homosexuality. Firstly, it is worth remembering that the episode of Lorca's conversation with Rivas Cherif is included in Gibson's biography and is, as Gibson himself points out, based on Rivas Cherif's own account.[33] 'If we are to credit Riva Cherif's reconstruction of that conversation,' writes Gibson, 'Lorca went on to relate his homosexuality to his early experience, saying that he had never recovered when, before he was seven, his best friend in Fuente Vaqueros school, slightly younger than himself, was taken away by his parents to another village' (Gibson 1989, p. 420). By highlighting his source (on this and other occasions), Gibson allows for the possibility that the episode need not be treated as fact; an ambiguity, however, that is not permitted by the biopic in which all events are treated equally as the truth, regardless of their source. Yet more to the point, in the biopic the moment of Lorca's important confession has not been prepared in the rest of the work. Indeed, the statement about his homosexuality makes little sense if anguish about sexual orientation has not been presented earlier. Yet the writers shy away from implying too much about Lorca's relationship with, for example, Salvador Dalí: this would have begun to provide some ground for the confession scene. The question is not whether Lorca was or was not tortured about his sexuality (or whether Rivas Cherif's version of events is accurate or not), but rather how to construct a through-line in the biopic to provide valid and effective dramatic moments. The authors of *Muerte de un poeta* attempt a balance between truth and the spectacular that forgets the dramatic. Ultimately, they are responding to the wrong dichotomy, for the choice they must make is not between truth and drama, but between consistent narrative, true to character, and the inconsistent collection of moments in the life of the writer.

---

33   See Ian Gibson, *Federico García Lorca: A Life* (London: Faber & Faber, 1989), 420–1.

Lorca as Thriller – *The Disappearance of García Lorca*

The difficulties of the biographical approach are circumvented in two other films with the presence of the poet: Marcos Zurinaga's *The Disappearance of García Lorca* and Jaime Chávarri's *A un dios desconocido*. Zurinaga's film is constructed as a thriller about a quest for the truth. The protagonist is Ricardo, a writer living in exile in Puerto Rico, to where he emigrated with his father after the Spanish Civil War, and who fleetingly knew Lorca as a child. Finding out the real reasons behind the writer's death becomes something of a life obsession for Ricardo, and he returns to Granada in 1958 to investigate what really happened. The premise feels forced: in the first place, the circumstances of the poet's death are more or less clear for audiences of the 1990s and have already been eluci-dated elsewhere by Gibson (co-writer of this film);[34] in the second place, the answers provided in the film do not contribute to a radically new perspective on the events.

Lorca is represented through Ricardo's childhood memories, in a series of flashbacks. In particular, the boy attends the first night of Lorca's *Yerma*, where conservative audiences protest that the play is against traditional Spanish values. After the curtain comes down he meets the writer briefly. This meeting will haunt him for the rest of his life. In light of this, one can understand why the issue of Lorca's sexuality is not present in this adaptation, as it would bring with it associations that might weigh dangerously on the narrative. As it is, the writers are at pains to stop such associations (the plot features the idea of betrayal between friends and, at most, only a 'particular friendship' between two adolescents).

For Ricardo, Lorca remains a figure that stands for the country he lost and misses. García Lorca becomes the excuse that sets the thriller in motion and is quickly pushed to the margins of the narrative. In good old Hollywood fashion, a love story is thrown in, there is a 'deep throat' character who supplies key infor-mation and the resolution is one that concerns the father–son relationship: the narrative pay-off is that it was Ricardo's father who was forced to pull the trigger at Viznar.

There is a forced parallelism between Ricardo and the poet as writers who want to speak out against external pressures. Lorca will die for it; Ricardo will have to live with the consequences. Lorca is, for the protagonist, just somebody who fought for freedom and lost. The quest for Lorca becomes an illustration of the impossibility to recover the past. The choice of Andy García to play Lorca is also odd. It can be understand in box office terms, but it is not clear what he contributes to the character. The irony is that García was a prominent anti-Castro

---

[34] In addition to his biography, see Ian Gibson, *The Assassination of Federico García Lorca* (Harmondsworth: Penguin, 1983); originally published in Spanish as *La represión nacionalista de Granada en 1936 y la muerte de Federico García Lorca* (Paris: Ruedo Ibérico, 1971).

activist; thus in his portrayal of Lorca, the fight for freedom becomes identified, potentially, with the struggle against Fidel Castro.

By turning the search for Lorca into a thriller, the film does at least allow the character of Lorca to be defined in dramatic terms. Whereas *Lorca: Muerte de un poeta* presented an inconsistent entity, here we have a simply outlined freedom fighter and peace activist who acquires, in this respect, a relevance to the present.

Lorca as Psychological Drama: *A un Dios desconocido*

A un dios desconocido constitutes the most complex cinematic take on Lorca, even if the poet himself only appears as a distant presence in white looking out of a window. The film is about dealing with the past in the post-Franco period, and the memory of Lorca becomes a bridge between the pre-Civil War years and the Spanish Transition. The protagonist is José (Héctor Alterio), who works as a magician in a nightclub. His parents were servants of a wealthy Granada family and he had an emotional and sexual attachment to the family son, Pedro, in the troubled summer of 1936. Forty years later, after Pedro's death, he goes back to visit the house where he spent his childhood (even if he never crosses the threshold of the main building).

The film opens on a sun-drenched afternoon before the war. José and Pedro play in the garden, although the latter's mother is against the servant boy being there. Someone, a visitor, is heard playing the piano. It will become clear that this person is García Lorca himself. Pedro seems to be fascinated by him (but too shy to come too close), and it is this fascination that will be passed on to José. This is the only moment the poet shares location (albeit mostly off-screen) with the protagonists. Still, his presence is key to the plot. Every night for the rest of his life, before going to bed, José goes through a strange ritual, which he keeps secret even from his lover Miguel (Xabier Elorriaga): he undresses slowly, while listening to a recorded version of Lorca's 'Oda a Walt Whitman' ['Ode to Walt Whitman']. During his visit to Granada, he steals a picture of Lorca owned by the deceased Pedro, which he will from then on keep by his bedside table. Lorca is presented as his link to the past and to his feelings for Pedro. Later in the film, during a party at the house he meets an older man who claims to have had an affair with Pedro and suggests that he also had sex with Lorca. In an extraordinary plot twist, this man performs fellatio on him, and there are connotations here of tradition and knowledge being transmitted. It will also work as catharsis for the protagonist. At the end of the film, José, somehow liberated by a series of events in the plot, will be able to let Miguel penetrate his intimacy by letting him watch his nightly ritual.

The presence of Lorca in this film has some elements in common with the *The Disappearance of Lorca*: the writer is represented via someone else's perspective and in terms of the impact he has on someone else's life. Lorca's influence is once more presented in the form of an inheritance from the pre-Civil War years (which in the film appear as some kind of utopia of desire), and this inheritance suggests freedom (for José, this can be read as sexual, rather than political). In both films, the character has to engage with the icon in order to be at peace with the past. In both narratives, this engagement is successful.

Yet one important difference is that Hollywood conventions are ignored in Chávarri's film. It is hard to pin down in narrative terms what really happened on those afternoons (such obscurity may have to do with certain problems attending the representation of homosexual desire in cinema at the time in Spain). Lorca is, for José, a presence that has to do with his inner self, with his sexual identity. There is also an element of class alienation: José was poor; Lorca, Pedro and the man at the party belong to the wealthier classes from which José is systematically excluded. At the same time, sex with Lorca becomes a metaphor for the handing down of a cultural heritage. José, therefore, has a spiritual link with the poet that goes beyond the mere image of Lorca as freedom fighter: in a way, Lorca becomes his guardian angel, somebody who brings comfort and spiritual advice from the tape recording of his ode. The film is clearly not about Lorca and it does not aspire to provide even a portrait of the writer. Instead, Lorca is treated as icon; his legacy makes sense only in terms of the way other characters conceive of it.[35]

[35] See also Chris Perriam, '*A un dios desconocido*: Resurrecting a Queer Identity under Lorca's Spell', *Bulletin of Hispanic Studies*, 76, 1 (January 1999), 77–91.

6

Religion

ERIC SOUTHWORTH

In this chapter we will refer to both religious belief and practice: to questions of a theological and metaphysical nature, relating to Christianity and other religions; and to ways in which religious belief impinges on people's lives, as individuals and as members of societies. Such an approach accommodates Lorca's central conviction, shared with Nietzsche, that 'God is dead', and his exploration of the human consequences of that. Art may assuage where metaphysics fails to satisfy. Considered within a context of the history of ideas, Lorca's is not an unusual case, given central trends of Spanish liberal thought: many serious-minded people were repelled by the Catholic Church's doctrinal and political intransigence, but could not quell their anxiety over big questions that refuse to go away.[1] One thinks here, for instance, of the lay ethos of the Residencia de Estudiantes that Lorca himself attended, or of the influence of a figure like Unamuno. The following survey cannot be exhaustive; it will aim, rather, to draw out a number of significant emphases within Lorca's writings.

The youthful writings

In 1986, Eutimio Martín's important study *Federico García Lorca, heterodoxo y mártir* made readers aware of the poet's early established interest in religious questions, closely linked to anxieties about matters of personal identity.[2] The publication of three volumes of Lorcan juvenilia in 1994 subsequently filled out the picture.[3] The main emphases within this sizeable corpus, having links

---

[1] The author's understanding of Spanish Catholicism in the modern period has been greatly aided by Frances Lannon, *Privilege, Persecution, and Prophecy: The Catholic Church in Spain, 1875–1975* (Oxford: Clarendon Press, 1987), and by two books by William J. Callahan: *Church, Politics and Society in Spain, 1750–1874* (Cambridge, MA: Harvard, 1984), and *La iglesia católica en España (1875–2002)* (Barcelona: Crítica, 2000).

[2] Eutimio Martín, *Federico García Lorca, heterodoxo y mártir* (Madrid: Siglo XXI, 1986).

[3] Federico García Lorca, *Poesía inédita de juventud*, ed. Christian de Paepe, Letras Hispánicas 374 (Madrid: Cátedra, 1994); Federico García Lorca, *Prosa inédita de juventud*, ed. Christopher Maurer, Letras Hispánicas 377 (Madrid: Cátedra, 1994); Federico García

with *Impresiones y paisajes* [*Impressions and Landscapes*] (1918) and *Libro de poemas* [*Book of Poems*] (1921), have been ably summarised by Ian Gibson and Christopher Maurer.[4] Briefly recapitulated, for Lorca neither the self nor the cosmos can be satisfactorily understood. An awareness of death and fear of personal extinction, coupled with other forms of religious doubt, for instance about the place of evil, are at the root of human suffering (see for example *Obras completas*, IV, pp. 820–3), and this focuses the issue of whether God exists at all; if so, what is he really like?[5] If he does, he must be an 'artista fracasado' [failed artist] (*Obras completas*, IV, p. 615), silent, absent, unperturbed by the sufferings of his own creation. The idea of Hell is a moral outrage. Jesus was a failure too. He did not bring redemption. A Jesus who is man, not God, was crucified, but never rose from the dead, a perception, this, that Holy Week celebrations and the relative 'deadness' of Easter Sunday in the South tends to confirm.[6] This perception is reflected also in ordinary Spaniards' ultra-realist iconography of the Passion (*Obras completas*, III, pp. 1334–5). Christ's followers have distorted his revolutionary preaching of self-giving love.[7] A major culprit has been a Church in league with other reactionary forces in society; a Church that aggravates human beings' alienated consciousness, by emphasizing a split between the spirit and the flesh. Individuals find lust conquers love, and their ensuing erotic frustration encourages a yearning to recover their lost innocence and the child's unalienated relationship with its mother. The self-defeating escapism of monastic life provides a further instance of the malaise that Lorca identifies. Insofar as there is any hope for man at all, though, it has been incarnated in the lives of certain saints, monastics albeit, whose love was creatively channelled in spite of everything: Francis; Teresa and John of the Cross; and, for their chastity in particular, Aloysius Gonzaga and Stanislaus Kotska. (Lorca's pantheon finds place as well for religious teachers outside Christianity: Mohammed and the Buddha among them.)

Reading Lorca's youthful writings can be heavy going. His expression is often turgid, foggy and clichéd; one cannot advance strong claims for it as finished art. Nor is the writer's thinking especially original for its time. What the early texts do demonstrate, however, is the rightness of one of Martín's fundamental claims: 'El sustrato religioso de los escritos juveniles nutrirá toda su

Lorca, *Teatro inédito de juventud*, ed. Andrés Soria Olmedo, Letras Hispánicas 385 (Madrid: Cátedra, 1994).

[4] Ian Gibson, *Federico García Lorca, 1. De Fuente Vaqueros a Nueva York, 1898–1929* (Barcelona: Grijalbo, 1985), ch. 9; Maurer, *Prosa*, pp. 13–49.

[5] With the exception of his correspondence, reference will be made to Lorca's work in Federico García Lorca, *Obras completas*, ed. Miguel García-Posada, 4 vols (Barcelona: Galaxia Gutenberg / Círculo de Lectores, 1997), [I, 'Poesía'; II, 'Teatro'; III, 'Prosa'; IV, 'Primeros escritos'].

[6] One eloquent expression of Lorca's early Christology is his 'Oración. Jesús de Nazareth' (*Obras completas*, IV, pp. 545–56).

[7] See especially 'El patriotismo' (*Obras completas*, IV, pp. 731–6).

obra' [the religious substrate to the youthful writings will feed all his subsequent work] (Martín, p. 321).

The poetry

Many of the concerns of Lorca's earlier writings 'go underground' after the publication of *Libro de poemas*. His next works often deal in questions of cultural identity. They explore how a more comprehensive understanding of Andalusian culture, with its complex, ancient roots and their survival into modern times, might underpin a critique of Spanish decadence and, more generally, of a Western culture in decline; provide refreshment, also, for modern man in search of his lost soul. The culture of the South can be a better guide to an understanding of the human heart, at an individual and at group level, than rationalizing, dogmatic, systems can. Images of the Passion and of the saints both reflect and mould ordinary rural people's intuitive self-understanding and self-expression.[8] Alongside questions of cultural identity, the poet of *Romancero gitano* [*Gypsy Ballads*] (1928), as of *Canciones* [*Songs*] (1921–4) and *Poema del cante jondo* [*Poem of the Deep Song*] (1921), quietly pursues questions posed already concerning interpersonal relationships and sexuality.[9] In 'Encuentro' [Meeting] from *Poema del cante jondo* (*Obras completas*, I, p. 315), no real meeting of hearts between two persons has taken place, for reasons deliberately left unclear. The speaker dramatizes his resultant pain by reference to Christ's pierced hands: 'En las manos, / tengo los agujeros / de los clavos. / ¿No ves cómo me estoy / desangrando?' [In my hands I have the holes made by the nails. Can't you see how I am bleeding to death?].

One of Lorca's main concerns is how much confusion, mutability and isolation art can allow itself to reflect, or whether it should confine itself to ideals and absolutes. At this stage, where suffering is admitted, it is explored in the

---

[8] In her guise as Our Lady of Sorrows or Virgen de la Soledad in religious processions, Mary figures as a picturesque complement to the Man of Sorrows (see, for example, 'Paso', *Obras completas*, I, pp. 318–19). But she can be sharply ironized also: St Francis holds out against Caperucita's wish to meet her for as long as he can, but when an encounter does take place, Mary appears as an old woman, even if she does attend to the little girl's wounded heart (*Obras completas*, IV, p. 514); in 'El poeta pide ayuda a la Virgen' [The poet asks the Virgin for help], Lorca's conventional opening leads into a prayer for an undivided consciousness like that of the smallest animals, who themselves suffer violent deaths in great numbers ('un millón de muertecitas' [a million little deaths]). It is disconcerting, to say the least, when the poet then addresses Mary once more: 'Tú, Madre siempre terrible' [the *mater terribilis* of a more ancient religion, also alluded to in *Llanto por Ignacio Sánchez Mejías* (*Lament for the Death of Ignacio Sánchez Mejías*)]. 'Ballena de todos los cielos. / Tú, Madre siempre bromista. Vecina del perejil prestado' [Thou, ever-terrible Mother. The whale in every sky. Thou, ever-unserious Mother. Neighbour who comes to borrow a bit of parsley] (*Obras completas*, I, p. 586). The ironies in 'San Gabriel' and 'Romance de la Guardia Civil española' are more mixed (*Obras completas*, I, pp. 431–3, 441–5).

[9] For a particular instance of this, see Eric Southworth, 'Lorca's "San Rafael (Córdoba)" and Some Other Texts', *Modern Language Review*, 94 (1999), 87–102.

context of a 'dehumanized' aesthetic, eschewing sentimentality, the confessional and the anecdotal. Much as Lorca was drawn to doctrines of purism for artistic reasons, very human fears of what he called 'the abyss' were also involved in his drawing back from direct confrontation with painful facts. He wrote to Sebastià Gasch in 1927, 'El abismo y el sueño los *temo* en la realidad de mi vida, en el amor, en el encuentro cotidiano con los demás' [I fear the abyss and dreams in my real life, in love, and in my day-to-day encounters with other people].[10]

Human suffering, however, can promote powerful aesthetic responses to our predicament without necessarily involving interference from the wrong sort of 'personality', as Eliot called it. One place where Lorca found this happening was in authentic *cante jondo* [deep song]. The art of his own *Poema del cante jondo* is concerned to explore the ethos of that form of song and dance, and of the culture in which they are embedded, a world dominated by a sense of *pena* [sorrow or grief], which he elsewhere glossed as 'una lucha de la inteligencia amorosa con el misterio que la rodea y que no puede comprender' [a battle between loving intelligence and the mystery that surrounds it but which it cannot comprehend] (*Obras completas*, III, p. 179). The poet believed in links between *cante jondo* and primitive forms of religion.[11] One section of *Poema del cante jondo* is devoted to the *saeta*, songs associated with Christian Holy Week processions. In large part, the texts of 'Poema de la saeta' are painting pictures in words, without great depth of implication, but one poem, 'Procesión', arguably takes us further (*Obras completas*, I, p. 318). It is generated by a visual similarity between a mythical beast, the unicorn, and the pointed headdress worn by the members of the *cofradías* [lay brotherhoods] that field and accompany the *pasos* of Semana Santa (richly adorned and lifelike religious images carried through the streets). The poem evokes the *paso* of the Ecce Homo, where Pilate shows Jesus to the crowds before his Crucifixion. The unicorn belongs to a different world of cultural reference, however, and its sexual symbolism is plain. So, a scene that turns on Jesus' suffering born of love for fallen humanity is associated with the profane unicorn. The penitents and the figure of Christ himself then imaginatively mutate into figures from romance: Merlin, Orlando and Durandarte. The poem thus as a whole explores connections between the ethos of sacred and sexual love in Andalusian culture, where, what is more, the expression of the sacred includes, but does not always confine itself to, orthodox Christian iconography.

Romancero gitano similarly explores varieties of Andalusian culture. The worlds of Tartessos, of the Romans, of Gypsies with their Oriental roots, of

---

[10] Federico García Lorca, *Epistolario Completo*, ed. Andrew A. Anderson and Christopher Maurer (Madrid: Cátedra, 1997), 520.

[11] 'El cantaor [. . .] celebra un solemne rito, saca las viejas esencias dormidas [. . .] Tiene un profundo sentido religioso del canto' [The *cante jondo* singer celebrates a solemn rite, bringing to light old essences that had been lying dormant. He has a deeply religious sense of the song he sings] (*Obras completas*, III, p. 51).

Christians, Jews and Muslims, all live on into the present in various guises and with different emphases from one place to another. There is a spiritually empty modern world to contend with also. Distinctive religious cultures are involved, as Lorca, the historically aware poetic anthropologist, constructs his complex poetic 'retablo de Andalucía' [exhibition of Andalusia: a *retablo* is both a retable or altar-piece, and a puppet show] (*Obras completas*, III, p. 179). One element in the *retablo*, common to the Jewish, Christian and Muslim worlds, are angels that appear in many guises, sometimes as bored and seedy witnesses to deeds of violence, and as such, possible cousins of those we find in the early play *Jehová* [*Jehovah*]. (Lorca suggests also how angels may be fanciful transpositions of natural phenomena, like clouds or birds of prey.) The heavens do not in any obvious way proclaim peace on earth or good will towards men. In his central triptych of poems about the three great cities of Granada, Cordoba and Seville (*Obras completas*, I, pp. 427–33) and their associated angel guardians, though, other topics remain in play: an awareness of forms taken by popular piety, and of the ways religious art reflects and influences how humans understand and project themselves.

'Romance de la luna luna' [Ballad of the Moon Moon] (*Obras completas*, I, pp. 415–16) personifies the spirit of *cante jondo* dance and its inland setting, with reference to a Cretan moon goddess in a figurine unearthed by Sir Arthur Evans at Knossos. An ancient religious sensibility, involving moon worship and irrational fears, is thus, in transmuted form, seen to live on into modern times, in the purest forms of Southern dance and song. In 'Preciosa y el aire' [Preciosa and the Wind] (I, pp. 416–18), a different mood of cultural expression, one incarnated in Cervantes' chaste and prudent *gitanilla* [little gypsy girl] but which still can yield to panics rooted in sexual fearfulness, is related to perceptions of a pagan deity Boreas, the classical god of the North Wind, and to the figure of Saint Christopher that adorns the wall of many a Christian church. The old gods figuratively live on in the sensibility of simple people. They transform themselves, and so survive, into images of the Christian saints, and this remains true even if the more jaded incoming sophisticates among whom rural people live cannot relate imaginatively to their world at all. In 'La monja gitana' [The Gypsy Nun] (I, pp. 423–4), Lorca returns in an intensely poeticized way to forms of cloistered frustration that his youthful work had lamented. When the gypsy Antoñito el Camborio is arrested by the Civil Guard for an artistic *acte gratuit* involving someone else's lemons (I, pp. 434–5), the poet draws on Christological imagery: the word *Prendimiento* in the poem's title, that usually refers to Christ's arrest; the reed the gypsy carries, echoing Matthew 27:29–30; the 'fuente de sangre, con cinco chorros' [a fount of blood, spouting from five places] recalling Christ's five wounds, alongside imagery from non-religious sources. Camborio is a version of the archetypal Man of Sorrows, and it comes naturally for him and his contemporaries to interpret their experiences as those of an *alter Christus*. Something similar is at work in the 'Romance de la Guardia Civil Española' [Ballad of the Spanish Civil Guard] (I, pp. 441–5) where the persecution of Gypsies is bodied forth in part with reference to folksy Christmas cribs, and, in the case of Rosa la de los Camborios, to the iconography of Christian virgin martyrs, specifically Zurbarán's Santa Águeda (Saint Agatha) calmly carrying her own severed breasts on a dish like egg custards. This representation of the saint embodies attitudes to suffering that gypsy culture still participates in, Rosa and the female martyr from Roman times exhibiting a common sensibility, which Lorca saw embodied also in the Roman Saint Sebastian. Three *romances históricos* [historical ballads] close the *Romancero*, alluding to three major cultural threads in Southern life: the Roman–Christian Eulalia, the later Christian Don Pedro, and the Jewish Thamar and Amnon. 'Martirio de Santa Olalla' [Martyrdom of Saint Eulalia] (I, pp. 446–8) is set in Mérida, but the tale's relevance concerns a clash of cultures to which Lorca referred repeatedly, that between, on the one hand, a decadent and decaying Roman world of rationality and order, imperturbably closed to any awareness of mystery, and on the other, spiritually fertile cultures open to a range and depth of experience not so easily rationalized. (We readily make a link between Olalla and the gypsy Rosa.) We find presented the paradox of how rationality seems to foster sadism and fruitless lust, whereas the virgin martyr, cut off in mid-prayer, connotes an opposing range of life-enhancing qualities. 'Tamar y Amnón' (I, pp. 451–4) tackles the subject of lust and sexual violence that so tormented Lorca in his teens and early twenties, through the recreation of a tale from the Old Testament, a source that otherwise is barely represented in Spanish balladry.

As the 1920s progressed, Lorca's suspicion of cold rationality returned with increasing force. Instrumental in clarifying his dissatisfaction with an art excluding all uncertainty, and eliding direct self-exposure, was his growing friendship with Salvador Dalí after 1923. The notion of pursuing the ode as a genre got going in earnest in summer 1925, when the poet began work on his 'Oda a Salvador Dalí' (*Obras completas*, I, pp. 457–61). In this poem, the dominant value he identifies in the art of his Catalan friend is anti-realism. This entails the pursuit of a cold beauty, rational control, precision and clarity of form, together with a strict avoidance of many areas of experience that Lorca's juvenilia had more readily examined. The poem praises Dalí's 'amor a lo que tiene explicación posible' [love for things that can be explained], but not so much the painter's execution of his ideals or his aspirations as such: it is the wounded artist whom Lorca admires, and how Dalí represents this wounding in his painting. The poet has become aware that aesthetic purism is pursued at a considerable cost.

A point of reference in this for both Lorca and Dalí again came from Christian iconography, in this case the figure of the Roman soldier-martyr, Saint Sebastian, patron of Cadaqués, killed for his faith beneath a hail of arrows. In September 1926, the poet asked Jorge Guillén for a photograph of Berruguete's polychrome wood image of the saint, kept in Valladolid (*Epistolario*, p. 374). He tells Guillén how Sebastian represents both ethical and aesthetic values; true poetry, 'que es amor, esfuerzo, y *renunciamiento*' [love, effort and renunciation]. Mainly, however, it was to Mantegna's treatment of the subject that Lorca and Dalí referred, and for the latter, the Roman martyr embodied the cult of Holy

Objectivity, as he called it, that he had embraced during his neo-Cubist phase, and about which the former had now begun to express some reservations. In August 1927, Lorca wrote Dalí a letter, in which he tried to identify differences between his view of Sebastian and that of his friend (*Epistolario*, pp. 511–12). In it, the poet again voices his unease about the studied 'dehumanization' of Dalinian painting. In the martyr he admires '*serenidad* en medio de la desgracia [. . .] no es un *resignado*, sino un *triunfador*, un triunfador lleno de elegancia y de tonos grises' [serenity in the face of disaster (. . .) not as a man resigned to fate, but as a victor, a victor utterly elegant and tinged with grey]. He sees the saint's 'salvation' coming precisely through an aesthetic response to the human predicament: 'Se salva por su *belleza* [. . .] se diferencia de todos, *posa y construye su cuerpo* dando eternidad a lo fugitivo y logrando *hacer visible* una abstracta idea estética. [. . .] Por eso yo lo amo' [His beauty saves him (. . .) he sets himself apart from others, poses, and constructs his body, making what is fugitive eternal and succeeding in making visible an abstract aesthetic ideal. (. . .) That is why I love him]. All Lorca's odes explore, in fact, however coolly, the relation of artistic creation, with an emphasis on the ideal, to the fallen world of mortality and suffering. Images of Christ's Passion and of certain saints supply natural points of reference, but the supernatural remains outside the frame; Jesus features as the Man of Sorrows, not as the second person of the Trinity.

By late 1928, purist aesthetics have been found unequivocally wanting.[12] We find a distinctly new, speculative cast to the texts the poet embarks upon around this time, this speculation being embodied in a taxing metaphorical language. A discursive note re-enters the scene, about topics that had preoccupied Lorca in his later teens, when things had, however, been very differently expressed. This return to more overtly articulated philosophical concerns is part of a trend correctly identified by Eutimio Martín. On the evidence of the Blessed Sacrament Ode, to which we shall turn later, Martín writes that immediately prior to the New York period and afterwards, 'La figura de Cristo seguirá siendo para Lorca una meta ética y una simbología estética' [For Lorca, the figure of Christ remains an ethical objective and an aesthetic source of symbolism] (Martín, p. 320). While Dalí became increasingly close to Surrealism, for Lorca, self-abandonment to the unconscious and the loss of all rational control in art remained a sticking point. By 1929, though, we find him speaking of art as itself a mystical religion, something that we should receive sacramentally, without seeking an analytical understanding of it.[13]

The poet worked on another ode, his 'Oda al Santísimo Sacramento del Altar'

12 For more detail, see Andrew A. Anderson, 'Lorca at the Crossroads', *Anales de Literatura Española Contemporánea*, 16 (1991), 149–73.

13 'La poesía [es] como la fe, algo que no debe comprenderse, sino recibirse en una especie de estado de gracia' [poetry is like faith, not something to be understood but to be received in as it were a state of grace] (*Obras completas*, III, p. 105; compare *Obras completas*, III, p. 635).

[Ode to the Blessed Sacrament of the Altar] (*Obras completas*, I, pp. 463–9) between early February 1928 and mid-September 1929. Its composition spills over into the American period, therefore, and its earlier-written lines anticipate *Poeta en Nueva York* [*Poet in New York*], both as to their manner and their content. It is subdivided into four parts: an opening section entitled 'Exposición' [Exposition], followed by three devoted to those enemies of the soul, the World, the Devil and the Flesh. Lorca draws on the central mysteries of Catholic Christianity to explore central personal, interpersonal and also artistic dilemmas. The Mass for him was liturgical drama, representing a subject that his youthful writings had treated with some disdain: God incarnate, and his sacrifice for the sins of the world. The personal anguish that the poet was undergoing around the time of writing[14] has influenced how he now writes about God made Man, present in the Sacrament of the Altar, and about the best aesthetic means of dealing with human pain: 'Sólo tu Sacramento de luz en equilibrio, / aquietaba la angustia del amor desligado. [. . .] Mundo, ya tienes meta para tu desamparo. / Para tu horror perenne de agujero sin fondo' [Your Sacrament of light in equilibrium alone could calm the anguish of a love estranged (or unrestrained). (. . .) Now, World, you have a reference-point for your helplessness, for the ceaseless horror of a bottomless shaft]. (The text combines relatively plain statements of this sort with more hermetic utterance, in a way that may remind us of *Poeta en Nueva York*.)

This ode pursues a topic also found in 'Oda a Salvador Dalí', that of an interplay, or opposition, between a cold art that idealizes and an art that takes cognizance of mutability and suffering. The mystery of the Eucharist miraculously succeeds in squaring a circle: the tangible presence of Christ in the consecrated Host, the sacrament in which bread becomes his body, entails a material reality that transcends the sinfulness and insubstantiality of mere earthly life, the 'carne que no sabe tu nombre' [flesh that does not know your name]. The Host is associated with whiteness, with light, with the rose, with geometrical clarity, in language that recalls the lexis of the Dalí ode, while submitting it to rigorous criticism.

Lorca seems to batten here on to a central emphasis of St Paul's preaching about Christ, the emphasis on a divine strength revealed in suffering, self-giving and vulnerability. Apparent ignominy and defeat attest to a crucial dimension to God's power. Thus the Host is seen as simultaneously strong and powerful, and as weak as a child: 'Dios en mantillas, Cristo diminuto y eterno' [God in swaddling clothes, Christ tiny and eternal]. Near the close, we read, 'Es tu carne vencida, rota, pisoteada, / la que vence y relumbra sobre la carne nuestra' [It is your flesh, vanquished, torn, and trampled underfoot, that shines and triumphs over our flesh]. Lorca uses the word *carne* in the Christian sense of everything subject to sin and death. Thus his poem rejects the sins of the flesh, involving lust, the worship of superficial beauty, living for the moment, using others as a

---

[14] For details of this, see Gibson, I, *passim*.

means of selfish gratification, extending its reference, as the Ode to Walt Whitman also does, to a world of work that turns human beings into machines: 'elevan tu columna de nardo bajo nieve / sobre el mundo de ruedas y falos que circula' [raise your column of snow-covered spikenard above the circling world of wheels and phalluses].

The title of the opening section 'Exposición' refers to a liturgical happening, but is also an exposition in a rhetorical sense, in which Lorca stakes out his ground. The remainder of the ode launches an all-out attack on the World. Even if the poem's lexis still employs references to science and technology, any purist glorying in modernity is absent. The poet bitterly attacks the ambit of cities, a world against nature, a world of alienation, of massiveness dwarfing the human individual, of moral disorientation and oppression. Insofar as art involves discipline still, it must also admit genuine and gentle human emotion ('la rosa templada' [temperate rose]), and reject directionless libertarianism ('lo libre sin norte' [freedom with no north]). The World is a place of death, suicide, bureaucracy, prostitution, frustrated desire, loss of innocence, 'living at speed'. We find much here that anticipates *Poeta en Nueva York*, except that *Poeta en Nueva York* ceases to invoke the Christian vision with anything approaching a positive evaluation. The ethos of the Blessed Sacrament Ode, on the other hand, is, unusually for Lorca, open to the Eucharist and its re-enactment of the central mystery of Christianity, without for now lambasting the Catholic clergy and their (he thinks) manipulation of liturgical ceremonies for worldly, fleshly, demonic, ends.

The section 'Demonio', actually written in New York, then concentrates on the pain of 'fleshly' sexuality, that topic that so many of Lorca's youthful writings had addressed. Explaining what 'amor desligado' and the 'cuerpo sin amor' [loveless body] amount to, the ode attacks superficial sensuality, a skin-deep cult of physical beauty and a directionless self-indulgence that is actually loveless, providing only a simulacrum of permanence for people actually terrified by their transitoriness and weakness. The Blessed Sacrament points towards Man's only hope: 'Sólo tu Sacramento, manómetro que salva / corazones lanzados a quinientos por hora' [Your sacrament alone is a manometer to save hearts hurtling at five hundred miles an hour].

Lorca took an active part in the Granadan Holy Week celebrations in 1929 (Gibson, I, pp. 595–6), and, in the letter to his family soon after arrival in New York that same year (*Epistolario*, pp. 626–7), he asserts the values of Spanish Catholicism against those of Protestantism and even American Catholicism, missing the transcendence of human isolation that Catholic worship in Spain involves: 'Lo que el catolicismo de los Estados Unidos no tiene es [. . .] calor humano. La solemnidad en lo religioso es *cordialidad* [. . .] Es como decir: Dios está con nosotros' [American Catholicism lacks all human warmth. What religious solemnity is all about is cordiality (. . .) Like saying 'God is with us']. But this affirmative evaluation of a central Catholic truth, based on the poet's renewed, intense personal unhappiness in love and on a heightened sense of cultural alienation on arrival in the New World, did not last for long.

Other poetry written in New York similarly attacks an urban, high-speed, mechanized environment. The modern capitalist city is in thrall not only to physical death but to spiritual death as well: a world of rootlessness, hopelessness, without creative restlessness, playfulness or imaginativeness. Love and religion have been corrupted; there is worship only of money, where value is reduced to financial terms and the individual no longer counts. There is cruelty and indifference towards all living things: thus, Lorca attacks a greedy and convenient anthropomorphism, and condemns the city's daily hecatombs of suffering animals of every size, down to the smallest. Appearances are everywhere deceptive and 'mystified' (as Marxists used to say); hypocrisy is all-pervasive, together with closed minds and complacency – these things most of all among the whites.

While some of his protests are directed against specific features of transatlantic culture, some of them have a more universal import. They may well attach to a socio-economic system that we now call developed or industrial capitalism, by which (most of) Spain was still untouched. And Lorca realized how, although 'mystified' on the surface, interpersonal relationships are coloured by such distinctive socio-economic conditions. However, if we ask if there is a realistic possibility of transcendence anywhere, the answer to that is 'no'. Human beings are everywhere alone in the cosmos and unable to connect with one another. Lorca still, though, values a creative effort to tell the truth and to make meaning where none is given, be that effort ultimately fruitless; anything rather than mindless acquiescence in cruelty and suffering; anything rather than the cowardly / tactical ignoring of mortality. As T.S. Eliot was to put it, 'For us, there is only the trying. The rest is not our business' ('East Coker'). Aspiration, though, for Lorca must be rooted in the reality of a God-less world. Death, instability, emptiness (the *hueco*) and solitude are everywhere, even in the beautiful landscape of rural Vermont. Likewise, the poet's concern with the lost innocence of childhood is not tied to urban America alone. He feels it intensely in himself, as those poems show in which he dreams back to his Andalusian childhood and painful passage into adolescence. Examples include '1910 (Intermedio)' [1910 (Interlude)] and 'Poema doble del Lago Eden' [Double Poem of Lake Eden] (*Obras completas*, II, p. 512 and pp. 537–8 respectively), in the latter of which sexual maturing, metaphysical anguish, linguistic alienation and poetic inauthenticity are interwoven in a vision of a Fall that Lorca yearns to reverse, but recognizes he cannot. The yearning will have to be its own reward.

What follows now is an analysis of those poems in *Poeta en Nueva York* that employ direct reference to Christianity. It is important to stress throughout, though, that the case for *Poeta en Nueva York* is an artistic case. As Maurer remarks, 'abstract concepts and perceptions turn into astonishingly *tangible* poetic figures'.[15] The poet's specific images and their concatenations and transi-

---

15 Federico García Lorca, *Poet in New York*, ed. Christopher Maurer (Harmondsworth: Penguin, 1990), xxiii.

tions often make for quite remarkable poetry. Lorca deliberately undercuts the paraphraseability and logical sense-making that his 1928 lecture 'Imaginación, inspiración, evasión' [Imagination, inspiration, evasion] (*Obras completas*, III, pp. 98–112) had already rejected. And crucial to his communicated vision is the structuring of his texts and their rhythmic design. So striking now is Lorca's mode of expression, that while returning in an overt fashion to many of the concerns first canvassed in his youthful writing, he does so with a poetic energy, concision and multiple suggestiveness that leaves the *fadeurs* of his earlier explorations far behind.

'Iglesia abandonada (Balada de la Gran Guerra)' [Abandoned Church (Ballad of the Great War)] (*Obras completas*, I, pp. 522–3) closes the collection's second section, 'Los Negros' [The Blacks] (perhaps because the 1917 US Expeditionary Forces to France could not have failed to include black soldiers). Lorca recreates the voice of a mother who has lost her soldier son. She recalls him as an altar server when a boy, and thus, imagery of the Mass is used to focus her grief and protest. We notice marked departures here from the stance of the Blessed Sacrament Ode. Death has severed her child from the church where he took part in public worship; the destruction wrought by war has led the survivors to lose hope, and to abandon the reassuring structures of the official cult: 'los muertos son más fuertes y saben devorar pedazos de cielo' [the dead are stronger and are able to devour chunks of sky]. The poem is laced with references to the paraphernalia of the liturgy – holy water, incense and candles – and to major moments in the Mass: the preparation at the foot of the altar between celebrant and server, the offertory, and what Lorca calls the *centro* [centre], the consecration. Here is the passage relating to the offertory, when bread and wine are placed upon the altar:

> En las anémonas del ofertorio te encontraré, ¡corazón mío!,
> cuando el sacerdote levante la mula y el buey con sus fuertes
> brazos
> para espantar los sapos nocturnos que rondan los helados paisajes
> del cáliz.

> [My love, I'll find you in the anemones of the offertory, when the
> priest elevates the ox and ass with his strong arms to frighten off
> the nocturnal toads that stalk the frozen landscapes of the
> chalice.]

Instead of bread and wine, the priest offers an ox and an ass, the animals present at Christ's birth in Bethlehem. These are symbols of meekness, and remind us that Christ was marked for death and suffering from the moment of his birth. All meek creatures, human and animals (as we are frequently reminded throughout the collection), are subject to a common fate. The forces of evil are not kept at bay by Christ's sacrifice, however; the chalice for the Precious Blood is not a cup of blessing. The mother thinks meekness is of little avail, once one remembers the savagery of the whole natural world, human, animal, vegetable:

> Si mi niño hubiera sido un oso
> yo no temería el sigilo de los caimanes,
> ni hubiese visto al mar amarrado a los árboles
> para ser fornicado y herido por el tropel de los regimientos.

> [If my boy had been a bear, I wouldn't fear the stealth of caymans
> nor would I have seen the sea tied against a tree to be raped and
> wounded by regiments of soldiers.]

Her son was not strong enough to survive, and so at the central moment of the Mass, the representation of Christ's atoning sacrifice, this parent finds not peace and reconciliation, but freedom only in her strident protest. The last four lines of the poem have a simple, direct force, and seem to echo with some sombre irony the gospel words: 'God so loved the world that he gave his only begotten son, to the end that all that believe in him should not perish, but have eternal life' (John 3:16). The poet can no longer, apparently, draw consolation from the Eucharist and its underpinning Christology.

In 'Navidad en el Hudson' [Christmas on the Hudson] (*Obras completas*, I, pp. 530–1) the poet once more sets before us a suffering, death-bound world, where people engage in frenetic escapism, 'sin enterarse de que el mundo / estaba solo por el cielo. // El mundo solo por el cielo solo' [without being able to understand that the Earth was alone in space. A lonely world set in a lonely space]. The birth of Christ is a 'fábula inerte' [idle fable] and has made no difference to anything: 'No importa que cada minuto / un niño nuevo agite sus ramitos de venas' [It doesn't matter if every minute some new child waves its tiny bunch of veins]. The poet tries to aid his fellow-sufferers, but to no practical effect: 'estoy con las manos vacías en la desembocadura' [I'm empty-handed in the estuary].

In 'Crucifixión' [Crucifixion] (I, pp. 559–60), Lorca again draws on imagery of Christ's Passion, familiar from his homeland, to elucidate not just America's alien Protestant culture but also things more universal. At one point we find plainly anti-clerical material, as when an ecclesiastical tailor who provides prelates with their purple robes locks up the women who in the gospels visit Christ's tomb on Easter morning, forcing them instead to confront the visual evidence of their Saviour's not having risen from the dead:

> Un sastre especialista en púrpura
> había encerrado a las tres santas mujeres
> y les enseñaba una calavera por los vidrios de la ventana.

> [A tailor specialising in purple
> had locked up the three holy women
> and was showing them a skull through the panes of a window.]

The Church in practice denies the risen Christ by its pomp and its commercialism. These prelates are closely related to the Pharisees whom we meet later in the poem. Christ's Passion continues unrelieved; [16] the Precious Blood finds no chalices to contain it now, only the shoes that are one of the poet's obsessive images of the brute fact of death; Christ's crown of thorns is worn by other human beings for all eternity; preparations for crucifixions still continue, as woodsmen and carpenters pursue their work; the Lamb of God fails to take away the sins of the world; we are left not with an earthquake or tombs opening as when Christ died, but with something far more humdrum and insidious – *polilla*, moth! Animals suffer as well as humans: particular attention in this poem being paid to a horse, with its connotations of force and masculinity, and, entering the scene half-way through the text, to a cow, an emblem of suffering innocence and nurturing, that as such, religious hypocrites punish, reject and refuse to hear spoken of. The horse has been castrated, but its suffering is ultimately assuaged; not so, the suffering of a child. This side of death, Christ is endlessly recrucified amidst scenes of pain and degradation that affect the guilty and the innocent alike; heaven is indifferent (we may remember Jesus' words from the cross, as He recites the beginning of Psalm 22, 'My God, My God, why hast Thou forsaken me?'), while others hardly care, unaware of the divine silence and the suffering of the innocent. The whole poem is as much a critical reflection on a certain brand of orthodox Christology (as Lorca sees it) as it is a restatement of his basic anthropology, for which his starkly demythologized imagery of the Passion serves as one vehicle among others.

The eighth section of *Poeta en Nueva York* opens with another powerful poem of denunciation, 'Grito hacia Roma' [Cry towards Rome] (I, pp. 561–3), denunciation this time specifically directed against the institutional Catholicism that had concluded a deal with Italian Fascism in February 1929. The rites of the Roman basilicas are denounced, as is a hypocritical, loveless form of religion that denies human equality and social justice. Christ himself may be able to provide living water (in a reference to John 4), but the Pope does not; the dispossessed require their daily bread in a literal as well as in a metaphorical sense, but the Church provides them with neither. Lorca again attacks escapist otherworldliness, the promise of rewards or compensations in some future state: modifying the Lord's Prayer, he writes, 'queremos el pan nuestro de cada día, [. . .] queremos que se cumpla la voluntad de la Tierra' [we want our daily bread (. . .) we want the will of the Earth to be done]. In the poem's two final lines we are given a revised reading of Christ's death, but the volcano that accompanies this, in an ironic allusion to the earthquake mentioned in the Bible (Matthew 27:50–3), sends into the air not magma and 'many bodies of the saints which slept' but, as in the poem 'Crucifixión' too, trembling rivers of moth, 'temblorosos ríos de polilla'.[17]

---

[16] The poem's first five lines may perhaps in part be read as an evocation of nightfall, as the blood-red sky gives way to moonlight. The red sky is associated with the circumcision of the child Jesus, in whose submission to that Jewish rite was prefigured his obedience to death.

[17] An anticipation of the anti-clerical sentiments of *Poeta en Nueva York* is 'Consideración amarguísima . . .' [Consideration most bitter] of October 1917 (*Obras*

Work on *Llanto por Ignacio Sánchez Mejías* [*Lament for the Death of Ignacio Sánchez Mejías*] (*Obras completas*, I, pp. 616–24) started quite soon after the bullfighter's goring and tragic death in August 1934, all four parts being published in April 1935. For Lorca, the *corrida* was a very ancient (*milenario*) religious spectacle, the rituals of which involve the worship and the sacrifice of a god (*Obras completas*, III, pp. 160, 264). He was temperamentally inclined to see in it multiple overlays of cultural accretion, running from the pre-Roman, through the Roman, to the Christian civilization of Andalusia, the successive gods of which do, or do not, inherit characteristics from the past.[18] The *Llanto* explores positive values already asserted in *Poeta en Nueva York*: the sense that heroism involves having the courage to look death and nothingness in the face, not flinching, not denying the truth, and feeling able to envisage, even make art of, pain and disorientation. It is another statement as much ethical as it is aesthetic.

As the second section opens, the poet still finds himself recoiling from the horror of his friend's death, unable, either, to face the fact that Ignacio's death is part of a millennial story, repeated over and over again. He saw styles of different bullfighters as reflecting the two key *corrida* ingredients that, in a 1928 text, he had called sun and shade, 'sol y sombra': the Roman spirit of clarity, control, discipline and geometry on the one hand, and on the other, things darkly primitive or Oriental, shadow and moonlight, the mysterious forces of what he called the *duende*. Some *toreros* even strike a balance between the two, between the metaphorical worlds of light and of darkness or *misterio* [mystery] (*Obras completas*, III, pp. 295–6). We are invited to conclude that if in life Ignacio was a 'sunny' bullfighter with virtues redolent of those of Roman civilization, in death he is closer to the suffering Saviour, priest-and-victim, of Southern Spanish, Baroque, Christian art: 'Por las gradas sube Ignacio / con toda su muerte a cuestas' [Ignacio ascends the altar steps, carrying on his shoulders the whole weight of his death]. The dead Ignacio is now seen aptly to resemble the image on a Holy Week *paso*, of Christ carrying his cross up to Calvary; the priest too, ascending the altar to say Mass, does so as an *alter Christus*. In a lecture first given in 1933 (*Obras completas*, III, p. 155), incidentally, the poet linked what he called *duende* with a sense of the divine and with the bullfight:

> En toda la música árabe, [. . .] la llegada del duende es saludada con enérgicos '¡Alá, Alá!', '¡Dios, Dios!', tan cerca del '¡Olé!' de los toros que quién sabe si será lo mismo, y en todos los cantos del sur de España la aparición del duende es seguida por sinceros gritos de '¡Viva Dios!', profundo, humano, tierno grito, de una comunicación con Dios por medio de los cinco sentidos, [. . .] evasión real y poética de este mundo.

completas, IV, pp. 617–20). Other striking instances of such attitudes in *Poeta en Nueva York* itself are provided by 'Danza de la muerte' [Dance of Death] (*Obras completas*, I, pp. 524–7), and 'La aurora' [The Dawn] (I, p. 536).

[18] For more detail, see Andrew A. Anderson, *Lorca's Late Poetry*, Liverpool Monographs in Hispanic Studies 10 (Leeds: Francis Cairns, 1990), ch. 3, especially 158–71.

[In Arabic music, the descent of the *duende* is greeted with enthusiastic shouts of 'Allah, Allah!', 'God, God!', so close to the 'Olés!' heard at the bullfight that it may well be the same, and in all southern folksong, the appearance of the *duende* is followed by sincere cries to God of 'Viva!', a profound, tender, human cry of communication with God through the five senses (. . .) a genuinely poetic escape from this world.]

In some of the texts of *Poeta en Nueva York*, Lorca praised a capacity to face mortality and uncertainty, squarely and bravely, in art as in life.[19] In the *Llanto*, though, he goes further, and dramatizes the process he goes through, from an inability to engage emotionally with his friend's death to a proper, unsimplifying, acceptance of it. His conclusion is that the only fit form of mourning for such a man as Ignacio is for those left behind to emulate his virtues, while also grasping how intelligence and prudence require the capacity to recognize where reason cannot reach. True courage is not a matter of bravado or temerity: it involves knowing what can and ultimately cannot be achieved. Physical extinction is a fact, but poetry may grant a measure of survival, although without religious consolation in terms of the resurrection of the body and the life of a world to come. The emphasis here is both at odds with that of the 'Oda al Santísimo Sacramento', and more upbeat than we find in *Poeta en Nueva York*, apart perhaps from 'Oda a Walt Whitman' (*Obras completas*, I, pp. 563–7). (Whitman, with his Apollinian, as opposed to Dionysian qualities, but with a lack of definition and softness of outline about him at the same time, had prophesied and yearned for, without tasting it, something better and more truthful than the modern world affords.)

After Lorca's return from New York in July 1930, and following the proclamation of the Second Republic in April 1931, religious allusions, while not wholly absent, figure relatively little in his poetry. The same goes for his writing for the theatre.[20] Lorca's political sympathies were clearly on the left; but he did not embark upon a politicized art (apart from the unpublished *El sueño de la vida* [*The Dream of Life*] of 1935–6, with its literally murderous Espectador 2° [2nd Spectator], self-appointed representative of the God of Battles). When working for the touring theatre group La Barraca indeed, if not before, he came

[19] In section V of a much earlier text, 'Fray Antonio (poema raro)' [Brother Antonio (strange poem)] (September 1917), the protagonist visits the *cámara mortuoria* [funeral chamber] of a childhood friend, Carlos, and sees his face uncovered, with terrifying consequences (*Obras completas*, IV, pp. 763–4). Some horrifying memory of this sort may have affected the young poet *in propria persona*. Compare the account of the death of *el compadre* Pastor in 'Autobiografías' [Autobiographies] (*Obras completas*, IV, p. 853).

[20] For an overview of Lorca's later drama, see Andrew A. Anderson, 'The Strategy of García Lorca's Dramatic Composition 1930–36', *Romance Quarterly*, 33 (1986), 211–29. Two British scholars who have made stimulating contributions to the study of the religious possibilities of Lorca's drama in general are Ronald Cueto, in his *Souls in Anguish. Religion and Spirituality in Lorca's Theatre* (Leeds: Trinity and All Saints, 1994), and Patricia McDermott, in her 'Death as a Way of Life. Lorca's Dramatic Subversion of Orthodoxy', *Leeds Papers on Hispanic Drama* (Leeds: Trinity and All Saints, 1991), 125–52.

to admire Calderón's religious drama, seeing links between the sacred dramas of both Eastern and Western Christian liturgies (see *Obras completas*, III, pp. 219, 244, 1354; *Epistolario*, pp. 633–4). Although Lorca's development as a dramatist, encouraged by his success in South America in 1933–4, was to some degree resultant upon his desire to get his work performed and in that way contribute to the 'edificación de un pueblo' [edification of a people], his plays seem unresponsive in any explicit way to, say, the deteriorating relations between church and state.

The plays

We should recall in passing some of Lorca's earliest theatrical essays, notably *Cristo. Tragedia religiosa* [*Christ. Religious Tragedy*] and *Jehová;* and there is also *El maleficio de la mariposa* [*The Butterfly's Evil Spell*] (1920) in which the cockroach Curianito's hapless pursuit of a butterfly dramatizes questions with which readers will already be familiar from the early prose. More interesting from our point of view are two plays from the earlier 1920s containing Christological allusions relatable to the poetry of the same period.

Mariana Pineda [*Mariana Pineda*] (first performed in 1927 but written between 1923 and 1925) makes a number of references to the Passion and Death of Christ. Given the play's immediate Romantic context, this is perhaps no more than one would expect. But Lorca is rarely merely folksy, and comparison is invited with those other places in his work where Christ's death is presented as an archetypal instance of the *muerte de amor* [death from love], the frustrated eros that crucifies, in that interplay between desire and death that so much of this dramatist's work is dedicated to exploring. Mariana's idolized Pedro at one point associates his own suffering with Christ's Passion: 'Tengo abierta / una herida que sangra en mi costado' [There's an open wound that is bleeding in my side] (*Obras completas*, II, p. 133), unconsciously echoing Mariana's earlier prayer for his safety, '¡Señor, por la llaga [wound] de vuestro costado!' (II, p. 104). But it is Mariana herself who, as well as being linked implicitly with Our Lady of Sorrows, is more sustainedly associated with Christ. Gender is not a primary issue. She undergoes her Gethsemane experience in the convent garden; envisages her past and present moral cowardice and fear of pain ('take away this cup from me'); and comes out the other side, obedient unto death. Rather than continue to displace or flee contradictions that in Lorca's view were inherent in the wider culture of Granada,[21] she herself becomes the battleground, and drinks the cup to the dregs. It is the fate (or paradoxical existential good fortune) of some, a few, in Lorca's theatre to embody conflicts, rather than to run away from them. And Mariana is not alone in making a connection between herself and the

---

[21] For some of Lorca's responses to Granadan culture, see his lectures 'Paraíso cerrado para muchos' [Paradise Closed to Many] and 'Cómo canta una ciudad' [How a City Sings], (*Obras completas*, III, pp. 78–87, 137–49).

sufferings of Christ: others make it also. Take the following exchange between Mariana and Mother Carmen in the second scene of Estampa [Engraving] III: 'MARIANA: ¡Estoy muy herida, hermana, / por las cosas de la tierra! // CARMEN: Dios está lleno de heridas / de amor, que nunca se cierran' [I'm gravely wounded, Sister, by earthly things! / God is full of wounds of love that never close] (II, p. 153). This Christological self-identification comes across plainly too as the heroine approches death: 'Doy mi sangre, / que es tu sangre y la sangre de todas las criaturas [. . .] ¡Yo soy la Libertad, herida por los hombres!' [I give my blood, which is your blood and the blood of every creature (. . .) I am Freedom, wounded by men] (II, pp. 172–3). Not only is this how Mariana sees herself; it is a way in which we the audience are invited to consider her also.

In *Amor de Don Perlimplín con Belisa en su jardín* [*The Love of Don Perlimplín for Belisa in Their Garden*] (probably substantially completed by late 1925 and therefore contemporary with some of the poems of *Romancero gitano*) we have another play whose meanings are substantially embodied in its recurrent imagery. We find knives (the lancet, the scalpel) and wounding spoken of, and, in association with this, there runs throughout a sequence of allusions to the archetypal *muerte de amor*, that of Christ. A stage direction at the start of the third scene (*cuadro*) alludes to primitive paintings of the Last Supper (*Obras completas*, II, p. 254); Perlimplín talks of self-sacrifice at the end of that same scene (II, p. 257); near the close of the play, Marcolfa refers to 'la sangre gloriosísima de mi señor' [the most glorious blood of my master] (II, p. 263). The garden setting once more recalls Gethsemane, a place of agony and bloody sweat; Perlimplín and Belisa's red cloak reminds us of the scarlet robe in which Christ was arrayed by Pilate at the time of his mocking (Matthew 27:28). Its red is the red of violence, of blood and sacrifice (life blood, blood spilt: Lorca's juvenilia were also fond of 'sacrifice' as a metaphor for the sexual act). Perlimplín immolates himself, but the dramatic question is what we make of such an overtly 'Christlike' action: its sources, complex motivation and uncertain outcome. Lorca's metaphors invite us to keep paradoxical meanings in our minds as such, as unresolved loci of uncertainty. Through such dramatic language, characters reveal their own unresolved ambivalences, and the poet helps us focus ours, as to the significance of his action.

The plays written in New York and afterwards involve religious allusion somewhat incidentally, as we have already noted. Thus, *El público* [*The Public*, or *The Audience*] (1930) explores how people, in what they are pleased to think of as 'real life', are perpetually play-acting, fantasizing about their identities to themselves and one another; it explores how most folk lie about their sexual feelings, how they shy away from the transitoriness and insubstantiality that really 'define' our fragile personalities and undermine our attempts at relating to others as insubstantial as ourselves. It is in such a context that we find a scene in which 'un Desnudo Rojo' [a red man naked] is 'coronado de espinas azules' [crowned with blue thorns] (*Obras completas*, II, p. 311). This naked figure shows the suffering that ensues when erotic frustration is faced up to; the form of a suffering Christ, belittled by the modern as by an older world, is an honest, not dishonest, representation, appropriate for Lorca's 'theatre beneath the sand'. In this work, though, Christ is but one among a number of other cultural intertextual references, pagan and otherwise.

Religious allusion is almost wholly absent from *Bodas de sangre* [*Blood Wedding*] (1932), and so stands out at the end, as a chorus of women, surrounding La Madre [The Mother], recite a lament as the four dead men are brought on stage:

NIÑA:	Ya los traen.
MADRE:	Es lo mismo.
	La cruz, la cruz.
MUJERES:	Dulces clavos,
	dulce cruz,
	dulce nombre
	de Jesús.
NOVIA:	Que la cruz ampare a muertos y a vivos.

(Obras completas, II, p. 474)

[Here they come. / Never mind. The cross. The cross. / Sweet nails, sweet cross, sweet name of Jesus. / May the cross avail the living and the dead.]

Such language may echoes lines from the Latin hymn 'Pange lingua gloriosi' [Sing, my tongue, the Saviour's glory] associated with the liturgy of Holy Week, but why is it introduced at all? A simple answer to that has already been supplied in our account of how the Crucified Christ had clearly come by now to represent the poet's tragic sense of life. (It may, further, be relevant to recall how in late medieval devotion, invocation of both the Name of Jesus and of the Nails of the Passion was held to be specially effective against 'life's ills and dangers'.[22]) The final act of *Bodas de sangre* shows us not even, principally, the immolation of its victims but rather how the survivors variously approach an understanding of what has happened, and why.

In *Yerma* [*Yerma*] (1933–4), there is little to suggest that God is to blame for the protagonist's childlessness. More at point are personal incompatibilities. We do, however, find the following exchange towards the end of Act I between Yerma and a *vieja* [an old woman]:

YERMA:	Que Dios me ampare.
VIEJA:	Dios, no. A mí no me ha gustado nunca Dios. ¿Cuándo os vais a dar cuenta de que no existe? Son los hombres los que te tienen que amparar.
YERMA:	Pero ¿por qué me dices eso?, ¿por qué?
VIEJA:	(*Yéndose.*) Aunque debía haber Dios, aunque fuera pequeñito,

---

22 See Eamon Duffy, *The Stripping of the Altars* (London: Yale, 1992), 284–6.

para que mandara rayos contra los hombres de simiente podrida que
encharcan la alegría de los campos.
YERMA: No sé lo que me quieres decir. (*Obras completas*, II, p. 490)

[May God come to my aid. / No, not God. I've never cared for God myself.
When are people going to realize he doesn't exist? It's other people that will
have to help you. / Why are you telling me that? Why? / (Leaving) There ought
to be a God, though, even if only a tiny one, to send thunderbolts against men
with rotten seed who muddy the happiness of the fields. / I don't know what
you mean.]

The old woman's sentiments here recall those of the playwright in his personal
capacity. However, this is dramatic dialogue, and we note Yerma's uncompre-
hending response, and also, how, when set in the context of the drama as a
whole, the Vieja's comments are tendentious, rather than authoritative and
straightforward. For the rest, the play's religious references involve folk beliefs:
about the efficacy of certain prayers, and above all, about attendance, in the final
cuadro, at a *romería* or pilgrimage, where we witness the mumming of two
masked figures, 'dos máscaras populares' (*Obras completas*, II, pp. 519–22).
This draws, in 'real-life' terms, on the *Romería del Cristo del Paño*, a
pilgrimage, held annually, to the shrine at Moclín near Lorca's birthplace, and so
is an example of the poetic transposition of popular customs. Both figures wear
large masks, but the stage direction insists, '*No son grotescas de ningún modo,
sino de gran belleza y con un sentido de pura tierra*' [They are not at all
grotesque, but rather, of great beauty and with the feel of pure earth]. One is
Male, El Macho, the other Female, La Hembra. (A group of children, however,
identify them as 'El demonio y su mujer' [the devil and his wife], but then, apart
from the figures' aspect of pagan survival, orthodox religion has always had a
tendency to demonize carnality.) He carries a bull's horn, she waves a string of
cowbells: the sexual symbolism is plain. These maskers voice the pain and frustration of many childless women, and also speak the language of a mere
carnality that Yerma quite rejects, and that, as we have seen many times already,
Lorca sees as intrinsic to human suffering rather than its remedy. The
pagan–Christian syncretism of the *romería* ceremonies, therefore, may not be
grotesque, but nor does it represent, in potential or in effect, so much a solution,
as the *mise au point* of an ongoing, deeply felt dilemma.

In *La casa de Bernarda Alba* [*The House of Bernarda Alba*] (1936) no
special emphasis is placed on Bernarda's entirely formal devotions. They are
just one element among others in the stifling atmosphere of a house in which,
even so, the women's names suggest oppressive religiosity: Martirio, Magdalena
and Angustias. Bernarda's name may indeed involve various ironies in the way
that it refers us to the multifaceted character of a great saint – Bernard of
Clairvaux, preacher of the Second Crusade, the austere Cistercian reformer, but
also, devoted to the Humanity of Christ and of his Mother, the author of treatises
on the Song of Songs and on the Love of God. When it comes to a passing

mention of Saint Barbara near the start of Act III, prompting Bernarda's comment that 'Los antiguos sabían muchas cosas que hemos olvidado' [the ancients knew a lot of things that we have forgotten] (*Obras completas*, II, p. 624), it is again Eamon Duffy who provides some useful points of reference. The Virgin Martyr Barbara defied patriarchy, rejected all her suitors, and endured a terrible death, it being precisely this that in popular devotion was supposed to guarantee her powerful intercession against all dangers, especially sudden death, caused by thunderbolts or other means (Duffy, pp. 171–6). How cleverly Lorca slips such details in. Then there is María Josefa's final eruption into the action (II, pp. 627–30). This crazed old lady enters, singing a macaronic carol-cum-lullaby-cum-nursery rhyme to the sheep she is carrying in her arms, which she deems a child. This goes on while Adela is making love with Pepe, and in its imagery, the grandmother's rambling speech makes a direct comment on the girl's hopeless attempt at 'slaking her thirst' in the dark yard outside. María Josefa draws attention to things that nobody in Bernarda's house, except the servants, dares voice directly: that the girls are all dying for men, and dying to have children, but are in fact condemned to frustration and sterility. Against this are set the resonances of carols and the stable at Bethlehem, allusion to the Lamb of God, and, through the old lady's name, to the Holy Family of a popular devotion much encouraged in the nineteenth century. The effect is disconcerting, as we are left with the contrast between conventional referents to the Christmas story and the situation in Bernarda's household, where hypocrisy and cruelty are rife.

Conclusion

This chapter has argued that Lorca's main religious preoccupations were well established in his teens and early twenties, but that they went underground for a period when he was influenced by artistic purism. However, friendship with Dalí and its tensions gradually helped focus the poet's dissatisfaction with an art that rejects the exploration of suffering and uncertainty. We see Lorca has matured towards a different stance by later 1928. His Blessed Sacrament Ode, spanning 1928–9, is an island of sympathy with Catholic sensibility, but this does not last for long. The poetry of the North American period clearly breaks with sympathy for the sacramental, and expresses overt anti-clericalism. Christ is only present as the Man of Sorrows, neither redeeming nor risen. After New York, religious concerns, while not wholly absent, figure relatively little in Lorca's poetry or theatre, the *Llanto* apart. His work is unresponsive in any explicit way to the political conflicts between church and state from 1931 onwards. If, though, in 1936 his murderers had been able to read his juvenilia and the texts of *Poeta en Nueva York*, this would only have confirmed their suspicions about his religious orthodoxy. The case for his writing cannot in any case rest on abstract summaries of his ideas, but on the art he made of them, at its most striking and intense, where religious matters are concerned, in the 'Oda al Santísimo Sacramento' and the poetry of New York.

7

Gender and Sexuality

CHRIS PERRIAM

Love

Directness and complication

In Act III of *El público* [*The Public*, or *The Audience*] Julieta – Shakespeare's Juliet – distances herself from her role within a role to exclaim 'Ya estoy cansada y me levanto a pedir auxilio para arrojar de mi sepulcro a los que teorizan sobre mi corazón y a los que me abren la boca con pequeñas pinzas de mármol' [I'm tired and I'm getting up from here to ask for help to cast out from my tomb all those who probe my heart with theories and open up my mouth with tiny marble pincers].[1] She longs for a moment when she might have been 'Julieta viva, alegrísima, libre del punzante enjambre de lupas. Julieta en el comienzo, Julieta en la orilla de la ciudad' [lively Juliet, most happy Juliet, free from stinging swarms of magnifying glasses. Juliet at the beginning, Juliet on the city's shore] (*Obras completas*, II, p. 494). Her despairing, tortured recognition of the loss of the possibility of being that 'Julieta en el comienzo' – in a simple place where feelings are direct, unmediated and unquestioned – is founded on a more fundamental recognition, in the same speech, that 'es el engaño la palabra del amor, el espejo roto, el paso en el agua' [the word of love is deception, a broken mirror, a footstep on the water] (p. 494). The sympathetic member of the public, thinking back to this rereading of the tragedy of the star-crossed lovers as she walks home from the theatre, might muse – if she knows her Lorca – on how often his words are themselves magnifying glasses trained on the vulnerable text of love. Words appear in the plays and poems (and, obviously, in the lectures and essays) as theorizing instruments, with as many stings in their looks as there are moments of extreme pleasure, virtuosity or apparently pure emotion in their sounds, deployment and implications.

Lorca often wishes to hide this fact by creating compelling illusions to the effect that love is unapproachable as an object of analysis. It is a common and well-enough founded view that many of the works 'have an extraordinary direct-

---

[1] Federico García Lorca, *Obras completas*, 2 vols, 21st edn (Madrid: Aguilar, 1980), II, 494.

ness of emotional address which explains their popularity far beyond the Spanish-speaking world'.[2] The most well-known aspect of this appeal is that which makes the social appear to be bound up in the natural and to make both of these appear to be lifted out of themselves by the supernatural in the form of folkloric motifs and myths.[3] It is love – or the lack of love – that is the catalyst for the processes that raise the social and the natural on to an apparently other plane. In those works that draw on oddly authentic yet never quite historically specific Andalusian rural contexts, the words of love and passion are given a dramatic intensity that creates the thrilling effect of an equivalence between feelings and the processes of the external, natural world. This occurs in the exchanges between the Novia [Bride] and Leonardo in Act II, Scene 1 of *Bodas de sangre* [*Blood Wedding*], in Amnón's address to Thamar in the ballad that bears their names, or, in a different mode, in frightening disturbances of the boundaries between the social and the natural in *Poeta en Nueva York* [*Poet in New York*], and in countless other moments. Lorca, as is well known, is skilled at making the equivalence of word and feeling seem real. Language, desire, the elemental and the more-than-real blend together. Only the chilliest readers or theatre-goers would not give themselves up, from time to time and for a while at least, to the conviction that 'la palabra del amor' [the word of love], rather than being an agent of deceit, is little less than a spell to access the forces of nature. Yielding to this, they suspend disbelief and put aside the querulous urge to theorize nature.

Conversely, though, Lorca can be gnomic, sceptical and cerebral, adopting what were to be thought of, after his time, as postmodern strategies of disruption, fragmentation and ironic self-awareness. Arguably his work reveals an aesthetics and a poetics that go beyond the crafty simulation of the natural and supernatural orders of things; and it is certainly a work aware of its embeddedness in a range of literary, philosophical and dramatic traditions; in other words, of its constructedness.[4] Many of the erotically oriented early poems display an awareness of the trickiness of their subject matter and, as D. Gareth Walters has observed, they set up diversions linked to a dynamics of aversion and use humour, indirection, masks and disguises (Walters, pp. 191–37). They reveal a tactic of the 'conspicuous concealment' of a given poem's emotional centre (Walters, p. 228). Perhaps because the results of such an analysis are unbearable to contemplate head on, in *El público* a sharp and unremitting analysis of love is deliberately scattered among distinct character groupings and is overlaid with

[2] Paul Binding, *Lorca: The Gay Imagination* (London: GMP, 1985), 12–13.

[3] See, among many others, Rupert Allen, *The Symbolic World of Federico García Lorca* (Albuquerque: University of New Mexico Press, 1972), 1–44.

[4] See Marie Laffranque, *Les idées esthétiques de Federico García Lorca* (Paris : Centre de Recherches Hispaniques, 1967); D. Gareth Walters, *'Canciones' and the Early Poetry of Lorca: A Study in Critical Methodology and Poetic Maturity* (Cardiff: University of Wales Press, 2002); Andrew A. Anderson, *Lorca's Late Poetry: A Critical Study*, Liverpool Monographs in Hispanic Studies 10 (Leeds: Francis Cairns, 1990), 406–15.

sudden pulses of verbal and physical unexpectedness that act like radio interference. Love, furthermore, is associated with a wide range of different forms of authenticity whose plurality at the very least complicates and more usually goes so far as to confound the purportedly simple operations of that 'extraordinary directness' alluded to above.[5] In *Así que pasen cinco años* [*Once Five Years Pass*] brazen caricature contrastively accompanies a subtle tracing of emotional dysfunction made up of frustration, sterility and existential distress.[6] Daring if sporadic experiments with narrative time (Ucelay, pp. 83–7) are interwoven with standard episodes, bits of in-and-out-of-the-bedroom stage business borrowed from farce, and touches of the circus. The shadings of angst and depth of feeling are countered by an eye-catching fascination with costume and period, such as when the Mask appears in 'un traje de 1900 con larga cola amarillo rabioso' [a 1900-style dress with a long train in violent yellow] in Act 3, Scene 1 (*Obras completas*, II, p. 431). Just as the Fiancée is reaching a pitch of passionate surrender to match that of her namesake (Novia) in *Bodas de sangre* and weaving a fine filter of words to capture her feelings at the start of Act 2, her bulky new boyfriend the Rugby Player is coarsely smoking a cigar. Even the *Romancero gitano* [*Gypsy Ballads*] veils its analysis through contradictory tactics: extreme, organic directness and, as Derek Harris has suggested, a cleverness that may or may not lead the reader anywhere but into admiration.[7]

Nothing of this should surprise those coming to Lorca first by way of the seductiveness of his representations of love and nature. Few terms, after all, are more heavily laden with their own constructedness and with their long history of still inconclusive attempts at definition as socio-cultural contexts shift. Love inevitably points to questions of power, oppression, repression, subjectivity and identity: there is no longer a Lorca without Foucault and Freud,[8] without feminisms, theories of the body,[9] without attendant questions about the bases and relationships between manifestations of heterosexuality and homosexuality,

5 On this last aspect, see María Clementa Millán, 'Introducción', in Federico García Lorca, *El público*, ed. María Clementa Millán, Letras Hispánicas 272 (Madrid: Cátedra, 1991), 13–115 (pp. 61–70). Millán's suggestion, however, is that the treatment of the theme of love determines the internal structure of the play (p. 61), as well as revealing the 'mundo interior' [inner world] of Lorca the playwright (p. 70), which implies a more coherent set of effects than that which is being pointed to here.

6 Margarita Ucelay, 'Introducción', in Federico García Lorca, *Así que pasen cinco años. Leyenda del tiempo*, ed. M. Ucelay, Letras Hispánicas 397 (Madrid: Cátedra, 1995), 9–184 (pp. 97–109).

7 Federico García Lorca, *Romancero gitano*, ed. Derek Harris, Grant & Cutler Spanish Texts (London: Grant and Cutler, 1991), 7–17 and 82–7.

8 Paul Julian Smith, *The Body Hispanic: Gender and Sexuality in Spanish and Spanish American Literature* (Oxford: Oxford University Press, 1989), 105–37; Paul Julian Smith, *The Theatre of García Lorca: Text, Performance, Psychoanalysis* (Cambridge: Cambridge University Press, 1998); and see Joseph Bristow, *Sexuality*, The New Critical Idiom (London: Routledge, 1997), 62–82 and 168–97 for an overview.

9 See, for example, Sarah Wright, *The Trickster-Function in the Theatre of García Lorca*, Colección Támesis 185 (Woodbridge: Tamesis, 2000), 48–56 and 105–25; and Lisa

between various emerging eroticisms (Bristow, pp. 197–228), and questions, not least, about the interrelatedness of romantic desire, sexuality, gender and social roles and conventions.[10]

Lorca's frequent deployment of a language of impulses and instincts formed around a terminology by turns animal, cosmic, mineral, elemental and earthy creates a highly unstable but highly persuasive equivalence between love, nature and sexuality (in the sense of a dynamics of desire). The modern readers and audiences of this modern writer, who was producing ideas and images at a time when, in the field of thinking about erotics, sexology was giving way to psychoanalysis,[11] might in some ways be surprised and even dismayed by Lorca's strategic construction of equivalences of sign and feeling, sex and the elemental, 'love' and 'nature', not least because these equivalences risk flattening out the sense of love by restricting its range variously to that of high passion or deep, undifferentiable desire. They also tend to lead to a misrepresentation of the scope of Lorca's writing on love, ignoring the fact that, especially in the poetry, there is a wide 'variety of perspectives on love' (Walters, p. 191). Lorca is strong on companionship, on family ties, on spiritual love, on love as commitment to others and to the fight against social injustice as it impacts on Gypsies, women, homosexual men and black people (Ucelay, p. 97).

Love, in its textualised habitat of gender and sexuality, is an obvious – inevitable – point of departure for readings of Lorca, as has been observed by Rafael Martínez Nadal, and many before and after him.[12] Along with death it is one of the most noticeably characteristic concerns of the plays and texts (Martínez Nadal, p. 133); as a term it can be extended to include the writer's affective outreach to the world (p. 133) or to mean a fiery passion that leads the writer to seek out 'el amor en todas sus formas' [love in all its forms] (p. 139).[13] The predominant mode of representation of love in Lorca, prior to *Poeta en Nueva York,* is sexual, carnal, argues Martínez Nadal: 'amor, deseo, lujuria, es uno y uno mismo' [love, desire, lust: they are all one] (p. 161). Throughout his career, though, the complications of love just as often take the audience and reader away from the bodily. Carlos Feal Deibe, for instance, studies the ways in which the difficulty or impossibility of love in Lorca's work intensifies, extends and complicates desire. While he argues that the violence of unrequited passions between men and women in Lorca's work is attributable to fear (in the dramatist as well as in some of the protagonists) of the woman as other (Feal Deibe 1973,

Clughen, 'Lorca's Anorexics: Hunger Strike in the Cause of Selfhood', *Bulletin of Hispanic Studies* (Liverpool), 79, 3 (2002), 309–24.

[10] See Mary Evans, *Love: An Unromantic Discussion* (Cambridge: Polity Press, 2003).

[11] On the general history of this shift, see Bristow, pp. 12–115.

[12] Rafael Martínez Nadal, *'El Público': Amor, Teatro y Caballos en la obra de Federico García Lorca* (Oxford: Dolphin Book Co., 1970). See also Carlos Feal Deibe, *Eros y Lorca* (Barcelona: EDHASA, 1973), although this is less revealing because of the way it plunges straight into close readings of texts without signalling what each has to do with the other.

[13] The coy formulation is part of a passage grappling with the issue of Lorca's homosexuality at an early stage in the history of this strand of Lorca criticism.

pp. 263 and 261), Smith (*The Theatre of García Lorca*) and Wright study engagement with and disengagement from the Other in a psychoanalytical sense, exploring how these motivate and paralyze many of Lorca's characters and voices when they get caught up in the terms of love. The operative connection here is not so much between sexuality and the body (a locus of extraordinary directness, of sensation and lust) as it is between sexuality and the mind (as configured by and as configuring the desires of the body).

Pleasure and surrender

It is important to remember, though, that Lorca is as compelling on the pleasures of love as he is on its painful complications, although in the final section of this chapter we shall see that the majority of readings suggest that the dynamics of desire carry his protagonists and voices far away from the full apprehension of pleasure into the pain of loss or into annihilation, even when considerable physical pleasure has already been captured or may be recalled (as it is by Adela in *La casa de Bernarda Alba* [*The House of Bernarda Alba*]). Pleasure may be simple, and direct enough, as in the case of 'Al oído de una muchacha' [In the Ear of a Girl] (*Obras completas*, I, p. 331), where the visual leads to a sense of almost touching as well as to a position of almost saying: 'Vi en tus dos ojos / dos arbolitos locos. / De brisa, de risa y de oro' [I saw in your two eyes two mad little trees. Of breeze, of laughter and of gold] (translation by Walters, p. 207). Although Walters opens up the possibility of this poem's 'turning away from love' and its being an instance of 'erotic aversion' (Walters, p. 207), it is also possible that there is a sense of enjoyment here of the deliciousness of postponement of crass oral expression in favour of the equally sensual, and mobile, delights of what can be seen: those two 'mad little trees' of Walters's translation are just as much, and perhaps less sinisterly, wild little trees, and the gold, the prize and blaze of sexual excitement. Even love cut short or only imagined to have had physical fulfilment can lead to pleasure, this time pleasure pointed up by pain for the projected protagonist, and developed and enhanced through literary skill by the poet himself. This is sharply presented in 'Murió al amanecer' [Died at Dawn], in the *Canciones* (I, p. 343), which mixes physicality with literary wit relating 'the moon to a lemon and a coin pressed into the palm as an ill omen' (Walters, p. 203): 'Llevo el No que me diste, / en la palma de la mano, / como un limón de cera / casi blanco' [I bear the No that you gave me, in the palm of my hand, like a wax lemon that is almost white] (translation in Walters, p. 203). From the male narrator protagonist of the ballad 'La casada infiel' [The Unfaithful Married Woman] in the *Romancero gitano* to La Poncia in *La casa de Bernarda Alba*, Lorca's work abounds in characters able to give bold, no-nonsense accounts of the meaning of love – it is carnal, it is fleeting, it is often illicit, but it is a ready and relatively simple pleasure.

Much more compelling though are Lorca's accounts of the psychologically and socially imposed barriers to understanding and exploitation of love. Compelling too is the complicated overlay both of the notion of love as impossible or difficult of access for certain subjects (women living an experience constructed through heteronormative patriarchy, or precarious poetic personae) and, on the other hand, of its representation as something simply and directly there to be apprehended by everyone. Sometimes there does seem to be a way through to finding love even though the characters or voices that name it might be destroyed or decentred in the process, like the Bride and Leonardo in *Bodas de sangre* identifying love with absolute physical dependency or like the risk-taking voice of *Poeta en Nueva York* defining love in terms of purity and other-ness. At other times, where love appears to be a given, and naturally there, as often as not, it leads on into a discourse connecting it with oblivion or absolute surrender, leaving no original subject there, as it were, to continue the process of reaching out to grasp it. The expertise in absolute absorption of Lorca's charac-ters and voices can as easily lead to the extremity of alienation as to ecstasy. By a familiar enough paradox where love is concerned, direct, transparent appre-hension of the feeling and its operation in experience contributes directly at best to its shifting its ground, and at worst to its fragmentation and self-perpetuating inaccessibility.

In *Mariana Pineda* [*Mariana Pineda*], Mariana seems to have achieved ecstatic communication in Act 2, Scene 5 when she tells the rebel leader Pedro 'cuando se quiere / se está fuera del tiempo, / y ya no hay día ni noche, sino tú y yo!' [in love, one is outside time, and there is neither day nor night, only you and me] (*Obras completas*, II, p. 170); but she realizes later in the act, when she is left to face Pedrosa the justice and to cover for Pedro, that 'soy una mujer / que va atada a la cola de un caballo' [I am a woman tied to a horse's tail] (II, p. 187). Having fled the loss of agency in the world imposed on her by her adoptive mother's relayed, conventional views of women and politics at the start of the play – '[Mariana] debe dejar esas intrigas, / qué le importan las cosas de la calle!' [shouldn't get involved. What can it matter to her what goes on outside?] (II, p. 124) – she moves on into an equally gendered disempowerment, through her abandonment by Pedro and then into absolute surrender of autonomy at the hands of justice. Her eventual death by execution, while on the one hand heroic, is on the other a violent representation of her disempowerment by her espousal of a conventional and irrational code of love, which has meant that she has sacri-ficed her very power of thought to Pedro and to a code of honour that in literary and social terms is based around patriarchal priorities. She tells Fernando, her disappointed suitor, of her surrender to Pedro: 'Yo he conspirado / para vivir y amar su pensamiento propio' [If I have been a conspirator it has been in order to live and love his very thoughts] (II, p. 222). When he pleads with her in the name of love – a pragmatic, but no less strong, sort of love, which has sustained him through the years of disappointment – it is open to the director and actors to make that very word, love, the trigger for a tragic apprehension of uncertainty and the definitive alienation of Mariana from all that, in yet another sense, she might indeed have loved:

> MARIANA (*Loca y delirante, en un estado agudo de pasión y angustia*)
> Y qué es amor, Fernando? Yo no sé qué es amor!

[. . .] Tus palabras me llegan
a través del gran río del mundo que abandono.
Ya soy como la estrella sobre el agua profunda,
última débil brisa que se pierde en los álamos. (II, p. 223)

[MARIANA (*Crazed and delirious, in an acute state of passion and anxiety*)
And what is love, Fernando? I cannot know.
[. . .] Your words reach me
from across the great river of the world I am leaving.
I am like a star poised on deep waters,
the last of the breeze in the poplar trees.]

Rather than finding herself, as Julieta so desired, as a new Mariana 'en el comienzo' [at the beginning], she is pulling – pulled – away from time and the material world, disintegrated by self-sacrificial love; not on the promising shores of the city, with the story yet to begin, as Julieta wished, but pushed to the edge by the word 'amor' and the consequences of loving.

Love as disturbance

We have already begun to see how some of the early poems also concern themselves sporadically with this big, destabilizing question, 'Y qué es amor?' In particular they do so by looking for clues or ways of sharpening the question in a range of traditions written and oral, as Walters explains (in *'Canciones' and the Early Poetry of Lorca*). In an unexpectedly abstract way in the *Romancero gitano* – in view of the initial impression that the collection can give of being specifically about just such grand themes as love – love keeps resurfacing as a dislocated and disorienting question. It flickers in the background, barely attached to any single enunciating subject in 'Muerto de amor' [Dead from Love] despite the clearly emblematic status of the dead male (god, hero, martyr, simple victim of street violence) being brought down from the high places as part of the story. In the famous 'Romance sonámbulo' [Sleepwalking Ballad] love colours the action, seems to explain the return of one of the speakers to the place of death, and is one of the elements bonding the two speakers together and both of them to the dead woman floating through the poem's impressionistic narrative landscape. But it is notoriously difficult to allocate a single, personal position from which that strange statement 'Verde que te quiero, verde' [Green, I love you, green] (*Obras completas*, I, pp. 400, 402 and 403) emerges.

In *Poeta en Nueva York* the very lovelessness of the experience of the city sets into high relief the poems and sections of poems that deal with love, but that intensity reveals vast gaps in understanding and in the graspability of love. 'Nocturno del hueco' [A Nocturne on an Empty Space] addresses love itself, both as an abstract concept and a lover in whom a tragically aestheticized absence as much as presence is being sought after – ambivalently love and the lover are desired in the refrain 'Para ver que todo se ha ido!' [Only to then see that all has gone away / In order to see that all has gone away] (*Obras completas*, I, pp. 504–6). In 'Tu infancia en Menton' [Your Childhood in Menton] love is (conventionally enough) represented in terms of extreme conceptual opposites: 'Amor de siempre, amor, amor de nunca' [The same love as always, love, the same love as never] (I, p. 453). Less conventionally (except perhaps in terms of simple structuring), the once more ambivalent 'amor' as idea and as person sits there at the pivot of the line reconciling and failing to reconcile the old contradiction (being in love with love but being uncertain whether love existed or exists), but also, more radically, reconciling and failing to reconcile a high lyrical seriousness with a deliberately banal sentimentality and easy rhythm. The following line sets this affective seesaw in motion with flailing words and broken sense: 'Oh, sí! Yo quiero. Amor, amor. Dejadme' [Oh yes. I want to. Love, love. Leave me be] (I, p. 453). In this collection an unknown addressee and unidentified onlookers (evoked in the plural of 'dejadme') are spoken to by an unhinged subject capable of combinations of words producing nostalgic intensity, a sense of great pain, anger, frustration and passion, all clustered around love, but this same subject also finds structures that allow a detached, experimental examination of the bleak absurdity of the discourses of love, belonging and sense.

After 1930, while the poems of *Diván del Tamarit* [*Diwan of the Tamarit*] display a more controlled set of feelings, carefully working through the complexities of the associations of love, death and sex (Anderson 1990, pp. 16–152), the *Sonetos de amor oscuro* [*Sonnets of Dark Love*] written in 1935 and 1936 are 'about the tormented experience of love, passion and suffering' (Anderson 1990, p. 307). Their title alludes, as Anderson suggests (p. 306), to qualities of intimacy and deep, dark, Dionysian passion; it hints at that connection between loving and death or annihilation which Lorca so frequently uses both to construct directness and to create obliqueness. Far from leading exclusively to the accustomed extraordinary directness in the representation of feeling, this situation of connectedness of all and nothing, vitality and the void, seems to favour extreme textual precaution too. The 'Soneto de la guirnalda de rosas' [Sonnet of the Garland of Roses] works with sudden contrasts, explores disparity in the exchange of love (Anderson 1990, p. 313), and is interested in the shuttling backwards and forwards between emotional positions of the speaking, loving subject, 'Entre lo que me quieres y te quiero' [Between how much you love me and I love you];[14] similarly, in 'El poeta dice la verdad' [The Poet Tells the Truth], love is caught up (willingly) in the eternal 'madeja / del que te quiero me quieres, siempre ardida / con decrépito sol y luna vieja' [the twine / of I love you you love me, forever singed / by enfeebled sun and tired old moon] (*Sonetos*, p. 31). These are tactics in the midst of unthinking passion intellectually and creatively to postpone or deny the fall into love as annihilation, to escape surrender.

There are, of course, further possible motives for the strange impassioned

---

14 Federico García Lorca, *Sonetos del amor oscuro; Poemas de amor y erotismo; Inéditos de madurez*, ed. Javier Ruiz-Portella (Barcelona: Ediciones Áltera, 1995), 25.

cautiousness of these texts. As Anderson puts it, with understatement designed not so much to be cautious as to acknowledge the extreme history of denial that lay behind the eventual double publication of these poems in 1983 and 1984 (in a clandestine, unauthorized edition and then in the conservative paper *ABC*),[15] '[t]here is little doubt that on one level' it also alludes to 'homosexual love' (Anderson 1990, p. 305). There is an 'agitation' (Binding, p. 206) in most of the poems, and it is closely linked to sexuality as well as to the gendered conventions of love poetry: the usual assumption of a heterosexual perspective of the tradition of love poetry is set aside in favour of a direct, scarcely veiled sexual language referring to two male bodies in erotic activity in 'Noche del amor insomne' [Night of Sleepless Love] and 'El poeta le pide a su amor que le escriba' [The Poet Asks His Loved One to Write] (Binding, pp. 208–9)[16]; alongside religious connotations in 'Llagas de amor' [Wounds of Love] (Anderson 1990, pp. 328–30) there is a resurgence of a queer subcultural thematics of sado-masochism, tacitly explored by Sahuquillo in relation to the 'Diálogo del Amargo' [Dialogue of the Bitter One] in *Poema del cante jondo* [*Poem of the Deep Song*] and in *El público* (Sahuquillo, pp. 135–49). There is also, by way of sharp and dynamic contrast, a deliberate anchoring of the sonnets to Spanish Golden Age, Petrarchan and spiritual traditions, and at times a tight, elegant, and meaningful control of form (Anderson 1990, pp. 396–8); and in *Así que pasen cinco años* and *El público* enigmatic terseness in dialogue is used as a foil to a certain outrageousness in *mise-en-scène*, which may be played up or down by different artistic directors and productions.[17]

The forms of love and the form of their expression – by playing on norms and deviations from them, by mixing abandon and control – return the reader and the audience to just what Julieta says she does not want, effectively a questioning politics of desire. Like Stendhal and Ibsen before him, Lorca has his voices and characters engage, willingly and not, with the fact of the social construction of emotional life. He develops in this regard a 'dimensión retórico-revolucionaria' [revolutionary-rhetorical dimension] (Sahuquillo, p. 391). Here perceptions of gender inequality and, particularly in *Poeta en Nueva York*, class inequality, intuitions about the power of sexual desire, and, as is persuasively argued by Sahuquillo, Lorca's own experience and feelings about being caught up in 'la situación de homosexual perseguido' [the position of being a persecuted homosexual man] (p. 391) train an analytical gaze on questions of normativity, appearances and resistance or surrender to social conventions (p. 393).

[15] Daniel Eisenberg, 'Reaction to the Publication of the *Sonetos del amor oscuro*', *Bulletin of Hispanic Studies*, 65, 3 (1988), 261–71.

[16] Also see Ángel Sahuquillo, *Federico García Lorca y la Cultura de la Homosexualidad* (Alicante: Instituto de Cultura 'Juan Gil-Albert' / Diputación de Alicante, 1991), 127.

[17] Also see Smith 1998, pp. 40–2 on versions of *Yerma* [*Yerma*].

Femininity / masculinity

Cross-gender identification

It is not unusual for Lorca's accounts of female sexuality and the experience of women to be approached by way of a partial account of his homosexuality in relation to questions of norms and conventions. The results of such approaches are very uneven, and Sahuquillo (pp. 67–99) and Smith (1998, pp. 109–11) give clear accounts of the difficulties that critics have had with co-locating the author, his sexuality, and gender and sexuality in the texts. Back in 1970 came the warning that 'del no hablar de lo que Lorca no temía escribir, se ha pasado a sugerir que cuando Lorca menciona una mujer en un poema amoroso es disfraz del sexo contrario' [from a position where nobody would speak of what Lorca himself was not afraid to write down we have come to one where it is suggested that when Lorca mentions a woman in a love poem this is a disguise of a person of the opposite sex] (Martínez Nadal, p. 138). By the 1980s Paul Binding was asserting, only slightly less extremely, that the 'homosexual writer' has a special insight into women's autonomy and its denial and that Lorca, in *Doña Rosita la soltera o El lenguaje de las flores* [*Doña Rosita the Spinster or the Language of Flowers*] and *La casa de Bernarda Alba* 'make[s] use of his experience as a homosexual to apprehend the lives of women trapped and suffocated by custom' (Binding, p. 184). The homosexuality question cast in such rather crude terms, and calling on an explanatory model of bisexuality, intermediacy or transitionality (Bristow, pp. 38–46) still appears to bulk large in the teaching of pre-university or early honours-years students. A characteristic passage, which starts off usefully and then perhaps less usefully takes its cue from Binding, comes in a web-based study guide:

What are contemporary readers to make of this male author and his female subjects? Is his use of these figures a true gesture of liberation or simply more sexism in a humanist disguise? Lorca had no interest in feminism per se and clearly did not portray his Spanish women with reference to a specific social or political program. Instead, like Ibsen, Chekhov, and Benavente before him, he used women as human beings and analyzed their problems as representative of broader human dilemmas. But at the same time, his heroines are distinctively modern women [. . .] The very heart of their drama is their struggle to gain control over their lives, and the fact that all but one of his leading women fail is a criticism of the society which makes tragedy out of such a struggle. As a homosexual, Lorca had a special sympathy for oppressed, powerless groups and individuals, especially women.[18]

While one can look in a straightforward manner for evidence in the political Lorca of a nuanced understanding (or not, as the case may be) of oppression of

[18] David Richard Jones and Susan Jones, *Federico García Lorca: Study Guide*, online at http://www.repertorio.org/education/pdfs/lorca.pdf, p. 14. Accessed 25 April 2005.

social groups in his times, the method for exploring his 'sympathy' in terms of identification across gender is a more complex matter. First, with varying degrees of obviousness, critical readings have their own agendas, emphases and blindspots (this one also, no doubt). Second, one needs to recognize the counter-intuitive nature of the notion that a city-dwelling, upper middle-class, homosexual writer in 1920s and 1930s Spain, who to judge by most biographical accounts was struggling with the various stages of internalized homophobia (not usually a propitious state for feeling at ease with, let alone bonding with, the other sex), might be well placed to develop true emotional and political sympathy with (mainly rural) women.[19] Binding, in fact, is taking the argument for sympathetic identification in yet another direction in his assertion that Lorca's 'personal investment' in *Yerma* stems from 'the most anguishing problem for a homosexual', that 'his love-making can never lead to a child'; this adds to the power of the drama, he argues, in part by allowing an identification with Juan as well as with Yerma (Binding, p. 175). Interesting though the last part of this is for an understanding of the play, that evocation of the universalized anguished homosexual is as serious a critical obstacle as is its apparent contradiction of emphatically anti-procreative Lorcas elsewhere in the works (Sahuquillo, p. 381) or as is the unquestioning supposition that a personal investment by a dramatist should play a major rather than a minor, indirect or vestigial role.

   Other arguments for reading Lorca as feminine-identified seem to be symptoms of the gestures of humanism, not so much in Lorca as in his audiences and readers (Clughen, 'Lorca's Anorexics', pp. 309–24). For Clughen (p. 309), 'the humanist approach to Lorca [. . .] knows that the subject is an amalgam of such binary forces as the rational and the emotional and it knows that the female self bears a distinct relation to the emotional side of the binary.' Furthermore, if 'liberal humanists seek to know the natural, essential self', when they read Lorca in order to uncover this, then woman as 'representative of nature' becomes a 'necessary element'and, for a range of critics from the 1970s through to the 1990s, a key to knowledge.[20] As both Clughen and Smith (1989, pp. 105–37) argue, an extension of this sort of critical project (as well, indeed, as of some versions of Freudianism) is to see the feminine in terms of (tragic) incompleteness (Clughen, 'Re-Reading Lorca', pp. 52–3; Smith 1989, p. 111). So many are the instances of representation of women as being in search of something absent that seems vital to them – representations both by themselves in character and by the semiotics of the drama or the framing of poetic descriptions – that Lorca

---

   [19] On the other hand it is a fair if overstated point that in certain lights and in certain texts – mainly essays and letters – 'resulta obvio que Lorca tenía una gran conciencia social' [it is obvious that Lorca had a great social awareness] (Allen Josephs and Juan Caballero, 'Introducción', in Federico García Lorca, *La casa de Bernarda Alba*, ed. Allen Josephs and Juan Caballero [Madrid: Cátedra, 1998], 11–114 [p. 86]).
   [20] Lisa Clughen, 'Re-Reading Lorca', unpublished M. Phil thesis, University of Newcastle upon Tyne, 2002, 48–9.

does appear to encourage this tragic empathetic reading of femininity. However, as suggested in the first section of this chapter, in Lorca directness overlaps with sharp theorization on matters of the heart, of gender, and of sexuality. The woman who is in search of the ineffable, ungraspable object of desire – more in the dramas than in the poems, it is true – is also the woman who knows all too well what she wants. The more symbolic her speech and action gets, the plainer is the problem she faces from a sociological, gendered perspective.

Feminist Lorcas

Throughout Lorca's mature work there are socially grounded representations of femininity that stress gender equality, superiority on the side of the feminine, or a radical and sustaining distance from the projects of masculinity altogether. Lorca can be read according to first- and second-wave feminisms simultaneously, both for enlightened representations of possible models of equality and for a non-androcentric recasting of gender difference as anti-oppressive.[21] Let us take the first-wave perspective first. In the women-centred plays there are a number of clear, if not always directly historicized, accounts of disempowerment and power from an equality-interested perspective, or a perspective that links sexuality and gender roles to social control, and these are elaborated on in the standard critical texts. C. Brian Morris sees the Bride – among other male and female characters – as imprisoned by conventions as well as desire.[22] Virginia Higginbotham focuses on Lorca's use of irony, the grotesque and the techniques of absurdist drama to point up his rebellious attitudes to norms;[23] for example, Bernarda is read as 'the personification of a social code that has become so fraudulent it is farcical' and as a character she is 'preposterous' (Higginbotham, pp. 111 and 118); just as María Josefa pokes cruel fun at the daughters, so the women in the last scene of *Yerma* joke at Yerma's expense (pp. 101–2 and 148). Robin Warner, while stressing a philosophical and psychological rather than plainly feminist perspective (exploring Yerma's estrangement from a reality felt as otherness) links Yerma's plight to social issues of the time stressing contemporary rights-based and legal debates and Yerma's ambivalent position with regard to tradition and conformism.[24] Martínez Nadal documents Lorca's denunciations in the poetry and early plays of socially imposed lack of sexual and social fulfilment for a range of women (Martínez Nadal, pp. 141–54). All

---

[21] Claire Colebrook, *Gender*, Transitions (Basingstoke: Palgrave / Macmillan, 2004), 118–35.

[22] C. Brian Morris, *Federico García Lorca. Bodas de sangre*, Critical Guides to Spanish Texts 26 (London: Grant & Cutler, 1996), 30–42.

[23] Virginia Higginbotham, *The Comic Spirit of Federico García Lorca* (Austin and London: University of Texas Press, 1976). The study also places the plays in a context of Spanish and European theatre history: pp. 121–50.

[24] Robin Warner, 'Introduction', in Federico García Lorca, *Yerma*, ed. Robin Warner, Hispanic Texts (Manchester: Manchester University Press, 1994), 1–25 (pp. 16–17 and 21).

these readings look at a discrepancy in arguments that are posited on a masculine / feminine binary and the notion of a struggle for a rebalancing of power within broadly patriarchal structures whose permanent displacement is not seriously contemplated.

Some of Lorca is, though, readable in terms of second- as well as first-wave feminism. Second-wave feminism emphasized how there is 'no direct relation between bodies and genders' and 'rejected the ways in which female bodies had been interpreted or gendered' (Colebrook, p. 127); it was (and is) interested in questioning from a range of perspectives the established primacy of social familial structures (Colebrook, pp. 132–44) and in focusing on the feminine from feminine perspectives, abandoning the relationality of equality feminism. While the Bride and Yerma might define their frustrations in relation to men and a male-oriented social order, and while they and the women's voices in the pre-1930 poetry presuppose an essential, timeless set of gendered qualities and experiences for women, by no means all of Lorca's women are caught up in a scenario of injustice and inequality. Characteristically, Lorca's intense directness in matters of bodily feeling opens up possibilities for questioning the way that bodies are felt, perceived, interpreted. Clughen ('Lorca's Anorexics') and Smith (1998, pp. 16–43) are able to engage Lorca in an important dialogue with body-centred tenets of the discourse of difference, identifying escape routes away from the violence of the rhetoric of binary oppositions (especially male/female; self/body) (Clughen, pp. 318–20), or reading *Yerma* in the wider terms of 'a drama of the woman's body' (Smith 1998, p. 18) in the sense of its conformation through contemporary medical discourses and psychoanalytical insights around the question of sexual inversion and intersexuality, bisexuality and the destabilization of sexual oppositions (Smith 1998, pp. 28–33 and 37–40). Sarah Wright suggests that *Amor de Don Perlimplín con Belisa en su jardín* [*The Love of Don Perlimplín for Belisa in Their Garden*] requires its audiences to ask 'What is the truth of femininity?' (Wright, p. 53) and says, to post-twentieth-century audiences at least, that 'femininity is contingent, staged, inessential' (p. 54). An ancient and fairly straightforward story of gender power relations – adultery, revenge, men's fears of women (Wright, p. 49) – becomes an intricate investigation of how gender is experienced in relation to perceptions of death and the imagination of limits (Wright's main themes). What is a woman, in Lorca, becomes as double-textured a question (with its simple, self-evident layer and its underlying criss-crossing of ideas) as Mariana's 'what is love?'

Masculinity

And what is a man? Attention to Lorca's representation of masculinity is an important contribution to the still rather slow change of emphasis in critical reception and the efforts to counter 'the pernicious and pervasive folkloric stereotypes that [. . .] determine foreign responses to Lorca and the concentration on the so-called rural trilogy' (Smith 1998, p. 4). The 'trilogy', of course, is itself as much about men as about women and is stocked, on stage and off, with a range of typical masculinities some of which are filled out and undermined by

textual and dramatic stategies that emphasize contradictions within and diver-
gences from conventional gendered positions. Folkloric stereotyping tempts
audiences, novice students and some critics into over-plain and binaristic interpretations of these plays, ignoring the complications of masculinity. Mischievously, Lorca has his patriarchs, adulterers, rugged men of the soil and the horse
(be they sucked dry or pumped up by their contact with nature) inhabit a
hyper-signifying space, which leads them into iconic stasis; so much so, in *La
casa de Bernarda Alba*, that Pepe el Romano is so impossibly handsome, so
much a virile force, that he has to become a *deus ex machina* as well as the local
stud. Much the same temptation is laid down, with less intensity, in the pre-1930
poems with their olive-skinned fighters, male Gypsies, boys, bandits and
matadors, and women's longings for the same. An interestingly persistent and
anachronistic, critical orientalization and typification of Lorca's men – and
particularly of his men in love – ignores his scope, his intellectual eclecticism,
his analytical aesthetic, and also his sense of humour. It also forgets that it is
around masculine figures and in masculine voices that another of the persistent
fascinations for Lorca criticism is focused – androgyny. In representing his men
Lorca is constantly drawn to exploring not gender difference but forms of
overlap that lead to a questioning of heteronormative interpretations of masculinity, sometimes through the strategies of camp.[25] So, if one sort of reading of
the ballad 'San Miguel (Granada)' [Saint Michael (Granada)] can privilege the
term of masculinity by speaking of the saint as 'afeminado' (made feminine,
effeminate) (Feal Deibe 1973, p. 195) and, by speaking in terms of a virility
reduced and threatened (Feal Deibe 1973, p. 196), can suggest that masculinity
is the true original and femininity the alteration or aberration, more (if not
totally) convincing is a reading of the poem as an affirmation through
homoeroticism and the operation of a camp perspective on traditional, religious
Andalusian culture of a dissident sexuality at work in the formation of the
writer's imagination (Binding, pp. 121–2). It might seem strange to seek such
gender- and sexuality-related instabilities in a collection where, even when its
complexities are recognized, they are literary, cultural or hermeneutic ones.
However, Luis Antonio de Villena rightly asks the readership of the magazine
Qué leer, 'Cómo no percibir el alto homoerotismo del *Romancero gitano*?'
[how could one not notice the high degree of homoeroticism in the *Gypsy
Ballads*?].[26] Conventionally enough Villena, like others (Anderson 1990, pp.

---

[25] This is explored amusingly in text and graphics in relation to the figure of the
androgyne in Gregorio Prieto, *Lorca y su mundo angélico* (Madrid: Sala Editorial, 1972), 195.
The whole book, in fact, by drawing out in graphic images homoerotic and camp aspects of
the poet and dramatist's work, seeks to enshrine Lorca as an 'Adán miguelangélico,
convertido en Angel y dios helénico [. . .] un ave de hermoso plumaje' [a Michelangelic
Adam, become Angel and Hellenic god [. . .] a bird of handsome pink feathers] (pp. 9 and
10), a Lorca who is now in tune with the spirit of the early 1970s, 'Federico, *in*. Federico,
camp. Federico, *pop*' (p. 173).
[26] Luis Antonio de Villena, 'Lorca: De mito rojo a mártir gay', *Qué leer*, 20 (March

412–13; Walters, pp. 1–39), is concerned to preserve the idea of the open-endedness of poetry, and insists that 'como todo gran poeta, García Lorca es un escritor plural, y ninguna lectura ciega otras' [like all great poets, García Lorca is a writer whose work is marked by plurality, and no one reading shuts off others] (Villena 1998, p. 66); he also wishes to protect Lorca from a ghetto-ization related to his sexuality that would be just as unproductive as his folklorization (Villena 1998, p. 66). In fact the collection probably saves itself from both through a knowing hybridization, around the male figures, of height-ened elements of both tendencies, mixing a highly fabricated essence of Gypsy masculinity with a distillation of a queer look at men and their doings.

In the poetry prior to *Poeta en Nueva York* this dissident interest in gender overlap, and this move to reinterpret masculinity are far from evident at first reading, it is true. They soon assert themselves, however. The early poems seem to play to a somewhat static, romanticized image of the Andalusian male. Some-times, though, there is a slightly destabilizing glamorization of masculinity through techniques of reduction learned from the old ballad and other traditions and put to new use, such as the evocative reduction to their horses, clothes, swords of the first seven suitors of the girl picking olives in 'Arbolé, arbolé' (*Obras completas*, I, p. 315) and to fragrant, magical, erotic and mythic 'rosas y mirtos de luna' [roses and myrtles of the moon] of the last. In the *Romancero gitano* masculinity begins to attract a more distinctive sideways glance as repre-sentational associations of men with swords, bright colours, knives and horses (the 'Romance sonámbulo' is among other things a compendium of such features: *Obras completas*, I, pp. 400–3) come close to fetishization while flashes of gleaming olive skin (I, pp. 417, 419), thighs, waists and shoulders (I, pp. 399, 413, 414), curled hair and eyes (I, p. 417) display a simpler, franker interest on the part of the text in drawing attention to male sexual beauty just as there is constant reference to female sexual beauty too (Martínez Nadal, pp. 162–73 and 189–90). Directness and complication again go hand in hand, not just through this kind of homoerotic objectification but also through an eroticization of violence, of blood and of death, which, while keying in to a major concern with the links between *eros* and *thanatos*, serves principally to add layers of varying implication to the brute representation of masculinity. 'Muerte de Antoñito el Camborio' [The Death of Antoñito el Camborio] (*Obras completas*, I, pp. 419–20), again deploying standard Lorcan tropes of masculine beauty ('moreno de verde luna, / voz de clavel varonil' [dark olive moonlit skin, a manly voice like the scent of carnations]), has a curiously destabilizing moment of proximity to camp seriousness in a context of violent death as the speaker witnessing the death (one Federico García) pays the dying man the hyperbolic compliment – such as no man would to another man in hetero-normative reality – of saying that he is 'worthy of an Empress' (I, p. 420). In

1998), 66–7 (p. 67). See also Luis Antonio de Villena, 'La sensibilidad homoerótica en el *Romancero gitano*', *Campus*, 11 (1986), 27–30.

'Muerto de amor' [Dead from Love] (I, pp. 421–2) blood itself is the metonym
for the dead man, or for dead love, at the poem's narrative core, and the blood is
'tranquila de flor cortada / y amarga de muslo joven' in a tortured syntax that
might suggest both 'deathly quiet because it is like a cut flower and bitter
because it flows from so young a thigh' and 'with the calmness of a cut flower
and the bitterness of a young man's thigh'. There is a hint here of a decadent
perversity fixed at the level of the image; at the level of literary reference
though, as has been noted,[27] the mythological, religious and ritualistic connotations of this representation of the Death Of Love bypass the poem's interest in
the eroticized male body. This is a characteristic sleight of hand. 'Reyerta'
[Duel] (*Obras completas*, I, pp. 398–9) – originally 'Reyerta de mozos' [Duel
Between Young Men] – with its vivid snapshot reversal and overlay of the
moment of fatal wounding and the moment of burial in the lines 'su cuerpo lleno
de lirios / y una granada en las sienes' [his body covered in lilies / and pome-
granate at his temples] (I, p. 398) – might seem a brilliant, stylized micro-drama,
with an argument over gambling or a simple sexual rivalry (over a woman) at its
core; but its structure of allusion refers out to iconic masculinities that are both
culturally too distant from Andalusia and too various to allow folkloricization or
any reduction down to a set of clichéd stories about men on the tough, Southern,
rural roads. Christ and Bacchus flicker in the background, and there are rapid
references to bullfighting and to war (in the Romans and Carthaginians).[28] The
poem also creates a dream or nightmare landscape of masculine resonance
where dark angels appear. As if in some sadomasochistic micro-drama, they
come both to tend the wounded man with bandages and ointment and to further
wound him with wings made of knife-blades. Lorca's own explication of it is
intriguing: it represents those fights between young men, he explains, that
happen 'por causas misteriosas, por una mirada, por una rosa, porque un hombre
de repente siente una mosca en su mejilla, por un amor de hace dos siglos' [for
mysterious reasons, because of a look, or a rose, or because a man suddenly
feels a fly settle on his cheek, because of a love some two centuries old].[29] Who
might look at whom with what intention, and whether that rose might provoke
envy as much as jealousy is left mischievously open.

Where jealousy and rivalry is most clearly and most famously at the core of
the plot is in *Bodas de sangre*, of course; and the play's men fit certain types:
two bands of feuding fathers and brothers; the just-male-enough but unexciting
Novio [Groom]; the uncontainable but self-recriminating force of virile desire

[27] See Christian de Paepe's notes in Federico García Lorca, *Romancero gitano*, ed. Christian de Paepe, Colección Austral 156 (Madrid: Espasa-Calpe, 1998), 157–62.

[28] Miguel García-Posada, 'Introducción', in Federico García Lorca, *Primer romancero
gitano. Llanto por Ignacio Sánchez Mejías. Romance de la corrida de toros en Ronda, y otros
textos taurinos*, ed. Miguel García-Posada (Madrid: Castalia, 1988), 9–73 (p. 42; also p. 118,
notes).

[29] Federico García Lorca, 'Conferencia-Recital del *Romancero gitano*', in Lorca,
Romancero gitano, ed. Christian de Paepe, 209–18 (p. 213).

Leonardo; the aloof visiting father of the bride and an anxious jockeying for patriarchal credibility between him and the Madre as substitute head of the family on the Groom's side; and all these masculine positions are so alien to the women in the play that the latter have constantly to redescribe them to themselves as if they were at constant risk of forgetting what a man is like. However, the play is also concerned with far less polarized representations of masculinity and in a strictly delimited way in Act 3 rehearses (off-stage) the radical experimentation with gender fluidity associated with *El público* (discussed below). Inverted gender roles and suggestions of an erotic death- and blood-bond between the two men, the Groom and Leonardo, in *Bodas de sangre* (Sahuquillo, pp. 277–8) – 'Morenito el uno / Morenito el otro' [One dark and handsome / the other one too], as Sahuquillo points out (p. 277) – have interested critics since the early 1980s.[30] Carlos Saura's dance film version of the play enhances the sensuality of the confrontation of the two men (Sahuquillo, p. 278) and, indeed, shows it (Smith 1998, p.4). Smith has argued that the climax of the play 'dramatizes [. . .] the young male body and its confrontation with that of the other and that within a context of "all-pervasive melancholia" – in the Freudian sense of a working through of the loss of the object (the other or the object of desire) – it enacts the missing relation "between desiring male bodies" ' (Smith 1998, pp. 5 and 65). This off-stage happening, otherwise very difficult to integrate into the play's meanings, thus links the event to the Madre's state of pathological mourning, the Bride's exhibition of melancholia (Smith 1998, p. 63). Images of savage orality that have their models in the Freudian incorporation of the (lost) object into the ego (Smith 1998, p. 64) make sense as part of an exploration by Lorca – another of his hidden theorizations – of a libidinal economy of which Smith (1998, p. 68) sees him in control, rather than fate just being in control of the characters.

In *Yerma*, although it is true that '[s]o dominating is Yerma's presence that other characters tend to serve as foils for different sides of her dramatic personality' (Warner, p. 11), the relationship between Juan and Víctor, which in Act 1, Scene 1 is based around economic exchange (of livestock), becomes one of mutual interest that will develop into a partial exchange of roles and an enclosure of both in the same gendered hell of oppression and repression. Victor in Act 1, Scene 1 is already passing on advice to Juan via Yerma (that he should worry less about work); in Scene 2 he remarks on Juan's lack of spark; he knows what is going on and has projected himself into the relationship as well as being constructed in Yerma's fantasies as a substitute husband. By Act 2, Scene 2, for Juan, unconsciously, the unnameable Víctor has become his rival and a threat to

---

[30] Andrew A. Anderson, 'De qué trata *Bodas de sangre*?', in *Hommage à Federico García Lorca*, Travaux de l'Université de Toulouse-Le Mirail, Série A20, ed. Michèle Ramond (Toulouse: Université de Toulouse-Le-Mirail, 1982), 53–64 (p. 60); Carlos Feal Deibe, 'El sacrificio de la hombría en *Bodas de sangre*', *Modern Language Notes*, 99 (1984), 270–87; Terence McMullan, 'Federico García Lorca's Critique of Marriage in *Bodas de sangre*', *Neophilologus*, 77 (1993), 62–73 (p. 71).

his honour, reinforcing not his desire for Yerma, or to be Víctor, but simply his position as husband. The presence of Víctor beyond the space of the marital relationship and beyond the terms of Juan's own uncommunicative masculinity has to be dealt with by a redefinition and shoring up of masculinity in terms of its superiority to a femininity lacking agency: 'quiero ver cerrada esa puerta y cada persona en su casa' [I want to see that door shut and each in their own house], 'piensa que eres una mujer casada' [remember that you are a married woman], 'obligarte, encerrarte, porque para eso soy el marido' [to have you obey me, shut you in, that's what my being your husband means I must do] (*Obras completas*, II, p. 709). By the time Víctor's father's decision to move his sons saves him from himself, he has reverted – though with a strong ironic undertow coming in from elsewhere in the play, and under pressure from the presence on stage of one of Juan's sisters – to a similar interpretation of labour and gender roles as is held to so desperately by Juan: 'La acequia por su sitio, el rebaño en el redil, la luna en el cielo y el hombre con su arado' [water following its course, the sheep in their pen, the moon in the sky, and a man with his plough] (II, p. 717). When Yerma explains her restlessness and her searching to Juan in terms of a quest for the man that he is not but might have been, her language operates a conflation of the two men: 'Te busco a ti. Es a ti a quien busco día y noche sin encontrar sombra donde respirar' [It's you I am searching for. You are the one I search for day and night without ever finding a cool and shady place to draw a breath] (II, p. 727).

Control and abandon

In his exploration of the dynamics of repression in Lorca's theatre and how it 'deconstructs the very idea of sexual gender',[31] Stephen Hart remarks of *La casa de Bernarda Alba* that it is 'intriguing that, given the critique immanent in Lorca's play, that the dramatic structure should be conventional' (Hart, p. 25), the structure thus all the more effectively 'conveying repression' (p. 26) by its tight control over the materials of desire. Lorca structures his masculinities similarly, not just, as suggested above, in broad-brush sketches in the poems, near-realist and conventional presentations of rural Mediterranean patriarchy, or fairly standard camp snapshots of prettified, well-built males, but across a wider range exploring the potential in the tensions he sets up between established patterns for realizing masculinity and, within those patterns, dramatically crucial deviations. His sociological instinct has his principal men anxiously performing masculinity in terms of a measuring up to others' masculinity or desirability as a male; but this pattern is radically disturbed when masculinity is all but displaced by its own excessiveness or by an apparent opposite – in the form of effeminacy, lack of agency, masochism – which turns out to be part of masculinity itself.

[31] Stephen M. Hart, *The Other Scene: Psychoanalytical Readings in Modern Spanish and Latin-American Literature* (Boulder, CO: Society of Spanish and Spanish-American Studies, 1992), 19–20.

First let us look at lack of agency and the abandonment of decision as an apparent non- or anti-masculine trait. Despite the considerable psychosexual complexity in the character of the Joven [Young Man] in *Así que pasen cinco años* – structured around 'reticence and postponement [. . .] and intermittent desire' (Smith 1998, p. 103) – and the difficult unconventionality of the play itself, the gender structuring of it is reassuringly schematic for an audience needing a way in. A range of non-human characters (as in *Bodas de sangre*) take on most of the business of building a problematic lyrical and libidinal structure on a shifting ground of misdirected desires, missed opportunities, lust and frustration, while the Young Man fills out as a fascinating study in what for audiences and readers with the late nineteenth- and early twentieth-century European repertoire in mind is a familiar enough masculinity made up of one part asexuality (Ucelay, p. 80), one part heterosexual desire that is out of synchronization, or 'stagger[ed]' (Smith 1998, p. 92), one part narcissistic bachelorhood, and a Buñuelesque dash of dangerous uptightness brought about by the burden of bourgeois living. Against him is set a Friend who represents robustness, vitality, omnisexuality (Ucelay, pp. 79–80) and tactile homosociality, and a Rugby Player who, with farcical obviousness, is no-nonsense, fully synchronized heterosexuality (in the simple but important enough sense that he finds his way into the Fiancée's bedroom at the right time and at least believes that he is able to sustain the right mood). When rejected by the Fiancée after the long wait imposed on her, the Young Man swerves away from confronting the immediate emotional pain, the responsibility, and the implications of her having, in her extremity, confused him with the Rugby Player, by an act of classic denial: 'Tú no significas nada. Es mi tesoro perdido' [You mean nothing. My lost treasure is what matters] (*Obras completas*, II, p. 413). This lost treasure is many, complex things: displaced desire, the misplaced abstract object of desire in a Freudian reading – 'the precious gift of the female genitals' or 'a relic of past psychic time', the object of analysis (Smith 1998, p. 102). It is also wounded masculine pride and an adherence to another sort of past. The Young Man sounds like a man of an older generation and of a rural rather than a modern urban space: he sounds like Juan, in *Yerma*, insisting in this scene that the Fiancée simply cannot break away, that she belongs to him; or, in a sudden reversal but in equally egocentric mode, he is like Leonardo at his most abandoned in *Bodas de sangre*: 'No hay más fuego que el mío' [No fire matches what I feel] (*Obras completas*, II, p. 411). He is the male hysteric, flailing out, regressing, doing anything but what in terms of gender power relations might be the right thing to do.

No less multifaceted and structurally demanding, and just as provocative psychosexually, *El público* nonetheless also displays a desire deceptively but pragmatically to schematize its men. In the midst of a dramatic discourse that fragments and extends bodily limits, and breaks down boundaries between categories and senses (Wright, pp. 106–25), there are some surprisingly solid points of reference for an understanding of male sexuality and masculine gender. Again there are bold contrasts designed to make a clear point for the sleepiest of audiences. The Artistic Director having trouble with his masculinity is set against a Centurion who is a grotesque parody of virile potency (Millán, p. 57). An Emperor represents both patriarchal power and one of its concomitants, pederasty. There are three White Horses who more or less represent socialized heterosexual masculinity (Millán, p. 58) and three Men who reveal heterosexuality's slippages. Man 1 uses his homosexuality, impelled by his now unrequited love for the Artistic Director, to theorize an alternative version of lived reality to that seen by the general public and the Horses, and he is doubled by a Figure in Vine Leaves who in Cuadro [scene] 2 sporadically evokes a manly homosexuality in the manner of the ideal, pure male in the 'Ode to Walt Whitman' in *Poeta en Nueva York* (Binding, pp. 131–42; Sahuquillo, pp. 103–12); Man 2 is fearfully alive to the fragility of sexual identity, is constantly counselling caution, acknowledges that he is enslaved to Man 3 (and to fear) (Cuadro 3: *Obras completas*, II, p. 490), and transforms into a woman in a black pyjama suit with a poppy motif; and Man 3 is a violent version of dysfunctional masculinity on the model of Don Juan, stripping Man 2 of her/his cross-dressing, and attempting to seduce Juliet. In a play whose themes are violence, pain and death as much as desire and lack of fulfilment (Wright, pp. 105–25), a classic duel between two men is a fitting way for Lorca to complicate his vision of masculinity, of gender and of sexuality. The transformative identifications of the play lead in part to a new vision of homosexual masculine identification where rivalry and love are neither sublimated nor repressed and where there is no misogynistic dynamic, no woman as object of fear or of exchange (Smith 1998, p. 132). But a price that Lorca pays for his conjuring with the tensions between the schematic and the fluidly new is that visions like this can waver. When Man 1 dares to go too close to the grain by refusing to acknowledge the presence of 'the mask' – which is, as in *Poeta en Nueva York*, death, but also convention – repression and oppression break back in. He feels he has fought the mask and won and can now see the Director metaphorically stripped bare (*Obras completas*, II, p. 501). For the latter, in denial and in fearful regression to a conservative position, 'la máscara oprime de tal forma nuestra carne que apenas si podemos tendernos en la cama' (II, p. 502) [the mask oppresses our flesh to such an extent that we can scarcely bear to lie down in our beds], and Man 1's openness and his embrace topples the Director back into homophobic self-loathing and urgent rejection:

> HOMBRE 1. (*Luchando*)   Te amo.
> DIRECTOR. (*Luchando*)   Te escupo. (II, p. 503)
>
> [MAN 1: (*Fighting him*)   I love you.
> DIRECTOR: (*Fighting him*)   I spit you out.]

This is that sting of theory in the tail of love that Juliet so regretted, and here is one answer at least to Mariana's naïve but necessary question – 'Y qué es amor, Fernando?' It is an answer that typically cuts through folkloricizing and ghettoizing readings of gender and sexuality in Lorca. It reminds the audience and reader of the dramas and micro-dramas of love that just when the ecstatic moment of absolute equivalence, of direct communication and full feeling, appears to have been achieved, the mood will change. Playfulness, extreme intertextual awareness, angry irony, fierce moments of empathy, disjunctures between form, utterance and performance, or sheer pathos – all or any may intervene movingly to complicate our apprehensions of how Lorca's characters and voices are caught up in and yet can often escape nature's and society's schemes of gender and of sexuality.

8

Politics

NIGEL DENNIS

In order to understand Lorca's politics we need to set him in the context of his times and to consider the events that shaped the sensibilities of the entire generation of writers to which he belonged. It is true that the collective experience cannot fully explain the sense of every individual case but it can legitimately draw attention to the range of social and historical circumstances to which all alert intellectuals of those years responded, directly or indirectly, positively or negatively, as they took stock of their place in the world and tried to define their role in it. Lorca was never a protagonist of political events, but nor was he an indifferent or neutral observer of them. Like his contemporaries, he reacted to what occurred around him and was prepared, when he thought the situation required it, to go on public record and state his beliefs, lending his support to a particular initiative or voicing his opposition to an incident or situation that troubled him. This did not necessarily make him a political writer, and we need to distinguish carefully between Lorca the man and Lorca the writer, between what the former said and what the latter wrote. It is easy to succumb to the temptation of hoisting an ideological agenda on to Lorca's writing in order to appropriate him for particular political ends. This happened during his lifetime and has certainly happened since his death, the circumstances of which transformed him, for better or for worse, into the martyred champion of a political cause. But we doubtless diminish his writings by stressing only the political charge they often seem to carry or can be made to bear. It is not the same, after all, to express an ethical impulse in favour of social justice and individual fulfilment as it is to be a revolutionary writer committed to the dissemination of a partisan political programme. We would do well to acknowledge at the beginning of this discussion that any approach to Lorca is bound to be partial, provisional and problematic. This is partly because of the complexity and elusiveness of the man, who oscillated between playing the public role of joyful entertainer and retreating into an intensely private world of acute uncertainties. It is also partly because of the very richness of his writing itself – revelatory and enigmatic at one and the same time, an invitation to endlessly divergent readings.

Like a good many of his friends and fellow writers, Lorca, born on 5 June 1898, grew up in a privileged, middle-class environment and remained financially dependent on his indulgent parents until he was into his thirties. However, he also absorbed the liberal atmosphere of his household and from an early age displayed the kind of progressive outlook that characterized his family. His father, Federico García Rodríguez, was a man of humble, working-class origins who only became an affluent property owner after the death of his first wife, Matilde Palacios, in 1894. He subsequently proved to be an astute and energetic businessman who prospered in the sugar market and extended his property hold-ings, becoming a well-known member of Granada's middle class after he moved his family there in 1909 from the rural isolation of Fuente Vaqueros. Concerned to consolidate his standing in the community, he became involved in local poli-tics and was elected to Granada's town council in 1916. While there was nothing notably radical about his political affiliations, he evidently took his duties seriously and discharged his civic responsibilities diligently. It is notable, however, that he counted among his friends the distinguished Socialist Fernando de los Ríos, an outspoken opponent of the dictatorship of Primo de Rivera (1923–30) and of the monarchy and a leading supporter of the Republican movement.

Despite his financial success and acquired social distinction, Lorca's father remained conscious of his origins and adopted an enlightened approach to the administration of his lands and to the treatment of the peasants who worked them. He became well known and admired for his philanthropic policies and acts of personal generosity. On one occasion, as Javier Herrero has noted, he tackled an acute problem of local unemployment by commissioning the construction on his land of a series of houses that he then rented out at low cost or else made available to people in need.[1] It was natural that he should welcome the advent of the Republic in 1931, seeing in it the vehicle for progressive social reform with which he instinctively sympathized. This was an unusual response in the archly conservative context of Granada, and we should not be surprised to learn that following the outbreak of Civil War he was labelled a 'rojo' [red] and his properties were confiscated.[2]

For her part, Lorca's mother was a cultured woman who shared her husband's liberal outlook as well as his compassionate approach to the agricultural workers based on family landholdings. Ian Gibson has noted how, fired with the evangel-ical idealism of the Institución Libre de Enseñanza [Free Teaching Institution],

---

[1] Javier Herrero, 'Don Federico García Rodríguez concejal del Ayuntamiento de Granada. Un enigma lorquiano', *Bulletin of Spanish Studies*, 81, 3 (2004), 309–23 (p. 321).

[2] Herrero notes that when this occurred, towards the end of 1936, Federico García Rodríguez was officially categorized as 'de los militantes del llamado "Frente Popular", o de las personas implicadas en manejos revolucionarios y actos contrarios a la causa del Ejército Nacional' [one of the militants of the so-called 'Popular Front' or among those people involved in revolutionary activities prejudicial to the cause of the National Army] (Herrero, p. 322). While he successfully regained possession of his lands and businesses before the end of the war, he continued to be identified as an enemy of the new regime. We should not forget that one of his daughters, Isabel, married Manuel Fernández-Montesinos, who was elected Socialist Mayor of Granada in 1936 and shot soon after the outbreak of war. His son Fran-cisco, the writer's brother, married the daughter of Fernando de los Ríos.

she personally taught 'hundreds of peasants' to read.[3] She seemed to attach little importance to class distinctions and lived comfortably alongside those less fortunate than herself, offering them support in their times of need.

While it is hard to say precisely what impact this family background – especially these parental examples – had on Lorca's own outlook, it seems reasonable to suppose that above and beyond a direct knowledge of and respect for the rural working class, their living conditions and cultural traditions, it gave him what must have amounted to a social conscience if not a political awareness. His parents' situation would have enabled him to temper an attachment to social and economic privilege with a liberal political outlook towards the marginalized and dispossessed, fostering a spirit of generosity and compassion that would manifest itself continuously in his adult life. Incorporated quite naturally into the circles in which his parents moved and conscious of the key presence of someone like Fernando de los Ríos, Lorca would in all likelihood have acquired a relatively clear understanding of the political issues facing the country. What better source of information than Fernando de los Ríos concerning the debates that took place among the enlightened middle class in the 1920s and 1930s about the problems facing Spain and the dangers attached to them? A natural consequence of these contacts, as we shall see, would be for Lorca to identify with the progressive, reforming spirit of Republicanism and to feel a desire to support the democratic initiatives it promoted.

When Lorca moved to Madrid in 1919 to continue his studies at the Residencia de Estudiantes, he entered a world that has conventionally been portrayed as largely indifferent to social and political issues. It is certainly true that for the select group of privileged young men at the Residencia, this was a relatively carefree time during which they were able to indulge their post-adolescent sense of playful ingenuity without paying too much attention to what was happening outside in the street. As Esteban Salazar Chapela was to comment in 1927, the entire Spanish avant-garde, the *residentes* included, seemed to have lived those years 'en el vacío [. . .] como si no existiera el mundo, España' [in a vacuum as if the world, Spain, did not exist].[4] Emblematic of this alleged apoliticism was the position taken by the journal *Revista de Occidente* – to which Lorca would regularly contribute – when it was launched in the summer of 1923: 'de espaldas a toda política' [with its back turned to politics].[5] Yet this perception of the 1920s as a period of aloofness or languid neutrality needs to be nuanced since it rests, on the one hand, on an implicit

---

[3] Ian Gibson, *Federico García Lorca: A Life* (London: Faber & Faber, 1989), 14. The Institución Libre de Enseñanza, founded in 1876 by Francisco Giner de los Ríos, was a lay college in Madrid renowned for its progressive ideas (see Gibson 1989, p. 21). Gibson's exhaustively documented biography, cited here, has proved an invaluable source, as will be evident from the frequency with which this chapter refers to it.

[4] Quoted by Javier Tussell and Genoveva G. Queipo de Llano, *Los intelectuales y la República* (Madrid: Nerea, 1990), 73.

[5] *Revista de Occidente*, 1 (July 1923), p. 2.

comparison with the 1930s, an emphatically more turbulent decade, which inevitably provoked a more combative response from writers and intellectuals, and, on the other, on the assumption that if a writer's work showed little if any trace of engagement with the realities of the time, the person wielding the pen lacked any political awareness or conviction.

The 1920s in Spain were, in fact, considerably less tranquil than standard accounts, especially those presented from a literary point of view, would have us believe. If cultural life flourished during that decade at the expense of active political involvement, it was not solely because of the emergence of a conjunction of exceptionally talented artists (Lorca among them) or because of their high-minded devotion to the ideals of pure art, but also because the stifling conditions of Primo de Rivera's dictatorship discouraged and curtailed political activity. Some notable writers like Unamuno did speak out vehemently against the regime and were duly subjected to severe punishment: prohibition and deportation. It is worth remembering that soon after *Revista de Occidente* appeared, with its sights fixed firmly on everything but politics, Antonio Espina, a companion of Lorca's who shared many of his interests at the time, urged his contemporaries – with the cry 'junamunámonos!' [let us be like Unamuno] – to follow his dissident lead.[6] If so few writers seemed to respond to such incitement, either in their lives or their work, it was not because of indifference to the national situation but rather because of a resolve to separate their writing from the world of prosaic socio-political realities they felt powerless to change. This, surely, is one of the implications behind the key observations José Ortega y Gasset made in his reflections on avant-garde art gathered in 1925 in *La deshumanización del arte* [*The Dehumanization of Art*]: 'vida es una cosa, poesía es otra'; 'el poeta empieza donde el hombre acaba' [Life is one thing, poetry is another; the poet begins where the man ends].[7] Far from advocating the separation of art and life or the exclusion of political interests from literary and artistic endeavours, Ortega was simply noting that the artists of the time, in the context of their own creative activities, had set the real and the mundane to one side. The simple fact is that it is impossible to determine the degree of political awareness (or otherwise) of any writer by dwelling solely on the content or style of his or her writing.[8]

---

6 Antonio Espina, 'Concéntricas panfletarias', *España*, 13 October 1923, n.p.

7 'La deshumanización del arte', in José Ortega y Gasset, *La deshumanización del arte y otros ensayos de estética*, Colección Austral 13 (Madrid: Espasa-Calpe, 1987), 45–92 (p. 72).

8 The reader should bear in mind that throughout the period under review, Ortega's attitude towards national political life oscillated between engagement and retreat, enthusiasm and remorse. Yet even in his moments of withdrawal and intense intellectual activity, he cannot be accused of being indifferent or uninformed about what was happening in the political arena. It is worth remembering, for example, that in November 1927 he began publishing in the newspaper *El Sol* a series of articles entitled 'Ideas políticas' [Political Ideas] in which he discussed, among other things, the prospect of a future Spain without a dictatorial regime and encouraged intellectuals to become involved in politics. A key statement was: 'España llega a un recodo histórico en el cual sólo puede salvarla, políticamente, la seria colaboración de los

It is difficult to document Lorca's ideas on non-literary or non-personal issues during the 1920s because of the scarcity of hard evidence. As his career gathered momentum, he may often have found himself under the spotlight of critical or public attention, but it is rare to encounter his name in any explicitly political context. It is evident, though, that even before he arrived at the Residencia, his writing had revealed a critical dissatisfaction with certain aspects of national life that is hard to dismiss as mere youthful nonconformity. Ian Gibson has shown how in a number of texts written in 1917 and 1918, for example, there are clear expressions of anti-clericalism, anti-militarism and a contempt for the bombastic rhetoric of exaggerated patriotism.[9] This helps to make sense of the comment made by the poet Emilio Prados about the Lorca he met in Madrid at the Residencia: 'his political ideals [are] at variance with his privileged social position' (quoted by Gibson 1989, p. 95). However, we know very little about what these 'political ideals' were and how they developed in subsequent years or the degree to which they determined his perception of national life or his approach to his own work.

It is not until the autumn of 1927, only a few months before he and a select group of friends would gather in Seville to pay homage to Góngora, the great Baroque poet of the seventeenth century and embodiment of the ideals of pure literary creation, that we get an insight into Lorca's response as a writer to the political realities and pressures of the time. This occurred following the Madrid première of his play *Mariana Pineda* [*Mariana Pineda*] in October of that year, when Lorca unwittingly set in motion one of the key critical debates of the decade concerning the relationship between politics and literature.

Mariana Pineda aroused a great deal of expectation in intellectual circles since many people imagined that Lorca would use the story of this nine-teenth-century champion of freedom to make some kind of statement regarding the current political climate under the dictatorship.[10] However, the melodramatic

intelectuales' [Spain has reached a point where it can only be saved, politically, by the serious involvement of intellectuals] (*El Sol*, 6 November 1927, n.p.). This series of articles came to an abrupt end in March 1928 owing to censorship. The official hostility towards Ortega at this time undoubtedly influenced the process of politicization that young intellectuals like Lorca underwent at the end of the 1920s.

[9] See Gibson 1989, pp. 71–2. The writer also quotes a letter from Lorca to Adriano del Valle of May 1918 in which the young poet says: 'Naturally I am a great admirer of France and hate militarism with all my soul' (p. 74).

[10] When *Mariana Pineda* was staged during the Civil War, in 1937, at the Second International Congress of Anti-Fascist Writers, the dramatist's friend, Manuel Altolaguirre, who directed the production, recalled: '*Mariana Pineda* [. . .] se estrenó en Madrid, durante la dictadura de Primo de Rivera. Aquel estreno, que constituye un verdadero acontecimiento literario, tuvo también un profundo sentido político. Toda la España amante de la libertad acudió a las representaciones. Federico García Lorca tenía escrita su obra desde hacía tres años [. . .] Los directores no se decidían a representarla, entre otras razones, porque *Mariana Pineda* era entonces un drama político' [*Mariana Pineda* was premiered in Madrid during the dictatorship of Primo de Rivera. The opening night was a real literary event but it also had a profound political sense. The whole of Spain that loved freedom attended the performances.

tone of the play disappointed most observers and its critical reception was largely negative.[11] Lorca found himself obliged to defend publicly his approach to the subject of his play. In an interview published in the Madrid press on 15 October, he commented:

> Hay mil Marianas de Pineda distintas [. . .]. Pero yo no las iba a 'hacer' todas. Puesto a elegir, me interesó más la Mariana amante [. . .] Aparte de que yo no creo en el mito de la Mariana Pineda liberal tal como lo han inventado los constitucionales [. . .] Además, mi Mariana Pineda la concebí más próxima a Julieta que a Judith, más para el idilio de la libertad que para la oda a la libertad.
>
> [There are a thousand different Mariana Pinedas (. . .). But I wasn't going to 'do' all of them. Faced with the need to choose, I was more interested in Mariana the lover (. . .) Apart from the fact that I don't believe in the myth of the liberal Mariana Pineda as invented by the constitutionalists (. . .) Moreover, I conceived my Mariana as closer to Juliet than to Judith, more apt for the idyll of liberty than the ode to liberty.][12]

These events were followed closely by Ernesto Giménez Caballero, the Director of *La Gaceta Literaria*, one of the most important literary journals of the decade, founded in January 1927. On 21 October, Giménez Caballero wrote to his friend and associate on *La Gaceta*, Guillermo de Torre, commenting that *Mariana Pineda* 'ha disgustado a las izquierdas como cosa cobarde' [has displeased the left wing who see it as a cowardly play] and explaining that he had decided to hold a banquet in Lorca's honour but with a hidden agenda: to oblige all those who attended to devote one minute of frank criticism to the play and to take part in a survey on the topic 'Arte y política' [Art and Politics], this being the fundamental issue that he believed *Mariana Pineda* had framed.[13] His

Lorca had written the play three years before (. . .) The directors couldn't make up their minds about staging it, among other reasons, because *Mariana Pineda* at that time was a political play]. See Manuel Altolaguirre, 'Nuestro teatro (1937)', in his *Obras completas*, I (Madrid: Istmo, 1986), 203–11 (p. 208).

11 The perceived shortcomings of the play are reviewed in Sumner Greenfield, 'El problema de *Mariana Pineda*', in Ildefonso Manuel-Gil (ed.), *Federico García Lorca* (Madrid: Taurus, 1975), 225–36. On 21 October 1927, shortly after the play opened, Pedro Salinas wrote to his friend Jorge Guillén: 'Siguen los comentarios al estreno de Federico. En su mayoría adversos' [The commentaries on Federico's play continue. Most of them unfavourable]. In Pedro Salinas and Jorge Guillén, *Correspondencia (1923–1951)*, ed. Andrés Soria Olmedo (Barcelona: Tusquets, 1992), 75.

12 Juan González Olmedilla, 'Los autores después del estreno. García Lorca, el público, la crítica y *Mariana Pineda*', *Heraldo de Madrid*, 15 October 1927, n.p. It is notable that Lorca signals here that he chose to focus on the dramatic and emotional rather than the political potential of the historical figure of Mariana Pineda. It suggests a reluctance – discernible in his later work – to allow political considerations to subjugate literary ones.

13 Cited by Francisca Montiel Rayo in her unpublished doctoral dissertation, 'Esteban Salazar Chapela en su época: Obra literaria y periodística (1923–1939)', 3 vols (Universitat

objective was to force Lorca's contemporaries, in the light of the hostile reception of the play, to clarify their view of the relationship between creative writing and political engagement.

The banquet was duly held but none of the sixty people who attended – among them many of Lorca's friends – was prepared to engage in the discussion that Giménez Caballero had prepared. Continuing his letter to Guillermo de Torre on 24 October, the Director of *La Gaceta* commented: 'Nadie se atrevió a disparar: enjuiciar de sobremesa la *Mariana Pineda* mostrando las disconformidades que por bajo tierra se dicen de ella. "Arte y política". (Pues están indignados [los viejos] de que no haya tocado el tema liberal)' [Nobody dared open fire: judging *Mariana Pineda* after the banquet by bringing out into the open the whispered judgements about it. 'Art and politics'. (Since some people – the old ones – are indignant that it didn't touch on the subject of liberalism)] (Montiel, p. 196). Having failed to provoke debate, Giménez Caballero pressed ahead with his plan to undertake a formal survey and to publish the results in his journal: 'En vista del silencio, Melchor [Fernández Almagro] y yo decidimos abrir la encuesta famosa a propósito de este *AntiHernani*, como yo la llamé a Marianita, y pedir a la juventud que contesten a dos preguntas' [In view of the silence, Melchor [Fernández Almagro] and I decided to undertake the famous survey about this *Anti-Hernani*, as I called Marianita, and to ask young writers to answer two questions] (cited by Montiel, p. 196).[14]

Viewed in retrospect, the survey can legitimately be described as one of the defining episodes in the evolution of the Spanish avant-garde, a kind of crossroads at which writers were invited for the first time to go on public record and answer the blunt question: '¿Debe intervenir la política en la literatura?' [Should politics intervene in literature?]. Implicitly, they were being asked to pass judgement on Lorca's reluctance or refusal to transform the historical Mariana Pineda, the heroine of the nineteenth-century liberal cause, into a champion of political freedom under Primo de Rivera's dictatorship; but this had become simply a pretext to explore and test something much more ambitious: the strength of ideological commitment among the most eminent of Lorca's contemporaries and their readiness to incorporate such a commitment into their writing. Although Lorca himself did not take part in the survey (a typically discreet absence), the published results showed that in late 1927, at a date that has been habitually signalled as the symbolic high point of his generation's defence of purist literary aesthetics, there were already clear signs of restlessness and a

---

Autónoma de Barcelona, 2005), p. 195. In her excellent thesis Montiel Rayo makes fruitful use of the unpublished correspondence between Giménez Caballero and Guillermo de Torre. This correspondence sheds important new light on the reception of *Mariana Pineda* in 1927 and its impact on subsequent events in the literary world in the late 1920s in Spain.

[14] The responses to the survey appeared in several issues of *La Gaceta Literaria*, beginning in no. 22 (15 November 1927). They have been collected in Carmen Bassolas, *La ideología de los escritores. Literatura y política en 'La Gaceta Literaria' (1927–1932)* (Barcelona: Fontamara, 1975), 193–225.

growing desire in certain quarters to establish closer links between writing and political beliefs. While it is true that there was a consensus among the majority of respondents that the two should be kept separate, a significant number of them – among them, Antonio Espina, José Díaz Fernández and Esteban Salazar Chapela – argued forcefully for the distance between them to be closed.[15]

Since he had been instrumental, albeit unintentionally, in providing the motive for the survey, Lorca would have been well aware of its impact and would doubtless have followed the repercussions it subsequently had, particularly among writers who openly advocated an engagement with socialist politics. He would have known, for example, of the vehement reaction voiced by Espina and Díaz Fernández in *Post-Guerra* [*Post-War*], the radical journal they had helped to found at the same time the survey was being undertaken. Denouncing the 'extravagancia reaccionaria' [reactionary extravagance] of their contemporaries who refused to make any literary concessions to political realities, they dismissed the survey as unrepresentative and misleading, seeing in it no reason to doubt the 'vitalidad y sentido político de los jóvenes españoles' [the vitality and political awareness of young Spaniards].[16] Similarly, Lorca would have seen how Giménez Caballero sought to exploit the survey's aftermath, pushing the avant-garde community into adopting a more defined, combative stance in the face of political events in Spain and abroad. Giménez Caballero developed this strategy throughout 1928, in the context of his own growing interest in right-wing politics, and the tone of his writings, both in *La Gaceta* and elsewhere, became progressively more strident and provocative. The strategy culminated in the publication in February 1929 of his 'Carta a un muchacho de la joven España' [Letter to a boy of young Spain], a text that is generally acknowledged to be the 'acta de nacimiento del fascismo español' [the birth certificate of Spanish fascism].[17] In it he set out to 'convocar a todos los jóvenes espíritus de nuestro país para preparar el resurgimiento hispánico – nuestro *risorgimento* –, aprovechando todas las fuerzas auténticas del pasado y del porvenir' [convene all the young minds of our country in order to prepare the Hispanic resurgence – our own *risorgimento* – by marshalling all the genuine forces of the past and the future]. This attempt to impose his personality and political ideas on *La Gaceta* brought out into the open the increasingly irrecon-

---

15 It is notable that Lorca's young friend, Francisco Ayala, declared unequivocally that bringing literature and politics together produced a 'mixtificación insoportable' [insufferable confusion]. Quoted by Bassolas, p. 210.

16 See the two editorials published in *Post-Guerra* at the end of 1927 and early the following year: 'Una encuesta interesantísima' [An Extremely Interesting Survey], no. 6 (20 December 1927), pp. 7–8; and 'Los jóvenes y la política' [Young People and Politics], no. 9 (1 April 1928), p. 2.

17 Giménez Caballero's 'Letter' was published in *La Gaceta Literaria*, 52 (15 February 1929), pp. 1 and 5. It appeared simultaneously as the prologue to his translation of Curzio Malaparte's *En torno al casticismo en Italia*. The description of the letter is taken from Jean Bécarud and Evelyn López Campillo, *Los intelectuales españoles durante la II República* (Madrid: Siglo XXI, 1978), 28.

cilable differences between him, his co-editors and the core of the journal's contributors, among whom Lorca figured prominently. Antonio Espina, for example, was irredeemably alienated by Giménez Caballero's stance and orchestrated what amounted, in the words of Pedro Salinas, to a 'declaración de fe liberal [. . .] contra el equívoco sembrado por Giménez Caballero' [a declaration of liberal faith in opposition to the confusion sown by Giménez Caballero].[18] In April 1929, Espina, who up to that time had been in charge of the visual arts section of *La Gaceta*, was replaced. A month later, the then Secretary of the journal, César Arconada, wrote ominously to Guillermo de Torre that they were all living through 'la hora de la política, y por lo tanto, la hora de las divisiones' [the hour of politics and, therefore, the hour of divisions] (quoted in Montiel, p. 415). Arconada himself resigned from his position in September of that year; this was followed by mass defections of contributors in subsequent months. Giménez Caballero would eventually find himself entirely alone, forced to maintain *La Gaceta* single-handedly, writing the entire contents of the journal – now under the apt new title of *El Robinsón Literario de España* [*The Literary Robinson Crusoe of Spain*] – on his own between August 1931 and February 1932.

What this episode and its various outcomes show is that as the issue of political involvement and its relationship with literature became a legitimate, if not unavoidable subject of public debate, writers were inspired – some more confidently than others – to take up positions to the right as well as to the left. The predictable effect was the progressive polarization of the intellectual world, a phenomenon that would become more and more acute as the time passed. To get an idea of Lorca's response, both as spectator and participant, to these circumstances, we need to consider two other important episodes in the late 1920s that signalled the increasingly untenable position of Primo de Rivera as dictator and the serious growth of Republicanism as a political force in the intellectual community.

In late 1928 and the early months of 1929, at around the same time as Giménez Caballero was framing his early call for a fascist offensive in Spain, the relative peace of Primo's dictatorship was broken by major street demonstrations that involved violent clashes between the authorities and the students of Madrid University's Federación Universitaria Escolar [University Student Federation], the same organization with which Lorca would soon be collaborating when he launched his travelling theatre company, La Barraca, in 1931. The students were protesting against the planned legislation to give degree-conferring rights to the country's Catholic universities and were supported by numerous intellectuals and university teachers.[19] These protests culminated in

---

18 See his letter to Jorge Guillén of 24 March 1929 in *Correspondencia*, p. 99.

19 Important links between students and intellectuals had already been forged in June 1928 with the creation of the Liga de Educación Social [Social Education League]. This organization brought together leading figures like Valle-Inclán, Pérez de Ayala, Azaña and Marañón and some of the young activists of the FUE like José López-Rey and María

the resignation from their posts of some of the most eminent academics of the day, among them Ortega, Jiménez de Asúa, Alfonso García Valdecasas and the family friend of the Lorcas, Fernando de los Ríos. Showing admirable initiative, the students of the FUE made arrangements for their teachers to continue giving their classes in various public venues, creating what was known as the 'Universidad Libre' [Free University], which functioned entirely outside the official system. As a result, Primo de Rivera was forced to withdraw the planned legislation and in so doing not only undermined his own personal credibility but also the viability of his regime. This, in turn, provided a key incentive to intellectuals who realized that the exercise of their civic responsibilities and their involvement in social issues could effectively engineer significant political change.

These events had a decisive impact on young writers like Rafael Alberti, Lorca's close friend, who, according to his own testimony, underwent a political awakening as a result. Alberti recalled in his autobiography how up to that point, like many of his fellow poets, he had lived 'entregado a mis versos solamente en aquella España hasta entonces de apariencia tranquila' [devoted solely to writing poetry in that Spain which up to then had seemed so peaceful], when suddenly:

> Mis oídos se abrieron a palabras que antes no había escuchado o nadie me dijera: como república, fascismo, libertad [. . .] Sin sentir, como por ensalmo, se había creado un clima de violencia que me fascinaba. El grito y la protesta que de manera oscura me mordían rebotando en mis propias paredes, encontraban por fin una puerta de escape, precipitándose, encendidos, en las calles enfebrecidas de estudiantes, en las barricadas de los paseos, frente a los caballos de la guardia civil y los disparos de sus máusers.[20]

> [My ears were opened to words I had not heard before or which no one had spoken to me: like republic, fascism, freedom (. . .) Imperceptibly, as if by magic, there had been created a climate of violence that fascinated me. The shouts and protests that gnawed away at me darkly within the walls of my own room finally found an outlet, spilling passionately out into the streets, milling with crowds of feverish students, to the barricades in the boulevards, face to face with the horses of the Civil Guard and the shots fired from their rifles.]

There is no way of knowing for certain if these events proved to be a revelation for Lorca too, but they do at least seem to have provided him with the incentive to respond directly to the mood of political unrest. The fact is that this wave of public demonstrations coincided with a notable run-in he had with the author-

Zambrano. It was declared illegal in March 1929 precisely because of student involvement in demonstrations against the dictatorship. Full details of student involvement in politics at this time and of the contribution of the FUE to the downfall of the dictatorship are given in José López-Rey, *Los estudiantes frente a la dictadura* (Madrid: Javier Morata, 1930).

[20] Rafael Alberti, *La arboleda perdida. Libros I y II de memorias* (Barcelona: Seix-Barral, 1975), 257–8.

ities, at the beginning of February 1929, over plans to stage his play *Amor de Don Perlimpín con Belisa en su jardín* [*The Love of Perlimpín for Belisa in Their Garden*] with the newly formed experimental theatre company *Caracol*, under the direction of his friend Cipriano Rivas Cherif. On the day scheduled for the play's première (6 February), the mother of King Alfonso XIII died and theatres were closed as a sign of respect. When the authorities discovered that despite this, rehearsals were continuing behind closed doors, they intervened and the entire production was shut down. Gibson describes the effect of this as 'intensifying Lorca's already vehement dislike of the Primo de Rivera regime' (Gibson 1989, p. 230). More significantly, in the context of this discussion, this experience – probably combined with the student demonstrations described by Alberti – seems to have provided him with the incentive, a few months later in April, to lend his explicit support to a proposal that sought to overcome the general lack of political activism in recent years and to steer Spain in a more liberal, progressive direction. The proposal took the form of an open letter addressed to Ortega that was widely publicized and discussed in the press at the time. As well as Lorca's, it carried the signatures of twenty-four other young writers and intellectuals, among them many of his friends and associates, from Francisco Ayala, Antonio Espina, Pedro Salinas and Eduardo Ugarte to José Díaz Fernández, Ramón Sender and Fernando Vela. The proposal amounted to a move to create what has been described as 'una especie de "partido de la inteligencia" ' [a kind of 'party of intellectuals'],[21] and the way the document frames the concerns of the signatories is highly revealing: 'Poco tiempo hace, surgió entre nosotros, unos cuantos escritores, la idea de organizar un grupo de carácter político, de la más amplia ideología dentro del horizonte de la libertad, y de tono y significación distintivamente intelectuales' [A little while ago, the idea occurred to some of us writers of organizing a group that would be political in nature, inspired by a broadly liberal ideology and distinctively intellectual in its tone and import].[22] This wording suggests that the initiative stemmed from the events of the relatively recent past and that Lorca had been a party to the intense discussions that followed on from them concerning the state of national political life. The document goes on to stress the sense of civic responsibility felt by young intellectuals who were now openly acknowledging that their cultural interests could not be pursued in isolation, on the margins of political realities:

Creemos que se impone con urgencia la necesidad de que los intelectuales españoles, muy particularmente los intelectuales jóvenes, definan sus diversas

---

[21] Gloria Rey, 'Presentación', in Antonio Espina, *Poesía completa* (Madrid: Fundación Banco Santander Central Hispano, 2000), xviii.

[22] 'Señor Don . . .', in José Ortega y Gasset, *Obras completas*, vol. XI: *Escritos políticos II (1922–1933)* (Madrid: Revista de Occidente, 1969), 102. The full text of this letter is also reproduced in Federico García Lorca, *Epistolario completo*, eds Christopher Maurer and Andrew A. Anderson (Madrid: Cátedra, 1997), 607–10.

actitudes políticas y salgan de ese apoliticismo, de ese apartamiento – no pocas veces reprochable – que les ha llevado a desentenderse de los más hondos problemas de la vida española. La política no es un ejercicio que se pueda desprender de los demás de la inteligencia, ni una reducida especialidad de profesionales. Es un objeto esencial del pensamiento y una parcela importantísima de la cultura.

[We believe that it is a matter of urgency for Spanish intellectuals, above all young intellectuals, to define their various political outlooks and to abandon that apoliticism, that often reproachable withdrawal that has led them to wash their hands of the most serious problems facing Spain. Politics is not an activity that can be separated from other activities of the mind; it is not a refined specialism of professionals. It is an essential object of reflection and an extremely important part of culture.]

The signatories then signalled their resolve to bring together like-minded people in the frame of a political party that would push for national regeneration:

Propugnamos una definición de actitudes, credos, convicciones y tendencias. Y convocamos por nuestra parte a todos los hombres 'nuevos' de España, cuya sensibilidad liberal sintonice con la nuestra, para que de la colectiva afirmación que hoy hacemos, nazca un partido fuerte y desinteresado. Un grupo de genérico y resuelto liberalismo.

[We advocate a definition of outlooks, beliefs, convictions and tendencies. And we invite all the 'new' men of Spain who share our liberal sensibility to join with us so that our collective declaration of today can bring into being a strong and disinterested party. A group bound together by an overarching and resolute liberalism.]

As it happened, this proposal came to nothing. It lacked an adequate ideological basis to make it viable and Ortega politely declined the invitation to act as leader of the envisaged party. However, as a snapshot of Lorca's political outlook at the time, it is unusually revealing. Here he is, in early 1929, alongside some of the most radical intellectuals of his generation, lending the prestige of his name to the expression of a shared concern about political life in Spain and showing his readiness to contribute towards a programme of forward-looking revitalization. Above all, it signals a willingness on the part of a significant sector of Lorca's contemporaries not simply to temper their activities as writers with an acknowledgement of socio-political realities but also to engage in political activity. In some notable cases, though not in Lorca's, this would lead to high-profile party activism.

As the dictatorship of Primo de Rivera unravelled, Spain found herself at something of a crossroads: one chapter of the nation's life was coming to an end and a new one, full of uncertainties and challenges, seemed about to begin. The historian Manuel Tuñón de Lara has described the impact of this situation on the general population:

El fenómeno esencial del momento [. . .] era la extraordinaria 'politización' de los españoles. Al cabo de un año (1929–1930), los temas políticos, el dilema básico de Monarquía o República, habían penetrado todos los hogares y dominado todas las conversaciones. Nunca hasta entonces [. . .] la cuestión del comportamiento del Estado y de las decisiones que tomar sobre el mismo se había adentrado tan profundamente en la conciencia de los españoles.[23]

[The essential feature of the time was the extraordinary 'politicization' of Spaniards. In the space of one year (1929–1930), political issues, the basic dilemma of choosing between a Monarchy or a Republic had entered into every household and dominated all conversation. Never before had the question of the conduct of the State and the decisions to be taken concerning its future had such a profound impact on the consciousness of the nation.]

This mood spread through the intellectual and cultural world, and was perfectly captured by the group of restless young writers who launched a new journal at the beginning of 1930 under the apt title *Nueva España* [*New Spain*]. Its appearance was announced in a manifesto published in the newspaper *El Sol* on 11 January of that year, signed by Antonio Espina, José Díaz Fernández and Esteban Salazar Chapela. It confidently stated that 'el período de los ismos se halla en su trance final en estos albores del año treinta' [at the start of this new year, the period of 'isms' is on its way out] and declared at an end 'la etapa en que el arte puro, sin compromiso político y basado en actitudes de vanguardia formal, había sido lo habitual' [the stage during which pure art, lacking political engagement and based on purely formal innovation, had been the norm]. Some months later, the publication of Díaz Fernández's programmatic text *El nuevo romanticismo* [*The New Romanticism*][24] confirmed this resolve to bind writers to 'las nuevas inquietudes del pensamiento' [the new concerns of thinking people] (p. 50) that had emerged in Spanish life. Advocating what he significantly described as a 'vuelta a lo humano' [return to the human], Díaz Fernández underlined the need to pursue 'un arte para la vida, no una vida para el arte' [an art for life, not a life for art] (p. 50). In effect, both *Nueva España* and *El nuevo romanticismo* are symptoms of a desire to engage more directly in social and political issues and to reflect that engagement in literature.

Lorca was absent from Spain during these months, having left for New York, accompanied by Fernando de los Ríos, in September 1929; but there is plenty of textual and biographical evidence to suggest that he shared this restlessness and had resolved to try to take his own writing in new directions. While in the States, he sought to overcome some of the perceived limitations of his earlier writings and to voice not only the unsettling sense of uncertainty and disorientation he felt as an individual but also a response to the social and political realities he encountered. This is to say that the poems dating from that long stay abroad –

[23] Manuel Tuñón de Lara, *La España del siglo XX*, vol. 1 (Barcelona: Laia, 1974), 243.
[24] José Díaz Fernández, *El nuevo romanticismo* (Madrid: Zeus, 1930).

subsequently collected under the title *Poeta en Nueva York* [*Poet in New York*] – combine an attention to the various predicaments he felt in his own life with a critical perspective on the cynicism and degradation of the city he observed. The poems about the Harlem Blacks and the commercial life of New York, for example, attack the materialism of a society too preoccupied with material wellbeing and profit to worry about its effect on the vulnerable, marginalized sectors of the population. In similar vein, 'Grito hacia Roma' [Cry towards Rome] takes issue with a corrupt Catholic Church that has abdicated its traditional responsibilities. *Poeta en Nueva York* is not a political tract or a sociological treatise, and it is an exaggeration to conclude, as Ian Gibson does, that in these poems Lorca moved closer to 'a Marxist analysis of the human condition' (1989, p. 273); but it is nonetheless true that the book reveals a caring, compassionate poet who felt indignant at the impact of industrial society on the individual or indeed at any social system that exploited and dehumanized the weak and dispossessed. It was doubtless this kind of conviction, rather than militant political dissidence, that lay behind the statements he made while in Cuba in 1930 in which he denounced all forms of dictatorship and oppression.

When he returned to Spain, Lorca would have followed political events in the country with the same intense interest as the rest of the population and, like his father and friends, would have welcomed the proclamation of the Republic in April of 1931 as a chance to reinvigorate national life through a programme of liberal reform. We should not forget that he had close personal ties with a good many eminent Republican politicians. Apart from Fernando de los Ríos, who enjoyed ministerial rank in the early governments of the new regime, he was on good terms with Manuel Azaña, soon to be Prime Minister, since Azaña was the brother-in-law of Cipriano Rivas Cherif, the theatre director with whom he worked before 1931 and who would continue to be one of his closest collaborators subsequently. There is little reason not to share Gibson's conclusion on this point that these personal contacts 'sharpened the poet's awareness of the issues at stake in the country and strengthened his determination to participate in the shaping of the New Spain' (1989, p. 320). The opportunity to participate came in December 1931 when Fernando de los Ríos, having moved from the Ministry of Justice to the Ministry of Public Education, made available the financial support for the creation of La Barraca, the travelling theatre company of which Lorca was named Director. Since the writer devoted an enormous amount of time and energy to this enterprise during the final years of his life, it is worth dwelling briefly on its social and political implications.

La Barraca should be seen as a part of a wider cultural and educational strategy set in motion by the new Republican government to combat Spain's backwardness and social inequalities. This strategy would involve, among other things, the renewal of the educational inspectorate and the development of new programmes at Madrid University, and was heralded already in May 1931 with the establishment of the so-called 'Misiones Pedagógicas' [Pedagogical Missions] under the presidency of Antonio Machado, a writer much admired by Lorca. Imbued with the spirit of the Institución Libre de Enseñanza and inspired by the educational idealism of Manuel Bartolomé de Cossío, these 'missions' were designed to enrich the lives of those sectors of the population that, by virtue of their isolation or poverty, were deprived of direct contact with any form of cultural expression beyond their own traditional practices. The 'missionaries' recruited by Cossío organized excursions to remote villages in different parts of the country, from Galicia to Andalusia, and armed with gramophones, film projectors, books and reproductions of paintings, took on the task of taking culture to the people. They numbered among them some notable writers such as Lorca's friend Luis Cernuda and the brilliant young painter Ramón Gaya, who directed the Missions' 'Museo del Pueblo' [People's Museum] and later collaborated with Lorca as a set and costume designer for one of La Barraca's productions.

Like the Missions, La Barraca was not the product of any specific political party programme but rather reflected the spirit of Republicanism in general. Obviously, despite the paternal benevolence of Fernando de los Ríos, Lorca would not have been entrusted with the responsibility of organizing its activities if he had not been viewed as a sympathetic supporter of the Republic's objectives on the cultural and educational fronts, and his appointment in itself was a confirmation of a clear political allegiance on his part, even if it was not tied to a particular party. As mentioned earlier, to maintain La Barraca Lorca relied on the collaboration of volunteers from the FUE, the student organization that had played such an important role in the downfall of the dictatorship. The fact that the male members of the troupe, Lorca included, chose the *mono azul* [workers' blue overalls] as their uniform was emblematic of a sensed affiliation with the working classes who were, after all, the intended beneficiaries of La Barraca's activities. Noteworthy too was the inclusion in the company's repertoire, alongside classical pieces by writers like Lope, Calderón and Cervantes, of items designed to pay homage to the popular folklore and traditional culture that Lorca knew so well from his own background.

All this would mean that the activities of La Barraca inevitably became charged with political meaning. For the Republican government it was a showpiece of its enlightened cultural policies and when the occasion arose, it made a point of supporting it. In December 1932, for example, Calderón's *La vida es sueño* [*Life is a Dream*] was performed before an audience that included Niceto Alcalá-Zamora, the President of the Republic, Manuel Azaña, the Prime Minister, and prominent ministers such as Julián Besteiro and Fernando de los Ríos. The latter's political enemies, on the other hand, as well as the enemies of the Republic in general, viewed the company with suspicion and open hostility, attacking it as a waste of public money and a vehicle for the promotion of 'Jewish Marxism' (quoted by Gibson 1989, p. 387). When they visited areas under right-wing political control, the members of La Barraca, like the missionaries of the Misiones Pedagógicas, were often denounced as Communist agitators 'determined to bring the Red Revolution to Spain' (Gibson 1989, p. 344) and were even victims of acts of sabotage perpetrated by reactionary Monarchist student groups. It is not surprising that the fortunes of Lorca's troupe were tied to the shifts in the world of Republican politics; its operating budget, for example, was severely cut when power passed into the hands of Gil Robles and his cohorts after the elections of November 1933.

Lorca cannot be said to have been a completely innocent party in the politicization of La Barraca. When he staged Lope's *Fuenteovejuna*, for example, in 1933, he deliberately introduced a number of changes – dressing the peasants in contemporary costume, for example, and eliminating references to the Catholic Kings – that would not only make the play more immediately accessible to the audiences that saw the production but also transform it into a work of social engagement and an expression of solidarity with the Republic. He cannot have been surprised that the production was condemned by the political right. However, Lorca was a man of the theatre rather than a political animal. He saw La Barraca primarily as a vehicle with which to develop his innovative interests in staging and performance and to devise ways to revitalize the classical repertoire and reach genuinely popular audiences. If what he did became enveloped in emotive ideological rhetoric, it was not so much because he consciously used La Barraca to advance a political agenda but because in the dramatic climate of unfolding events in Spain and abroad in the early and mid-1930s, practically any cultural initiative, especially if it embodied a concern for the welfare of 'el pueblo' [the people], became irredeemably politicized. In this sense, it is legitimate to see Lorca in the final years of his life caught up in events and conflicts that were not of his own making. Whether he sought it or not, he attracted political attention; his work, whether it consciously contained a political message or not, was often a pretext for others to express a political point of view.

With his customary clearsightedness, Antonio Espina had already noted in 1930 that writers were beginning to square up to political realities 'empujados por las circunstancias' [pushed by circumstances].[25] The pressure of those circumstances only increased in the years following the proclamation of the Republic as the pace of political change, both in Spain and abroad, quickened alarmingly and writers of all persuasions found it progressively more difficult to avoid being drawn into public discussions of and responses to the events occurring around them. These events posed serious threats to the survival of the Republic and suggested that even democracy itself was at risk. Within Spain, for example, the period 1932–5 witnessed an abortive military uprising, the foundation of the right-wing Falange, the growing political influence of José María Gil Robles, a self-declared enemy of the Republic, and an attempted general strike that led to one of the most violent episodes of the nation's life in those years: the so-called Asturian Revolution of October 1934, in the aftermath of which hundreds of people in the mining villages of northwest Spain were killed, imprisoned or tortured. Outside the country, international attention was riveted on the situation in Germany, where Hitler had risen dramatically to power in

[25] 'La cultura y el espíritu proletario' [Culture and the Proletarian Spirit], *El Sol*, 18 July 1930, n.p.

1933, and in Italy where Mussolini, having taken control of the country, invaded Abyssinia in pursuit of imperial glory. In such circumstances, few writers, if any, could allow themselves the luxury of remaining detached or silent, and it is unsurprising that Lorca felt compelled to respond to them, in the shape of public expressions of protest or solidarity, and did so in a way that was in harmony with the overwhelming majority of his friends and fellow writers. In April 1933, for example, he joined the Association of Friends of the Soviet Union and signed a protest against the 'fascist barbarism' of Hitler's regime (see Gibson 1989, p. 349). At around the same time, he became affiliated to Socorro Rojo Internacional [International Red Aid], an organization to which he would make a donation in Granada a few days before the military uprising of 18 July 1936.[26] Since his friend Fernando de los Ríos was a member of the parliamentary commission set up to investigate the way the incident had been handled, he was well informed of the repercussions of the Asturian Revolution and shared the general indignation in liberal circles at the imprisonment and mistreatment of those involved in the uprising. It was in this context that he made the famous statement: 'In this world I am and always will be on the side of the poor' (quoted by Gibson 1989, p. 396). In November 1935, along with Antonio Machado, Fernando de los Ríos and other prominent Republican politicians, he signed a manifesto of protest against Mussolini's foreign policy.

What these facts indicate is that during those turbulent years, and especially during the period of right-wing government in Spain in 1934 and 1935, Lorca's views on political events at home and abroad became steadily more radical and he became less and less inhibited about voicing them publicly. In this sense, he was no different from many of his contemporaries who underwent a similar process, reassessing their priorities and responsibilities and reconsidering – often vigorously reaffirming – where their loyalties lay in an increasingly conflictive situation. But Lorca had a particularly high public profile, which meant that what he had to say on these matters, however brief or general, acquired a special resonance and could be used, just as his work could, either positively or negatively, for political ends.[27] This is evident, for example, in the

---

[26] See Ian Gibson, *The Assassination of Federico García Lorca* (London: W.H. Allen, 1979), 177.

[27] Robert Marrast quotes the testimony of the Argentinian writer Raúl González Tuñón concerning the politically subversive use to which Lorca's play *El retablillo de don Cristóbol* [*The 'retablillo' of Don Cristóbal*] was put by Miguel Prieto, Director of the *Teatro Guiñol Octubre*, the puppet theatre of the radical left-wing journal *Octubre*, founded by Rafael Alberti. González Tuñón recounts how, without Lorca's knowledge or permission, his play was used in the company's street performances during the Feria del Libro [Book Fair] of 1935, using 'frases intencionadas que ridiculizaban a los 'leaders' cavernícolas' [using loaded phrases to ridicule the reactionary leaders]. González Tuñón commented: 'Y no sonaba mal en el retablillo de don Cristóbal oír hablar de "La Internacional", de Goicoechea, de "La Marsellesa", de Gil Robles [. . .] No sé cómo no se llevaron preso a Cristobita' [And it didn't sound bad in the 'retablillo' of Don Cristóbal to hear mentioned The International, Goicoechea, The Marseillaise, Gil Robles [. . .] I don't understand how Cristobita wasn't

critical responses to the plays of his that were staged at the time where consideration of their artistic merits was sometimes subordinated to their social and
political implications. In the case of *Yerma* [*Yerma*], Ian Gibson has shown that
opinions about the play at the time were largely determined by the political affiliations of the newspapers in which they were published: 'if all the liberal,
Republican and left-wing press came up with rave reviews, the right-wing newspapers were unanimous in their condemnation of what they considered an
immoral, anti-Spanish, irreligious and odious play' (1989, p. 398). Whether
either side did justice to Lorca the dramatist and whether *Yerma* constitutes the
socio-political work that those commentators identified is an issue that each
reader or spectator has to resolve. What is undeniable is that in the highly
charged atmosphere in Spain in that period before the outbreak of civil war,
Lorca was clearly perceived to have aligned himself with the political left – not
with any particular party but with a broad body of liberal, democratic opinion.

Little that happened in the final year of Lorca's life would alter this perception. On the contrary, his public statements on social and political issues
became, if anything, more explicit and provocative. In September 1935, for
example, he gave an interview to *L'Hora*, the weekly publication of the Trotsky-
ists in Barcelona, in which he voiced his contempt for fascism and his admiration for the Soviet Union (see Gibson 1989, pp. 413–14). He also stated that he
considered the mission of the theatre to 'educate the masses' and suggested,
albeit obliquely, that *Poeta en Nueva York* should be read as a protest against the
injustices of contemporary capitalist society. In the following year, in the
build-up to the crucial elections of February 1936, he pledged his support to the
Popular Front, an alliance of left-wing parties and workers' organizations forged
to combat the threat of fascism. His name appeared at the very top of a list of
more than three hundred signatories of a document entitled 'The Intellectuals
and the Popular Front' that was published in *Mundo Obrero* [*Workers' World*],
the leading Communist daily paper. Gibson has reported how at around the same
time Lorca gave a poetry reading at a mass meeting in Madrid's Workers' Club
and joined both the Association of Friends of South America – dedicated to
combating the dictatorship of Miguel Gómez in Cuba and Getulio Vargas in
Brazil – and the Friends of Portugal, whose mission was to inform the Spanish
public about the dictatorship of Oliveira Salazar. On the occasion of the May
Day celebrations of 1936, which saw huge public demonstrations organized by
the United Socialist Youth Movement as an expression of opposition to fascism,
Lorca sent a message of solidarity that appeared in the Communist publication
Ayuda. It read: 'My greetings to all the workers of Spain, united this First of
May by the desire for a more just and fraternal society' (Gibson 1989, p. 433).

That all these gestures, and others like them, were political in themselves and
were perceived as such goes without saying. Yet Lorca was not acting out of

carted off and arrested]. See Robert Marrast, 'El teatro durante la guerra civil española', *El
Público*, 15 (June 1986), 18–31 (p. 20).

partisan loyalty but rather with that same compassion and social conscience that he had always showed. As he put it candidly – and no doubt with absolute sincerity – in an interview in the Madrid press in June 1936: 'Yo soy hermano de todos' [I am a brother to all men] (translated by Gibson 1979, p. 56).[28] This important distinction between an instinctive liberal humanitarianism, inspired by a sense of solidarity with all mankind, and a specific political allegiance comes up again in another interview conducted in those unsettled months before the outbreak of war. The tone of Lorca's statements on this occasion was blunt and belligerent:

> Mientras haya desequilibrio económico, el mundo no piensa. [. . .] El día que el hambre desaparezca, va a producirse en el mundo la explosión espiritual más grande que jamás conoció la Humanidad. Nunca jamás se podrán figurar los hombres la alegría que estallará el día de la Gran Revolución.
>
> (*Obras completas*, III, pp. 674–5)

> [As long as there is economic injustice in the world, the world will be unable to think clearly. (. . .) The day when hunger is eradicated there is going to be the greatest spiritual explosion the world has ever seen. We'll never be able to imagine the joy that will erupt when the Great Revolution comes.]
>
> (Gibson 1989, p. 431)

But the journalist conducting the interview recorded that having said this, Lorca, as if surprised by his own words, remarked: '¿Verdad que te estoy hablando en socialista puro?' [I'm talking like a real Socialist, aren't I?] (*Obras completas*, III, p. 675 / Gibson 1989, p. 431). It was as if he had unexpectedly realized the link between his hopes for the material and spiritual liberation of mankind and a particular partisan rhetoric. His way of expressing his opinions was not a product of ideological training or party discipline but signalled, rather, a natural convergence of aspirations. However, in the conflictive atmosphere of the time, such statements would be interpreted as those of a dangerous political agitator and would be enough to seal his fate in Granada.

In 1948, Dámaso Alonso, a companion and admirer of Lorca and another prominent figure in the pre-war literary world, recalled the occasion in Madrid when Lorca read his recently completed play *La casa de Bernarda Alba* [*The House of Bernarda Alba*] to a group of friends. This occurred on the night of 12 July 1936, at a time of acute social and political unrest, in a city plagued by acts of violence. Following the reading, Lorca is reported to have voiced his doubts about the ability of any politically committed writer to write anything of serious literary value. This was understood to be a reference to his close friend Rafael Alberti who, since 1932, had been a card-carrying member of the Communist party and whose poetry had adopted the hectoring rhetoric of revolution. Alonso

---

[28] Spanish original in Federico García Lorca, *Obras completas*, III, ed. Arturo del Hoyo, 3 vols, 2nd edn (Madrid: Aguilar, 1986), 683.

quotes Lorca's words: 'Yo nunca seré politico. Yo soy revolucionario, porque no hay un verdadero poeta que no sea revolucionario. ¿No lo crees tú así? [. . .] Pero politico no lo seré nunca, ¡nunca!' [As for me, I'll never be political. I'm a revolutionary, because all poets are revolutionaries – don't you agree? – but political, never!'].[29] We are entitled to view these recollections with some scepticism. After all, the dead – especially if they were famous during their lifetime – are always vulnerable to manipulation, and it is easy to invoke their oral testimony in order to serve someone else's agenda. Whatever Lorca may have said that night and whatever meaning Alonso might have sought to attribute to his words, there may well be an important truth here that is worth salvaging. If Lorca did indeed see himself as a revolutionary, it was clearly not in a political sense. Politics for him seems to have implied party organization, collective discipline, a willingness to make concessions when required and to toe the line. While he might sympathize with particular political objectives and outcomes, he valued his creative independence too highly to become an obedient instrument of policy. This, no doubt, was why he chose never to join a political party. His concept of 'revolution' was broader and more spiritual than Socialism or Communism and seems to have rested on the Romantic concept of the solitary writer whose only duty was to himself and who felt bonded only to his fellow writers. What he instinctively knew he shared with them was his own bold commitment to authenticity, innovation and originality, a commitment rooted in a concern for the elemental values of truth, justice and individual self-fulfilment.[30]

[29] 'Una generación poética (1920–1936)', in Dámaso Alonso, *Poetas españoles contemporáneos*, 3rd edn (Madrid: Gredos, 1978), 155–77 (pp. 160–1). The translation is Gibson's (1989, p. 443).

[30] Lorca's words of 1936, as recollected by Dámaso Alonso, can be set alongside those he is reported to have spoken to Manuel Altolaguirre towards the end of his life: 'Yo no soy politico, ni pertenezco a ningún partido; pero amo al pueblo, y sobre todo a la parte del pueblo que sufre' [I'm not political and I don't belong to any political party; but I love the people and especially that sector of the people that suffers]. See 'El poeta García Lorca (apunte biográfico) (1937)', in Manuel Altolaguirre, *Obras completas*, vol. 1, 211–14 (pp. 213–14).

SUGGESTED FURTHER READING

The contributors to this volume have used a number of different editions of Lorca's *Obras completas*. For some time the standard reference for scholars was Arturo del Hoyo's three-volume edition (Madrid: Aguilar, 1986), although more recently this has been displaced by Miguel García-Posada's four-volume edition (Barcelona: Galaxia Gutenberg / Círculo de Lectores, 1997), which collects all of Lorca's known works. In addition there is Mario Hernández's multi-volume edition of the works (Madrid: Alianza), the first volume of which was published in 1981. Hernández's volumes include excellent introductory essays, interviews and chronologies. Cátedra (Madrid) has also produced a number of important editions of the works by different editors in its Letras Hispánicas series, all of which include introductory essays. Among these it is worth noting the collections of Lorca's unpublished juvenilia: Christopher Maurer's, Christian de Paepe's and Andrés Soria Olmedo's editions of the prose, poetry and theatre respectively (all 1994). Noteworthy too are Andrew A. Anderson's edition of the prose poems, *Poemas en prosa* (Granada: Comares / La Veleta, 2000) and Christopher Maurer's two-volume collection of Lorca's lectures, *Conferencias* (Madrid: Alianza, 1984). Maurer has also produced editions of the poetry and prose in English translation, including the extremely useful revised bilingual edition of *Collected Poems* (New York: Farrar, Straus and Giroux, 2002) and the collection *Deep Song and Other Prose* (London: Marion Boyars, 1980). Reliable translations into English of the plays include John Edmunds's *Federico García Lorca: Four Major Plays*, in the Oxford World Classics series (Oxford: Oxford Paperbacks, 1999), which brings together *Blood Wedding, Yerma, The House of Bernarda Alba* and *Doña Rosita the Spinster*; Robert G. Havard's bilingual edition of *Mariana Pineda* (Warminster: Aris & Phillips, 1987); the bilingual edition of *Yerma* by Ian R. McPherson, J. Minett and John E. Lyon (Warminster: Aris & Phillips, 1987); and Caridad Svich's *Federico García Lorca: Impossible Theatre* (Lyme, NH: Smith and Krauss, 2000), which includes *The Love of Don Perlimplín for Belisa in Their Garden* and *Once Five Years Pass*. To this list we should also add John London's translations of miscellanea in his *The Unknown Federico García Lorca. Dialogues, Dramatic Projects, Unfinished Plays and a Filmscript* (London: Atlas Press, 1996). Indispensable for the study of Lorca's drawings is their reproduction in Mario Hernández's *Libro de los dibujos de Federico García Lorca* (Madrid: Tabapress / Fundación Federico García Lorca, 1990), translated by Christopher Maurer into English under the title *Line of Light and*

Shadow: The Drawings of Federico García Lorca (Durham, NC: Duke University Press, 1991).

As regards Lorca's biography, the standard references are Ian Gibson's *Federico García Lorca: A Life* (New York: Pantheon / London: Faber & Faber, 1989) and Leslie Stainton's immensely readable portrait of the artist in *Lorca: A Dream of Life* (London: Bloomsbury, 1998 / New York: Farrar, Straus and Giroux, 1999). Gibson's groundbreaking work, to which Stainton's is indebted, is an exhaustive chronological study, excellently indexed, and an indispensable source of information concerning, among other things, the writer's encounters with the socio-political realities of his time. Even more detailed are the Spanish originals on which this biography is based – *Federico García Lorca, 1. De Fuente Vaqueros a Nueva York, 1898–1929* and *Federico García Lorca, 2. De Nueva York a Fuente Grande, 1929–1936* (Barcelona: Grijalbo, 1985, 1987) – while Gibson's account of the political context of Lorca's death remains unsurpassed: *The Assassination of Federico García Lorca* (Harmondsworth: Penguin, 1983), originally published in Spanish under the title *La represión nacionalista de Granada en 1936 y la muerte de Federico García Lorca* (Paris: Ruedo Ibérico, 1971). The world of the Residencia de Estudiantes is well described in John Crispin's *'Oxford y Cambridge en Madrid'. La Residencia de Estudiantes, 1910–1936, y su entorno cultural* (Santander: La Isla de los Ratones, 1981), and the best history of La Barraca is still Luis Sáenz de la Calzada's *'La Barraca'. Teatro universitario* (Madrid: Revista de Occidente, 1976). Lorca's letters have been collected together in their most complete form to date in Andrew A. Anderson's and Christopher Maurer's helpfully annotated *Epistolario completo* (Madrid: Cátedra, 1997). There are also a number of interesting and useful memoirs, including José Mora Guarnido's *Federico García Lorca y su mundo: Testimonio para una biografía* (Buenos Aires: Losada, 1958), that of Lorca's brother, Francisco, entitled *Federico y su mundo* (Madrid: Alianza, 1981), and, more recently, that of his sister, Isabel, entitled simply *Recurdos míos* (Barcelona: Tusquets, 2002), as well as Jorge Guillén's vivid portrait, *Federico en persona. Semblanza y epistolario* (Buenos Aires: Emecé Editores, 1959), also reproduced in the first volume of Arturo del Hoyo's edition of the complete works. Key texts concerning Lorca's relationship with Salvador Dalí include Christopher Maurer's collection, in English translation, of letters, lectures and mementos important for our understanding of Lorca's Dalí period and, vice versa, Dalí's Lorca period: *Federico García Lorca, Salvador Dalí, Sebastian's Arrows: Letters and Mementos of Salvador Dalí and Federico García Lorca* (Chicago: Swan Isle Press, 2004); Antonina Rodrigo's *Lorca–Dalí: Una amistad traicionada* (Barcelona: Planeta, 1981); Rafael Santos Torroella's *La miel es más dulce que la sangre: Las épocas lorquiana y freudiana de Salvador Dalí* (Barcelona: Seix Barral, 1984); Agustín Sánchez Vidal's *Buñuel, Lorca, Dalí: el enigma sin fin* (Barcelona: Planeta, 1996); and Ian Gibson's *Lorca– Dalí: El amor que no pudo ser* (Barcelona: Plaza & Janés, 1999).

There are so many critical studies worthy of our interest that we cannot cite them all here. Instead we will limit ourselves mainly to good introductory studies in English, important general surveys and criticism that has applied modern literary or cultural theories to the study of Lorca's work. Marie Laffranque's *Les idées esthétiques de Federico García Lorca* (Paris: Centre de Recherches Hispaniques, 1967), in French, is still one of the most thorough introductions to Lorca's aesthetic ideas. Among the best critical guides to arguably Lorca's best-known poetry is Derek Harris's introduction to his edition of *Romancero gitano* (London: Grant & Cutler, 1991) and his study of *Poeta en Nueva York* in the Grant & Cutler Critical Guides series (London, 1978). Equally accessible is H. Ramsden's *'Romancero gitano': Eighteen commentaries* (Manchester: Manchester University Press, 1988), which, like Harris's edition, provides succinct introductory readings of each of the poems. A more theoretical and highly demanding approach to *Poeta en Nueva York* is provided by Martha J. Nandorfy's recent study, *The Poetics of Apocalypse: García Lorca's 'Poet in New York'* (Lewisburg, PA: Bucknell University Press / London: Associated University Presses, 2003), which includes an excellent section on Lorca's drawing from 1929 onwards. Norman C. Miller's book, *García Lorca's 'Poema del cante jondo'* (London: Tamesis Books, 1978), and Edward F. Stanton's *The Tragic Myth. Lorca and Cante Jondo* (Lexington: University Press of Kentucky, 1978) are a good starting point for the study of *Poem of the Deep Song*, as are the relevant chapters in the more recent and broader studies of Lorca's work in the context of Andalusian culture provided by C. Brian Morris's *Son of Andalusia. The Lyrical Landscapes of Federico García Lorca* (Nashville: Vanderbilt University Press / Liverpool: Liverpool University Press, 1997) and Rob Stone's *The Flamenco Tradition in the Works of Federico García Lorca and Carlos Saura. The Wounded Throat* (Lewiston / Queenston / Lampeter: Edwin Mellen Press, 2004). A clear-headed appraisal of Lorca's knowledge and use of traditional and popular Andalusian music can be found in Félix Grande's *García Lorca y el flamenco* (Madrid: Mondadori, 1992). D. Gareth Walters emphasizes the reading process in his book, *'Canciones' and the Early Poetry of Lorca: A Study in Critical Methodology and Poetic Maturity* (Cardiff: University of Wales Press, 2002), in which he produces informed, detailed and sensitive readings of examples from Lorca's juvenilia, *Libro de poemas*, *Suites* and *Poema del cante jondo*, as well as a more substantial treatment of *Canciones*. Melissa Dinverno's forthcoming edition of *Suites* for Cátedra will provide a much needed, additional introduction to one of Lorca's most enigmatic collections, while Andrew A. Anderson's *Lorca's Late Poetry: A Critical Study* (Leeds: Francis Cairns, 1990) is still the most substantial and thorough treatment of Lorca's later poetic texts.

Critics have adopted a number of theoretical approaches to the study of Lorca's theatre, including psychoanalysis and performance studies. Indispensable in this respect are Paul Julian Smith's *The Theatre of García Lorca: Text, Performance, Psychoanalysis* (Cambridge: Cambridge University Press, 1996), Christopher C. Soufas's *Audience and Authority in the Modernist Theater of Federico García Lorca* (Tuscaloosa and London: University of Alabama Press, 1996), which looks at the writer's attitudes to the theatre in relation to his contemporary audience and Modernist aesthetics, and the relevant sections of María Delgado's *Other Spanish Theatres: Erasure and Inscription on the Spanish Stage* (Manchester: Manchester University Press, 2003). In addition, there is Sarah Wright's *The Trickster-Function in the Theatre of García Lorca* (Woodbridge: Tamesis, 2000), which draws on anthropology, psychoanalysis and literary theory to explore *Amor de Don Perlimpín con Belisa en su jardín, Así que pasen cinco años* and *El público* in terms of their representation of gender and in the context of the notions of masquerade and the carnivalesque. To this list we should also add Luis Fernández-Cifuentes's *García Lorca en el teatro: la norma y la diferencia* (Zaragoza: Prensas universitarias de Zaragoza, 1986). A good starting point for the study of the plays is Gwynne Edwards's *Lorca: The Theatre Beneath the Sand* (London: Marion Boyars, 1980), which places Lorca's theatre in its literary and historical context, and also David George's well-written and comprehensive study, *The History of the Commedia dell'arte in Modern Hispanic Literature with Special Attention to the Work of García Lorca* (Lampeter: The Edwin Mellen Press, 1995). As regards Lorca's interest in cinema, there is little criticism devoted entirely to the subject, but C. Brian Morris's *This Loving Darkness: Cinema and Spanish Writers, 1920–1936* (Oxford and New York: Oxford University Press, 1980) provides an important point of entry with its discussion of the creative responses of writers (Lorca among them) to the new medium. Of the books devoted wholly, or in part, to Lorca's drawings, Cecilia J. Cavanaugh's *Lorca's Drawings and Poems: Forming the Eye of the Reader* (London: Associated University Presses, 1995) is certainly one of the most enquiring and suggestive. Finally, in the context of Lorca's homosexuality, Ángel Sahuquillo's monograph is still the most comprehensive study of the codification of sexual identity in the writer's work: *Federico García Lorca y la cultura de la homosexualidad: Lorca, Dalí, Cernuda, Gil-Albert Prados y la voz silenciada del amor homosexual* (Alicante: Instituto de Cultura 'Juan Gil Albert' / Diputación de Alicante, 1991).

BIBLIOGRAPHY

The existing body of Lorca criticism is vast and there are countless editions of his poetry and plays. The entries below correspond to those texts cited in this *Companion*, but also include a number of titles signalled by contributors as being of particular interest. For a more comprehensive and up-to-date bibliography of Lorca publications, see Andrew A. Anderson's 'Bibliografía lorquiana reciente' (1984–present), which appears in each issue of *FGL. Boletín de la Fundación Federico García Lorca*, Madrid.

Lorca editions

Amor de Don Perlimplín con Belisa en su jardín, ed. Margarita Ucelay, Letras Hispánicas 313 (Madrid: Cátedra, 1992)

Así que pasen cinco años. Leyenda del tiempo, ed. Margarita Ucelay, Letras Hispánicas 397 (Madrid: Cátedra, 1995)

Bodas de sangre, ed. Allen Josephs and Juan Caballero, Letras Hispánicas 231 (Madrid: Cátedra, 1999)

Canciones y primeras canciones, ed. Piero Menarini (Madrid: Espasa-Calpe, 1986)

Canciones (1921–1924), ed. Mario Hernández, revised edition (Madrid: Alianza Editorial, 1998)

La casa de Bernarda Alba, ed. Allen Josephs and Juan Caballero, Letras Hispánicas 43 (Madrid: Cátedra, 1998)

La casa de Bernarda Alba, ed. María Francisca Vilches de Frutos, Letras Hispánicas 43 (Madrid: Cátedra, 2005)

Collected Poems, ed. Christopher Maurer (New York: Farrar, Straus and Giroux, 1991)

Collected Poems, revised bilingual edition, ed. Christopher Maurer (New York: Farrar, Straus and Giroux, 2002)

Conferencias, ed. Christopher Maurer, 2 vols (Madrid: Alianza, 1984)

Deep Song and Other Prose, ed. and trans. Christopher Maurer (London: Marion Boyars, 1980)

Diván del Tamarit. Llanto por Ignacio Sánchez Mejías. Sonetos, ed. Mario Hernández (Madrid: Alianza Editorial, 1981)

Diván del Tamarit. Seis poemas galegos. Llanto por Ignacio Sánchez Mejías. Poemas sueltos, ed. Andrew A. Anderson (Madrid: Espasa-Calpe, 1988)

Doña Rosita la Soltera o El lenguaje de las flores, ed. Mario Hernández (Madrid: Alianza, 1998)

Epistolario completo, ed. Andrew A. Anderson and Christopher Maurer (Madrid: Cátedra, 1997)

Federico García Lorca: Dibujos, ed. Mario Hernández (Ministerio de Cultura, Museo Español de Arte Contemporáneo, 1986)

Federico García Lorca: Four Major Plays, trans. John Edmunds, Oxford World Classics (Oxford: Oxford Paperbacks, 1999)

Federico García Lorca: Impossible Theatre, trans. Caridad Svich (Lyme, NH: Smith & Krauss, 2000)

Federico García Lorca. Textes inédits et documents critiques, commentary and trans. Jacques Comincioli (Lausanne: Éditions Rencontre, 1970)

Federico García Lorca e il suo 'Libro de poemas': Un poeta alla ricerca della propria voce (Introduzione. Testo critico. Commento), ed. Marco Massoli (Pisa: C. Cursi Editore, 1982)

How a City Sings From November to November, ed. and trans. Christopher Maurer (San Francsico: Cadmus Editions, 1984)

In Search of Duende, ed. and trans. Christopher Maurer (New York: New Directions, 1998)

Libro de los dibujos de Federico García Lorca, ed. Mario Hernández (Madrid: Tabapress / Fundación Federico García Lorca, 1990)

Libro de poemas (1921), ed. Ian Gibson (Barcelona: Ariel, 1982)

Libro de poemas [1918–1920], ed. Mario Hernández, revised edition (Madrid: Alianza Editorial, 1998)

Line of Light and Shadow: The Drawings of Federico García Lorca, by Mario Hernández; trans. Christopher Maurer (Durham, NC: Duke University Press, 1991)

Llanto por Ignacio Sánchez Mejías, con dos grabados de José Hernández y otros textos de Ignacio Sánchez Mejías, Francisco García Lorca, y José Bergamín, ed. Mario Hernández, 2 vols (Madrid: Ayuntamiento de Madrid, 1997)

Lola la comedianta, ed. Piero Menarini (Madrid: Alianza, 1981)

Manuscritos neoyorquinos: Poeta en Nueva York y otras hojas y poemas, ed. Mario Hernández (Madrid: Tabapress / Fundación Federico García Lorca, 1990)

Mariana Pineda, bilingual edition, trans. with intro. and commentary by Robert G. Havard (Warminster: Aris & Phillips, 1987)

Obras completas, 13th edn (Madrid: Aguilar, 1967)

Obras completas, 2 vols, 21st edn (Madrid: Aguilar, 1980)

Obras completas, ed. Arturo del Hoyo, 3 vols, 22nd edn (Madrid: Aguilar, 1986)

Obras completas, ed. Miguel García-Posada, 4 vols (Barcelona: Galaxia Gutenberg / Círculo de Lectores, 1997)

Plays, trans. Gwynne Edwards, 3 vols, Methuen World Classics (London: Methuen, 1990)

Poema del cante jondo, ed. Christian de Paepe, Clásicos Castellanos, Nueva Serie, 2 (Madrid: Espasa-Calpe, 1986)

Poema del cante jondo. Romancero gitano, ed. Allen Josephs and Juan Caballero, Letras Hispánicas 66 (Madrid: Cátedra, 1989)

Poema del cante jondo (1921) seguido de tres textos teóricos de Federico García Lorca y Manuel de Falla, ed. Mario Hernández, revised edition (Madrid: Alianza Editorial, 1998)

Poemas en prosa, ed. Andrew A. Anderson (Granada: Comares / La Veleta, 2000)

Poesía inédita de juventud, ed. Christian de Paepe, Letras Hispánicas 374 (Madrid: Cátedra, 1994)

Poeta en Nueva York, ed. José Bergamín (Mexico: Editorial Séneca, 1940)

The Poet in New York and Other Poems of Federico García Lorca, ed. and trans. Rolfe Humphries (New York: W.W. Norton, 1940)

Poeta en Nueva York, ed. María Clementa Millán, Letras Hispánicas 260 (Madrid: Cátedra, 1987)

Poeta en Nueva York / Tierra y luna, ed. Eutimio Martín (Barcelona: Ariel, 1981)

Poet in New York, ed. Christopher Maurer (Harmondsworth: Penguin, 1990)

Poet in New York: A Bilingual Edition, ed. Christopher Maurer; trans. Greg Simon and Steven F. White (New York: Farrar, Straus and Giroux, 1998)

Primer romancero gitano. Llanto por Ignacio Sánchez Mejías. Romance de la corrida de toros en ronda y otros textos taurinos, ed. Miguel García-Posada (Madrid: Castalia, 1988)

Primer romancero gitano (1924–1927), ed. Mario Hernández, revised edition (Madrid: Alianza Editorial, 1998)

Primeras canciones. Seis poemas galegos. Poemas sueltos. Colección de canciones populares antiguos, ed. Mario Hernández (Madrid: Alianza Editorial, 1981)

Prosa inédita de juventud, ed. Christopher Maurer, Letras Hispánicas 377 (Madrid: Cátedra, 1994)

El público, ed. María Clementa Millán, Letras Hispánicas 272 (Madrid: Cátedra, 1991)

Romancero gitano, ed. Derek Harris, Grant & Cutler Spanish Texts (London: Grant & Cutler, 1991)

Romancero gitano, ed. Christian de Paepe, Colección Austral 156 (Madrid: Espasa-Calpe, 1998)

Selected Poems, ed. with an intro. by Christopher Maurer, trans. Francisco Aragón et al. (London: Penguin, 1997)

Sonetos del amor oscuro, with drawings by Miguel Rodríguez Acosta Carlström, introd. by Jorge Guillén and notes by Mario Hernández (Barcelona: Maeght, 1980)

Sonetos del amor oscuro (1935–1936) [ed. Victor Infantes] (Granada: privately printed, 1983)

Sonetos del amor oscuro; Poemas de amor y erotismo; Inéditos de madurez, ed. Javier Ruis-Portella (Barcelona: Ediciones Áltera, 1995)

Suites, ed. André Belamich (Barcelona: Ariel, 1983)

Suites, ed. Melissa Dinverno (Madrid: Cátedra, in press)

Teatro inédito de juventud, ed. Andrés Soria Olmedo, Letras Hispánicas 385 (Madrid: Cátedra, 1994)

The Unknown Federico García Lorca. Dialogues, Dramatic Projects, Unfinished Plays and a Filmscript, ed. and trans. John London (London: Atlas Press, 1996)

Viaje a la luna [Guión cinematográfico], ed. Antonio Monegal (Valencia: Editorial Pre-Textos, 1994)

Viaje a la luna (Barcelona: Edicions de l'Eixample-Centre de Cultura Contemporània de Barcelona-Comisión del Centenario de Federico García Lorca-Institut d'Edicions de la Diputació de Barcelona, 1998)

Yerma, bilingual edition, trans. with intro. and notes by Ian R. McPherson, J. Minett and John E. Lyon (Warminster: Aris & Phillips, 1987)

Yerma, ed. Ildefonso Manuel-Gil, Letras Hispánicas 46 (Madrid: Cátedra, 1991)

Yerma, ed. Robin Warner, Hispanic Texts (Manchester: Manchester University Press, 1994)

Works on Lorca

Aisa Pampols, Ferran, *Salvador Dalí i Federico García Lorca: la persistencia de la memoria* (Barcelona / Viena : Generalitat de Catalunya, Departament de Cultura, 2004)

Allen, Rupert C., *The Symbolic World of Federico García Lorca* (Albuquerque: University of New Mexico Press, 1972)

——, 'A commentary on Lorca's *El Paseo de Buster Keaton*', *Hispanófila*, 48 (1973), 23–35

——, *Psyche and Symbol in the Theatre of Federico García Lorca. Perlimpín. Yerma. Blood Wedding* (Austin and London: University of Texas Press, 1974)

Anderson, Andrew A., 'De qué trata *Bodas de sangre*?', in *Hommage à Federico García Lorca*, Travaux de l'Université de Toulouse-Le Mirail, Série A20, ed. Michèle Ramond (Toulouse: Université de Toulouse-Le-Mirail, 1982), 53–64

——, 'The Strategy of Federico García Lorca's Dramatic Composition, 1930–36', *Romance Quarterly*, 33 (1986), 211–29

——, 'Who Wrote *Seis poemas galegos* and in What Language?', in C. Brian Morris (ed.), *'Cuando yo me muera . . .' Essays in Memory of Federico García Lorca* (Lanham, MD: University Press of America, 1988), 129–46

——, *Lorca's Late Poetry: A Critical Study*, Liverpool Monographs in Hispanic Studies 10 (Leeds: Francis Cairns, 1990)

——, 'Lorca at the Crossroads: "Imaginación, inspiración, evasión" and the "Novísimas estéticas"', *Anales de Literatura Española Contemporánea*, 16 (1991), 149–73

——, '*El público, Así que pasen cinco años* y *El sueño de la vida*: tres dramas expresionistas de García Lorca', in Dru Dougherty and María Francisca Vilches de Frutos (eds), *El teatro en España: entre la tradición y la vanguardia, 1918–39* (Madrid: CSIC / Fundación FGL / Tabacalera, 1992), 215–26

——, 'New Light on the Textual History of García Lorca's *Sonetos del amor oscuro*', in David T. Gies, *Negotiating Past and Present: Studies in Spanish Literature for Javier Herrero* (Charlottesville, VA: Rookwood Press, 1997), 109–26

——, *García Lorca: Yerma*, Critical Guides to Spanish Texts 69 (London: Grant & Cutler, 2003)

——, and Nigel Dennis,' The Manuscript of Lorca's "Tu infancia en Menton"', *Bulletin of Spanish Studies*, 82, 2 (2005), 181–204

Auclair, Marcelle, *Enfances et mort de García Lorca* (Paris: Seuil, 1968)

Bacarisse, Pamela, 'Perlimplín's Tragedy', in Robert Havard (ed.), *Lorca: Poet and Playwright* (Cardiff: University of Wales Press, 1992), 71–92

Beltrán Fernández de los Ríos, Luis, *La arquitectura del humo: una reconstrucción del 'Romancero gitano' de Federico García Lorca* (London: Tamesis, 1986)

Binding, Paul, *Lorca: The Gay Imagination* (London: GMP, 1985)

Bonaddio, Federico, 'Lorca's *Poeta en Nueva York*: Creativity and the City', in 'The Image of the City', *Romance Studies*, 22 (Autumn 1993), 41–51

——, 'Lorca's "Romance sonámbulo": the Desirability of Non-Disclosure', *Bulletin of Hispanic Studies*, 72 (1995), 385–401

Butt, John, 'I'm not a happy poet', *London Review of Books*, 1 April 1999, pp. 27–8

Cavanaugh, Cecilia J., *Lorca's Drawings and Poems: Forming The Eye of the Reader* (London: Associated University Presses, 1995)

Clughen, Lisa, 'Lorca's Anorexics: Hunger Strike in the Cause of Selfhood', *Bulletin of Hispanic Studies* (Liverpool), 79, 3 (2002), 309–24

——, 'Re-Reading Lorca', unpublished M. Phil thesis, University of Newcastle upon Tyne, 2002

Cockburn, Jacqueline, 'Learning from the Master: Lorca's homage to Picasso', in *Fire, Blood and the Alphabet: One Hundred Years of Lorca*, ed. Sebastian Doggart and Michael Thompson (Durham: University of Durham, 1999), 23–42

——, 'Gifts from the Poet to the Art Critic', in Federico Bonaddio and Xon de Ros (eds), *Crossing Fields in Modern Spanish Literature* (Oxford: Legenda [European Humanities Research Centre], 2003), 67–80

Cueto, Ronald, *Souls in Anguish. Religion and Spirituality in Lorca's Theatre* (Leeds: Trinity and All Saints, 1994)

Dalí, Salvador, 'Federico García Lorca. Exposició de dibuixos acolorits', *Nova Revista*, Barcelona, September 1927, pp. 84, 85

Delgado, María, 'Lluis Pasqual's unknown Lorcas', in Doggart, Sebastian and Michael Thompson (eds), *Fire, Blood and the Alphabet: One Hundred Years of Lorca* (Durham: University of Durham, 1999), 81–106

Dempsey, Andrew, *A Life of Lorca. Drawings, Photographs, Words* (Norwich: University of East Anglia, 1997)

Dennis, Nigel, *Vida y milagros de un manuscrito de Lorca: En Pos de 'Poeta en Nueva York'* (Santander: Sociedad Menéndez Pelayo, 2000)

——, '*Viaje a la luna*, de Federico García Lorca, y el problema de la expresión', *Revista Canadiense de Estudios Hispánicos*, 25, 1 (2000), 137–49

——, 'Lorca en el espejo: estrategias de (auto)percepción', in Luis Fernández Cifuentes (ed.), *Estudios sobre la poesía de Lorca* (Madrid: Istmo, 2005), 143–58

Devoto, Daniel, 'Notas sobre el elemento tradicional en la obra de Federico García Lorca', in Ildefonso Manuel-Gil (ed.), *Federico García Lorca* (Madrid: Taurus, 1975), 25–72

——, *Introducción a 'Diván del Tamarit' de Federico García Lorca* (Paris: Ediciones Hispanoamericanas, 1976)

——, '¿Tesis, o prótesis?', *Bulletin Hispanique*, 89, 1–4 (1987), 331–58

Dier, Richard, 'Introduction to Federico García Lorca, *Trip to the Moon*', *New Directions*, 18 (1964), 33–5

Doggart, Sebastian and Michael Thompson (eds), *Fire, Blood and the Alphabet: One Hundred Years of Lorca* (Durham: University of Durham, 1999)

Edwards, Gwynne, *Lorca: The Theatre Beneath the Sand* (London: Marion Boyars, 1980)

Eisenberg, Daniel, 'Reaction to the Publication of the *Sonetos del amor oscuro*'. *Bulletin of Hispanic Studies*, 65, 3 (1988), 261–71

——, 'Lorca and Censorship: The Gay Artist Made Heterosexual,' *Angélica* (Lucena, Spain), 2 (1991), 121–45. Updated version posted at http://users.ipfw.edu/jehle/deisenbe/

Feal Deibe, Carlos, 'Los *Seis poemas galegos* de Lorca y sus fuentes rosalianas', *Romanische Forschungen*, 83 (1971), 555–87

——, *Eros y Lorca* (Barcelona: EDHASA, 1973)

——, 'El sacrificio de la hombría en *Bodas de sangre*', *Modern Language Notes*, 99 (1984), 270–87

——, *Lorca: tragedia y mito* (Ottawa: Dovehouse Editions, Ottawa Hispanic Series 4, 1989)

————, *Federico García Lorca (1898–1936)* (Madrid: Comisión Nacional del Centenario de Federico García Lorca / Museo Nacional Centro de Arte Reina Sofía / Fundación Federico García Lorca, 1998)

Fernández-Cifuentes, Luis, 'Anatomía de una transgresión', *Modern Language Notes*, 99, 2 (March 1984), 288–307

————, 'Ian Gibson, *Federico García Lorca 1: De Fuente Vaqueros a Nueva York, 1898–1929* (review article)', *Nueva Revista de Filología Hispánica*, 34 (1985–6), 224–32

————, *García Lorca en el teatro: la norma y la diferencia* (Zaragoza: Prensas Universitarias de Zaragoza, 1986)

————, ¿Qué es aquello que relumbra? (Una última cuestión): Examen de agotamientos', in Andrés Soria Olmedo, María José Sánchez Montes and Juan Varo Zafra (eds and introd.), *Federico García Lorca, clásico moderno (1898–1998)* (Granada: Diputación de Granada, 2000), 223–5

————, *Cartografías de desasosiego: el teatro de García Lorca* (Madrid: Ediciones del Orto / University of Minnesota, 2003)

Fernández-Montesinos, Manuel, *Descripción de la biblioteca de Federico García Lorca (Catálogo y estudio). Tesina para la licienciatura presentada en la Universidad Complutense de Madrid*, 13 September 1985

Foster, David William, 'Reiterative Formulas in García Lorca's Poetry', *Language and Style*, 9, 3 (Summer 1976), 171–91

Fuentes Vázquez, Tadea, *El folklore infantil en la obra de Federico García Lorca* (Granada: Universidad de Granada, 1991)

García Lorca, Francisco, *Federico y su mundo*, ed. Mario Hernández, 2nd / revised edition (Madrid: Alianza, 1981)

————, *De Garcilaso a Lorca*, ed. Claudio Guillén (Madrid: Istmo, 1984)

————, *In the Green Morning. Memories of Federico*, ed. Mario Hernández, trans. Christopher Maurer (New York: New Directions, 1986)

García Lorca, Isabel, *Recuerdos míos* (Barcelona: Tusquets, 2002)

Gasch, Sebastià, 'Lorca Dibujante', *La Gaceta Literaria*, 30, 15 March 1928, p. 4

George, David, *The History of the Commedia dell'arte in Modern Hispanic Literature with Special Attention to the Work of García Lorca* (Lampeter: The Edwin Mellen Press, 1995)

Gibson, Ian, 'Lorca's *Balada triste*: Children's Songs and the Theme of Sexual Disharmony in *Libro de poemas*', *Bulletin of Hispanic Studies*, 46 (1969), 21–38

————, *La represión nacionalista de Granada en 1936 y la muerte de Federico García Lorca* (Paris: Ruedo Ibérico, 1971)

————, *The Assassination of Federico García Lorca* (Harmondsworth: Penguin, 1983)

————, *Federico García Lorca, 1. De Fuente Vaqueros a Nueva York, 1898–1929* (Barcelona: Grijalbo, 1985)

————, *Federico García Lorca, 2. De Nueva York a Fuente Grande, 1929–1936* (Barcelona: Grijalbo, 1987)

————, *Federico García Lorca: A Life* (New York: Pantheon / London: Faber & Faber, 1989)

————, *Lorca's Granada. A Practical Guide* (London: Faber & Faber, 1992)

————, *Lorca–Dalí: El amor que no pudo ser* (Barcelona: Plaza & Janés, 1999)

Grande, Félix, *García Lorca y el flamenco* (Madrid: Mondadori, 1992)

Guarnido, José Mora, *Federico García Lorca y su mundo: Testimonio para una biografía* (Buenos Aires: Losada, 1958)

Guillén, Jorge, *Federico en persona. Semblanza y epistolario* (Buenos Aires: Emecé Editores, 1959)

———, 'Federico en persona', in Federico García Lorca, *Obras completas*, I, ed. Arturo del Hoyo, 3 vols, 22nd edn (Madrid: Aguilar, 1986), xvii–lxxxiv

Harris, Derek, *Federico García Lorca: Poeta en Nueva York*, Critical Guides 24 (London: Grant & Cutler, 1978)

Havard, Robert G., 'Lorca's Buster Keaton', *Bulletin of Hispanic Studies*, 54 (1977), 13–20

Hernández, Mario, 'Jardín deshecho: Los "sonetos" de García Lorca', *El Crotalón. Anuario de Filología Española*, 1 (1984), 193–228

Higginbotham, Virginia, *The Comic Spirit of Federico García Lorca* (Austin and London: University of Texas Press, 1976)

Huélamo Kosma, Julio, 'La influencia de Freud en Federico García Lorca', *Boletín de la Fundación Federico García Lorca*, 6 (1989), 59–83

Jerez-Farrán, Carlos, *Un Lorca desconocido: análisis de un teatro 'irrepresentable'* (Madrid: Biblioteca Nueva, 2004)

———, 'Mundo étnico y circunstancia personal en el *Romancero gitano* de García Lorca', *Cuadernos Americanos*, 109 (2005), 103–31

Johnston, David, *Federico García Lorca* (Bath: Absolute Press, 1998)

Jones, David Richard and Susan Jones, *Federico García Lorca: Study Guide*, online at http://www.repertorio.org/education/pdfs/lorca.pdf

Keenaghan, Eric, 'Jack Spicer's Pricks and Cocksuckers: Translating Homosexuality into Visibility', *Translator*, 4, 2 (November 1998), 273–94

Kolbert, Elizabeth, 'Looking for Lorca: A Poet's Grave and a War's Buried Secrets', *The New Yorker*, 22 and 29 December 2003, pp. 64–78

Laffranque, Marie, *Les idées esthétiques de Federico García Lorca* (París: Centre de Recherches Hispaniques, 1967)

———, *Federico García Lorca: Teatro inconcluso. Fragmentos y proyectos inacabados* (Granada: Universidad de Granada, 1987)

Londré Hardison, Felicia, *Federico García Lorca* (New York: Frederick Ungar, 1984)

López Quero, Salvador, 'Formas de atribución en la poesía de Federico García Lorca', *Alfinge*, 13 (2001), 143–7

Loughran, David K., *Federico García Lorca: The Poetry of Limits* (London: Tamesis Books, 1978)

McDermott, Patricia, 'Death as a Way of Life. Lorca's Dramatic Subversion of Orthodoxy', *Leeds Papers on Hispanic Drama* (Leeds: Trinity and All Saints, 1991), 125–52

———, 'Subversions of the Sacred: The Sign of the Fish', in Derek Harris (ed.), *The Spanish Avant-garde* (Manchester: Manchester University Press, 1995), 204–17

———, 'Lorca's Trip Back to a Future Surrealist Theatre and Cinema', in Robert Havard (ed.), *A Companion to Spanish Surrealism* (Woodbridge: Tamesis, 2004), 183–203

McMullan, Terence, 'Federico García Lorca's *Santa Lucía y San Lázaro* and the Aesthetics of Transition', *Bulletin of Hispanic Studies*, 67 (1990), 1–20

————, 'Federico García Lorca's Critique of Marriage in *Bodas de sangre*', *Neophilologus*, 77 (1993), 62–73

Manuel-Gil, Ildefonso, ed., *Federico García Lorca, El Escritor y la Crítica* (Madrid: Taurus, 1975)

Martín, Eutimio, *Federico García Lorca, heterodoxo y mártir. Análisis y proyección de la obra juvenil inédita* (Madrid: Siglo XXI, 1986)

Martínez Nadal, Rafael, '*El Público': Amor, Teatro y Caballos en la obra de Federico García Lorca* (Oxford: Dolphin Book Co., 1970)

————, *El público: amor y muerte en la obra de Federico García Lorca* (Madrid: Ediciones Hiperión, 1970)

————, *Lorca's The Public* (London: Calder & Boyars, 1974)

————, *Federico García Lorca. Mi penúltimo libro sobre el hombre y el poeta* (Madrid: Editorial Casariego, 1992)

Maurer, Christopher, 'Lorca y las formas de la música', in Andrés Soria Olmedo (ed.), *Lecciones sobre Federico García Lorca* (Granada: Edición del Cincuentenario, 1986), 235–50

————, 'Perspectivas críticas: horizontes infinitos. Two Critical Editions of Lorca's Early Poetry (A Review Article)', *Anales de Literatura Española Contemporánea*, 14 (1989), 223–37

————, 'Millonario de lágrimas', *El Pais*, 3 December 1989, p. 15

————, *Federico García Lorca y su 'Arquitectura del cante jondo'* (Granada: Comares, 2000)

————, *Federico Garcia Lorca, Salvador Dalí, Sebastian's Arrows: Letters and Mementos of Salvador Dalí and Federico García Lorca*, ed. Christopher Maurer (Chicago: Swan Isle Press, 2004)

Miller, Norman C., *García Lorca's 'Poema del cante jondo'* (London: Tamesis Books, 1978)

Mira, Alberto, 'Modernistas, dandis y pederastas: articulaciones de la homosexualidad en "la edad de plata" ', *Journal of Iberian & Latin American Studies*, 7, 1 (2001), 27–35

Monegal, Antonio, 'Las palabras y las cosas, según Salvador Dalí', *El aeroplano y la estrella: El movimiento de vanguardia en los Paises Catalanes (1904–1936)*, ed. Joan Ramon Resina (Amsterdam / Atlanta: Rodopi, 1997), 151–76

————, 'Shall the Circle Be Unbroken? Verbal and Visual Poetry in Lorca, Buñuel, and Dalí', in *Lorca, Buñuel, Dalí: Art and Theory*, ed. Manuel Delgado Morales and A.J. Poust (London and Toronto: Associated University Presses, 2001)

Mora Guarnido, José, *Federico García Lorca y su mundo*, ed. Mario Hernández, 2nd edn (Granada: Caja General de Ahorros, 1998)

Morla Lynch, Carlos, *En España con Federico García Lorca: páginas de un diario íntimo (1928–1936)* (Madrid: Aguilar, 1957)

Morris, C. Brian, *Federico García Lorca. Bodas de sangre*, Critical Guides to Spanish Texts 26 (London: Grant & Cutler, 1996)

————, *Son of Andalusia. The Lyrical Landscapes of Federico García Lorca* (Nashville: Vanderbilt University Press / Liverpool: Liverpool University Press, 1997)

Nandorfy, Martha, *The Poetics of Apocalypse: García Lorca's 'Poet in New York'* (Lewisburg, PA: Bucknell University Press / London: Associated University Presses, 2003)

Newton, Candelas M., *Lorca, una escritura en trance: 'Libro de Poemas' y 'Diván del Tamarit'* (Amsterdam: John Benjamins, 1992)

————, *Understanding Federico García Lorca* (Columbus, SC: University of South Carolina Press, 1995)

Oppenheimer, Helen, *Lorca, The Drawings: Their relation to his Life and Work* (London: The Herbert Press, 1986)

Perri, Dennis, 'Lorca's Suite "Palimpsestos": Keeping the Reader at Bay', *Romance Quarterly*, 38, 2 (May 1991), 197–211

Predmore, Richard L., *Lorca's New York Poetry: Social Injustice, Dark Love, Lost Faith* (Durham, NC: Duke University Press, 1980)

Prieto, Gregorio, *Lorca y su mundo angélico* (Madrid: Sala Editorial, 1972)

————, *Federico García Lorca y la Generación del 27* (Madrid: Editorial Biblioteca Nueva, 1977)

Ramond, Michèle (ed.), *Hommage à Federico García Lorca*, Travaux de l'Université de Toulouse-Le Mirail, Série A20 (Toulouse: Université de Toulouse-le-Mirail, 1982)

————, *Psychotextes. La question de L'Autre dans Federico García Lorca* (Toulouse: Editions Eché, 1986)

Ramos-Gil, Carlos, *Claves líricas de García Lorca. Ensayos sobre la expresión y los climas poéticos lorquianos* (Madrid: Aguilar, 1967)

Ramsden, H., *Lorca's 'Romancero gitano': Eighteen commentaries* (Manchester: Manchester University Press, 1988)

Robertson, Sandra Cary, *Lorca, Alberti, and the Theatre of Popular Poetry* (New York: Peter Lang, 1991)

Rodrigo, Antonina, *García Lorca en Cataluña* (Barcelona: Planeta, 1975)

————, *Lorca–Dalí: Una amistad traicionada* (Barcelona: Planeta 1981)

————, *Memorias de Granada. Manuel Ángeles Ortiz. Federico García Lorca* (Barcelona: Plaza & Janés, 1984)

————, *García Lorca en el país de Dalí* (Barcelona: Editorial Base, 2004)

Ros, Xon de, 'Science and Myth in Lorca's "Llanto"', *Modern Language Review*, 95, 1 (2000), 114–26

————, 'Ignacio Sánchez Mejías Blues', in Federico Bonaddio and Xon de Ros (eds), *Crossing Fields in Modern Spanish Culture* (Oxford: Legenda [European Humanities Research Centre], 2003), 81–91

Sahuquillo, Ángel, *Federico García Lorca y la Cultura de la Homosexualidad: Lorca, Dalí, Cernuda, Gil-Albert, Prados y la voz silenciada del amor homosexual* (Alicante: Instituto de Cultura 'Juan Gil Albert' / Diputación de Alicante, 1991)

Sánchez Vidal, Agustín, 'El viaje a la luna de un perro andaluz', in *Valoración actual de la obra de García Lorca*, eds Alfonso Esteban y Jean-Pierre Étienvre (Madrid: Casa de Velázquez / Univ. Complutense, 1988), 141–61

————, *Buñuel, Lorca, Dalí: El enigma sin fin*, 2nd edn (Barcelona: Planeta, 1996)

Santos Torroella, Rafael, *La miel es más dulce que la sangre: Las épocas lorquiana y freudiana de Salvador Dalí* (Barcelona: Seix Barral, 1984)

————, *Salvador Dalí escribe a Federico García Lorca [1925–1936].* Special issue of *Poesía. Revista Ilustrada de Información Poética*, 27–28 (1987)

————, *'Los putrefactos' Dalí y Lorca: Historia y antología de un libro que no pudo ser* (Madrid: Residencia de Estudiantes / Consejo Superior de Investigaciones Científicas, 1995)

————, *Dalí. Época de Madrid. Catálogo razonado* (Madrid: Residencia de Estudiantes, 2004)

Smith, Paul Julian, 'Lorca and Foucault', *The Body Hispanic: Gender and Sexuality in Spanish and Spanish American Literature* (Oxford: Oxford University Press, 1989), ch. 4, 105–37

———, *The Theatre of García Lorca: Text, Performance, Psychoanalysis* (Cambridge: Cambridge University Press, 1998)

———, 'New York, New York: Lorca's Double Vision', *Journal of Iberian and Latin American Studies*, 6, 2 (2000), 169–80

Soria Olmedo, Andrés, *Federico García Lorca* (Madrid: Editorial Eneida, 2000)

———, *Fábula de fuentes: Tradición y vida literaria en Federico García Lorca* (Madrid: Residencia de Estudiantes, 2004)

Soufas, C. Christopher, *Audience and Authority in the Modernist Theater of Federico García Lorca* (Tuscaloosa and London: University of Alabama Press, 1996)

Southworth, Eric, 'Lorca's "San Rafael (Córdoba)" and Some Other Texts', *Modern Language Review*, 94 (1999), 87–102

Stainton, Leslie, *Lorca: A Dream of Life* (London: Bloomsbury, 1998 / New York: Farrar, Straus and Giroux, 1999)

Stanton, Edward F., *The Tragic Myth. Lorca and Cante Jondo* (Lexington: University Press of Kentucky, 1978)

Stone, Rob, *The Flamenco Tradition in the Works of Federico García Lorca and Carlos Saura. The Wounded Throat*, Spanish Studies 26 (Lewiston / Queenston / Lampeter: Edwin Mellen Press, 2004)

Tinnell, Roger D., *Federico García Lorca y la música*, 2nd edn (Madrid: Fundación March, 1998)

Tubert, Silvia, 'The Deconstruction and Construction of Maternal Desire: *Yerma* and *Die Frau ohne Schatten*', *Mosaic*, 26, 3 (1993), 69–87

Valente, Angel, 'Pez luna', *Trece de nieve: homenaje a Federico García Lorca*, 1–2 (Madrid, 1976), 191–201

Valis, Noel Maureen, 'The Culture of Nostalgia, or the Language of Flowers', in Noel Maureen Valis, *The Culture of Cursilería: Bad Taste, Kitsch, and Class in Modern Spain* (Durham, NC and London: Duke University Press, 2002), 244–76

Vilches de Frutos, María Francisca and Dru Dougherty, *Los estrenos teatrales de Federico García Lorca (1920–45)* (Madrid: Tabapress / Grupo Tabacalera / Fundación FGL, 1992)

Villena, Luis Antonio de, 'La sensibilidad homoerótica en el *Romancero gitano*', *Campus*, 11 (1986), 27–30

———, 'Lorca: De mito rojo a mártir gay', *Qué leer*, 20 (March 1998), 66–7

Walters, D. Gareth, 'The Queen of Castile and the Andalusian Spinster: Lorca's Elegies for Two Women', in Robert Havard (ed.), *Lorca: Poet and Playwright* (Cardiff: University of Wales Press, 1992)

———, *'Canciones' and the Early Poetry of Lorca: A Study in Critical Methodology and Poetic Maturity* (Cardiff: University of Wales Press, 2002)

———, 'Parallel Trajectories in the Careers of Falla and Lorca', in Federico Bonaddio and Xon de Ros (eds), *Crossing Fields in Modern Spanish Culture* (Oxford: Legenda [European Humanities Research Centre], 2003), 92–102

Warner, Robin, *Powers of Utterance: A Discourse Approach to Works of Lorca, Machado and Valle-Inclán* (Bristol: Hiplam, 2003)

Williams, Merryn, 'Translating Lorca', *Vida Hispánica*, 18 (September 1998), 25–8

Wright, Sarah, *The Trickster-Function in the Theatre of García Lorca*, Colección Támesis 185 (Woodbridge: Tamesis, 2000)

Works of general interest

Ades, Dawn, 'Morphologies of Desire', in *Salvador Dali: The Early Years* (exhibition catalogue) (London: The Hayward Gallery, 1994), 129–59

Aguilera Sastre, Juan and Manuel Aznar Soler (eds), 'Cipriano de Rivas Cherif: Retrato de una utopía', *Cuadernos el Público*, 42 (Madrid, December 1989), 61–100

Alberti, Rafael, *La arboleda perdida. Libros I y II de memorias* (Barcelona: Seix-Barral, 1975)

Alonso, Dámaso, *Poetas españoles contemporáneos*, 3rd edn (Madrid: Gredos, 1978)

Altolaguirre, Manuel, *Obras completas*, ed. James Valender, 3 vols (Madrid: Istmo, 1986)

Álvarez de Miranda, Ángel, *Obras*, vol. 2 (Madrid: Ediciones Cultura Hispánica, 1959)

Anderson, Andrew A., *El veintisiete en tela de juicio: Examen de la historiografía generacional y replanteamiento de la vanguardia histórica española* (Madrid: Gredos, 2005)

Apollinaire, Guillaume, 'The New Spirit and the Poets', *Selected Writings of Guillaume Apollinaire*, trans. with an intro. by Roger Shattuck (London: Harvill, 1950), 227–37

Arenas, Reinaldo, *Halley's Comet*, trans. Dolores M. Koch, *Hopscotch: A Cultural Review*, 2, 1 (2000), 74–82

Bassolas, Carmen, *La ideología de los escritores. Literatura y política en 'La Gaceta Literaria' (1927–1932)* (Barcelona: Fontamara, 1975)

Bécarud, Jean and Evelyn López Campillo, *Los intelectuales españoles durante y la II República* (Madrid: Siglo XXI, 1978)

Blokker, Roy, with Robert Dearling, *The Music of Dmitri Shostakovich: The Symphonies* (Cranbury, NJ: Associated University Presses, 1979)

Bly, Robert, *American Poetry: Wildness and Domesticity* (New York: Harper & Row, 1990)

Bourdieu, Pierre, *The Field of Cultural Production. Essays on Art and Literature*, ed. and introd. Randal Johnson (Cambridge: Polity Press, 1993)

Bradbury, Malcolm and James McFarlane (eds), *Modernism* (Harmondsworth: Penguin, 1976)

Breton, André, *Mad Love*, trans. Mary Ann Caw (Lincoln and London: University of Nebraska Press, 1987)

Bristow, Joseph, *Sexuality,* The New Critical Idiom (London: Routledge, 1997)

Buñuel, Luis, *Mi último suspiro* (Barcelona: Plaza y Janés, 1982)

———, *My Last Breath*, trans. by Abigail Israel (London: Fontana, 1985)

Calinescu, Matei, *Five Faces of Modernity* (Durham NC: Duke University Press, 1987)

Callahan, William J., *Church, Politics and Society in Spain, 1750–1874* (Cambridge, MA: Harvard, 1984)

———, *La iglesia católica en España (1875–2002)* (Barcelona: Crítica, 2000)

Chase, Gilbert, *The Music of Spain*, 2nd revised edn (New York: Dover Publications, 1959)

Crichton, Ronald, *Falla*, BBC Music Guides (London: British Broadcasting Corporation, 1982)

Crispin, John, *'Oxford y Cambridge en Madrid'. La Residencia de Estudiantes, 1910–1936, y su entorno cultural* (Santander: La Isla de los Ratones, 1981)

Culler, Johnathan, *Structuralist Poetics: Structuralism, Linguistics, and the Study of Literature* (Ithaca, NY: Cornell University Press, 1975)

Cummins, J.G., *The Spanish Traditional Lyric* (New York and Oxford: Pergamon Press, 1977)

Dalí, Salvador, *Collected Writings*, ed. Haim Finkelstein (Cambridge: Cambridge University Press, 1998)

Delgado, María, *Other Spanish Theatres: Erasure and Inscription on the Spanish Stage* (Manchester: Manchester University Press, 2003)

Derrida, Jacques, 'The Theater of Cruelty and the Closure of Representation', in A. Bass (trans.), *Writing and Difference* (London: Routledge, 1990), 232–50

Descharnes, Robert, *The World of Salvador Dalí* (New York: Macmillan, 1962)

Díaz Fernández, José, *El nuevo romanticismo* (Madrid: Zeus, 1930)

Dougherty, Dru and María Francisca Vilches de Frutos (eds), *El teatro en España: entre la tradición y la vanguardia, 1918–39* (Madrid: CSIC / Fundación FGL / Tabacalera, 1992)

Duffy, Eamon, *The Stripping of the Altars* (London: Yale, 1992)

Epstein, Jean, 'On certain characteristics of Photogenie' (1924), in Richard Abel (ed. and trans.), *French Film Theory and Criticism: A History/Anthology, 1907–1939*, 2 vols (Princeton: Princeton University Press, 1988), I (1907–1929), 314–18

Espina, Antonio, *Poesía completa*, ed. Gloria Rey (Madrid: Fundación Banco Santander Central Hispano, 2000)

Evans, Mary, *Love: An Unromantic Discussion* (Cambridge: Polity Press, 2003)

Falla, Manuel de, *Escritos sobre música y músicos* (Madrid: Espasa-Calpe, 1972)

———, *On Music and Musicians*, intro. and notes by Federico Sopeña (London: Marion Boyars, 1979)

Fish, Stanley, 'Biography and Intention', in William H. Epstein (ed.), *Contesting the subject: essays in the postmodern theory and practice of biography and biographical criticism* (West Lafayette, IN: Purdue University Press, 1991), 9–16

Foucault, Michel, 'What is an author?', in David Lodge (ed.), *Modern Criticism and Theory. A Reader* (London and New York: Longman, 1988), 196–210

Freud, Sigmund, *Beyond the Pleasure Principle* (1920), in J. Strachey (ed.), *The Standard Edition of the Complete Psychological Works of Sigmund Freud*, 23 vols (London: The Hogarth Press, 1974), VIII, 1–64

Fuentes, Victor, *La marcha al pueblo en las letras españolas, 1917–1936* (Madrid: Ediciones de la Torre, 1980)

Gance, Abel, 'A Sixth Art' (1912), in Richard Abel (ed. and trans.), *French Film Theory and Criticism: A History/Anthology, 1907–1939*, 2 vols (Princeton: Princeton University Press, 1988), vol. I (1907–1929), 66–7

Garraty, John A., *The Nature of Biography* (New York: Alfred A. Knopf, 1957)

Gibson, Ian, Rafael Santos Torroella, Félix Fanés, Dawn Ades and Agustín Sánchez Vidal, *Salvador Dalí: The Early Years*, ed. Michael Raeburn (New York: Thames & Hudson, 1994)

————, *The Shameful Life of Salvador Dalí* (London: Faber & Faber, 1997)

Gubern, Román, *Proyector de luna: La generación del 27 y el cine* (Barcelona: Anagrama, 1999)

Hart, Stephen, *The Other Scene: Psychoanalyitcal Readings in Modern Spanish and Latin-American Literature* (Boulder, CO: Society of Spanish and Spanish-American Studies, 1992)

Herrero, Javier, 'Don Federico García Rodríguez concejal del Ayuntamiento de Granada. Un enigma lorquiano', *Bulletin of Spanish Studies*, 81, 3 (2004), 309–23

Hirsch, Edward, *The Demon and the Angel. Searching for the Source of Artistic Inspiration* (New York: Harvest Books, 2003)

Irizarry, Estelle, *Painter-Poets of Contemporary Spain* (Boston: Twayne, 1984)

James, Burnett, *Manuel de Falla and the Spanish Musical Renaissance* (London: Victor Gollancz, 1979)

Josephs, Allen, *White Wall of Spain. The Mysteries of Andalusian Culture* (Ames: Iowa State University Press, 1983)

Jung, Christof, 'Cante flamenco', in *Flamenco: Gipsy Dance and Music from Andalusia*, ed. Claus Schreiner (Portland, OR: Amadeus Press, 1990), 57–87

Lannon, Frances, *Privilege, Persecution, and Prophecy: The Catholic Church in Spain, 1875–1975* (Oxford: Clarendon Press, 1987)

Lewis, A., *The Contemporary Theater* (New York: Crown Publishers, 1971)

Livermore, Ann, *A Short History of Spanish Music*, (London: Duckworth, 1972)

López-Rey, José, *Los estudiantes frente a la dictadura* (Madrid: Javier Morata, 1930)

Marrast, Robert, 'El teatro durante la guerra civil española', *El Público*, 15 (1986), 18–31

Mauss, Marcel, *The Gift*, trans. W.D. Halls (London: Routledge, 1990)

Mitchell, Timothy, *Flamenco Deep Song* (New Haven: Yale University Press, 1994)

Monegal, Antonio, *En el límite de la diferencia: Poesía e imagen en las vanguardias hispánicas* (Madrid: Editorial Tecnos, 1998)

Montiel Rayo, Francisca, 'Esteban Salazar Chapela en su época: Obra literaria y periodística (1923–1939)'. Unpublished PhD dissertation, 3 vols, Barcelona: Universitat Autónoma de Barcelona, 2005

Morris, C. Brian, *This Loving Darkness: Cinema and Spanish Writers, 1920–1936* (Oxford and New York: Oxford University Press, 1980)

Ortega y Gasset, José, *Obras completas*, vol. XI: *Escritos políticos II (1922–1933)* (Madrid: Revista de Occidente, 1969)

————, 'La deshumanización del arte', in José Ortega y Gasset, *La deshumanización del arte y otros ensayos de estética*, Colección Austral 13 (Madrid: Espasa-Calpe, 1987), 45–92

Papenbrok, Marion, 'History of Flamenco', in *Flamenco: Gypsy Dance and Music from Andalusia*, ed. Claus Schreiner (Portland, OR: Amadeus Press, 1990), 35–48

Perriam, Chris, '*A un dios desconocido*: Resurrecting a Queer Identity under Lorca's Spell', *Bulletin of Hispanic Studies*, 76, 1 (January 1999), 77–91

Plato, *The Symposium*, trans. and intro. Christopher Gill (London: Penguin, 1999)

Rhode, Eric, *A History of the Cinema: from its Origins to 1970* (London: Penguin, 1978)

Rozas, Juan Manuel, *La Generación de 27 desde dentro: Textos y documentos*, 2nd edn (Madrid: Istmo, 1986)

Sáenz de la Calzada, Luis, *'La Barraca'. Teatro universitario* (Madrid: Revista de Occidente, 1976)

Said, Edward W., *The World, the Text, and the Critic* (Cambridge, MA: Harvard University, 1983)

Salinas, Pedro and Jorge Guillén, *Correspondencia (1923–1951)*, ed. Andrés Soria Olmedo (Barcelona: Tusquets, 1992)

Sontag, Susan, 'Against Interpretation', in Susan Sontag, *Against Interpretation and other essays* (London: Eyre & Spottiswoode, 1967), 3–14

———, 'Introduction', Walter Benjamin, *'One-Way Street' and Other Writings*, trans. Edmund Jephcott and Kingsley Shorter (London: Verso, 1985), 7–28

Tuñón de Lara, Manuel, *La España del siglo XX*, 2 vols (Barcelona: Laia, 1974)

Tussell, Javier and Genoveva G. Queipo de Llano, *Los intelectuales y la República* (Madrid: Nerea, 1990)

Venuti, Lawrence, 'Translation as Cultural Politics: Regimes of Domestication in English', *Textual Practice*, 7, 2 (1993), 208–23

INDEX

A un dios desconocido 123, 126, 127–8
Ades, Dawn 88–9
Albéniz, Isaac 24–5, 64, 65, 66, 73
Alberti, Rafael 65, 92, 179, 188
Alcalá-Zamora, Niceto 184
Allen, Rupert 3
Almodóvar, Pedro 57
Alonso, Dámaso 92, 188–9
Alterio, Héctor 44, 127
Altolaguirre, Manuel 26
Amat, Frederic 117, 121
Amero, Emilio 115–16
El amor de don Perlimplín con Belisa en su jardín 18, 41, 49, 145, 161
   run-in with authorities 180
   scenography 110
   unstageable love 44–8
Amor Intelectualis 96–7
'Anda jaleo' 68
Ángeles Ortiz, Manuel ('Manolo') 22, 74
Apollinaire, Guillaume 101
Arconada, César 178
'La Argentinita' *see* López Júlvez, Encarnación
Artaud, Antonin 49
Así que pasen cinco años 41, 42, 110, 115, 151, 167
   mise-en-scène 157
   postponing desire 53–5
Ayala, Francisco 177n, 180
Azaña, Manuel 183, 184

Bach, Johann Sebastian 18, 81–2
Bardem, Juan Antonio 124
La Barraca 34, 37, 42, 178
   religious drama 143–4, 178
   spirit of Republicanism 183–5
   theatre in crisis 103
Bécquer, Gustavo Adolfo 19
Beethoven, Ludwig van 64
Belitt, Ben 38
Bello, Pepín 30
Beltrán Fernandez de los Ríos, Luis 3
Benedicto, Sonsoles 44

Bergamín, José 34, 92
Bermúdez Cañete, Diego 75
Besteiro, Julián 184
Blanco Amor, Eduardo 36
Bly, Robert 16, 38
Bodas de sangre 34, 41, 42, 151, 154, 167
   Almeida Theatre, May 2005 51–3
   Bach's influence 18, 81–2
   Buenos Aires 35
   feelings and natural world 150
   feminism 160
   folk songs 68, 69
   jealousy and rivalry 164–5
   Luís Pasqual 57
   'Pange lingua gloriosi' 146
La bola negra 41
Borges, Jorge Luis 28, 92
Borges, Norah 92
Bourdieu, Pierre 11–12, 14
Breton, André 54
Buñuel, Luis 109, 112, 114
   dedication in *Canciones* 108
   eye-motif 106
   L'Âge d'Or 54
   relationship with Lorca and Dalí 6, 30, 98
   rising interest in film 102, 103
   Un chien andalou 116, 118

Caballero, José 92
Cabezón, Antonio de 20
Cal, Ernesto da 36
Campbell, Roy 38
Camus, Mario 124
'Canción' 70
Canciones 25, 26, 80, 108, 131, 153
La casa de Bernarda Alba 34, 41, 153, 158
   absurdist drama 160
   masculinity 162, 166
   mother-figure 57, 59–61
   oppressive religiosity 147–8
   photographic documentary 18, 108
   politics 40, 188
Castro, Fidel 127
Cavanaugh, Cecilia 89

Cela, Camilo José 92
Cequeira, Daniel 51
Cernuda, Luis 184
Cerón Rubio, Miguel 74, 92
Chaplin, Charlie *see* 'Meditaciones a la muerte de la madre de Charlot'
Chávarri, Jaime 126
Cocteau, Jean 30
Comedia sin título 41
'Cómo canta una ciudad de noviembre a noviembre' 18
Concurso del cante jondo 74–6
'Corazón bleu y Coeur azul' 31
Cossío, Manuel Bartolomé de 184
Cristo. Tragedia religiosa 41, 144
Crommelynck, Fernand 48
'Los cuatro muleros' 68

Dalí, Salvador 53, 148
  Dalmau Gallery 84
  eye-motif 106
  influence on Lorca 30–2, 111, 114
  L'Âge d'Or 54
  Lorca's correspondence 9n
  Lorca period 88
  'Oda a Salvador Dalí' 134
  relationsip with Lorca and Buñuel 6, 98
  Retrato de Salvador Dalí 93–5
  Romancero gitano 29, 98, 112
  Saint Sebastian 92–3, 135
  Un chien andalou 116
Dalmau, Josep 95, 98
Darío, Rubén 10n, 20, 28, 80
Debussy, Claude 20, 23, 25, 26, 66
La destrucción de Sodoma 41
Diaghilev, Sergei 73
Díaz Fernández, José 177, 180, 182
Diego, Gerardo 28
Diez-Canedo, Enrique 24
The Disappearance of García Lorca 123, 126–7
Diván del Tamarit 17–8, 35–6, 156
Domínguez Berrueta, Martín 64, 65
La doncella, el marinero y el estudiante 41
Doña Rosia la soltera o El lenguaje de las flores 18, 35, 41, 55–6, 108, 158
Dragón 41
Duse, Eleonora 107

Elorriaga, Xabier 127
Epstein, Jean 102, 104
Ernst, Max 31
Espert, Nuria 57, 124

Espina, Antonio 173, 177, 178, 180, 182, 185
Esplá, Oscar 23

Falla, Manuel de 64, 92
  Concurso del cante jondo 22, 74–5
  influence on Lorca 23–5, 30, 70, 72–3, 76, 77
Feal Deibe, Carlos 152
Fernández Almagro, Melchor 87, 176
Fernández-Montesinos, Manuel 171n
Fernández-Cifuentes, Luis 5–6, 7–8
Ferrant, Manuel 92
Fish, Stanley 3–4, 14
Foix, J. V. 92
Foucault, Michel 4, 11, 151
Franco, Francisco 37–8
Freud, Sigmund 8, 52, 53, 54, 151

Gades, Antonio 82
Gance, Abel 103
Gaos, Lola 124
García, Andy 39, 126–7
García Bernal, Gael 51, 52
García Gómez, Emilio 35, 36
García Lorca, Francisco (FGL's brother) 16, 20, 36, 63–4, 67–8, 171n
García Lorca, Isabel (FGL's sister) 171n
García Lorca, María de la Concepción ('Concha') (FGL's sister) 63
García Maroto, Gabriel 20
García Rodríguez, Baldomero 63
García Rodríguez, Federico (FGL's father) 8, 171
García Valdecasas, Alfonso 179
García Vargas, Antonio (FGL's great-grandfather) 63
Garraty, John A. 6–7
Gasch, Sebastiá 30, 94
  Amor Intelectualis 97
  Lorca's drawings 84–5, 92, 95–6, 98–9
  'Sketch de la Nueva Pintura' 85–6
Gautier, Théophile 25
Gaya, Ramón 184
Gebser, Hans 'Jean' 92
Gerhard, Roberto 66
Gibson, Ian 5–6, 7, 8, 10, 39, 123, 124
Gide, André 54
Gil Robles, José María 185
Giménez Caballero, Ernesto 103, 175–6, 177–8
Gómez, José Luis 44
Gómez, Miguel 187
Gómez de la Serna, Ramón 20, 28

Grace, Nickolas 124
Granados, Enrique 64, 66
Guerrero Ruiz, Juan 92
Guillén, Jorge 26, 82, 92, 134

Halffter, Ernesto 23
Haraldsson, Björn Hlynur 52
Hernández, Mario 87
Hitler, Adolf 185, 186
Hoyo, Arturo del 38
Hoyos, Cristina 58
Humphries, Rolfe 34, 38

'La imagen poética de don Luis de
    Góngora' 28–9, 32, 104, 111, 114
'Imaginación, inspiración, evasión' 32, 113
'Importancia histórica y artística del
    primitivo canto andaluz llamado "cante
    jondo" ' 76–7
Impresiones y paisajes 130
Ingres, Jean-Auguste-Dominique 30

Jardín de los sonetos 37
Jehová 41, 133, 144
Jiménez, Juan Ramón 20, 26, 29
Jiménez de Asúa, Luis 179
'Juego y teoría del duende' 35

Keaton, Buster *see* 'El paseo de Buster
    Keaton'

Lanz, Hermenegildo 92
Le Corbusier 32
Libro de poemas 22, 68
    preface 5–6
    musical influence 19, 80
    themes 20, 130, 131
Linehan, Rosaleen 52
Lieder heroico 65–6
Llanto por Ignacio Sánchez Mejías 36–7,
    39–40, 142–3, 148
Lola la comedianta 41, 73
Londré, Felicia 87
López Júlvez, Encarnación 14, 19, 65, 67,
    114
Lorca: Muerte de un poeta 123–5, 127
Lorca Romero, Vicenta (FGL's mother)
    171–2
Loughran, David 87
Lozano, Margarita 124

Machado, Antonio 29, 65, 183, 186
Machado, Manuel 23, 24, 25, 77
Magritte, René 51

El maleficio de la mariposa 41, 43, 144
Manrique, Jorge 37
Marañón, Gregorio 92
Mariana Pineda 18, 30, 41, 144–5, 154–5,
    174–6
Martín, Eutimio 129, 130
Mauss, Marcel 91–2
'Meditaciones a la muerte de la madre de
    Charlot' 111–14
Méliès, George 109
Menéndez Pidal, Ramón 22, 27, 68
Milán, Luis 20
Místicas 41
Molinari, Ricardo 92
Mompou, Federic 66
Mora Guarnido, José 22, 74, 75
Morla Lynch, Carlos 92
Morris, C. Brian 102–3
Mussolini, Benito 186

'Nana' 72
'Nana de Sevilla' 69–70
Nandorfy, Martha 89–90, 98
Neruda, Pablo 92
'La niña que riega la albahaca y el príncipe
    preguntón' 74
Nono, Luigi 82

'Oda a Salvador Dalí' 31, 134, 136
'Oda al Santísimo Sacramento del
    Altar' 23, 135–7, 148
Onís, Federico de 63
Oppenheimer, Helen 88
Orense, Eduardo 63
Ortega, Manuel 75
Ortega y Gasset, José 26, 173, 179, 180,
    181

'El paño moruno' 70
Palacios, Matilde 171
Palencia, Benjamín 92
Paredes, Marisa 57
'El paseo de Buster Keaton' 41, 102–3,
    104–8
Pasqual, Lluís 50, 57, 61
'Los pelegrinitos' 70
Picasso, Pablo Ruiz 83
Plato 45–7, 50, 52
Poema del cante jondo 18, 22–5, 26, 27, 73
    musicality 77–9
    continuity 81
    Shostakovich's Fourteenth Symphony 83
    relationships 131
    Holy Week 132

Poeta en Nueva York 18, 32, 87, 114, 115, 168
  anticipated in 'Oda al Santísimo Sacramento del Altar' 136, 137
  autobiography 6
  connections with *Llanto por Ignacio Sánchez Mejías* 142, 143
  imagery and film 110
  inequality 157
  love 150, 154, 155–6
  overview 33–4
  politics 183, 187
  religion 138–41, 148
'Polo' 70–1
Pomès, Mathilde 92
Pou, José María 124
Poulenc, Francis 82
Prados, Emilio 26, 80, 92, 174
Prieto, Gregorio 91, 92, 98
Primo de Rivera, Miguel 178, 179
El público 34, 41, 42, 43, 115, 157
  cinema 108–10
  love 149, 150–1
  masculinity 167–8
  religion 145–6
  unstageable love 48–50

Quimera 41, 44

Rachmaninoff, Sergei Vasilyevich 64
Ramos-Gil, Carlos 2–3, 12
Raphael 30
Ravel, Maurice 23
'Las reglas de la música' 19–20
Residencia de Estudiantes 172
Retrato de Salvador Dalí 93–4
Reuten, Thekla 52
Río, Ángel del 92
Ríos Urruti, Fernando de los 179, 186
  La Barraca 183, 184
  Lorca's mentor and friend 64, 171, 172
  New York 182
Rivas Cherif, Cipriano 125, 180, 183
Rodríguez Rapún, Rafael 37
Romancero gitano 3, 18, 73, 97, 112, 131
  cinema 110–11
  Dalí's criticism 31–2
  Falla's influence 25
  homoeroticism 162–3
  love 151, 153, 155
  musicality 81
  overview 27–30
  religion 132–4
Ronder, Tanya 51

Rostand, Edmond 48
Rubinstein, Artur 72
Rueda, Salvador 20, 23, 24
Ruiz Aguilera, Ventura 24

Said, Edward 12–14
Salazar, Adolfo 22, 24, 73
Salazar, Antonio de Oliveira 187
Salazar Chapela, Esteban 172, 177, 182
Salinas, Pedro 178, 180
San Sebastián 96, 97
Santa Lucía y San Lázaro 31
Santos Torroella, Rafael 30–1
Saura, Carlos 82, 165
Scarlatti, Domenico 18
Schoenberg, Arnold 66
Segura Mesa, Antonio 19, 63, 67
Seis poemas galegos 36
Sender, Ramón 180
'Sevillanas' 69
Shakespeare, William 48
Shostakovich, Dimitri 83
'Sketch de la Nueva Pintura' 85–7
Smith, Paul Julian 1–2, 40, 42
Sombras 41, 44
Sonetos del amor oscuro 37, 156–7
Sontag, Susan 9–10
Stainton, Leslie 5n, 7, 8, 10, 12, 14
Stravinsky, Igor 23, 66, 72
El sueño de la vida 42, 143
Los sueños de mi prima Aurelia 41
Suero, Pablo 42
Suites 20, 22, 25–6, 80–1

Teorema de la Copa y la Mandolina 83
'Los títeres de Cachiporra de Granada' 25
Torre, Guillermo de 28, 104, 176, 178
Tragicomedia de don Cristóbal y la Señá Rosita 41

Ugarte, Eduardo 180
Unamuno, Miguel de 173

Vargas, Getulio 187
Vela, Fernando 180
Verdi, Giuseppe 19, 63
Verlaine, Paul 26
Vermeer, Johannes 30
Viaje a la luna 34, 108, 109, 114–22
Villaespesa, Francisco 20
La viudita que se quería casar 41

Whitman, Walt 33
Wiene, Robert 110

Xirgu, Margarita 43, 53, 55, 59n, 92

Yerma 34, 41
  feminism 160
  folk songs 68, 69
  Lorca's childlessness 14, 159
  mother-figure 57–9
  politics 187

  religion 146–7, 159
  rivalry 165–6

Zandry, Assly 52
La zapatera prodigiosa 41, 53, 73, 108
Zurbarán, Francisco de 134
Zurinaga, Marcos 40–1, 126

Printed and bound by CPI Group (UK) Ltd, Croydon, CR0 4YY

13/04/2025

14656523-0003